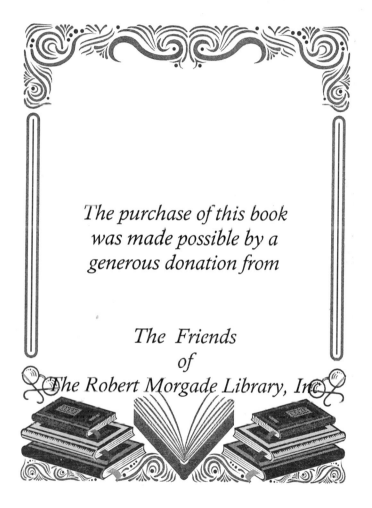

ANSWER THEM NOTHING

ANSWER THEM NOTHING
Bringing Down the Polygamous Empire of Warren Jeffs

Debra Weyermann

CHICAGO
REVIEW
PRESS

Library of Congress Cataloging-in-Publication Data

Weyermann, Debra.
 Answer them nothing : bringing down the polygamous empire of Warren
Jeffs / Debra Weyermann.
    p. cm.
 Includes bibliographical references and index.
 ISBN 978-1-56976-531-9 (hbk.)
 1. Polygamy—United States. 2. Jeffs, Warren, 1955–. 3. Fundamentalist
Church of Jesus Christ of Latter Day Saints. 4. Forced marriage—United
States. 5. Mormon fundamentalism—United States. I. Title.
 HQ994.W49 2011
 306.84'23—dc22

                               2011007722

Interior design: Visible Logic, Inc.

Published by Chicago Review Press, Incorporated
814 North Franklin Street
Chicago, Illinois 60610
ISBN 978-1-56976-531-9
Printed in the United States of America
5 4 3 2 1

For pro bono lawyers, who give justice a fighting chance.

CONTENTS

Map ... ix

Note on Sources ... xi

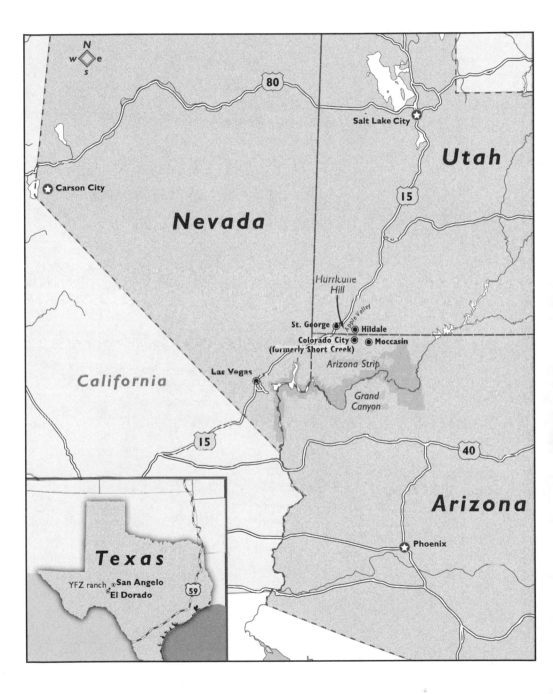

Note on Sources

In unraveling such a complicated, contemporary story like FLDS, heavy use must be made of current media sources. There is no shortage of information about FLDS in every form of media. The difficulty lies with making sense of the haphazard manner in which the sect is covered, usually in bits and pieces by journalists who are assigned a one-time task with no background or intended follow-up.

Gathering, collating, and comparing the reams of media coverage would have been nearly impossible without the Hope Organization website. Founder Elaine Tyler has spent a good chunk of her life gathering tens of thousands of print and electronic stories about FLDS (only the *Salt Lake Tribune* refuses permission to reprint), organizing them by topic and date. The website also posts many of the legal documents referenced in this book, as well as links to documentaries and other FLDS-related information. Hope Organization is one website to which I regularly returned. There are dozens of FLDS-related websites. Many are less than reliable. Others, like the ones listed in the bibliography, reprint original documents or other source material to support their headlines and discussions. Though designated an anti-FLDS website by some, FLDS Texas reprinted or provided links to hundreds of original documents, correspondence, and news film, and I visited the site almost daily to track legal developments in that state.

I was fortunate to know people in Utah, Arizona, and Texas who provided me with full court files and then sent new documents as they were filed. In this way, I was able to follow court cases not through the media but from actual legal filings as they occurred. I was also able to obtain most of Warren Jeffs's dictations seized in the 2008 Texas raid. These voluminous and damning diaries containing illuminating details not available to FLDS members allowed me to re-create life in Short Creek in a way not possible before.

Finally, dozens of people were interviewed for the book, many in person. Almost as important were the people who refused to be interviewed for various reasons. No current FLDS members agreed to speak with me. Some *ex*-FLDS members agreed to anonymous interviews, but many more feared retribution either against themselves or against relatives still inside

FLDS. Some individuals, like Dan Fischer, initially granted interviews but withdrew their cooperation as FLDS attorneys drew their personal lives into the escalating court battles. All the judges, as well as the attorneys general for Texas and Arizona, declined requests for interviews with regrets, explaining that they did not want to risk remarks that sect lawyers might construe as legally actionable. Their actions have been reconstructed from the voluminous public record.

ANSWER THEM NOTHING

Prologue
THE RAID

On July 26, 1953, the fully eclipsed moon didn't afford the lookouts any light, but they knew what to expect. Polygamist sympathizers in Salt Lake City had tipped leaders of the Fundamentalist Church of Jesus Christ of Latter-Day Saints (FLDS) that Arizona governor Howard Pyle intended to raid their isolated stronghold on the Utah-Arizona border, and he meant to do it conclusively. The boy sentries stationed on the highest ground of the unofficial town of Short Creek felt the rumble of heavy military transport trucks well before the darkened column's silhouette appeared against the desert's star-blurred horizon, affording them ample time to race back to town before Pyle's two hundred troops—more than Short Creek's entire adult population—poured into the settlement. Some accounts record that fully alerted FLDS leaders shattered the predawn silence with dynamite blasts, the signal for the faithful to gather and greet their oppressors.

The alarming ordnance display reassured Pyle that his decision to bring a heavily armed, overwhelming force into a dirt-farming community bursting with women and children was justified. After a five-month investigation, his investigators had informed him that this collection of child rapists and welfare embezzlers had amassed a dazzling arsenal for defense against the imminent apocalypse, stashing guns and explosives in the giant caves pocking the soaring red cliffs behind the town. Pyle also never second-guessed his decision to invite truckloads of press well marinated in the lurid details of his five-month investigation into FLDS, an investigation that proved myriad crimes, not least of which was the appalling practice of marrying girls as young as twelve to old men who'd accumulated up to twenty other women.

"We could do no less than this!" an emotional Pyle declared during an address describing the plight of FLDS children he called "innocent chattels" victimized by a handful of foul men from whom the children were "without hope of escaping their degrading slavery from the moment of their birth." Once his reporters told Americans the truth about Short Creek, Pyle knew a raid that might seem extreme at first blush would be not only understood but embraced.

But FLDS leaders knew the press was coming too. As armed-to-the-teeth American lawmen flooded into an ostensibly American community, the FLDS faithful waited in their modest town hall, erupting into a rousing chorus of "God Bless America" as the swarm of increasingly bewildered reporters filtered through the doors.

Where were the evil child molesters and degenerate "white slavers" promised in Pyle's voluminous report? The people before the reporters were spindly and plain, poor farmers barely squeaking by. The pitted streets and weather-beaten houses spoke to poverty, not wickedness. Children in thread-bare nightclothes and cardboard shoes issued heart-wrenching wails as they were torn from their mothers' arms. Anguished women, their faces stamped with the ravages of backbreaking work, sobbed and implored as the stony-faced American soldiers loaded their men into ominous prison buses.

Cameras rolled and clicked for days as Pyle processed his pitiful-looking prisoners, feeding long queues of stunned women and children what appeared to be cups of gruel from a kind of chuck wagon truck. And then, the horrifying coup de grace: after most of the men were hauled away, the dead-faced women and children were lined up in front of their humble but clean American houses holding numbered cards across their chests for identification. Less than ten years after the end of World War II, it wasn't quite a concentration camp picture, but it was close enough. Whatever traumatized Short Creek women Pyle didn't remove to Phoenix fled to relatives in neighboring communities trying, they said, to evade the jackboots of government. The press ate it up.

The media Pyle had enlisted to document his defeat of a criminal enter-prise—and perhaps launch the presidential bid he mulled—now savaged him from coast to coast. Constituents who had demanded an end to the polyga-mists in their midst turned on him. Legislators who'd shared Pyle's revulsion and appropriated hundreds of thousands of dollars for Pyle's investigation and raid now denounced him. Pyle and any other official discovered to be a part of the raid were drawn as big, fat ogres in editorial cartoons and excori-ated as heartless fiends in print. But the worst fallout came from the ocean of depressing photographs epitomized by *Life* magazine's September 14, 1953, pictorial essay of the raid and its aftermath.

In the article entitled "The Lonely Men of Short Creek," *Life* photogra-phers flexed their renowned artistry with photo after photo of Short Creek's remaining damaged yet stoic men, determined to do their level best to keep life normal for their motherless children. Essay editors outdid themselves with a half-page photo of a forlorn black dog abandoned to a bad fate on a bleak dirt road with the caption: "Deserted puppy, left behind when his young master was taken by state troopers to Phoenix, sits in the deserted main street of Short Creek." Without any evidence whatsoever, angry *Life* editors blamed the fatal heart attack suffered by an eighty-four-year-old man a full month after the raid on Governor Pyle's heartless actions.

Text accompanying "The Lonely Men of Short Creek" was perplexing to say the least. Crimes the arrested men were accused of actually committing—child rape, bigamy, fraud—were dismissed in a throwaway sentence, implying the charges were an obvious ruse concocted so that Pyle might storm into a perfectly idyllic American town and ruin everyone's lives. *Life* offered no speculation as to why Pyle might have nourished such an odd ambition, but the rest of the article was pure prophecy of the media's velvet-gloved approach to FLDS from that time until this day. With a few notable exceptions, American media continue to fail the public comprehension of what, exactly, FLDS is by modeling its coverage of the sect on a half-century-old *Life* article.

Concerning the young girls who would be assigned without consent to men old enough to be their grandfathers, *Life* impatiently insisted that polygamy "was the only life they'd ever known." The peeved writer explained that FLDS men were lonelier than most because they were "used to having as many as five women and 21 children around the house," yet they "stolidly" managed to fix their own breakfasts without assistance. Also recommending them were activities like corn husking, cow milking, and hymn singing. *Life* characterized the required underage marriages, polygamy, and welfare abuses as "tricky" legal questions, but the magazine's readers were reminded often and sternly that this hardy stock of pioneer folk were practicing a religion upon which no one could form an opinion, much less a judgment.

Pyle was floored, astonished, unable to beat back the tidal wave of public disgust by reminding the public that they themselves had demanded the removal of the polygamous, tax dollar–siphoning FLDS from their midst in noisy, sometimes raucous, public demonstrations just months before. Pyle couldn't find work as a street sweeper after he was hounded from the governor's mansion, a fate shared by a dozen other raid participants who couldn't get clear of the flying wreckage. Their ghosts would whisper in every politician and police officer's ear for the next half century: *Go there at your peril.*

For FLDS leadership, the 1953 raid was the ultimate cloud with the silver lining. Flabbergasted by the unexpected tsunami of public sympathy, FLDS leaders moved swiftly to solidify their unlikely new identity as paragons of American family values, besieged by a dangerously secular government. Immediately understood was the power of pictures and that a goodly chunk of professional photographers would overlook a lot of "tricky" questions for the photogenic smorgasbord of women and kids dressed in old-timey pioneer clothes doing old-timey stuff, all against a backdrop of spectacular vistas in the ethereal Southwestern light photographers treasure.

As the decades passed, FLDS leaders sporadically invited carefully pre-screened media folks who were not too picky about statutory rape into compounds otherwise fortified against intrusion by the tax-paid FLDS police force. Like the *Life* staff before them, photographers appreciated the opportunity to step back in time, producing montages of apple-cheeked children glowing under golden sunsets as they pulled carrots, played on swings, and of course prayed in the wholesome, somehow reassuring pigtail-and-pinafore garb representing a simpler, better time when butter was churned fresh and no one locked their doors.

The only adults in the essays are quaint, prairie dress–clad FLDS women, who might be snapped braiding one another's hair or sharing a carefree laugh as they bake bread from scratch. Photos of adult FLDS men are conspicuously absent, a glaring omission that suggests a prearranged complicity between the publications and FLDS men who know there is still a remote chance, however absurd, that a post-'53 raid police officer will prosecute them for taking "brides" as young as twelve. With media help, FLDS over the past fifty years has cultivated the mistaken impression they are a wholesome, if somewhat eccentric, American religion—sort of like the Amish but without the horse carriages. As in the *Life* article in 1953, texts accompanying photos admit polygamy is illegal, but so what? The ferocious American commitment to religious freedom—a bedrock of American society—trumps the admittedly odd practices of a small group far, far away. Nobody wanted to ever again see pictures of armed Americans dragging anguished women from their children and homes.

FLDS wore the 1953 raid like armor against nosy child welfare workers, outside cops, and fraud investigators, and the armor worked. By 2000, the FLDS population in Short Creek—comprising the twin cities of Colorado City, Arizona, and Hildale, Utah—had swelled from five hundred to ten thousand, with additional known FLDS enclaves in Utah, South Dakota, Colorado, Nevada, New Mexico, California, Canada, and Mexico, and suspected communities in a dozen other states. The sect's United Effort

Plan—a "trust" that held all land titles of all FLDS members—was worth $110 million in property alone, even as the vast majority of FLDS members subsisted on millions bestowed from various welfare programs, while millions more in tax dollars to support local government, schools, and police disappeared every year into FLDS bank accounts. Dozens of FLDS businesses in construction, lumber, concrete, and agriculture, staffed by unpaid FLDS members, flourished without the pesky labor costs other firms had to include in competitive project bids. The sect's leaders built 40,000-square-foot homes with trout ponds and wine cellars. They dined on fresh lobster while FLDS mothers parsed food stamps to feed thirty children. They traveled at will in their own aircraft, the only customers for the multimillion-dollar airport built outside Short Creek with a federal grant awarded to "encourage tourism."

Even a little curiosity would have revealed that tourism was the very last thing FLDS leaders wished to encourage. Little by little, Short Creek was transformed from a poor farming community of a few dozen families who governed themselves with a semblance of democracy into a wealthy fortress ruled by the iron words of a single man, the prophet, deemed to be God's only representative on earth.

The FLDS prophet controlled not only the wealth but also the daily lives of every man, woman, and child. The prophet decided who would work in a dairy or a construction site or a lumber mill, and on what days at which times. The prophet decided which men would be allowed a family and assigned girls without their consent to the men he selected. No books or magazines save those approved by the prophet were allowed. Television, music, radio, and movies were strictly forbidden. Tape recorders were allowed but only to listen to hour upon hour of droning religious instruction. Education, which had included the sciences until as late as 1986, was effectively ended. The FLDS teachers drove spanking new, high-end SUVs purchased by taxpayers and kept a good eye peeled for children not sufficiently "sweet" while teaching that God lived inside the sun and the fossil record was a nefarious government hoax.

Disobedience, however unintentional, was catastrophic. It would seem the FLDS doctrine of "blood atonement" murder, condoned from the pulpit by FLDS prophets, was too extreme a measure for actual practice, but who needed murder when you could erase an FLDS member's existence with a simple, declarative sentence? Because they did not own homes or cars or even the clothes on their backs, FLDS members had to keep sensitive antennae on the prophet's shifting moods lest they find themselves dropped in the middle of nowhere without a dime, stripped of home, family, and eternal salvation forever. Without explanation or appeal, the prophet could and did disappear a man in the middle of the night by throwing him in the back of a van, driving him out of town, and dumping him with orders that he never contact his family again. By dawn, his weeping wives and children would be reassigned to more favored brethren who would see to it the expelled man's name was never spoken again.

Women were so low on the heavenly totem pole they required their husband's postmortem consent to even get to heaven, but they were invaluable as child-bearing wives.

In a closed religious society that required each man to obtain a minimum of three wives before he could ascend to the celestial kingdom and rule a planet after death, the fifty-fifty gender birthrate was a killer. Many men had more than three wives. The prophet Rulon Jeffs was rumored to have upward of sixty, adding a fourteen-year-old girl when he was eighty-six. Women were too scarce a commodity to be given the boot for even the gravest indiscretions. So long as they could produce children, misbehaving females were isolated for "reflection," locked in secret houses or even abandoned in the cliff caves far above town for "behavior modification," which might involve beatings or deprivations of food, water, or sleep.

Even for FLDS members who might have wanted it, there was nowhere to turn for relief. There had never been a contested election in the governments of Hildale or Colorado City. Every tax-paid position was held by favored FLDS men. The police forces comprised FLDS men who reported not to state government but to the prophet, as did the firemen who might or might not respond to your burning home should you break a rule or be even suspected of harboring a bad thought. Outside police didn't want to get involved. Even when those young girls fleeing forced marriages to men several times their age managed to get out of town, skittish officers heeding the ghosts of 1953 simply returned them to their parents. And the situation was about to get so much worse.

By 2000 the pool of girls available for assignment had run critically low. Prophet Rulon Jeffs tried to remedy the situation by "plucking," as he called it, younger and younger girls, pulling them from school after the fourth or fifth grade to ready them for his impatient supporters. Yet the measure only extended the problem to a new generation. Now there were teenage boys, as well as young men in their twenties and up, without a single unattached girl in their age bracket, practicing a religion that required them to reproduce with at least three wives to enter the celestial kingdom. Without enlightening these bachelors to their forever single status, scores of young men were shuffled around the country like damaged playing cards to work in FLDS businesses and construction projects. Eventually, boys as young as twelve were also pulled from school to travel the United States as FLDS laborers.

When even those steps did not lessen the pressure, Rulon Jeffs and later his son, Warren, hit upon a solution of unbearable cruelty. Concocting the flimsiest of offenses, the prophet ordered parents to eject their own sons, some as young as thirteen, from the only community they'd ever seen without a penny, scrap of food, or change of clothes to their names. Fathers and mothers obeyed the prophet, driving their children into the yawning desert or to a faraway city. They'd be abandoned on the side of the road, left with these loving words from the parents who'd given them life: "You are eternally damned to hell, and we will never think of you or speak to you again." Terrified, bewildered, and devastated boys watched their fathers' taillights vanish into the night, their small bodies wracked with hopeless sobs. Many tried to kill themselves right away. Some succeeded, little sacrifices to the prophet's supporters' insatiable appetites for young girls.

Hundreds and hundreds of boys were severed this way, their own parents setting them adrift onto the mean streets of Las Vegas or Phoenix without educations, skills, or knowing a single soul, believing only hell awaited them. There were so many, the press was forced to create an entire classification to describe the drug-soaked, despairing boys who often turned to prostitution—the only skill they could learn on short notice—to eat. The "lost boys" became the shame of Utah and Arizona alike, their inhuman stories eventually printed in newspapers from coast to coast. Yet politicians and police still under the influence of the 1953 raid did nothing, knowing that interference with FLDS spelled political disaster.

Anti-FLDS activists screamed about the young girls and boys whose lives were being shattered with the support of tens of millions of tax dollars. They presented cases of appalling incest, rape, and assault, of mothers permanently separated from their children on a prophet's power whims, not to mention outrageous abuse and misappropriation of education and law enforcement funds. They issued press releases about missing FLDS persons for whom the authorities would not search—frantic girls running for their very lives who were returned to their oppressors without investigation and dead boys for whom no one grieved.

In the unassailable name of religious freedom, the entire nation averted its eyes, preferring instead the sanitized, wholesome picture stories that showed up on newsstands every eighteen months or so. FLDS judges, policemen, teachers, city councilmen, and public utilities administrators all abused their authority with impunity, blindly obedient to the self-proclaimed prophet Warren Jeffs and his increasingly draconian and bizarre revelations. Short Creek was allowed to morph into a dictatorship on U.S. soil with a dictator who openly and defiantly rejected U.S. law, declaring that snippets from his incoherent dreams were the only true laws from God.

"Fifty years of darkness" is what despairing activists call the madness allowed to flourish in the years between 1953 and 2000. They feared that the wall of darkness around Short Creek was too thick to breach. But in 2001, it cracked from within.

I

RUTH CROSSES THE RUBICON

Sisters, do you wish to make yourselves happy? Then what is your duty? It is for you to bear children in the name of the Lord, that are full of faith and the power of God— to receive, conceive, bear, and bring forth in the name of Israel's God.
                                    —Brigham Young, *Journal of Discourses*, Vol. 9

The devil uses a certain weakness. He whispers selfishness, and that weakness in a girl—since I am talking to girls—is vanity, wanting to be noticed, wanting to be looked at. Vanity is something useless where you want it, but it gets you nowhere, and when girls want to be where the boys are, look at them, that is called vanity. The good boys won't even pay you any attention. Faithful and good Priesthood men won't pay you attention and try to get you to like them. The boys that pay you attention and tries [sic] to get you to like them are the boys that would destroy you, and you can see that difference.
                            —Warren Jeffs, lecture to eighth grade girls, November 1, 2002

I just want to eat sugar or drink a cup of coffee without asking permission. I want to take my kids across town to the park without being followed. I want to get off all the welfare and be a real person. I want to be free and my kids to live free and I want my kids to have an education and have hope. I just want to be a real person.
                    —Journal of Ruth Stubbs, nineteen-year-old plural wife, June 2001, Phoenix

On a night nearing Christmas 2001, a resolved Ruth Stubbs stroked the perfect faces of her two sleeping toddlers, reviewing her deliriously dangerous plan to save their lives. If it worked, and that was a big qualifier, the plan would save her life as well, but Ruth didn't care about her own messed-up life. Looking back on the eternity of her nineteen years on earth, she understood she had never cared. FLDS had tricked her into self-loathing from birth, and tomorrow they'd begin hunting her like an animal.

The last three years had been the most monstrous. So monstrous it was sometimes hard to remember what had come before the prophet, out of the blue, "gave" her to a guy twice her age whom she didn't know. Until that surreal day almost exactly three years ago, Ruth felt she'd enjoyed a pretty OK childhood despite living it around the utterly twisted Fundamentalist Church of Jesus Christ of Latter-Day Saints, with "around" being the operative word. Looking back on it, Ruth realized she'd never truly been *in* FLDS. Until recently, her life had not been the physically battering, emotionally hopeless existence that she'd handed her own children, but in her defense, Ruth never imagined there would *be* any children in this picture. She'd only just turned sixteen when they'd literally thrown her in a pickup truck and driven her to hell.

That her father had helped them had been completely out of character and very difficult to accept, but Ruth didn't really blame him anymore. David Stubbs was FLDS raised. He'd acquired the three wives needed to enter the celestial kingdom and rule a planet after death before Ruth was born in 1982. That was lucky, because not so many men got a shot at the celestial kingdom after Rulon Jeffs and his son Warren took over Short Creek in 1986. After that, you had to be on the good side of Uncle Rulon, as he was called, to get the not-quite-ripe young girls assigned to you, and the Jeffs had some high-handed notions about strengthening Israelite bloodlines when making the assignments.

Until the Jeffs happened, David Stubbs had been kind of like FLDS royalty, being descended from one of the oldest polygamist families since The Work—as FLDS used to be called—got started in Short Creek during the 1930s. Consequently, the Stubbs family had some of the best lands with the most water rights—very important in the desert. Stubbs women had married into all the important Short Creek families who were also there from the beginning, and everybody was cool with the Lord and one another. Not to be too profane or anything, but Ruth had observed that the bonds of a more terrestrial nature could make the day-to-day business of living go a lot smoother.

Which was probably why David Stubbs wasn't too impressed with the Johnny-come-lately Jeffs family when they moved from Salt Lake City to Short Creek after the former prophet, Leroy Johnson, died. Naturally, Ruth hadn't known Uncle Leroy personally because she was just four years old when he died in 1986, but she did know he was beloved by a lot of Short Creek people, her dad included. When Rulon Jeffs just up and announced he was the new prophet when he'd lived in his Salt Lake all that time, a lot of Short Creekers didn't buy it. The first prophet, Joseph Smith, said that only God selects the prophet, and Uncle Leroy, who was the only one talking to God at the time, hadn't said squat about Rulon Jeffs before he passed on.

Plus, it was very cheeky, the way Uncle Rulon moved down from his big house in Salt Lake to take over Short Creek. Rulon and his favored son, Warren, had always been a little snotty to the Short Creek folks, who were still in shock that the prophet Leroy Johnson had died at all. Like all the prophets before him, Uncle Leroy said he'd *never* die until the apocalypse, which FLDS people have been expecting just about any day now from the beginning. Uncle Leroy predicted the end of days about three times, even anointing with sacred oil the ATVs God's chosen people—FLDS people— would need to hightail it to higher ground once the wholesale butchery of all the disbelievers started.

The descriptions of it could just make you sick with all the Gentiles' guts and blood flying everywhere and getting on your clothes. FLDS held survivalist skills classes where you learned how to slit cows' throats and everything, but nothing ever happened. People were disappointed when the world didn't end, but they felt even worse when Uncle Leroy explained that it hadn't happened because the FLDS people hadn't been pure enough for Joseph Smith and Jesus to ride their heaven cloud back to earth. The people felt really bad they'd let Jesus down that way. Uncle Leroy said that everybody had to double down and do better to help end the world, but he never said *anything* about the stuck-up Rulon Jeffs being elevated.

There was a big fight over it with a good number of people, Ruth's dad included, saying that Rulon Jeffs was not the prophet. But Uncle Rulon had his supporters too. They got kind of ugly about it, forming what some dubbed enforcement "God squads"—men who did what Uncle Rulon told them to do, including men in the police force. Uncle Rulon started "poofing" people, sometimes in the middle of the night, which meant they were excommunicated and driven away. Their wives and kids got reassigned to guys Uncle Rulon liked, and nobody could ever say the other guys' names again.

There were too many dissenters to poof them all, though, and it might have turned into a standoff, except the people on the wrong side of Uncle Rulon were alarmed about the rough exuberance of his support, so the dissenters banded together and moved onto land adjoining Short Creek. They were still fundamentalist Mormon polygamists, but they called themselves the Centennial Park group, later naming their town Centennial Park City.

The men were allowed to wear short-sleeved shirts, which Uncle Rulon said just proved how they already had one foot in hell.*

David Stubbs still didn't accept Rulon Jeffs as the prophet, but he didn't want to abandon his choice lands by moving to Centennial Park either, so he stayed put. This was unheard of. Living in Short Creek without acknowledging Rulon Jeffs as God's prophet pretty much made David Stubbs an apostate, and everybody knew that those who renounced FLDS were stripped of everything they owned and run out of town. But David Stubbs didn't take the hint, so in 1986, Jeffs sent notices all over Short Creek that FLDS folks were "tenants at will" of the prophet, and it was the prophet's will that Ruth's father and twenty other guys get the hell out of town. When this legal-sounding declaration, along with all the preceding threats and harassment, still failed to persuade the upstart FLDS men to abandon their lives, Rulon Jeffs was stumped. He'd never needed a backup plan in the past, but before he could fully consider his next move, Stubbs and the others hit Jeffs with the unimaginable. They filed a lawsuit against Rulon Jeffs in federal court claiming that they actually owned their lands under the terms of the UEP trust.

This was a lot more serious than the Centennial Park insurrection. That had been a stone shocker too, but those people had run away like they were supposed to. If people who didn't believe that Rulon Jeffs was God's prophet were allowed to live among those who did, it could really mess up Jeffs's power, which was utterly dependent on blind obedience coupled with Jeffs's ability to destroy the lives of anyone who opposed him. If the twenty-one families refusing to leave their lands won, what kind of message would that send? If Jeffs couldn't take away a man's home and family, would people still fear him? Would they still do what he told them to do? Jeffs didn't want to know the answer to those questions, so he dialed up FLDS's trusty Salt Lake City law firm of Snow, Christensen, and Martineau and the most dedicated FLDS attorney of all: Rod Parker.

Like he always did, Rod Parker just blistered the apostates led by David Stubbs in court, saying that a religion is untouchable in America, and religious

*   The FLDS offshoot known as Centennial Park or the Second Ward was actually founded in the early 1980s after the prophet Leroy Johnson arbitrarily switched the sect's internal system of governance from a quasi-democratic council headed by the prophet to "one-man rule" in which the prophet decided everything unilaterally. A sprinkling of families opposed to one-man rule left Short Creek, and in 1984 Johnson evicted the FLDS leaders and potential threats J. Marion Hammon and Alma Timpson. Centennial Park City did not achieve its current population of about two thousand until Rulon Jeffs increased the authoritarian style, driving more families away by choice or decree.

leaderships—not the courts—have the right to decide who stays and who goes. This argument had always prevailed, so you could have knocked everybody in FLDS over with a feather when, after years of battling, the Utah Supreme Court ruled against Rulon Jeffs in 1998, meaning that David Stubbs and the others got to stay put without declaring Rulon Jeffs the prophet.

Sure, the court had ruled only on a small technicality concerning the definition of the trust. It had not addressed the overall religious questions, which were still open for the legal hunt. But technicalities—life's little details—have a strong historical track record of tipping events in one direction rather than another, and so it was with the 1998 decision in *Jeffs v. Stubbs*. In seven years, the case would act as the explosives in a legal bomb that would leave the FLDS leadership fighting for their lives in three states, or at least fighting to retain control over every aspect of the members' lives, which was more or less the same thing.

Though they weren't planned or intended, the unrelated actions of three members of the Stubbs family would undo fifty years of FLDS untouchable status imparted by the disastrous raid of 1953. On the night nearing Christmas 2001, Ruth hadn't a clue that her desperate bid for freedom would be the timer set upon the ticking bomb, but Ruth and David Stubbs hadn't been the only family rebels. Ruth had another example from which to draw strength.

WHEN RUTH WAS five years old, her full-blooded sister, Pennie, accomplished the impossible. Threatened with the prospect of an intolerable marriage, Pennie fled Short Creek and got away clean. She'd been fourteen years old with flashy blue eyes, a beautiful brunette child with a woman's full figure, one that had not been overlooked by Rulon Jeffs. Without fanfare, Jeffs gave Pennie to a fifty-eight-year-old loyalist the girl absolutely detested, a swaggering bully with five other wives and something like seventy kids, many of them far older than Pennie. Ruth expected the guy must have been a serious Uncle Rulon fan to be given this juicy young girl, but Pennie wasn't having it.

In FLDS fashion, Pennie had only twenty-four hours to get herself together. As their mother worked on the wedding dress with other FLDS women, Ruth could just barely remember Pennie's loud despair, screaming at their mother, who was urging her to obey the prophet in the strongest terms. In an astonishing display of independent thinking, Pennie shrieked that her life was worth something and she would not forfeit her future to become a pedophile's concubine. Their mother, Sally Stubbs, told the girl to hush up and accept her place like all FLDS women before her. Sally did not go after her daughter when the girl stormed from the house. Where on earth could she go?

Even today there is no public transportation in Short Creek, not even taxis. Girls are closely monitored. A girl even walking alone on the streets would be reported to the cops, who'd come pick her up.* Even if she managed to get to the main road and hitchhike, the first person who stopped would be driving her straight back to town. Walking out of the desert southwest was laughable, and even if, wonder over wonder, she did get past Short Creek, they'd be coming after her for sure. She might get flat out kidnapped from wherever she landed. Or FLDS would sic one of their law firms on her. Parental rights were tried and true. If she had kids, they'd go after them through her husband. If she were a kid, they'd come after her through her parents. If all else failed, some women had been legally committed to insane asylums.

But Pennie Stubbs beat them. Keeping to the bushes, flattening herself against walls when camouflage was scarce, the scared but steady girl made her way though Short Creek's dark streets to the two-lane blacktop leading out of town. In those days, getting past the polygamy-sympathetic town of St. George forty miles away was imperative. A fleeing girl had to make it almost to Las Vegas to be truly clear of FLDS influence. Between the FLDS police, the members, and the fact that nobody outside of these two groups would be afoot at the late hour in the remote area, Pennie's chances were as close to zero as it got.

But as a confident Sally Stubbs continued the wedding dress as she waited for her daughter to be returned, the impossible materialized behind a lone set of headlights on the highway, illuminating a quivering, bedraggled teenage girl with a tear-stained face and her thumb out. The driver who should have been an FLDS cop or member was instead a businessman who'd elected to take the back roads on a whim, then decided he felt fresh enough to push

---

*   Police departments in both Colorado City, Arizona, and Hildale, Utah, are certified state law enforcement agencies supported by tax dollars. Despite this, the officers in both departments, some of them polygamists, openly declare their allegiance to the FLDS prophet above all other laws. FLDS girls do not consider reporting abuse to the Short Creek police. In the past, abused girls are also unlikely to find relief with outside police agencies, who might be polygamist sympathizers or unwilling to risk bad publicity by failing to return minors to their parents.

through the night to his Las Vegas destination. Most staggering of all, the man knew all about FLDS, and he didn't like anything he knew. Although the businessman was inviting big trouble by driving a runaway minor girl across state lines without parental permission, that is exactly what he did. The man Pennie still regards as heaven-sent risked his own arrest rather than return her for the rape and misery that awaited her. He drove out of his way to bring her to a women's shelter, which would not report her presence, and left her with all the money in his wallet, $200, and an order to have a good life.

That is exactly what Pennie intended. Today, she is Pennie Petersen, happily married mother and a scourge for FLDS, one of a half-dozen people denounced from FLDS pulpits by name. Her outspoken public activism is irritating enough, but it has been her success in helping dozens of young girls escape Short Creek that has proved most devastating for a sect that needs to keep every single female born into the cocoon available for its older men.

WHEN RUTH STARTED thinking about leaving, she was sure glad she had Pennie for a sister because everybody knew that getting out of town was just part of the fight. Like most FLDS girls, Ruth had been pulled from school, such as it was, in the fifth grade. With abbreviated educations, FLDS girls have no job or social skills. More insurmountable than that, they don't know anyone in the outside world who can offer support and guidance. They've nowhere to live and have never handled money outside of food stamps. They end up frightened and destitute, usually with small, wailing children for whom they cannot provide. Disoriented, confused, terrified, it is usually not difficult for FLDS to lure them back with promises of forgiveness and love.

For the less persuadable, there were always the FLDS lawyers and the polygamy-friendly Utah courts bordering Short Creek. Going after a girl's children killed two birds with one stone, because once FLDS lawyers got custody of a woman's children, she almost always returned to the sect. Ruth was sure she'd react to losing her kids the same way other FLDS women had: unable to bear life without her children, she would return.

When she did, there would be terrible punishment. The loss of eternal salvation wasn't always deterrent enough for the most desperate FLDS girls. Elders had to be certain potential runaways suspected more corporeal consequences. The possibilities were whispered shadows, elusive as snow on the wind. Women weren't supposed to know anything at all about FLDS worldly workings, and damn few men did either, but Ruth figured the elders let just enough slip out, oopsy-like, to give the community a shudder of what "uppity" women could expect. Maybe you'd be stuck up in one of those caves in the vermillion cliffs with not enough food or water. Cold, hungry, scared, with only sporadic visits from these gnarly old men who would yell at you or even hit you. You might be shipped off to some other FLDS settlement for the same treatment. After a few weeks of that, girls would be just begging for that sealing ceremony. It was known definitely that if you had kids, they'd be taken away, maybe forever. This was a measure that could be taken in the open, with the full support of folks who agreed a hell-bound, disobedient woman shouldn't be taking her kids with her.

Ruth knew all this, but it had just come to the point where staying was scarier for her kids than being caught. Pennie was her ace in the hole, the sister who knew the ropes. And Ruth's father had given her another set of skills most FLDS girls didn't have: the freedom to think for herself.

To the horror of his three wives and everybody else in Short Creek, David Stubb allowed Ruth to wear pants. Don't ask her why, but Ruth had fallen in love with tractors as a little girl. Her dad let her work on the family's tractors while wearing pants, a double whammy scandal that first set the harsh Short Creek rumor mill churning. Ruth was a natural, the ultimate tomboy. She worked alongside her brothers loading timber, digging fence posts, and laying pipe. For a while, she had a tomboy twin, her sister Jinny, who was born the same year as Ruth by a different mom. They were like the two musketeers, sacrificing the sacrosanct FLDS modesty for such disturbing activities as fishing, camping, and hunting, although she didn't enjoy the death part of hunting.

David Stubbs also allowed Ruth to have friends, even friends who were boys, as she got older. That was another bad scandal, made worse by the fact she could also talk to boys and girls from excommunicated or apostate families. This behavior was so shocking, the fact that Ruth smoked the occasional cigarette and drank a watered down, convenience store beer now and again was practically overlooked, except by the FLDS cops. They kept picking her up, giving her tickets, and threatening to take her before the prophet for hanging around the wrong people and having fun. Ruth sure got tired of getting those stupid, expensive tickets from the police, but David Stubbs always straightened her legal difficulties out quietly. One day she'd be facing hundreds of dollars of tickets and court dates, and the next day her troubles would disappear as easily as did the guys the prophet didn't like.

"Don't get caught again," Stubbs would advise her with a jocular wink and no insight into the true meaning of the tickets. But then, Ruth's perceived idyllic relationship with her father deteriorated with the rest of his life. David Stubbs's marriages had never been what you'd call happy. Like many FLDS men, Ruth's father kept a house separate from his wives and children, but that didn't ensure peace among "sister wives" afflicted with the same jealousies, insecurities, and need for affirmation as the rest of the human race.

Ruth's biological mom, Sally, was particularly unpredictable, displaying wild, sometimes violent mood swings. The family of three wives and forty-two children seemed dependent on David's second wife for what structure there was, and when she died of cancer, everything fell apart. David started drinking too much and carrying on with apostate women. Sally divorced him—as his first wife, she could do this legally, in court—and he kind of disappeared.

It was a wrenching development for Ruth, who clung to her family—or at least the good idea of one—like a buoy on pitching seas. Most FLDS children remain single-mindedly devoted to their families no matter what those families do to them in the name of the religion. Ruth was no exception. As more and more of her siblings fell away from FLDS, it became Ruth's mission in life to reunite her clan under one happy umbrella of camping, fishing, cookouts, and reunions. She didn't care one way or the other about the religion, but she was open to it, if that's what it took to reclaim family unity.

Ruth certainly had her work cut out for her, especially after her mom took up with the independent, slickly handsome FLDS grifter and convicted pedophile, Orson William Black.*

It wasn't long before Sally was trying to convince her fourteen-year-old daughter to share Black's bed. Even at that tender age, Ruth knew her mother's behavior was crazy reprehensible, but she refused to give up hope the family could be mended. To that end, she stayed in her mom's house instead of moving in with one of her adult siblings. While trying to break through to her mother, Ruth developed escape strategies to skitter away from the offensive Black when he was in the home.

---

* Raised in FLDS, Orson William Black left the sect with his own converts after discovering he was an archangel who could speak directly to God whenever he pleased. In one of his chats, God instructed Black to marry as many twelve- to fifteen-year-old girls as he could find. It is alleged boys were not exempt from his attentions, either. Black never got to Ruth, but he did marry and abuse two of her sisters, both under the age of fifteen. One of them has serious, ongoing emotional challenges due to the abuse. In 2002, Arizona indicted Black on two counts of conspiracy and sexual abuse of a minor. He fled to Mexico, where he is believed to preside over his own sect in the state of Chihuahua.

It was difficult because Black and every other man in Short Creek had their eyes on Ruth Stubbs, who'd blossomed into something of the town beauty. By the time she was fifteen, Ruth could be accurately described as a wholesome blond bombshell. Her statuesque five-foot-eight-inch frame supported 135 pounds of curves toned by a lifetime of tomboy exercise, but her figure wasn't even her most outstanding feature. Ruth possessed a dazzling, welcoming smile that made people happy to be alive, eager to be in her company. Tumbling, thick blond hair set off dancing eyes of the brightest blue. She was honest, quick to laugh, and quicker to sympathize, console, and encourage. Ruth Stubbs didn't have a bad bone in her body.

It was a package Hildale police officer Rodney Holm certainly understood when he started singling her out for all those moral turpitude tickets. Without her father's intervention, the tickets were a hassle, but Ruth didn't excite herself over it. She never even glanced at the cop who wrote her up. There were worse things happening in her life than tickets for smoking.

Confused, without guidance, and isolated in a fundamentalist religious community that condemned her daily, Ruth's confidence began to teeter, and she went a little crazy. She further damaged her self-esteem by keeping secret company with boys who couldn't acknowledge her existence on the street in daylight. Her cigarette consumption soared to four a day. Her weak 3.2 beer consumption put her perilously close to drunkenness a few times.

What if she were truly damned? What if it were true that Satan controlled her very soul? Dreams once populated by happy scenes were now invaded by visions of the eternal flames, so real her skin felt singed as she bolted awake in cold sweats. All the FLDS teachings carelessly discarded under her father's protection came surging back, strengthened by the fact that David Stubbs now seemed to be on the fence about Rulon and Warren Jeffs. She'd been fooling herself. They'd been right all along. Why else would this be happening? She'd turned a defeated sweet sixteen, not knowing where to turn.

Then, a miracle. Visiting a girlfriend who would still see her in daylight, Ruth saw the man of her dreams, her deliverance from the abyss. His name was Carl Cook, her friend's cousin from Salt Lake City and a strict Rulon Jeffs FLDS guy. Though he was twenty-six—a man, really—he was too adorably shy to look at her, but he was her white knight for sure. Brave, honest, and true blue. Ruth just knew it. She could die, he was so cute. From that point on, there was no one else. She would marry Carl Cook or die trying. What Ruth didn't—couldn't—possibly know about Carl Cook would soon shatter her heart and issue her a lifetime of aching regret.

Carl Cook was one of possibly thousands of unavoidably excess men endemic to a closed society that bestows multiple women upon certain men. After the Centennial Park debacle, Rulon Jeffs was accused of using young girls as currency to solidify support among his aging supporters, a practice with precedent. From the earliest days of polygamy, youthful women were used as rejuvenators for older loyalists and, by the late 1990s, Uncle Rulon was pushing ninety with his inner circle not far behind. In addition, three wives were required to reach the celestial kingdom, but more was better. The more wives, the more children who would populate your planet. The more populated the planet, the more exalted the rule.

Adding more and more women to a small group of men further diminished not just the supply of girls but also the pool of men who could hope to marry at all, ever. By the late 1990s, the permanent expulsion from Short Creek of boys, some as young as thirteen, was becoming alarming to anti-polygamy groups watching the sect as best they could.

But excommunication wasn't Uncle Rulon's only tool for culling the herd of hopeful grooms. FLDS boys had always been raised with a hands-off policy toward girls, but now they were taught females were "poisonous snakes" with depraved designs on their hapless male victims' salvation. In lieu of excommunication, suitably obedient boys as young as twelve who, through no effort of their own, happened to capture the fancy of any girl, might be yanked from school and sent away to work in FLDS construction, lumber, agriculture, or manufacturing businesses around the country. Told that they were invaluable cogs in the building up of Zion, scores of grown men were also banished to such unpredictable assignments for weeks, months, or years at a time. Even inside FLDS, they were called "eunuchs." Carl Cook was one of them.

Carl's inability to look Ruth in the eye was not a sign of the adorable modesty she imagined but of a ravaging, living fear that doing so would expose him to expulsion from FLDS into the licking flames of hell. It was likely Carl had never been close to any woman outside of the female relatives Ruth now pestered for an introduction. When the astonishingly beautiful, vivacious Ruth Stubbs made her intentions plain to Carl Cook, the shock may have overwhelmed him. It certainly stirred his dormant loins.

Carl's programmed aversion to the "poisonous snakes" was no match for Ruth's single-minded determination to make him hers. After a few sputtering starts, Ruth masterminded a two-day, eight-person, co-ed camping trip to which Carl was innocently invited by a third party. The group rode ATVs in the wilderness for a while, then went for a refreshing swim in a crystalline pond, a perfect day to be enjoyed and savored. Ruth spent every minute of it worried sick she'd lose sight of Carl and miss the critical but so far elusive opportunity to get next to him. After the men bagged and dressed a wild turkey, Ruth managed to snare a seat next to him as the bird roasted over an open campfire. Success! He still couldn't really look at her, but as people drifted away to their sleeping bags, Carl opened up with monologues on topics Ruth later couldn't remember but knew she could have listened to for the rest of her life. When he finally stretched and announced he was going to bed in the backseat of the pickup truck, Ruth was frantic to keep the evening going.

In a bold and reckless move, Ruth persuaded the guy who was supposed to share the backseat with Carl to give her the spot. Carl was asleep when she slid into place, conceding something to modesty when she lay down with her head at Carl's feet and drifted off. She was awakened by klutzy hands fumbling at her breasts with an inept urgency that bordered on painful. Charmed by the inexpert advance, Ruth repositioned herself so the couple might share their first magical kiss, but Carl was pretty worked up, and Ruth had to back him off a bit. She was a real believer in virgin marriage. *Her* white dress was going to be big and fluffy, and it wouldn't be just a symbol of purity. Well, close to purity. Ruth had a little experience with kissing and light petting, although she was pretty sure Carl had not and did not know the limits. It was very cute, although it was hard to snap him out of it long enough to explain they couldn't let things get out of hand. Carl was so *apologetic*, so *contrite* over his ungentlemanly mistake Ruth thought he'd melt from embarrassment. It was proof Carl was the most gallant white knight ever.

After that night, it was smooth sailing. The couple saw each other as often as they could. Because Ruth was in apostate limbo and Carl was devout FLDS, getting together required imagination, but they managed. Carl wanted to marry Ruth as much as she wanted to marry him, and—this was the coolest part—Carl wanted a monogamous marriage just like her. She didn't even have to talk him into it! He cared about her more than the celestial kingdom, like their minds and souls were already one. Ruth couldn't say when she'd concluded that polygamy was a bad idea, but there wasn't a doubt in her mind that it was. For her, there would be a white wedding, a huge party after, and then a boatload of kids and true blue, everlasting love—just her and Carl and their kids against the world.

Carl, however, was ulcerous with worry. Ruth had not yet been branded an apostate, but plenty of her family members—including the notorious Pennie Petersen—were. Their marriage was absurd, impossible. The prophet had not assigned Ruth to Carl. He would never accept such a marriage. But, unbeknownst to Carl, Ruth had anticipated the trouble and hatched a plan. Oblivious to Carl's terror, Ruth explained the particulars, which were simple and drastic at the same time: she'd just go on bended knee to Uncle Rulon and ask for readmittance to FLDS so she could marry Carl. The life change was admittedly bigger for her than Carl, but he was worth it.

In Ruth's mind, her return to FLDS was conditional upon her marriage to Carl, but that is not how Uncle Rulon and his increasingly powerful son, Warren, would see it. Ruth didn't understand that there would be no question about readmitting a beautiful, young, blue-eyed blond to FLDS. The only question before Rulon and Warren Jeffs would be how to get rid of Carl Cook. Ruth never understood that Carl Cook was doomed the moment she uttered his name.

Ruth also didn't understand that she could have called Uncle Rulon from a Las Vegas casino with her offer and he might have sent the Jeffs family plane to pick her up. She mistakenly believed a lowly sort like herself would need an intermediary to approach a man who spoke with God. She felt she had few options on this one. Most of the Stubbses were out of the religion, but she did have a much older full-blooded sister, Susie, who was married to an up-and-coming muckety-muck, Hildale police officer Rod Holm, whom Ruth believed she'd never met. (She didn't know that Officer Holm had been the one to single her out for those annoying moral turpitude tickets.)

Holm was some sort of enforcer for the prophet, which meant he sometimes beat people up. Distasteful as that was, Holm had been given two wives already, meaning he was on the prophet's good side.* Ruth felt she could use clout like that to get an audience with the prophet and decided she'd ask Susie for the introduction. When she explained the plan to Carl, he was all for it. Then he beat a hasty retreat to the relative safety of Salt Lake City to await the verdict.

Susie Holm was none too pleased to find an apostate sister begging favors at her door. Susie didn't even want Ruth—a frequent subject of the

---

* One of Holm's wives was Wendy Holm, the former wife of Rod Holm's own excommunicated brother. Wendy came into the marriage with two children, Rod Holm's nephews. Along with their mother, they were forbidden to speak of their father ever again, and the children were forced to call Rod "father."

town's humiliating rumor mill—to be *seen* standing at her door. She'd only tended Ruth a few times as an infant and, as she recalled, hadn't enjoyed it then either. Susie had an important position now as the *legal* first wife of Officer Holm. She guarded it with everything she had.

For instance, first wives are entitled to "correct" other wives and their children, a task Susie particularly enjoyed when Wendy came on board with distraught children disobedient enough to miss their real father. It secretly galled Susie that Wendy had the same legal last name of Holm, but Susie was still in charge of the household, which included falsifying the welfare paperwork to maximize payments.* Maybe the prophet realized that Wendy having the last legal name and all would simplify that job for Susie. At least that's what Susie told herself when the Devil got in her head, making her pissed off that this one little splash of honor—the legal name—had been diluted.

Still, Wendy's reassignment signaled the prophet was looking at Rod as a guy deserving a third wife, and that meant they were all going to the celestial kingdom to rule a planet after their deaths. Well, Rod would rule and make Susie a "goddess" if he saw fit, but Susie felt her obedience and sweetness was way above par, and she'd been "training" and "correcting" Wendy well too, like the first wife was supposed to. They were so close to salvation Susie could taste it, so even though she didn't care for Ruth, Susie held her nose, because in reality, they all needed that third wife.

As for Ruth, she had to grovel a little harder than she'd expected, but in the end Susie agreed to mediate the meeting with the prophet, and that's what mattered. Ruth never knew that Susie had in fact taken her bubbly sister's request to Rod Holm, who approved it. Holm was the person who wanted Ruth to request readmittance to FLDS. Susie may have recognized the writing on the wall, but even if Ruth had known about Holm, it's

---

*   As a part of the record for Ruth Stubbs's custody battle in Utah's Third District Court (*Holm v. Stubbs*, No. *014500891*), Ruth's Tucson attorney, William G. Walker, subpoenaed the welfare applications completed by Susie Holm for the three years Ruth was in the Holm house. Among the many questionable entries is Susie Holm's assertion that she is the natural mother of both Ruth and Ruth's children. Susie's frequent misrepresentations are standard operating procedure for FLDS members, of whom upward of 80 percent receive some form of welfare, also called "manna from heaven." Authorities in Utah and Arizona accept that FLDS members falsify government forms, as well as muddling birth and marriage records to disguise polygamy and underage marriage. FLDS leaders openly encourage these practices, freely characterizing them as "lying for the Lord" or "bleeding the beast." Sect members are taught that Jesus approves of both techniques.

doubtful she would have allowed anything to penetrate her happy delirium. Ruth's heart was just too full of stars to make room for caution.

Instead, Ruth began rehearsing her heartfelt presentation to Uncle Rulon. In her mind's eye, she saw him kind of tearing up as she expressed her regret at past misunderstandings and explained the purity of her and Carl's love. She wanted a poetic touch for that and complete sincerity in her promise to live her married life in faithful FLDS fashion, completely overlooking the fact that monogamous marriage didn't exist in FLDS, nor did women have any say in who they married. Ruth dreamed of her big white dress and a ranch house she'd decided would be painted blue. She was thinking maybe five to eight kids. She and Carl both came from big families, so it could go more. They'd figure it out together, like they'd figure everything out together. All Ruth's planning pushed everything she knew about FLDS clean out of her mind.

In early autumn 1998, the newly minted sixteen-year-old Ruth Stubbs appeared before the prophet Rulon Jeffs to plead her case. As she launched her polished presentation, she was a little concerned that the vacant-eyed Uncle Rulon appeared to be drooling, but when no one acknowledged this condition Ruth pressed on with the passion of her cause. Only Jeffs's closest advisors and Rulon's omnipresent son, Warren, knew that the eighty-eight-year-old year old Jeffs had suffered a series of strokes so debilitating he sometimes didn't know where he was. The strokes were a bad turn of events since Uncle Rulon had declared, and the people believed, that he would live to be 350 years old, unless the world ended first, but Jeffs's condition increasingly prevented him from making the most basic FLDS business decisions, much less inspire a flock of thousands depending on him to direct their daily activities.

Before anyone could think, Warren Jeffs had slipped into the power vacuum, demonstrating the heretofore unknown ability to channel his father's thoughts. Jeffs's power grab alarmed many who believed the spindly, anemic-looking man's monotone droning, endless religious training tapes, and suspect sexual proclivities were only the tip of an iceberg of cruel, unstable ambition to be executed with an autocracy even more severe than his father's. Their fears would prove accurate beyond expectation, but their hope that Warren, as the middle son with no church title, could not ascend to prophet proved to be wishful thinking. By the time Ruth presented herself for readmittance and marriage in FLDS, Warren Jeffs had become synonymous with his ailing father in the minds of the faithful and would adjudicate Ruth's life from that day on.

Her heart bursting with light, Ruth failed to appreciate the intensity of
Warren Jeffs's interest in her presentation. Warren was known to be scouring Short Creek and the group's Canadian outpost as well, "plucking" the
prettiest, youngest girls for his family's celestial kingdom, but Ruth directed
her vigor toward Uncle Rulon. To her great relief, he seemed to have recovered himself by the end of her speech. Before his bodyguards shuffled him
out, he told Ruth she was back in FLDS, no sweat, and he'd take her other
little matter up with God and get back to her.

That was good enough for Ruth, who knew from her reading that a man
of God such as Uncle Rulon would never stomp on a love so pure as hers
and Carl's. It seemed that, under all the layers of pants and tractors, Ruth
Stubbs still had faith in the only religion she'd ever known. A jubilant Ruth
departed the meeting to begin digging through bridal magazines. She was
disappointed but not worried when she could not find Carl to share the joyous news. Ruth wasn't panicked even after weeks passed without word from
her future husband. FLDS was forever moving him around job sites. Some
of them were so far out in the boonies you'd expect overlooked tribes of
wild Indians to attack the settlements, and there weren't always phones.

But Carl wasn't building up a remote FLDS outpost, nor was he without
phone service. Where Ruth Stubbs was concerned, Warren Jeffs was leaving nothing open to interpretation. Within hours of Ruth's meeting with
the prophet, Warren dispatched a slew of emissaries not just to Carl but to
Carl's father's home in Short Creek, meaning the entire Cook family would
be dragged into the dead zone unless Carl heeded this bit of unfriendly advice:
never speak to Ruth Stubbs again. Nobody needed Warren Jeffs's enforcers to
spell it out for them, and Carl didn't need to be told twice. He never placed or
returned a call to Ruth again. He never told her the wedding was off.

Oblivious to the disaster, Ruth continued her breezy wedding plans,
but after months passed, impatience overwhelmed her natural inclination
to await the prophet's decision with polite decorum. Returning to Susie
on December 10, 1998, Ruth was surprised to find her formerly aloof sister eager to assist. Deciding to interpret Susie's change of heart as a good
omen, Ruth floated into the new meeting with the prophet (and Warren) on
cloud nine. Although she hadn't talked to him since the first meeting, Ruth
expected to leave this one with a wedding date her beloved Carl could hang
his hat on. She knew he must be dying for news.

There were more people in the room at this meeting. It was probably her
imagination, but it felt like they were crowding her. Her sister was there, and

a few others she recognized. More whom she didn't recognize. Why were they there? She decided to ignore the fact that they'd closed ranks behind her, and when the prophet finally did speak, Ruth felt certain her happy anticipation was blurring his words.

Ruth heard Uncle Rulon confirm that God wanted her married. *Duh,* Ruth thought. But the next part was jarring, not even close to right. Uncle Rulon said God wanted her married *in the morning* to *Rodney Holm.* Ruth felt like she was in an earthquake movie where you're helpless, stumbling around like an imbecile trying to keep footing on ground disappearing beneath your feet. She was reeling as the prophet said he "felt like she belonged" to a man twice her age—a man who was her sister Susie's husband, with another wife and eighteen kids. He said it as if it were nothing, with an almost shrug, as if the rest of her life were of so little matter as to be almost boring. Ruth felt like she'd been punched in the stomach.

Later, Ruth would remember Holm as the cop who'd singled her out of a group of kids to issue tickets to her alone. But on that day, even though he was her brother-in-law, she didn't know Rod Holm from the man in the moon. Now she heard Prophet Jeffs's surprisingly gentle voice reminding her about her salvation, asking if Ruth planned on obeying God's will to be sealed to Rod Holm in about twenty hours. The people in the room seemed to close in on her, cutting off her air as they waited for her to choose between salvation and hellfire, and Ruth felt like she was floating toward the ceiling. Hot and cold flashes rocked her body as she turned her face upward to deal with the stream of burning tears flowing from her eyes. Trembling with shock, she heard her own disembodied voice agreeing to submit for her salvation and her family's.

Though it came from a shaking, weeping child on the verge of physical collapse, Ruth's affirmative answer was good enough for Rulon and Warren Jeffs. The drama over, Ruth was forgotten as everyone turned their attention to the chore of escorting the frail Rulon Jeffs from the room. It was as if the whole room let out a collective breath, exactly the intermission Ruth needed to snap out of it. Knocking grasping arms from her body, she bolted from the building in a blur, leaping into her father's pickup and burning rubber as she peeled away in a desperate search for her knight and savior, Carl Cook.

She found him on a side street, lounging against a truck like the handsome cowboy he was, talking with some of his fellow dudes as if nothing was amiss in the whole wide world. Ruth was ecstatic. Carl didn't know! If he had, Ruth knew he'd be racing to her rescue this minute and nothing would stand in his way! Flooded with relief, filled with hope, Ruth ignored the FLDS trucks and vans now screeching down on her from every street. How could they have gotten here so fast? How did they even know where she was going? She floored her truck, trying to get past the first gelling line of a blockade. If she could just get to Carl, it wouldn't matter if they boxed her in. Carl would save her. They could escape in *his* truck and never stop until they reached the safety of Phoenix or Las Vegas or even Los Angeles.

The sudden appearance of a van in her windshield forced her to stomp the brakes, momentarily losing sight of her beloved. Flinging her door wide, Ruth hit the ground running, streaking toward the spot she'd last seen Carl as happy tears wet her cheeks. She reached the spot and stopped, but where was Carl? Had she run the wrong way? Whipping her head in every direction, Ruth could not see Carl or his friends. But then she did see something familiar: the taillights of Carl's truck, tires spitting gravel as he deserted her. He must have taken off as soon as he'd seen Ruth. Carl was abandoning her to the FLDS members he knew would surround her, return her to the prophet. At that moment, the only thing of Ruth Stubbs left alive was a physical body she wished was as dead as her soul. She longed for a gun, a knife, or a handful of deadly pills as her captors emerged from their trucks.

She was vacant, numb, as they approached her cautiously, like you'd come up on a dumb, spooked animal. They spoke in low, soothing tones Ruth didn't care to decipher. Susie was there. Rod Holm was there, for God's sake. Had he been there all along? Her father was there. *How could that be?* she wondered idly. David Stubbs would *never* approve of this. She felt herself being loaded into Susie's pickup, not knowing or caring what they did with her.

They took Ruth to a house. There were a bunch of women there getting ready to sew her wedding dress. Rod Holm went and asked her dad for her hand, and her dad said: "Yes. It will calm her down." Ruth stayed up all night without eating or drinking, vaguely hearing the women jabber as they sewed a dress Ruth mournfully observed was not big or fluffy or even a nice shade of white.

Ruth was spinning, spinning inside her own head. She was certain she'd cleverly disguised the spinning and the women saw only a silent girl, motionless as a statue but still with a small smile on her face. Because Ruth had surely figured it out. *She had figured it out!* They couldn't fool *her*. This was one big, fat, elaborate game of switcheroo. A test! Just like the prophets were always saying the Lord threw tests at you, and this was hers! Carl had *not* run away, that was just part of the theater. And she was *not* going to marry Rodney Holm in a few hours. That would be stupid. She loved Carl, and Carl loved her. This was *exactly* like a movie she'd heard about where everybody conspires and makes the girl *think* she's going to marry this one guy, but then the guy she *really* loves shows up at the last minute and takes the *wrong* guy's place. That was *exactly* what was going on here.

As the women sewed, Ruth's smile expanded. How dumb did they think she was? Maybe the dress was a bust for the ceremony tomorrow, but she'd get the big, fluffy one later. Maybe have a vow renewal ceremony or something down the road. She sure hoped Carl had remembered she wanted a big reception party while he was planning all this silly stuff. *Men*, she snorted inside her head, hearing it the way her mom used to say it. Kind of scolding but with affection. She didn't know why Carl was doing all this unnecessary and upsetting stuff, but she was sure there was a reason.

WHEN RUTH'S MOTHER heard that her sixteen year old daughter had been "given" to Rod Holm, she hit the roof. Sally Stubbs was indeed a changed woman. A mere two years earlier, she'd tried and failed to place her then fourteen-year-old daughter in the bed of a sadistic pedophile. But in 1999 she was prepared to fight like a tigress to keep Ruth away from Rod Holm, away from polygamy and FLDS altogether.

Sally called her successfully escaped daughter Pennie Petersen in for reinforcements, but as much as they desperately tried, the women could not break through to Ruth, now wrapped in her own catatonic delusions of a practical joke wedding. Ruth kept smiling as Pennie tried to make her understand this was not a movie, Carl would not appear to take Rod Holm's place, and by nightfall, Ruth would find herself imprisoned in a hell on earth. Nothing worked. A serene Ruth only pitied her furious older sister's willful ignorance of such an obvious ruse. In a few hours, Ruth insisted, she would be happily married to Carl, not Rodney Holm.

That's exactly what Ruth thought as she smiled dopily through her "sealing" ceremony to Holm, conducted by the again indisposed prophet's clairvoyant son, Warren. Overexposed "wedding" photographs, which double as a kind of FLDS marriage certificate for the illicit, and in this case criminal, union tell the tale. Seated in the foreground is a disinterested Rulon Jeffs, flanked by a somber Warren and another, elderly man wearing a severe expression. Standing behind them, Rod Holm offers the camera a look of insipid complacency while Susie Holm regards her beautiful, much younger sister with pinched resignation. Wendy Holm is there, looking lost. Apparently unaware of the camera or anything else on the planet, a bouffanted Ruth smiles dazedly toward the doors at the rear of the room, doors from which she still expects Carl Cook to emerge any second to end the movie properly.

Some FLDS brides don't get much breathing room between the "sealing" and the small room off the ceremony area furnished only with a bed, but Rod Holm had grander plans for the honeymoon of his lovely and critically important third wife. He'd booked a room at the FLDS-owned Mark Twain Hotel located on the main highway across from the glaring florescent towers of CJ's convenience store, where Ruth would shortly be assigned to fourteen-hour workdays with no pay.*

Unlike the mainstream Mormon Church, FLDS does not prohibit any type of "strong drink," and the room was stocked with at least two bottles of champagne. Ruth knows there were at least two because she downed that much by herself before entering blackout territory, her intended destination from the moment she'd rejoined reality and realized the movie had ended badly. She remembered nothing of her "first time" or any other part of the evening except one: she was absolutely certain Carl was parked outside the Mark Twain all night, weeping and drinking himself into a stupor in the cab of the truck he'd used just over twenty-four hours prior to desert her. She never saw him or heard him speak, but to this day, Ruth remains dead sure he was there, keeping watch.**

Ruth was glad to get out of the depressing Mark Twain Hotel, but an hour later the honeymoon suite seemed like nirvana. Rodney Holm disappeared

---

*   Like most FLDS wives working outside the home in FLDS businesses, Ruth's paychecks were cut and delivered directly to her husband. During the custody fight, Susie Holm denied the family received any income from CJ's (no such income was listed on the welfare applications either), insisting that Ruth's salary was mediated in barter or trade for other family necessities as needed. Although the criteria for who must actually do so in what amounts are unclear, FLDS leaders maintain all members—male and female—return their income, including those incomes supplied by tax dollars like Rod Holm's, to the church. Bartering is part of the FLDS economy. However, some members appear to be able to barter for high-end, late model SUVs and enormous, meticulously manicured homes while others drive old Fords and live in trailers.

**   Carl Cook's audacious hope for a family did not go unnoticed, nor was the dangerous nature of such a desire unpunished. Within months, he was excommunicated and ejected from Short Creek.

after dropping his new wife off at the house that just yesterday belonged nowhere in her thoughts. It turned out Holm spent a lot of time in the splendid isolation of his separate apartment/office elsewhere on the property, and no wonder. Chaos prevailed in a house teeming with eighteen largely unsupervised kids under age twelve. Even if it were possible for three women to keep up with the more than a dozen toddlers prone to falling out of windows, the sister wives were awfully busy indulging their own venomous jealousies, sometimes erupting into fisticuffs with one another or, if the offending sister wife was unavailable, her proxy children. Ruth wasn't in the house a day before each of her new sister wives lobbied her to be their new best friend, an ally in never-ending crusades to settle scores and outdo each other in the eyes of their shared husband. Because she was Ruth's sister, Susie was particularly adamant that Ruth join forces with her against Wendy and her children. When Ruth tried to steer clear of the whole thing, she earned the hostilities of both women, whose ultimate goal in sabotaging each other was always to gain more favor, time, or attention from the man they called "father"—Rod Holm.

FLDS provided women with ovulation kits to encourage continuous pregnancies, but Ruth found she didn't need them. The sixteen-year-old became pregnant almost immediately, deepening her already terrible misery. Available to all FLDS men is instruction in techniques for "breaking" or "breaking in" young wives, the latter intended mostly to "correct" young girls who demonstrate fear, reluctance, or the rare outright opposition to sex with their aging husbands. Frustrated husbands might seek out "breaking in" instructions from elders, or elders sensing trouble in a fresh marriage may take it upon themselves to give instruction in bringing wayward young FLDS women back to their senses. The paramount goal and only acceptable behavior for every FLDS woman is to "keep sweet," essentially to be completely obedient and passive. In that she did not refuse Rod Holm sex, Ruth presented a different challenge. Her good nature wasn't sweet or obedient enough. She offered that radiant smile to people she didn't know. She was too free-spirited, too effervescent to be the kind of wife FLDS demanded. If he didn't do something, there would be talk.

Rod Holm immediately placed Ruth on a strict diet, requiring her to get verbal permission from him before consuming most of the foods she liked. He wrote up a daily schedule that accounted for every minute of her day. If Ruth could not be located by phone or sight within seven to ten minutes of the time Rod had scheduled her to be at any given place, calls were made in an effort to locate her or cars were sent out to search. Rod conducted regular searches of Ruth's room, confiscating anything that could be considered remotely personal. Her treasured diaries and photographs of her apostate family were taken away. Rod apparently never intended to keep the wedding promise he made Ruth that she could continue her close relationships with her mom, dad, brothers, and sisters after her sealing. In an act of heartless cruelty, Rod instantly forbade Ruth from seeing any member of her family except Susie. She was not allowed to speak to them on the phone or even speak *of* them ever again. They were to be dead to her.

Increasingly jealous of Ruth's youth and beauty, her sister wives watched her like malicious hawks, making certain Rod's orders were obeyed. Under Rod Holm's diet, Ruth lost thirty pounds even as her pregnancy progressed. The robust, fit, 135-pound tomboy Rod Holm "married" is not recognizable in photographs taken six months after the sealing. Pale, with gaunt cheeks and recessed eyes, Ruth smiles wanly into the lens, a stick-thin apparition of her former self. Ruth didn't care. A part of her died once she realized Carl would never be in her life. Listless, hopeless, Ruth viewed the pregnancy as just another nail in her coffin. Even if it could be dreamed, how could she ever get away with a baby weighing her down?

Certain she'd be a terrible mother, Ruth was deeply surprised by the explosion of love she felt for her new daughter, Maranda. She'd never felt love like this before. It was like pure light, pure water. A boy, Winston, followed twelve months later, and the love impossibly deepened. Her children made her sane. For her children, she resolved to try to make the marriage with Holm work. She resolved to throw herself into the FLDS imperative to keep sweet. Holm was their father, after all, and her children deserved good family memories like hers.

Ruth's efforts went unappreciated in a house where three wives behaved like fractious grade-schoolers jockeying for the tiniest of acknowledgments from their remote and disinterested headmaster. Ruth suffered a permanent facial scar from the time Susie tackled her like a madwoman, knocking the breath out of her as the older woman straddled her chest, choking with all her might with one hand while punching and clawing at Ruth's face with the other. Susie's tipping point? On Rod's instructions, Ruth had attempted to put one of Susie's daughters to bed, igniting a jealous firestorm.

When the women weren't battling one another, the children were targeted for beatings always justified as standard discipline, though Ruth suspected other motives. She found she could not bear to watch toddlers punched, slapped, and scratched, their little heads rammed into doorjambs by women whose fists were embedded in their hair. Little boys were strad-dled and whacked with sticks or hit unawares in the back of the head with heavy religious books, driving them forward and downward, their faces col-liding with the floor. Occasionally, Father Rod made his presence felt with wide, arcing kicks to a child's backside, kicks with sufficient force to lift them off their feet.

Ruth worried about fires. As the first and legal wife, Susie was the only wife not required to work outside the home. Ruth suspected she used her "on mother" time to settle sister wife disputes through proxy children, but equally nerve-wracking was Susie's indulgence in solo "going visiting" trips. Not even the demanding Susie judged the oldest Holm child—a thirteen-year-old girl—capable of supervising nineteen other little kids, so Susie locked the babies and toddlers in closets, bathrooms, and laundry areas for safekeeping, pocketing the keys. And whereas no fires ever ignited, a two-year-old boy did manage to tumble out a second-story window, lying on the ground cold and pale as death with a broken pelvis for hours before he was discovered. For all of Susie's on mother time, Ruth consistently slogged home after a grueling workday at CJ's to find Winston and Maranda scratched, bruised, and unsu-pervised, wallowing in stinking, sopping diapers Ruth expected were intended to punish her for whatever slight Susie had imagined.

The most violent arguments erupted over the "visitation" schedule Rod Holm had established for equitable sexual intercourse with his "ladies." Sex is a critical, if desperate, tool for FLDS women starved for individual atten-tion and who have few other private opportunities to plead their own cases or those of their children. FLDS wives are also expected to essentially remain pregnant from puberty forward, and it is not unusual for a single FLDS woman to give birth to twenty children. Unusually long gaps between infants are regarded with pity at best and potential devil's work at worst, but any lapse will start tongues wagging. Women who aren't pregnant are assumed to be out of favor with their husbands, a shameful condition in FLDS.

The Holm wives weren't in danger of the latter disgrace. Rod Holm "vis-ited" each woman in her own bedroom every third night, 365 days a year. This even-stephen system was designed to eliminate the well-known potentials for jealousy and hurt feelings. The problem was, Rod Holm kept violating his own rules with unscheduled trysts in garden sheds, pickup trucks, and, most galling of all, the kingdom of his private quarters. The women were not allowed in Holm's locked apartment except to clean or pick up his dirty laundry, so when

Wendy Holm discovered Rod had been entertaining his young, beautiful third wife on off days in his private quarters, the roof came off.

Susie and Wendy Holm could hardly attack Ruth on the basis of her extra sex sessions. That would directly challenge Rod's unassailable choices, behavior neither sweet nor obedient and a serious offense. Instead, Ruth's sister wives finally managed their own alliance against Ruth. They tattled to Rod that she was not sweet, and worse, she was "selfish." A "selfish" charge leveled at a woman was extremely damaging in FLDS society.

Rod Holm did not have the integrity or fortitude to deal with the destructive forces in his household. Rather than take on two united women, he'd admonish everyone to "keep sweet" before fleeing to his sanctuary. When the charges against Ruth persisted, he mollified Susie and Wendy by behaving rudely and hatefully toward Ruth in their presence. He'd treat Ruth as if she were invisible and stopped "visiting" her room, leading the sister wives to assume he was no longer bestowing his important sexual favors upon the youngest wife who would consequently fail to become pregnant, making her disfavor known to all. Ruth's adversaries couldn't wait.

In fact, Rod was summoning Ruth frequently, sometimes more than once a day, for groping, panting sex on a grimy desk in the police station during his shift, in the cab of a friend's pickup, in a friend's toolshed, and a dozen other places too humiliating to think about. Mocked or ignored in public, Ruth felt like she'd become Rod's sex toy. The clandestine nature of the trysts seemed to make his excitement even more repugnant. Ruth's misery deepened when Susie, believing she'd been victorious in her battle against her own little sister, encouraged her children to address Ruth as "bitch" and allowed them to disregard anything she said.

Just when Ruth thought she couldn't feel any more worthless, Rod delivered the knockout punch. Another room toss had revealed a pitiful collection of matchbook covers and calendar scraps upon which Ruth had been keeping a secret journal. Even though her entries revealed nothing more than a dull litany of thankless work, Rod mocked her "selfishness" as he dumped the miserable little paper pile on the kitchen table and set it afire for the entertainment of her triumphant sister wives, their faces flushed and glowing with the pleasure of her humiliation.

Looking back on it in December of 2001 on the night before her escape, Ruth couldn't decide if the sad diary incident was the proverbial straw on the camel's back. The turning point might have been the diaries, but it could have been the time Rod coldly refused her permission to eat a piece of cake at her own daughter's birthday party—the only person in the room so refused. It could have been the routine, fresh scratches on the tender faces of her children or her agony that her precious parents had never laid eyes on their own grandchildren. Ruth had nightmares about her children, knowing FLDS would deny Maranda and Winston educations, pirating Maranda into someone's bed when she was still a child, and who knows what would become of Winston? A construction job at thirteen? Thrown out of town to make room for old men?

Ruth thought it was no doubt all of those things, thrown on a big pile and fused by the electric jolt that coursed through her soul when she discovered she was pregnant with a third child. She vowed they would not get this child. They would never even *know* about this child, and no matter what happened to her, she was getting all her children out to be educated, to live free, and most importantly, to exist with hope.

After the wedding debacle three years earlier, Ruth could not be certain that Pennie, or Sally for that matter, would help her escape. Ruth would not have blamed them if they'd told her to jump off a cliff and sleep in the bed she'd made, as it were, but Ruth knew she could not leave without help. Rod Holm's destruction of her personal property, his mandates that she never speak to any member of her family, had not damaged Ruth's memory. She knew her family's phone numbers by heart. That heart nearly burst with joy when both her mother and sister never once said, "I told you so," but vowed to do everything in their power to get her out—and keep her out—of FLDS.

Now that her daughter had come to her senses, Sally wanted to get Ruth out of Short Creek immediately. Several of Ruth's apostate brothers lived in Alaska, and although Sally didn't even think that far-flung state was safe from FLDS lawyers or impromptu child kidnappings, it would have to do.* She ordered Ruth's brothers to work overtime, double shifts, to scrape together airfare for Ruth, Winston, and Maranda. They had the money in a week.

Although Ruth was totally grateful, not to mention humbled by her family's support, she did think Sally's overall plan could use some work. Having

---

* FLDS activists and women who have escaped the sect report that the kidnapping of children from their mothers is their greatest fear. Once sect members discover the residences of the defecting women, their children are often shadowed, then kidnapped from their yards or on their way to school, prompting many women to keep their children out of school and indoors. Even if the mothers of kidnapped children could afford lawyers, they face long, uphill court battles because the children are ostensibly returned to their fathers. Consequently, the vast majority of women whose children are taken return to the sect.

her burly Alaskan brothers beat the crap out of anyone who tried to stop them from escorting Ruth and the kids to their muscle car, then peeling out of town in what would amount to 110 miles of high-speed chase, all the way to Las Vegas's McCarran International, struck Ruth as problematic. She had a less conspicuous idea.

Following the omniscient Warren Jeffs's orders that he patch things up with his desirable convert, Rod Holm had proposed a lavish second honeymoon trip for the couple's upcoming third anniversary. Jeffs had provided an FLDS credit card to book an entire suite at an opulent ski lodge in the Wasatch Range outside of Salt Lake City—a trip virtually unheard of for any FLDS woman. The furious, bitter hatred radiating off Susie and Wendy was palpable as Rod witlessly described the accommodation's jacuzzi and fireplace, even promising to use *room service*.

"It sounded so sweet, I was sorry I wouldn't be there," Ruth remembered wryly, but her convincing enthusiasm for rekindling the marriage relaxed Holm's guard, while her sister wives' venomous jealousy provided the solution for the biggest problem Ruth had: including her kids in a second honeymoon scenario. Ruth guided the other women into demanding that the happy couple take some of the kids with them to mar the romance, then pretended to pout when Rod Holm saw his way out of the jam he'd created. The couple would take five kids, Ruth's included. Wendy and Susie smirked. It was a consolation prize for sure, but nobody was getting naked in a hot tub with a bunch of little kids underfoot.

The trip allowed Ruth to pack suitcases without arousing suspicion, a pursuit Pennie considered a needless complication. "You're going to have to buy all new clothes anyway," Pennie reminded her sister during one of their rushed, hushed phone calls. "They can't wear those crazy pioneer clothes in real life, so why risk the extra step?" But Ruth was sentimental, an optimist at her core who looked for the good memories in any situation. Besides, she'd sewed many of the clothes herself and was not in a mood to leave them for her sabotaging sister wives.

The night of her escape, Ruth sneaked from the house to hide the suitcases in some roadside bushes for later retrieval, then returned to wait for the gray light of dawn. It had been decided that her former tomboy sister, Jinny, would drive Ruth out of town. Besides Susie, Jinny was the least suspicious member of the Stubbs family. If she weren't already, Sally Stubbs would be put under surveillance as soon as Ruth's absence from the breakfast table was noted. Warming to her role in the subterfuge, Sally came up with a great idea to take a decoy trip. Once Ruth and Jinny were away, Sally would pretend to be rushing off someplace, luring at least some of Ruth's pursuers on a wild goose chase. But first, Ruth had to get out of the house without arousing suspicion in two women whose bitter resentment over the luxury trip would translate into scrutiny of Ruth's every breath.

Ruth was shaking as she ran a brush through her children's shiny hair, hoping they would not sense her fear. Winston's various food allergies had always worried his mother, but they'd become a blessing—like God had planned on helping her out all along. Cow milk was too rich for Winston. Every morning, Ruth trekked up to the dairy for his goat milk, a chore neither Susie nor Wendy had ever offered to perform. Would they question that she took both children that morning? Ruth didn't know. Still trembling, she bent to her fidgeting children's ears. "You all be quiet and do what Mama says," she whispered, "and we'll play that fun game Mama promised." Clamping their tiny hands in hers, Ruth drew a deep breath, stepping out of the room for the last time.

Ruth felt light-headed, kind of like she was floating as she made her way down the hallway to the kitchen. She didn't feel real as she tried to anticipate the calm that would be required if either Susie or Wendy became suspicious and ran tattling to Rod. What should she do if that happened? Pennie had instructed her to keep going no matter what, but that seemed so silly now. Ruth could not push past three people, and Rod would call the entire police department out to stop her. Her whole body quaked in fear as she stepped into the kitchen.

Miraculously for Ruth, Susie and Wendy were engrossed in a fresh fight between themselves. Susie brandished a serving spoon in Wendy's face, yelling and flushed. The women barely looked up as Ruth entered the room and paid no attention when she announced her usual trip to the dairy. No one called after her as she stepped out the back door, into what looked like a day of glorious sunshine.

Walk, do not *run,* Ruth repeated under her breath like a mantra as she tottered along the rutted streets in her ankle-length pioneer dress, passing the crazy-quilt construction of homes pieced together from whatever materials presented themselves as new wives were acquired and families exploded. Useless, rusting machinery cannibalized for parts melted into the yards of poorer homes. Dilapidated trailers that looked like they could blow over in the next rainstorm sat in throwing distance of high-end construction, mansions with manicured yards and twelve-foot-high concrete fences discouraging the riffraff—the FLDS version of shared wealth.

Ruth saw no one observing her as she neared the broken-down dairy where waste from chemicals and listless, thin cattle wallowing in thick mud sometimes dribbled into the town's drinking water. As it came into sight, she was panicked by a scenario she hadn't considered during all the hours of meticulous planning: what if the dairy workers called Rod after watching her just walk on by without getting the goat milk? How could she have overlooked such a real possibility?

Horrified, Ruth realized she was *running* in her heavy dress, her own ragged breath like a hurricane in her ears, her children squalling as she dragged them behind her. She knew she should slow down—the running would attract attention—but another frantic thought launched her forward with even greater speed. What if Jinny hadn't been able to make it to the meet-up spot? What if she'd been challenged by Rod's own colleagues who even now were reporting the suspicious event? The tears were like rain on her face as she ran on, expecting rough hands to seize her from behind at any moment. *Oh, I am a stupid, stupid girl*, Ruth despaired. *It's not too late. I can turn back anytime under the ten minutes . . .*

But Ruth did not turn back. Something stubborn and strong welled up from inside her, pushing the doubt and tears away even as Maranda's mere protests turned to shrieks of fear. Behind a thicket of trees in the near distance, Ruth saw shards of pure light shoot between the leaves like a heavenly lighthouse—sun bouncing off a car windshield—and there was Jinny standing by the open door, framed like an angel in the white light, beckoning wildly and yelling ferocious encouragement. *Come on! Come on!* Bundling her toddlers before her, Ruth dove into the car she realized was running, had been running the whole time, and this was no dream, no theoretical exercise.

"We're gonna play that fun game Mama promised now, 'kay?" Ruth instructed her tearful children. The unexpected steadiness of determination in her own voice calmed the bewildered toddlers, who tucked themselves on the floorboards under the dash with their mother. "Whoever stays like this the longest wins a prize, 'kay?"

As much as she wanted to, Jinny did not smile at, speak to, or even cast a downward glance at the children. She couldn't give the pedestrian on the street or the person driving the oncoming car any hint there was anyone but her in the cab of her truck. Ruth held her breath, hugging her kids close, as the adrenaline of fear infused Jinny with the power to retrieve the luggage lickety-split, tossing the suitcases in the bed like paper balls that disappeared under a weighted tarp. Ruth hadn't even been forced to exhale before Jinny was back in the truck and cruising past the Mark Twain Hotel, the boundary of bitter memory. Short Creek might have had the invisible security of Fort Knox, but it was still a small space without a single traffic light. Once past the only major intersection, Highway 59 spilled into open country and Ruth's first real belief they could pull this off.

Keeping to the maddeningly restrictive sixty-five mile per hour speed limit to avoid attention, Jinny kept one eye on the road, the other glued on the rearview mirror checking for pursuit, which might take the form of flashing police lights or a caravan of pickups and SUVs with black tinted windows favored by the goon squads. There was nothing, and no drivers took an interest in them as they snaked down Hurricane Hill and passed through the hamlet of Hurricane unmolested.

In another half hour, Ruth was joyous as they arrived in St. George, a fast-growing mecca for outdoors enthusiasts where the once powerful influence of FLDS had been shattered by booming secular population growth. Not very long ago, Ruth and her children would have been obliged to remain concealed on the floorboards in St. George, but in December 2001, they bounded from Jinny's truck in a chorus of giddy squeals, racing into a gas station restroom to change out of their prairie clothes.

After hugs and tears, which confused the children, the group melted into the interstate traffic going eighty miles per hour toward Las Vegas, singing their hearts out, which delighted the children. They were an hour and a half clear. Right now, Rod and every cop in Short Creek were scouring the streets looking for her. The God squad would have already been to her mother's and probably her father's house. Sally Stubbs would not be able to spit for a month without Warren Jeffs knowing about it.

After a while, the children nodded off while the reunited sisters fell into a comfortable, contented silence. Before entering Las Vegas, Jinny exited the interstate, pulling into a crowded truck stop. Putting the car in park, Jinny grinned again. "Mom left the Crick two days ago."

As Ruth's mouth dropped open, Sally Stubbs emerged from the unfamiliar car beside them.

"There's been a change of plans," Sally stated matter-of-factly. "We're going to Pennie's in Phoenix." She motioned for the dumbfounded Ruth to help with the suitcases.

"We're gonna fight. We're gonna stop runnin' and we're gonna *fight back*."

2

SECTION 132

Verily, thus saith the Lord unto you, my servant Joseph, that inasmuch as you have inquired of my hand to know and understand wherein I, the Lord, justified my servants Abraham, Isaac, and Jacob, as also Moses, David and Solomon, my servants principle and doctrine of their having many wives and concubines . . .

For behold, I reveal unto you a new and everlasting covenant; and if ye abide not that covenant then are ye damned; for no one can reject this covenant and be permitted to enter into my glory.
—Joseph Smith, revealing the plural marriage mandate from God, *Doctrines and Covenants*, Article 132, July 12, 1843, Nauvoo, Illinois

Brother Cannon remarked that people wondered how many wives and children I had. He may inform them that I shall have wives and children by the million, and glory and riches and power, and dominion, and kingdom after kingdom, and reign triumphantly.
—Brigham Young, *Journal of Discourses, Vol. 8*

At certain times and for His specific purposes, God, through His prophets, has directed the practice of plural marriage (sometimes called polygamy), which means one man having more than one living wife at the same time. In obedience to direction from God, Latter-day Saints followed this practice for about 50 years during the 1800s, but officially ceased the practice of such marriages after the Manifesto was issued by President Woodruff in 1890. Since that time, plural marriage has not been approved by The Church of Jesus Christ of Latter-day Saints and any member adopting this practice is subject to losing his or her membership in the Church.
—Official website of the Church of Jesus Christ of Latter-Day Saints position on polygamy

In the heart of Salt Lake City are the Mormon prophet Brigham Young's two stately mansions, national landmarks treasured by the Church of Jesus Christ of Latter-Day Saints (LDS)—the church Young nearly singlehandedly saved from extinction after its founder, Joseph Smith, was murdered in 1844.

The Beehive and Lion Houses were built in 1854 and 1856, respectively, a dozen years after Young organized the extraordinary exodus of thousands of Saints from their Mississippi River settlements to wild Utah, a new Zion far from the reach of violent mobs and an American government not too crazy about certain principles of the new American religion.

Today, the Lion House is available for private functions, but LDS offers public tours of the reverently restored Beehive House. For thirty minutes, friendly guides transport waves of tourists back in time so they can imagine themselves in the top hats or laced gowns displayed around the home's sumptuous rooms furnished with the original nineteenth-century Victorian appointments. They may float through a music room luscious with rich, red drapes and a golden harp or parlors with plush sofas and elegant, crystal chandeliers, and everywhere there are the warm woods of exquisite staircases, chairs, and canopy beds. A walking cane and tall pioneer hat casually set upon a table suggest that Brigham Young himself has only just stepped out for a moment, a whimsical proposition many Mormon polygamists wish were true.

Explaining the homes' importance, official literature offered by LDS or the state of Utah say, somewhat vaguely, that important meetings transpired in the Beehive House during pioneer days. Also, after the Young family sold the home to LDS, it was used as a residence for church presidents including Lorenzo Snow, who died there in 1901. LDS restored both homes in the 1960s, the literature advises, adding that the completely faithful restoration offers touching insights into the prophet Brigham Young's warm and industrious family life.

Not volunteered, or even suggested, is the fact that Brigham Young's family life involved an estimated fifty-seven wives, probably more. The Lion House was constructed two years after the Beehive House because one mansion was not nearly enough to accommodate all of Young's women.* More than a century later, men in Short Creek faced the same problem. The Beehive and Lion Houses were born of the same necessity as the

---

*   When he first arrived in Salt Lake City, Young constructed a row of log cabins to house his wives and children. The cabins were known collectively as Harmony House. Some of the cabins were of crude construction, with dirt floors and lacking full roofs. Young constructed finer homes, including the Beehive and Lion houses nearby on what came to be called Brigham Street (now South Temple Street) but continued using the cabins to house wives. Some of them, including one of Joseph Smith's widows subsequently "sealed" to Young, felt bitter about their shabby accommodations that often left them exposed to the elements, without enough food from the pantries in the grander homes housing Young's presumably more favored women.

30,000-square-foot houses erupting with such startling incongruity from Short Creek's creaky grid: polygamy, the bane of Mormonism.

"Polygamy sanctified Mormon lying," remarks acclaimed Utah author and historian Will Bagley. "It became a condoned habit."

"Even if you're open to a discussion of polygamy as a religious tenet," argues Roger Hoole, a Salt Lake City attorney whose lawsuits against FLDS would spark the sect's legal upheaval, "how can you justify the lying it requires? The deceit? Not for the outside world, but within families. Deceit is endemic to polygamy, a requirement. How can that be a good thing?"

Modern LDS leaders do not much care to discuss the excruciating subject of polygamy, a practice that produced venomous public outrage along with legal disenfranchisement in the nineteenth century and stoked a sense that Mormonism was a crackpot sect in the twentieth. When the Saints first entered Utah in 1846, their goal was complete isolation, but soon after Young's death in 1877, the church began a ferocious drive to join mainstream American society, working assiduously to dispel any lingering unfavorable perceptions by promoting mainstream qualities like the Beehive House tours and the Mormon Tabernacle Choir. Singing groups like the Osmonds promoted a wholesome, family-oriented image LDS loves; politicians like Mitt Romney embody Mormon conservatism, work ethic, and business acumen.

After devoting the early years to theocratic isolationism, Mormon leaders made an about-face after the turn of the last century, zealously pursuing acceptance, inclusion, and, perhaps most importantly, respect from the rest of America. LDS has made impressive inroads into American government in the one hundred years since polygamy was renounced, holding some of the most important positions in a Congress once bent on legislating Mormonism out of existence. Mormons include the Udall political dynasty in Arizona and Colorado, U.S. Senate majority leader Harry Reid, and longtime Senate fixture Orrin Hatch. After Barack Obama's election in 2008, Mormon leaders traveled to Washington to present the new president with his genealogy chart.* Received into the White House with éclat, the resulting photographs of Mormon leaders explaining their work to an attentive president of the United States was exactly the kind of publicity LDS craves—an exclamation

---

* The visit was singed with controversy when it came to light that LDS had baptized Obama's late mother into the church with its dubious practice of using proxies to stand in for the dead at the ceremony without alerting the deceased's living family members. Mormon leaders were obliged to walk back the Obama baptism quietly, but outraged Jewish leaders forced a public retraction of LDS postmortem baptisms of Jews murdered in the Holocaust.

point to the church's assertions that polygamy is so far in the past it's like the practice never happened at all.

Undermining LDS's drive for closure is a plague of self-proclaimed "fundamentalist" Mormon groups practicing "spiritual wifery" from Salt Lake City's finest neighborhoods to the most isolated corners of the state.* FLDS is the largest of a dozen or so whack-a-mole polygamous sects popping up with surprising and always unnerving regularity, showcasing behavior often found repulsive to American sensibilities. Driving LDS leaders to distraction are opinion polls, some of them commissioned by the church itself, showing up to 44 percent of Americans believe LDS and fundamentalist polygamous Mormons are the same thing, a belief that might be closer to the truth than LDS wants to project.

Political operatives are sometimes alarmed, if not surprised, upon discovering political party delegates are polygamists. Nearly everyone has a story about attending school with the children of polygamists, and many can identify polygamist families on their own residential streets. "Do not buy into the myth that there's the mainstream silo of LDS and a lot of little *Beverly Hillbillies* silos of polygamists," warns journalist and author Jon Talton, whose family has lived in heavily Mormon Mesa, Arizona, for five generations. "There's a porous border between mainstream Mormons and polygamists. There's a lot of ambiguity in mainstream Mormons' will to enforce laws forbidding polygamy."

Off the record, Mormons in state government say the FLDS polygamists, at least, make them want to tear their hair out. "I think they're just really embarrassed and frustrated," says one Utah official of his church leaders' sentiments toward FLDS in particular. "But they don't know what to do about them."** On occasion, LDS has consulted with public relations firms for advice on promoting the wholesome, hardworking image it wants. LDS's own efforts to minimize its polygamous past could be tagged as dangerous revisionism if they weren't so silly.

Ex-Mormons and recanted converts are well represented on the Internet in websites projecting a mixture of wounded anger, betrayal, and shock upon

---

*   In 2010, the TLC cable network debuted a reality show called *Sister Wives*, documenting the lives of Nehi, Utah, polygamist Kody Brown, his four wives, and their thirteen children. Though religious discussion is strictly avoided on the show, the Browns are members of the Apostolic Brethren, a group which spit from FLDS in the 1950s.

**   LDS representatives declined all requests to be interviewed for this book.

discovering huge chunks of what they'd been taught of Mormon history was false.* Every religion tends to whitewash its wartier moments, but many of the world's religions were born thousands of years ago, producing sacred texts that cannot be fact-checked against court records or media reports. Founded less than two hundred years ago, the version of history LDS wants is often disadvantaged by the reality that the events unfolded in a literate, record-keeping era. Even the diaries early church leaders strongly encouraged of their members work against LDS efforts to sanitize its polygamous roots, another reality LDS essentially concedes by locking in a secret vault the journals and reams of other historical treasures an army of eager historians would love to study.

But even without the zealously guarded material, the ocean of known, demonstrable facts about the early Mormon Church are so plain that simply denying them seems almost unstable. LDS leaders themselves concede that Mormonism's former title of world's fastest-growing religion has been lost to groups like the Jehovah's Witnesses, whose conversion methods and material Mormons now study for pointers. Historian Will Bagley estimates that enthusiasm for LDS began waning in the mid-1990s. News articles and studies documenting LDS's struggle to halt declining membership began appearing in the early 2000s. By 2005, some studies indicated LDS for the first time had become dependent upon members born into the church and was having difficulty keeping its young people. Some estimates put the dropout rate for disillusioned converts at a whopping 50 percent.

The fact is, most Americans know little to nothing about Mormon history or beliefs, a condition LDS apparently finds satisfactory. While denying that it had anything to do with an anticipated presidential run by Utah favorite son and Mormon Mitt Romney, LDS launched a national television ad campaign in the summer of 2010 depicting a variety of next-door neighbor–type individuals engaging in wholesome activities, after which they simply declare, "I'm a Mormon!"

Though the ads do not address what Mormonism entails, the inference seems to be that whatever that is can't be very bad if these fine folks embrace

---

* In one example, LDS published a training manual in 1998 that portrayed Brigham Young as a monogamous husband. Polygamy is mentioned nowhere in the manual. Among the work's significant omissions is Mormon doctrine holding that God is himself a polygamist, as is Jesus Christ, whose wives included Mary Magdalene. When questioned by reporters, LDS officials Ronald L. Knighton and Craig Manscill staunchly defended the omissions, saying the manual was not intended as a historical document, only a broad introduction to the Mormon faith. The officials insisted the failure to mention polygamy was legitimate because the practice had been stopped in 1890.

it. Overall, LDS seems content to avoid discussing some of Mormon theology's more startling premises until potential converts can be warmed to such beliefs as Jesus was a polygamist or that the Garden of Eden was located in western Missouri or that God lives near or on a planet called Kolob.*

Because such premises are not commonly known, they are easily avoided in the rare press interviews granted by LDS officials, but polygamy is one characteristic associated with Mormonism that everyone seems to know. It doesn't happen often, but when LDS officials expose themselves to free-wheeling questions from the mainstream press, the ostrich technique isn't effective. In these instances, church representatives generally minimize their polygamous roots by characterizing it as a quaint, little practiced, and short-lived experiment, part of a past so hazy it might not have happened at all.

"The figures I have are from—between 2 percent and 5 percent of our people were involved in it [polygamy]," the late LDS president Gordon B. Hinckley told CNN's Larry King, giving what is still the stock LDS answer to unduckable polygamy queries. "It was a very limited practice, carefully safeguarded. In 1890, it was discontinued. The president of the church . . . went before the people, said he had, oh, prayed about it, worked on it, and had received from the Lord a revelation that it was time to stop, to discontinue it then. That's 118 years ago and it's behind us now."

---

*   Both Latter-day Saints and FLDS believe that Mormons and Mormon converts are descended from the Old Testament Abraham or one of his sons and have ancient Israelite blood flowing in their veins. FLDS believes these bloodlines can be strengthened or diluted through marriage. American Indians, called Lamanites, also carry the blood of ancient Israel but, like many Gentiles who have not yet been converted, don't realize it. The *Book of Mormon* teaches that ancient Hebrews traveled to the New World around 600 B.C. in a submarine-like boat, creating an advanced civilization with a number of nineteenth-century amenities. This population eventually split into the "good" tribe of Nephites and the "bad" tribe of Lamanites, who became embroiled in a centuries-long war. After Christ's crucifixion, he visited the New World and was able to remind the Lamanites of their roots, but they soon forgot and eventually wiped out the Nephites. God cursed the Lamanites with dark skin for their wickedness, but Mormon prophets taught they would again become a "white and delightsome" people when their memories were restored after the apocalypse. In the interim, God chose LDS founding prophet Joseph Smith to regather and remind the original good tribe members of their true identities and destinies. Smith taught that Mormonism was the only true faith and it was imperative that his followers find and convert all the amnesiac Israelites before God slaughtered the rest of the world's population who had angered him by, among other things, establishing all the other apostate Christian faiths. Neither LDS nor FLDS is deterred by the absence of archeological evidence of an advanced New World population or the genetic and DNA testing showing that native people in the North, South, and Central Americas as well as the Polynesian islands originated in Asia, not Israel.

One problem with the "it's behind us" presentation is that the plural marriage commandment—Article 132 of Joseph Smith's *Doctrine and Covenants*—is still active as a divine revelation in one of Mormonism's most sacred books, fueling at least a little speculation that LDS may see Smith's polygamy resurrected in its future. Contemporary LDS leaders don't help matters when they sporadically confirm that polygamy will be a part of heaven, although in the modern version, plural wives in the planetary-ruling afterlife will have been obtained if the man had been a remarried widower.

Hinckley's numbers are off as well. LDS's own church historian, Larry Logue, has estimated that polygamy was practiced by 33 percent of Mormons. While it is true that polygamous Mormons were a minority, it was a hefty minority—as much as 40 percent in some areas. It had to be a minority. The fifty-fifty male-female birthrate made it impossible for every Mormon man to practice polygamy. Hinckley represents that the practice was instantly concluded after then LDS president Wilford Woodruff issued what is known as the Manifesto of 1890, but this is also untrue. Renouncing polygamy was a nonnegotiable condition for the statehood Utah received in 1896. Though LDS leaders furiously insisted the practice was ended, they continued sanctioning plural marriage on the sly for another fifteen years after the Manifesto, even developing 007-style code names and language to describe both the men ordained to perform the marriages and the operations themselves, which usually took place in Mexico or Canada.

A rudely awakened Congress was so enraged by the subterfuge that its members refused to seat Utah-elected Mormons until hearings could be held to get to the bottom of things. Named for the in-limbo status of Utah senator-elect Reed Smoot, the Smoot Hearings became even more contentious when it came to light that no less a personage than LDS president Joseph Fielding Smith, Joseph Smith's nephew, had been bald-faced lying to Congress about the cessation of plural marriage and was openly living with five wives in Salt Lake City in defiance of state and federal laws as well as the conditions for Utah's statehood. In addition, Congress harbored suspicions that Smith may have himself performed a plural marriage, albeit one on a ship off the California coast. Smith forcefully denied the charge, but even the Mormon leadership understood they had a dire credibility problem. "We are considered two-faced and insincere," LDS apostle Francis M. Lyman wrote in a letter trying to persuade hardcore polygamy supporters within LDS to relent and follow the law. "We must not stand in that light before the Saints or the world."

But there is some suggestion the Manifesto was insincere from the start. "Inasmuch as laws have been enacted by Congress forbidding plural marriages, which laws have been pronounced constitutional by the court of last resort," Woodruff's statement read, "I hereby declare my intention to submit to those laws, and to use my influence with the members of the Church over which I preside to have them do likewise." Even at the time, Mormons and non-Mormons alike noted the statement did not contain the proper verbiage—such as "saith the Lord"—to qualify as a Mormon policy–altering revelation from God. In April 1891, a little more than a year after he'd issued the Manifesto, Woodruff told an LDS quorum meeting: "The principle of plural marriage will be restored to this church, but how or when I cannot say." Two years before the Manifesto, Smith wrote a cousin, saying, "It looks to me as if the only chance on that score [statehood] is to give the whole business [polygamy] away renouncing our faith save for five years and then taking it up again when once inside the great, government fold."

Smith's emotional pleas for understanding fell on congressional hearts already hardened by decades of cat-and-mouse wrangling with Mormon polygamy, and they were not in a forgiving mood. A number of prominent Mormons like Reed Smoot, who wanted his Senate seat, had also had enough, bringing internal pressure on church leaders to get serious about ending polygamy. In 1904, Smith was obliged to issue another manifesto— this time using the correct "saith the Lord" language—and he personally pleaded guilty to violating Utah's antipolygamy laws in 1906. Polygamy in *mainstream* Mormonism was on its way out, but that it ever got that far to begin with is both a testament to its importance as a tenet of the Mormon faith and evidence of the church's historically repetitive, astonishingly oblivious estimation of how polygamy would be received by the world.

The commonly used, Hinckley-style explanations as to *why* polygamy was ended always make it seem as if Woodruff just woke up one day with an impulse to seek God's thoughts on plural marriage, but that's just flat-out misleading. By the time Woodruff took the polygamy issue up with God, both Congress and the courts had provided him no shortage of excellent incentives to do so. In fact, Woodruff had no real choice at all. Congress had passed a series of strict legislation, upheld by the courts, disenfranchising Mormons, criminalizing polygamy, and allowing for unbridled federal seizure of church property and money. The Republican Party Mormons embrace today made the "Mormon question" its rallying cry, calling slavery and polygamy the "twin relics of barbarism." And if laws stripping Mormons of property and citizenship rights like voting didn't do it, the military could. More than one U.S. president toyed with sending troops into Utah.* Ending polygamy was not a meaningless concession. It was the only way Woodruff could save the Mormon Church from legal extinction.

The energy LDS has spent on polygamy seems almost tragic given the fact that the practice was not even part of the movement's original theology. Even when the charming and dynamic prophet Joseph Smith wedged polygamy into his doctrine years after starting the church, most of his followers were aghast and repulsed. "Just imagine what Mormonism would be like today if polygamy had never been a factor," groaned Roger Hoole. "There are so many good things in Mormonism, but polygamy overshadowed all of it. The good messages get lost in the endless justifications of polygamy, which has also ruined thousands of lives, maybe tens of thousands." No less a personage than Brigham Young reportedly told a select group that Smith himself had entertained second thoughts about polygamy before his murder, but by then, the charismatic Smith had already stamped American history with his self-described "peculiar people."

Mormon founder and prophet Joseph Smith came of age in a period of American history dubbed the Second Great Awakening, a period roughly between 1800 and 1840 in which the land was gripped with an apocalypse-themed religious frenzy mined by dozens, perhaps hundreds, of preachers and prophets scouring the countryside for believers in their particular brand of salvation. The mines were moneymakers. As they have been from the dawn of history, people were willing to part with a little hard-earned cash for a guaranteed ticket to heaven. Only about 15 percent of Americans were card-carrying members in any denomination at the time, and even they were open to persuasion, intrigued by the new religious buffet that included everything from kooky sex communes to doomsday cults.

---

*   Although the 1857–58 exercise became known as "Buchanan's Blunder," president James Buchanan sent troops into Utah to end what was viewed as a theocracy in open rebellion headed by Brigham Young. Although the action produced a few skirmishes, it accomplished little outside of providing grist for Young's feverish commitment to isolating Mormons as well as his drive for an extreme religious revivalism that prompted an explosion of polygamous marriages and may have aided Mormon hostility toward outsiders culminating in the Mountain Meadows Massacre.

As a youngster, Smith sampled the religious road shows with great inter- ✓
est. The intelligent, naturally curious Smith was of a dirt-poor farming
family, strangling in debt as they trudged from one rocky, worn-out patch
of upstate New York farmland to the next. As a young man, Smith, along
with his father and other male family members, made a sideline of "money
digging." A digger utilized magical "peep stones" to inform his client of the
location of buried treasures; people of the time believed Spanish conquista-
dors had buried treasure troves everywhere, just waiting to be discovered.*

LDS goes apoplectic when Smith's money-digging career is broached,
even blindly denying Smith's 1826 misdemeanor conviction as "a disorderly
person" after his only unsatisfied customer complained, but the Mormon
Church's distress seems unnecessary. Money digging was a perfectly acceptable profession in Smith's time, endorsed by newspapers and practiced by
hundreds of entrepreneurs. Ownership of peep stones was also common,
and Smith was actually a popular money digger, receiving many recom-
mendations from enthusiastic clients even though none of them discovered
Spanish treasure.

Money digging also failed to lift the Smith family from its dire financial circumstances, which weighed heavily on the young man who often
expressed a bitter resolve to elevate his family from the demeaning and
miserable condition of endless debt. In the late 1820s, after sampling the
traveling theaters of dozens of new messiahs, Smith began traveling with
his own message. Smith said he'd prayed to the Lord, asking which religious
presentation was correct so that he might throw himself into the critical
battle to save souls, not as a leader but a foot soldier.

Perhaps predictably, the Lord had answered that *all* of the preachers
Joseph had seen were hucksters and heretics, but Smith was as surprised
as anyone when the Lord informed him that Smith alone was now tasked
with setting the record straight and returning souls to the true church Smith
would lead. To this end, Smith was visited by a fearsome and sometimes tem-
peramental angel named Moroni, who showed Smith a set of gold tablets
inscribed in an ancient language Smith identified as "reformed Egyptian."

Although the Old and New Testaments were still valid, Moroni's gold
tablets explained the true history of Jesus Christ and the world, detailing

---

* Smith's career as a money digger is fairly well known, but in his book *Early Mormonism and
the Magic World View*, excommunicated Mormon historian D. Michael Quinn discusses at good
length the Smith family's dabbling in other areas of magic and the occult, including necro-
mancy, in which spirits of the dead are conjured up to reveal the future.

amazing events somehow lost to the collective human memory.* Iconic American author Mark Twain once called the story Smith produced from the tablets "chloroform in print," but interestingly, it seems that Smith once did entertain notions of becoming an author himself. Smith's mother, Lucy Mack Smith, told numerous people that her son had always been fascinated by the burial mounds sprinkled around New York State. When Smith was a young man, it had not yet been determined that the mounds were grave sites for the Iroquois tribe, which was decimated when Europeans arrived in the New World centuries earlier. Without knowing how the mounds got there, New York residents speculated liberally about their origins, the favored theory being that they were stashes for conquistador loot. Lucy Mack Smith indicated that her son wanted to research the matter to produce an authoritative scientific and historical book that would end all debate about the mounds, but he became discouraged when he realized he did not have the education or training to tackle the academic research.

Some historians suggest that Smith's speculations about the origin of the burial mounds may have morphed into the story he told in *The Book of Mormon* (a work Smith described as a supplement to the Bible) containing the startling foundations for Mormon theology: that Jesus Christ and his Father were once flesh-and-blood men who became gods and were now offering Smith the roadmap for his followers to accomplish the same transformation. Smith held that human beings exist prenatally as "spirit children"; their time here on earth is more like a training ground, a step in their evolution toward becoming Gods themselves. They are instructed in this process by the Mormon prophet, who receives his guidelines directly from God in the form of revelations all are expected to obey. Although there is but one God for humans, the theology naturally allows for the existence of other Gods, as human deification is the goal.**

---

* Only the Lutheran Church Missouri Synod equivocates its position on whether Mormonism is a Christian faith. All other major Christian denominations, including Catholics, Baptists, Presbyterian, Episcopalian, and so on, have position statements advising that, among other things, the Mormon belief that there are many gods, that God was a man, that men may become gods, that God and Jesus Christ were polygamists (a detail Smith added after he'd introduced polygamy years later), and that God and Jesus Christ are separate entities, not part of the holy trinity, are inconsistent with Christianity.

** Until 1978, only white males could attain the end goal of deification. Depending on how they felt about their wives, husbands could choose, or not choose, to elevate their women to "goddess" status in the afterlife, a handy threat for disobedient spouses.

Smith realized he could translate the reformed Egyptian with his money-digging peep stones. To accomplish the translation, Smith sometimes placed the stones in the bottom of a tall hat placed on a table upon which also rested the gold tablets, which were covered by a sheet. Burying his face in the hat, Smith's peep stones would transform the reformed Egyptian into a form of English that sounded suspiciously like the King James version of the Bible. A "scribe" physically separated from Smith by a sheet hung from the ceiling would then write down what Smith saw in the stones for what would become *The Book of Mormon*. Entire books have been written dissecting Smith's variety of stories concerning the angel Moroni's sporadic appearances and the gold tablets, which Moroni sometimes snatched away from Smith in fits of pique prompted by vile doubters before the angel either destroyed or returned them to God altogether.

Smith's intelligence was complemented by a curious nature. In addition to sampling the hellfire preachers of the Second Awakening, he studied other religions such as Islam, languages such as Hebrew, and cultures both ancient and contemporary. The details of his own story would evolve, even transform over time, but much of it was not original for the era. His story about being called to faith by a heavenly visitation from an angel of God was not new. There was even a previous variation on Smith's story of discovering an ancient holy text inscribed on golden tablets (they were copper in the competing version) guarded by an angel named Moroni (there was no named angel in the other version). What set Smith apart was his fully realized, easily visualized, and detailed description of the afterlife and the fact that men could get there by following a doable, no-guesswork program. "Whatever his lapses," Yale professor Harold Bloom writes in his book *The American Religion*, "Smith was an authentic religious genius, unique in our national history."

But even the most hardworking of geniuses can use a stroke of good luck and timing now and again, and for Smith, that stroke of fortune was named Martin Harris. A very wealthy farmer known for his lengthy conversations with woodland creatures he believed to be temporarily inhabited by Jesus Christ, Harris was an early convert who initially served as scribe for Smith's translation of the golden tablets. When Smith could find no one willing to publish the 588-page opus that would become *The Book of Mormon* without substantial money up front, Smith had a revelation from God that Harris should foot the bill.

Harris had already been divorced by a wife disgusted by Smith, the gold tablets nobody had seen, and her husband's determination to squander their fortune, so Harris balked at parting with the last of his cash, even for Smith. But Smith prevailed, convincing Harris with further divine revelations that he "shalt receive, if thou wilt slight these counsels; yea even the destruction of thyself and property. . . . Pay the printer's debt!" Harris forked over his remaining fortune of $10,000, the equivalent of $300,000 today, to get Smith's book published and bound in fine leather. Now, instead of arriving in a town with cheap penny pamphlets that blew away in a stiff wind, Smith could produce a somber book with heft and authority, like a Bible.* Within ten years, membership in Smith's church had soared from six thousand to twenty-six thousand. One thing is certain: if Smith hadn't added polygamy, the LDS trajectory would have been vastly different.

No one is sure when the tall, handsome, and charismatic Smith began "marrying" other women outside of his marriage, but Mormon polygamy came to widespread public attention in the 1840s, as the slavery issue was rolling toward the Civil War. Americans may have heard something about Joseph Smith before then, but when rumors of Mormon polygamy leaked into the general population, the backlash was ferocious. It was the era of Victorian morals, and Smith knew better than to walk down the street with a half-dozen pregnant young women in tow, but not much better.

In the first of what would become perpetual miscalculations of American public opinion by Mormon leaders, Smith allowed publication of a polygamy-advocating pamphlet called *The Peace Maker* in 1842. The pamphlet was purportedly authored by Udney Hay Jacob, but many believe Smith himself wrote *The Peace Maker* as a trial balloon to test public tolerance for polygamy, a remarkable piece of wishful thinking in itself. This, combined with the indiscreet statements from soon-to-be-excommunicated blowhards in his inner circle, threatened the enormous political power and security Smith had achieved, first in Missouri and later in Illinois, by promising and delivering large blocks of Mormon votes to politicians who would legislate in the Saints' favor. But just as he underestimated the public revulsion for polygamy, Smith seemed oblivious—or at least unconcerned—that the block voting he

---

*   Smith may not have regarded his work with biblical reverence, however. The Smith family was still having serious debt and cash-flow problems. Soon after its publication, he had a revelation that God wanted his brothers to travel to Canada to sell *The Book of Mormon* copyright for $8,000 to "relieve the family from all pecuniary embarrassment." Harkening back to his money-digger days, Smith also had a revelation that his brother Hyrum needed to travel to Salem, Massachusetts, to dig up a treasure there. Neither revelation bore fruit, a letdown Smith blamed on his brothers' faulty execution of his directions.

demanded of his Saints created antagonism among their pioneer neighbors. People who had not been overly interested in the "peculiar" religion before now feared it would be foisted upon them by the politicians Smith was purchasing with votes.

In Missouri, the savage persecution of Mormons was actually condoned by a state government that allowed the rape of Mormon women, the burning of Mormon farms, and the murder of Mormon people, culminating in the horrifying 1838 Haun's Mill Massacre in which seventeen unarmed Mormon men, women, and children were cornered and slaughtered by a Missouri mob. After a Mormon "extermination order" was issued by governor Lilburn Boggs, the Saints fled Missouri, settling in Illinois, where they were largely welcomed by a population revolted by the violence of their Missouri neighbors. Using the block vote to elevate mostly Democratic politicians, Smith was able to secure a charter for the astonishing Mormon city he built that basically gave him his own country, much like Short Creek today.

Politicians continued currying Smith's favor, but when the Mormon leader began testing the social waters for polygamy, the elected men got skittish, explaining to Smith that they still wanted to help him out but could not be tied to something as rankly scandalous as polygamy. To take the pressure off, Mormon publications began printing heated and indignant polygamy denials, accusing their bigoted, jealous enemies of mounting scurrilous slander campaigns intended to ruin the Mormon people. In an early example of the "lying for the Lord" embraced by modern fundamentalists, Smith the prophet delivered an actual divine revelation from the Lord in 1835 that condemned polygamy as a crime, even though he is thought to have had a half-dozen "wives" at the time. The revelation insisted "that ONE man should have ONE WIFE; and one woman, but one husband, except in the case of death, when either is at liberty to marry again."*

Some historians speculate that Smith may have started "marrying" outside women as early as 1831, telling a few intensely close associates at the time, but he told his mostly utterly horrified inner circle about God's mandate for "plural marriage" around 1841. Among the most horrified was his long-suffering wife, Emma Hale Smith, who had ejected more than one comely servant girl from the Smith's household employ after stumbling upon evidence of

---

*   Explaining that the 1835 revelation was inconsistent with church dogma, LDS leaders removed it from the *Doctrines and Covenants* in 1876. Despite the fact that it would now appear to be consistent with church dogma, it has not been reinstated.

her husband's extracurricular activities.* Emma had been obliged to hold her nose through a series of indiscretions. Some of them, like alleged incidents in Harmony, Pennsylvania, required only dead-of-night flight from the territory, but others were potentially fatal. In March 1832, when the Saints were head-quartered in Ohio, Smith was dragged from his bed to be tarred, feathered, and beaten senseless by a mob led by the brother of a teenage girl Smith was suspected of seducing. Smith was not permanently injured, but only because the surgeon enlisted to castrate him lost his enthusiasm for the job.

In addition to the headache of concealing polygamy from the larger pub-lic, Smith lived in dread of the lovely but aging Emma's wrath, especially after she allegedly threw one of her pregnant rivals down a flight of stairs and banished two sisters Smith had married in the same day to a hard life on the outskirts of civilization. In an attempt to make Emma toe the line, Smith clari-fied the polygamy edict with another divine revelation from the Lord, who had apparently overlooked Emma's possible resistance the first time around. Now, however, the Lord said his "handmaid" Emma would be "destroyed" should she continue opposing Smith's heavenly mandate to take extra wives.

Having known her husband for some little time, Emma was under-whelmed by the new death threat from God, rebuffing all future attempts to persuade her with vicious tongue lashings delivered to whichever unfor-tunate emissary Joseph had chosen to make the argument in his stead. So upset was Emma over her husband's philandering ways, she retreated into a better reality created inside her own head in which Joseph wasn't a polyga-mist at all and never had been. Until the day she died, Emma heatedly denied that her murdered husband had ever even thought about polygamy, much less taken up with other women. After Smith's death, Emma and her sons eventually joined the Reformed Church of Jesus Christ of Latter-Day Saints, which denied the church had ever sanctioned plural marriage. But no matter what turmoil raged inside his home or out during his life, Joseph Smith was unable or unwilling to control his marrying ways.

Most historians are comfortable with evidence for at least twenty-seven Smith wives, but there is reason to believe he could have obtained upward of

---

*   One of these girls, Fanny Alger, is believed to be the first of Smith's estimated twenty-seven-plus wives. Described as a girl of exceptional beauty with a lovely figure, Alger was sixteen when she was "sealed" to her employer, Joseph Smith. After Emma Smith evicted her, Fanny moved west with her family, eventually settling in Indiana where she married monoga-mously and raised a family. She refused to discuss her relationship with Joseph Smith until the day she died in 1889.

forty, and conquests that did not result in marriage could have reached into the hundreds.* Smith was not discouraged by tender age or wedding bands when making his selections. Girls as young as thirteen, as well as the daughters and wives of his closest friends, were all fair game for Joseph, who didn't flinch from a little heavenly extortion to get what he wanted. Occasionally Smith cultivated sympathy by saying that God would kill *him* if the intended girl rejected his advances. More often, though, balky celestial brides could find themselves cornered in locked rooms with the looming, six-foot-plus-tall prophet threatening not only their salvation but those of their entire families if they did not submit. Most did. Smith slurred as whores many of those who refused in spiteful whisper campaigns, and, in a supreme irony, Joseph's reckless fury following his rejection by the wife of one of his closest advisors would set the dominoes tumbling toward his murder in the Carthage, Illinois, jail.

In her groundbreaking biography of Joseph Smith, the late excommunicated-Mormon historian Fawn Brodie proposes a combination of psychological and sociological factors shaping Joseph's preoccupation with women, causing misery and heartache for tens of thousands in history and to this day. Still considered the gold standard for Smith biographies, Brodie's *No Man Knows My History* is often characterized as a contentious portrayal of the Mormon prophet, certainly the first to approach Smith as a human being confined to a historical era instead of the near contemporary of Jesus Christ LDS prefers. But Brodie seems to enjoy her rakish and charming subject's company very much, casting him as a likable but somewhat reckless opportunist who used his superior imagination and people skills to lift his family from hopeless debt and grinding poverty with a tale no taller than others being sold all over the country at the same time.

Brodie is not the only historian whose ears pricked up at Joseph's reported confession to a friend: "When I see a pretty woman, I have to pray for grace." His appreciation of the fairer sex was in large part reciprocated. Giddy diaries and letters penned by women favorably impressed with the tall, dark, and mysterious Smith record near-swooning episodes when the prophet,

---

*   Although he is a far from reliable source, river gambler and self-confessed scoundrel Joseph H. Jackson claimed to have infiltrated Smith's inner circle as sort of investigative journalism public service, publishing an account of his discoveries in 1844 titled *A Narrative of the Adventures and Experience of Joseph H. Jackson, in Nauvoo. Disclosing the Depths of Mormon Villainy.* Among other things, Jackson claims that Smith kept a list of four hundred women he'd bedded and that he targeted women of "high virtue."

often wreathed in ethereal light, rested his deeply blue, electric eyes upon their faces. Smith was definitely a ladies' man, but perhaps a conflicted one. Brodie writes: "But Joseph was no careless libertine who could be content with clandestine mistresses. There was too much of the Puritan in him, and he could not rest until he had redefined the nature of sin and erected a stupendous theological edifice to support his new theories on marriage. By the spring of 1840, this edifice was almost complete and had become so integral a part of his metaphysical system that he probably completely lost sight of the fact that it *had not figured at all in the original design.*" [Emphasis added.]

Smith knew that introducing the morally questionable polygamy into a theology that had never required it before might be abhorrent, even to his most devout followers. Many historians speculate that Joseph might have researched other religions looking for clues as to how polygamy might be justified. Smith is said to have taken great interest in Islam, even reading the Koran, because it was a major religion that embraced plural wives. In the end, though, Smith didn't need to stray any further than the Bible.

To help the uninitiated wrap their minds around plural wifery, Smith reminded his recoiling converts that polygamy was standard in Old Testament relationships, proving that polygamy was God's true intent for man. Smith explained that over the millennia, people had *mistakenly* fallen away from polygamy, tricked by Satan-infused political structures. All the world religions the Saints now knew were heretical fakes believed *monogamy* was God's plan, but nothing could be further from the truth. Monogamy, Smith said, was actually repugnant to God, because it hindered man's own path toward Godhood.

Having made the historical case for polygamy, Smith was able to fuse it onto his original premise. There couldn't be monogamy, he argued, because the kingdoms men would rule as Gods after their deaths were to be populated by that man's children. The more children, the greater the riches of the world. Obviously, one woman could not produce enough children for a respectable kingdom. Anyone demanding monogamy was trying to trick you out of a decent afterlife.

Polygamy created massive fissures in the church from the start. There are accounts of Smith's closet advisors literally collaring him on the street, hanging onto his neck as they begged him to relent. Smith was excommunicating resisters right and left, men and women. Some of them left to start new Mormon churches; others penned lurid missives detailing the "free love" goings-on in Nauvoo, accounts printed in newspapers that shocked Nauvoo's neighbors. Even the stalwart Brigham Young admitted that

Smith, toward the end of his own life, had expressed a "weariness" of polygamy and all its disasters, but the prophet had no idea how to get the horses back in the barn.

The horses were running wild in the streets of 1840s Nauvoo, Illinois, the astounding city Smith transformed from a foul swamp to a staggeringly beautiful metropolis with a population rivaling Chicago in under a dozen years. Mormons enthusiastic about "the principle" contributed to Nauvoo's exploding out-of-wedlock birthrate, undermining Smith's frantic efforts to douse the wildfire of Mormon polygamy rumors with regular, spirited denials. In addition to unmarried pregnant girls, a league of married women whose husbands had been absent for years doing Smith's missionary work found themselves unable to explain their conditions.* Some writers describe Nauvoo after dark as a kind of comic soap opera of men and women creeping through backyards, half their clothes draped over their arms, as they tried to make it home undetected before dawn.

The Saints could not afford any more bad publicity. Although he was genuinely sympathetic to Smith and his followers, Illinois governor Thomas Ford was becoming increasingly uneasy with the manner in which Smith was running his city-state. As they had in Missouri, locals were beginning to grumble that Smith was practically a king who offered safe haven to Mississippi River pirates and other scallywags, possibly for a percentage of their ill-gotten gains. Illinoisans felt queasy about public Mormon sermons promising to "exterminate" all the "Gentiles," or non-Mormons, usurping their property with the help of American Indians. Also unpleasant was Smith's personal army of two thousand men, half the size of the entire United States military, and his personal cadre of rough boys and assassins known as Danites with members such as the Smith-idolizing sociopath Porter Rockwell, who was feared by Mormons and non-Mormons alike. Anger was rising again, and the last thing Smith needed was a polygamy sex scandal. But incredibly, he provided one himself.

Even though Smith attempted to disgrace them as harlots, women resisting Smith's marriage ultimatums were gaining courage. Nancy Rigdon, the

---

*   It's been suggested that Smith often took married women as celestial wives because it eliminated gossip about unexplainable pregnancies. However, Smith's ardor undermined the tactic when he began using missionary assignments as a wedge to separate those married women rejecting polygamy from their husbands for years at a time, breaking down their resistance while creating a large pool of married women with long-absent husbands and obvious pregnancies.

nineteen-year-old daughter of Smith's early convert and apostle Sidney Rigdon, famously announced that when the prophet tried to teach her about plural marriage, "I told him to teach it to someone else." Undeterred by rejection, Smith went a woman too far in 1844. Not only was the pretty and vivacious Jane Law unimpressed with the prophet's proposition and subsequent threats upon her salvation, she took the whole sorry episode straight to her husband, Smith's friend and first counselor William Law. Shocked, hurt, and enraged, Law threatened to expose Smith's "principle" once and for all. As he did with all dissenters, Smith promptly excommunicated both William and Jane Law, ordering them from the area.

Most people excommunicated by Joseph Smith were delighted to obey the legally baseless order, as the violent proclivities of loyal Smith Danites were common knowledge. William Law also feared for his life, but Smith's political position was precarious enough that Law felt he could risk staying in the area to wreak his revenge. Smith's previous failure to separate William Law from his considerable fortune now came back to haunt him. The independently wealthy were rare converts to Mormonism, but Law was never so besotted with his prophet that he succumbed to Smith's honey-coated arguments that Law turn all his money over to the church. His fortune intact, Law now purchased a printing press, announcing in the first edition of his newspaper, the *Nauvoo Expositor*, that subsequent issues would provide all the tawdry evidence anyone could hope to digest about Joseph Smith's false prophecy and church.

This, Smith could not allow. He sent a mob of his bully boys to destroy Law's printing press in the dead of night, going so far as to splinter its pieces, scattering the shards throughout the surrounding countryside. Brodie speculates Joseph may have, by this time, come to believe his own publicity, thinking he was himself so close to Godly evolution, he was practically on equal footing with the Savior himself. If he did, that notion was about to be disabused.

News of Smith's assault on the sacrament of American free speech and destruction of private property was like a match tossed onto a lake of gasoline. Governor Ford, who felt genuine sympathy for the trials of Smith's Mormons and had given the prophet many favors, was now obliged to bring treason charges against him to keep Illinois from exploding into the same mob violence suffered in Missouri. At least Ford thought the charges would prevent it.

Finally grasping the grim consequences of the printing press debacle, Joseph fled Nauvoo with his brother Hyrum, intending to cross the

Mississippi River into Iowa to regroup. Joseph had for years toyed with the idea of permanently relocating his Saints to the American West, eyeing Texas as a land where Mormons might even establish their own country. In that light, the charges might actually be seen as providence. But bad weather, a flooded river, and shortages of the creature comforts like money and food to which Joseph had become accustomed dampened his adventurous spirits. When he received a note from Emma begging him to return and informing him that his Saints were fracturing under the depression of what they saw as his desertion, Joseph dismissed Hyrum's objections and turned back.

A great deal is said about Joseph's statement that he was going "as a lamb to slaughter" when he returned to face the charges against him, but it seems unlikely that a man with Smith's resilience, talent, and ambition intended to willingly present himself for his own execution. Ford had personally guaranteed Smith's safety, promising the Mormon leader they would ride into Nauvoo together to smooth things out after Smith had been booked into the Carthage jail. Whether Smith believed Ford or not, he had a backup plan. He still commanded a loyal, disciplined army of two thousand men, a contingent of which was preparing to march on Carthage and free Smith by armed force if necessary.

Ford got Smith into the Carthage jail safely, although the promise to ride with him to Nauvoo later seems to have slipped his mind. A few days after Smith arrived in Carthage, Ford ordered the militia he had called up to apprehend him disbanded immediately, an order the militia appeared to obey. Smith believed his own army was on its way to Carthage when Ford and his military escort rode out of town toward Nauvoo, leaving Smith, his brother Hyrum, the future prophet and polygamy champion John Taylor, and apostle Willard Richards in the upstairs living quarters of the jail.

That night, militia men who'd pretended to melt away earlier reorganized in the darkness outside of town, their faces painted a cowardly black. They encountered zero resistance from guards assigned to protect Smith and his visitors as they stormed the jail, stampeding upstairs and bursting through the living quarter's doors in a hail of gunfire. The ambushed prisoners were armed with smuggled pistols, but Hyrum was killed instantly. Richards was spared when he went unnoticed behind the flung-open door. In a fluke worthy of fiction, Taylor was spared when the bullet meant for his chest was deflected by a pocket watch, but the mob's intended target never had a chance.

Joseph Smith fired as he retreated toward the unbarred second-story window, but several bullets caught him before he could attempt the risky leap. It would have been futile anyway. Joseph cried out, "Oh Lord!" as he tumbled out the window and hit the ground, where he was instantly surrounded by a throng of waiting, blackened-faced men. In a revolting display, these men proceeded to taunt, stab, kick, and beat the lifeless Smith before bleeding back into the night. No one was ever convicted for the murders of Joseph and Hyrum Smith.

After the murders, a mortified Governor Ford encircled Nauvoo with troops to protect the inhabitants from the gathering Missouri-style mobs. After lengthy negotiations, Young and Ford met like generals of opposing armies under tents in a field outside the city, where Ford reluctantly advised Young to leave Illinois. Ford told the new prophet that public sentiment was running so white-hot against the Mormons, Ford could no longer guarantee their safety. In a curious talk Ford made part of the public record, he expressed sadness that "so many intelligent men" had chosen to worship a mere man with bad habits and that the hardworking Mormons would still be welcome in Illinois if they'd stop their controversial behavior and act like regular people. Otherwise, Ford could see no alternative for them but to get as far away from the United States as possible and form their own country. With their weird ways, it was the only way they'd be safe.

Not surprisingly, Brigham Young told Ford he'd "see him in hell" before abandoning the religion. Besides, Joseph Smith had already concluded the Saints would have to set up their own country after Smith's 1844 bid to become president of the United States failed in a big way. At that time, most of the present-day American West was still Mexico, but apparently neither Smith nor Young saw that as an obstacle to creating their own Mormon country. As the Saints agreed to leave Illinois, Young decided upon the parched but irrigable Salt Lake Valley as a capital of a country that would eventually swallow Texas along with most of today's American West.

Murdered and burned out of Missouri and forced to leave their spectacular city in Illinois, no one could have blamed Brigham Young and his followers for harboring rage toward the United States and its entire population. As he marched his Saints over thousands of miles of belligerent wilderness to an uncertain future, Young chose to nourish that hatred with abandon, without a single concession to the roles each side played in the tragic Mormon expulsions from several states. Brigham Young was no Joseph Smith. Smith could be easygoing, forgiving, generous, empathetic, and personal. Young's humor ran to sarcasm, his demeanor hard. He could be cold, ruthless, distant, calculating, and severe.*

It has been argued that Young was exactly the sort of man the Saints needed after the Smith murders left them in confused disarray, that they would have fallen apart without Young's iron hand, but it is also true that Young set the gold standard for demanding unquestioned obedience to what he frequently described as his divine infallibility. It was Young's intent to form a theocracatic domain in the West that would openly shun the rest of the United States, an edict he drove home with verbose predictions of Gentile country's gruesome destruction with tiresome regularity.

To accomplish this, Young set about fulfilling the *Book of Mormon* prophesies about the American Indians—the Lamanites—sending out agents to remind the tribes of their true Israelite roots. Young's agents informed all area tribes that only Mormon white men could be trusted. Mormons and Indians had to stick together, Young explained, because the other white men Young called "Americrats" were coming to Utah to destroy both of them, and it was the Indians' destiny to join forces with Young.

Young had apparently not considered the possibility that American Indian tribes would receive this news without enthusiasm. Although he would not interfere with the tribes' raids on interlopers in his territory, Young basically gave up on plans to convert the uncooperative males into Gentile slaughtering units. He instead urged Mormon men to marry as many of the Indian women and buy as many of the children as they could, but this plan also ran into trouble when the Indians began demanding reciprocation in the form of Mormon women and children.

Young's plans for an independent country hit another snag when the United States acquired all of the prophet's target territories in the 1848 Treaty of Guadalupe Hidalgo ending the Mexican American War. The always pragmatic Young changed strategies, deciding to seek statehood, a condition he believed could still produce independence for the huge territory he'd not yet populated. The ultimate believer in states' rights, Young

---

*   In a letter to a publisher, Stephen Harding, a former Utah governor who knew Young well, argued that the Mormon prophet could not have believed much of the "foolery" he preached. "[I]t is nonsense to say that a man of his coldness, executive ability and acuteness can be fooled by such stuff as makes his system," Harding wrote. "[I]t is all rabbit tracks—all rabbit tracks."

reckoned U.S. states were granted just enough autonomy that he could run rings about the feds. Once he got his state of "Deseret" populated and self-sufficient, he could have his country anyway.*

But if Young intended to sweet-talk anyone into statehood, he was off to a bad start. In 1856, a catastrophic drought and a series of crop-devastating grasshopper scourges pushed the Saints to the brink of starvation, and Young decided they all needed to recommit to the religion. The Mormon Reformation of 1856–58 was an unbridled festival of fire and brimstone, stoked by fanatical Smith devotees, incendiary speakers who traveled from settlement to town raging against the impure, the undedicated, the apostate devils in their midst and in the government. Men were castrated for some offenses, scores were rebaptized to rededicate themselves to the church, and all lived in trepidation of the efficient spy network Young boasted knew the movements of every man, woman, and child in the territory. If that weren't enough, the Saints were aware of Young's cadre of cold-blooded killers known as "destroying angels." Some, like Porter Rockwell, were graduates of Joseph Smith's Danites, but Young had other recruits like assassin "Wild Bill" Hickman, an ancestor of Utah's current attorney general.

Young also used the Reformation to push polygamy hard. Declaring that "any man who denied plural marriage was damned," Young had his followers, to prove their Sainthood, scrambling to marry wives at a frenetic pace, ironically causing the future prophet Wilford Woodruff, who would ban polygamy, to remark, "All are trying to get wives, until there is hardly a girl fourteen years old in Utah, but what is married, or is just going to be." So savage was the battle for extra wives among older men that there was at least one event in which a young man who refused to give up his betrothed to a Mormon elder was castrated and exiled. Young's Utah bore an uncanny resemblance to FLDS's modern Short Creek.

Young had a firm grip on Utah, but the California gold rush put the Utah Young thought nobody would want smack in the middle of new westward immigration routes traveled by hundreds of wagon trains. Alarmed by this unexpected influx of the godless, Young redoubled his exhortations that Saints steer clear of non-Mormons. The wagon train interlopers were

---

* According to Smith's translation of the reformed Egyptian tablets, the word *deseret* meant "honeybee," a symbol of symbiotic hard work. The symbol of a beehive is still used throughout Utah, including on state highway signs, ultimately inspiring Utah's nickname as the Beehive State.

harassed and their livestock rustled, and they were subjected to ridiculous and illegal tolls. Young ordered his Mormons to refuse to sell food, grain, or any goods to the travelers, and at least one Mormon man who violated this order by giving onions to a hungry man he'd known from Missouri days was beaten so badly he sustained disabling, permanent brain damage.

Young could generally rely upon the native tribes to at least stay out of his way. For everyone else, look out. Young's dissenters had a way of turning up dead, and the prophet also made life so miserable—and dangerous—for federal authorities sent to Utah, such as judges and Indian agents, that many fled the territory. Some of the "runaway judges," as they were called, said they feared for their lives under what they described as Young's iron-fisted dictatorship in open rebellion of U.S. law.

Needless to say, Congress was not amused, especially when Young's demonization of new settlers, combined with his zealous revivalism, culminated in the Mountain Meadows Massacre of 1857, the execution-style murders of 120 men, women, and children on their way from Arkansas to California, traveling in the richest wagon train to ever pass through economically disadvantaged Salt Lake City. Although some Mormon-recruited Indians participated at the start of the five-day tragedy, they quickly lost interest after sustaining unexpected casualties from the surprisingly spirited defense mounted by the besieged pioneers. Thereafter, Mormon men painted as Indians continued the assault but could not dislodge the defenders until they sent an undisguised white man in under a truce flag, promising to deliver the pioneers to safety if they'd relinquish their arms. Running low on food, water, and ammunition, the settlers walked unarmed with their presumed saviors for a quarter mile before Mormon men and some Indians shot, clubbed, and stabbed all but seventeen children to death as they pleaded for their lives. The attackers even stripped the bodies of clothes and jewelry while dividing up the train's other livestock and riches.

The outbreak of the Civil War distracted legislators from the polygamous theocracy in Utah, but not forever. Before the war became a total distraction, the antipolygamy Morrill Act passed in 1862. After the war, the Edmonds Act again outlawing polygamy passed in 1882, followed by the merciless 1887 Edmonds-Tucker Act, a furious wrecking ball aimed directly at Brigham Young's Mormons. Edmonds-Tucker allowed for the seizure of church property valued at more than $50,000 and disincorporated the LDS Church and its Perpetual Emigrating Fund Company critical for bringing thousands of European converts to Utah on the grounds that both entities promoted illegal polygamy.*

President James Buchanan had already removed Brigham Young as territorial governor in 1857, but that hadn't loosened his power one whit. Edmonds-Tucker sought to remedy that by yanking civil and criminal authority from the local magistrate judges Young selected for their personal loyalty and religious fervor and placing it with U.S. district attorneys, opening the door for hundreds of arrests of Mormon men and women—so many that some had to be moved to Detroit, of all places, when Utah ran out of jail space. The U.S. attorneys also filed suit against Mormon Church holdings, looking to seize an estimated $3 million in property.

Given their antigovernment rhetoric, it seems incongruous for Mormon leaders to trust American courts to overturn the legislation, but they did. Although Joseph Smith never seemed concerned with any provision of the U.S. Constitution save the one guaranteeing religious freedom, he did publicly declare the document to be divinely inspired. Apparently taking Smith at his word, Mormon leaders and prosecutors agreed to allow a "test case" to go forward. Willing Mormon guinea pig George Reynolds was arrested for polygamy in order to challenge the laws on First Amendment religious freedom grounds that Mormon leaders were certain the courts would support. As planned, the case made it all the way to the U.S. Supreme Court, where, as not planned, it blew up in their faces. In a landmark 1878 decision, the U.S. Supreme Court ruled that religion did not trump U.S. law, period. *United States v. Reynolds* was a truly unexpected shock.

But the Congress and courts weren't the only problems confronting LDS. Responding to the public uproar over polygamy and the lawless territory that harbored it, president James Buchanan dispatched 2,500 troops to bring the Mormons to heel as early as 1857. That effort fizzled, becoming something of a joke. But after the Civil War, Mormon leadership was faced with the prospect of a superbly trained, restlessly unemployed Union Army still dedicated to the irascible antipolygamist Ulysses Grant. By 1890, the whole of America would have supported an all-out invasion of the Utah territory, and some were openly demanding it. The hardcore and unrepentant

---

* Edmonds-Tucker also required antipolygamy oaths of prospective voters, required civil marriage certificates, abrogated common law spousal privilege, annulled territorial laws allowing illegitimate children to inherit, disenfranchised women who had been allowed to vote in the territory, and removed school textbook selections from local control. Apparently wishing to leave nothing to chance, Congress waited until 1978 to repeal the bill.

Brigham Young might never have acknowledged it, but his death in 1877 left Mormon leaders free to realistically contemplate their chances. Even counting the unreliable American Indians they'd converted or bribed, they were seriously outnumbered.

The final punch to the gut came in May 1890 when the U.S. Supreme Court ruled in the case of *Late Corporation of the Church of Jesus Christ of Latter Day Saints v. United States*, upholding the Edmonds-Tucker provision allowing the government to seize LDS property. The order green-lighted the territorial U.S. attorney to act on the suits they'd filed years earlier when the act had passed, allowing the government to seize Mormon property. Just three months later, in August 1890, a besieged Wilford Woodruff delivered the Manifesto ending plural marriage.

But abandoning that divine revelation was not accepted with the indifferent shrugs Hinckley and others imply. Far from it. Smith, and certainly Young, had inexorably established polygamy as a *requirement*—not an option—for admittance to the celestial kingdom, which was the whole point of being Mormon. From the instant the Manifesto left Woodruff's lips, Mormon polygamists argued the explanation was an insultingly transparent political capitulation to a secular entity with no authority to override God's laws. This is the position still taken by modern polygamous sects like FLDS, who argue it is the LDS Church that has apostated, not them.

It's not an indefensible argument. When LDS tries to put daylight between the mainstream church and FLDS in Short Creek, it's hard to get around one simple truth: except for polygamy, both groups believe the same theology, use the same holy books, sing the same hymns, and preach the same sermon themes. Though LDS officials are squeamishly evasive about the multistory, fifteen-barrel silo outside Salt Lake City stuffed with four hundred thousand pounds of grain, the food is there to sustain Mormons during the worldwide chaos that will precede the Second Coming. Both LDS and FLDS plan for this event, which could be imminent.

Both churches accept Joseph Smith as a prophet so divine he was just barely a man, practically a contemporary of Jesus Christ, with whom he will stand shoulder to shoulder at the upcoming apocalypse. Both churches believe Smith's revelation and commandments as set forth in *Doctrines and Covenants* were instructions directly from God. Despite two manifestos from separate prophets who were also talking to God, LDS has not removed the plural marriage revelation. To the contrary, LDS has not *restored* Smith's 1835 revelation condemning polygamy—a revelation LDS deleted from the *Doctrines and Covenants* in 1876 because it conflicted with the revelation *ordering* polygamy.

Even after the Manifesto, it took a suspicious Congress six more years to award statehood to a territory it whittled with deliberate glee to less than a third of Young's original design. It took another fifteen years after that for LDS to make an earnest commitment to ending polygamy. But there is still a sense that the effort was made under duress, that had the church its druthers, polygamy would have remained.

For hardcore FLDS members spurning LDS at the turn of the century, polygamy *has* remained. Like Brigham Young, they selected the beautiful but parched terrain known as the Arizona Strip precisely because it was out of the law's reach, too isolated and unforgiving for anyone else to desire. In fact, if Brigham Young's vision of a Mormon Utah had been realized, untouched for generations by outside influence, his followers might look a lot like those of the Fundamentalist Church of Jesus Christ of Latter-Day Saints in Short Creek, straddling the Utah-Arizona border.

Eventually, the Americrats did arrive.

3

BILL WALKER
AND THE FIRST CASE

If I had 40 wives in the United States, they did not know it, and could not substanti-
ate it, neither did I ask any lawyer, judge or magistrate for them. I live above the law,
and so do these [Mormon] *people.*

— Brigham Young, *Journal of Discourses*, Vol. 1

I was sick this morning, up since 2:30 A.M. praying. Had a hot soak. The Lord burned
the sickness out of me by 9 A.M. While I lay there, the Lord told me several things.
1) There was a conspiracy against me here in this community. I am not fully aware
of who they all are. 2) In Sunday School talk to the obedient about Zion . . . 3) Warn
the people about the apostates, especially the women.

—Warren Jeffs dictation, November 3, 2002

In January 2002, Tucson attorney Bill Walker received a call from a former satisfied client who knew that his recently retired lawyer was a sucker for the downtrodden. Like many folks, Bill's dreams of luxury retirement included nice cars, exotic travel, and cool summer homes, but for Walker, those hadn't been his primary goals. Walker had always dreamed of building a nest egg large enough to allow him to work for nothing on behalf of all the people he'd seen trampled in American courtrooms because they couldn't afford to defend their rights, but unlike many who entertain philanthropic notions in moments of euphoria or inebriation, Bill was serious.

The son of a philosophical army major and a musical genius mother who could play every band instrument and conducted the Harrisburg, Pennsylvania, symphony orchestra when she was seventeen, Bill was reared in countries from Asia to Europe and credits his passion for social justice to his childhood exposure to human diversity. After leaving the military, the family settled in spectacular Flagstaff, Arizona, for what amounted to a sedentary life after all of the family's adventures, but it was not to be.

Days before a life insurance policy was to take effect, Bill's fifty-three-year-old father drowned in a freak boating accident, leaving the family next to destitute. Barely eighteen, Bill willingly sacrificed the Ivy League education he'd earned to instead support his mother and younger siblings in what was often a desperate struggle to keep the lights on, days whose memories still cloud his face with dark worry. Though he's well-off now, Walker is a man who remembers what disenfranchised poverty means.

Bill's defiant refusal to register for the draft during the Vietnam War prevented him from practicing law for five years until he won exoneration before the American Bar Association, which, at that time would have been more inclined to catgut "draft dodgers" than send them off with the well-wishing backslaps. Good lawyers are not always good courtroom litigators, but Walker was both, and he didn't lose much. Irascible, provocative, tenacious, fearless, and scary smart, Walker had little use for unnecessary diplomacy, and opposing counsel generally did not enjoy their time with him. A mere letterhead from Walker's office often triggered morose decisions to settle cases with a checkbook rather than proceed to trials where juries responding to Walker's persuasion had awarded tens of millions to his clients in a single pop.

Still, it wasn't the passport inked with exotic destinations or the assortment of getaway homes on northwestern islands or warm, Mexican waters that moved Walker. He was teased about these indulgences by friends who were frequently exposed to Walker's crusading orations, but the fact remained that Walker backed his sermons about social justice up with pro bono action. By age fifty-six, though he was mostly retired from paying work, his schedule was booked for months in advance with unpaid service on the boards of international nonprofits and opportunities to level the playing field for people like the girl in such inconceivable circumstances described that day on the phone.

"You're such a do gooder?" Saul Bly challenged. "Put your money where your mouth is and help this girl."*

Walker was not a religious man. He'd heard of Mormons, of course, but knew nothing of the faith. He did know the client-turned-friend who called him that day was a nonpracticing Mormon, but as he listened to Saul Bly lay out the facts surrounding Ruth Stubbs, Bill tried to recall if his friend

---

*   Saul Bly is not a real name. Bill's former client remains an FLDS activist involved with helping young girls flee the sect and prefers to remain anonymous.

had ever demonstrated an appetite for irritating—and time squandering—practical jokes. Having been involved in Arizona law and politics for the past thirty-five years, Bill had never seen or heard of this FLDS—this doomsday polygamous cult on the Utah border—in any courtroom or crime blotter.

Bill felt the possibility that he'd missed a group like this was slim, because what Bly portrayed was laughably illegal—nearly every word of it. The word "slavery" sprang to mind as Saul described Ruth's ludicrous "marriage" and subsequent escape like a thief in the night. Even Saul's language evoked slavery as he explained his loose affiliation with activist antipolygamist groups trying for years to draw attention to polygamy in general and FLDS in particular. The Colorado City Underground Railroad, for instance, was a group of ex-FLDS women endeavoring to help girls escape the group. Walker felt that any group in modern America that would compare themselves to the famous network that helped slaves to escape was beyond absurd.

"Saul," Bill said evenly, applying as much patience as he could muster. "Everything you're telling me is against the law. So call the police."

"You don't understand, Bill," Bly answered in a dead voice. "They are the police."

In another moment, Bill would learn the thirty-two-year-old man who'd married the sixteen-year-old Stubbs was a policeman himself. Not a church parking lot policeman or a gated community rent-a-cop, but an actual policeman paid with actual tax dollars on a real police force, and Rod Holm was certified to work in both Utah and Arizona. Bill had seen his share of corrupt cops over his career, but most went bad for money, gambling, or drugs, not some prophet character. And bad cops had to be discreet. Even if they were popular with their fellows, their vices could not come to higher attention or they'd be fired at a minimum, possibly prosecuted. If they were going to bed an underage girl, they didn't advertise it by keeping her continuously pregnant, in the open, with two other women. And what were these "smoking tickets" this guy had issued Ruth prior to their "marriage"? Bill thought smoking was a stupid habit, but he knew of no laws against it.

Which raised bigger questions: What kind of police force was this? Why was Rod Holm still certified, and where was the state supervision? When Bly told him that the entirety of the twin cities of Hildale, Utah, and Colorado City, Arizona—city government, fire and water departments, electric, police, public schools, everything—was staffed by FLDS members, Bill could not get his head around it. It was impossible that the states of Arizona and Utah had allowed what amounted to a separate country to operate not only unfettered by state and federal law but funded by state and federal tax dollars. Laws were being broken in the open. Laws were being fabricated in the open. Everyone knew. How was it possible that the attorneys general of these states could be ignoring a man who'd set himself up as God's representative on earth, controlling the lives of thousands? How was that even accomplished?

Bly admitted that convincing the general public of the severity of the brainwashing inflicted upon FLDS members was one of his greatest hurdles. *Why don't they just leave?* potential donors to antipolygamy causes ask with exasperation. Or *Why don't they just get help?* Without real-time contact with sect members, it's difficult to illustrate the cradle-to-grave indoctrination, a constant, pervasive, and relentless reinforcement of FLDS dogma occurring virtually every hour of every day. Baking bread, doing laundry, and cooking dinner may all be accompanied with the endless, droning religious tapes Jeffs encouraged all to keep in their ears to drown out impure thoughts. Television, radio, "worldly" books, magazines, and movies are banned. FLDS children are reminded constantly they are "special" and "chosen" and will be spared when the world ends at any time. Literally at any day—maybe tomorrow—FLDS members expect the end to come and Jesus to ride a cloud down from heaven with Joseph Smith.

People in the outside world don't know this special information given only to FLDS members. Outside people are depraved, evil, lying in wait to steal your eternity of happiness. Even conversing with a Gentile jeopardized your salvation, and for women it was harder. As in LDS, FLDS men become members of the priesthood. To the degree that they followed the prophet's every command, men have some control over their admittance to heaven, but women have none. Barred from the priesthood, they had to rely upon their husbands' good graces, a dogma true for both LDS and FLDS to this day. Only men have the power to elevate their wives into heaven. Permission will not be granted without total obedience from women who must answer first to their fathers and later to their husbands. The obedience must be "sweet" as well. No questioning, balking, or, heaven forbid, arguing will be tolerated. From the time they can understand English, girls comprehend that their very existence depends on how well they please a man and that their only contribution of serious value will be the number of children they produce.

Still, things can get so desperate for some women they find the yawning jaws of hell preferable to their situations in FLDS, but the well of courage needed to escape must be deep enough to carry them beyond Short Creek's physical boundaries, if they even manage to get that far. Culture shock in the outside world is profound. FLDS escapees commonly cannot name the president of the United States and have no idea what Washington, D.C., is, much less what it does. Having been told their welfare checks are "manna from heaven," they don't know what government is. They can generally read and write on at least a grade-school level but have never read anything more than FLDS religious material. Their handwriting is strained, childish, with hesitating signatures that look like they belong at the bottom of a finger-painting project. They don't know there is such a thing as history outside of the life of Joseph Smith. They know nothing of science, the fossil record, the Sistine Chapel, World War II, or the Pilgrims. They would scoff in your face upon hearing that men had landed on the moon forty years ago, another apostate trick intended to shake their faith with lies.

One woman in her thirties escaping with her eight children in the dead of night was nearly recaptured because she ran out of gasoline before getting a safe distance. The woman had managed to pilfer a single thin dime before fleeing, and she was saved only because that coin was enough for her to place a phone call to an activist whose number had been smuggled into her possession. The young woman pushed the family station wagon off the road and huddled in the brush for hours, trying to shush her whimpering children, terrified she'd be discovered by the men she knew were out looking for her before the activist could get there.

The story is known because the activist did get there before FLDS, but these outcomes have been few and far between. Ruth's sister, Pennie Petersen, was saved by a Good Samaritan, but no one knows how many girls did not encounter one of these or did not have a dime and a phone number when they ran out of gasoline and were reclaimed by FLDS searchers and then disappeared into the sect's endless hiding places.

Better known are stories of those defectors who made it to geographical safety only to be overwhelmed by insurmountable culture shock, fear, poverty, depression, and loneliness. Girls in this state are emotionally unequipped to withstand the intense pressure levied by family and religious leaders offering false promises of forgiveness and reconciliation. Once reclaimed, the runaways are subjected to various forms of "behavior modification," which always meant separation from the children they'd often fled to protect. Some were plucked off the street by FLDS men in darkened vans, or the retrieval posses might snatch any children they'd be fortunate enough to find playing in the front yard or walking to school unattended. Cocooned in the generally sympathetic Utah courts, the high-dollar attorneys FLDS kept on retainer would mount a custody battle on behalf of the wronged fathers, alleging abandonment, abuse, neglect, and mental instability. They'd never lost.

"The children are the key," Bly went on. "They control these girls first through pregnancy and later by exploiting her love for her children. This girl made it all the way to Phoenix, and she has a little help from a sister there, but they're coming after her kids, Bill. If they get the kids, they get her too."

In addition to his overall revulsion for FLDS, Walker found himself developing a surprisingly healthy rage over Ruth's dreadful love story. The idea of a young girl's first love stolen from her, replaced with servitude to an older man she'd never met, a concubine who earned favor only through sex and endless pregnancy, was personally offensive to him, reminiscent of cruel, poverty-stricken third world countries. The fact that this girl had no recourse, no relief from the government charged with protecting her and was forced to rely for her salvation upon a loose patchwork quilt of disorganized activists and a pro bono attorney who wouldn't have existed a few years ago was an outrage. "The bottom line," Walker said, "is that there is no way any of this should be happening in the United States of America. To call it outrageous doesn't even start to cover what this is. I couldn't stand by and let this happen."

Walker worked for nothing, but pro bono cases still cost money. He usually recouped the office overhead, travel expenses, and costs of research, depositions, and court filing fees by prevailing in his wronged clients' civil suits, but Ruth's was a custody suit with no automatic fee awards for the victor. FLDS's Salt Lake City law firm was the prestigious and expensive Snow, Christensen, and Martineau with downtown offices in a historic edifice listed with the Beehive House as one of Utah's most revered and architecturally rich historical buildings. A firm like this represented the well-heeled, and if they couldn't win outright on merits, these clients were rich enough to drown the opposition in rivers of legal motions too costly to fight.

On its face, Walker looked like a one-man legal show with a destitute teenage mother for a client, easy pickings for a firm like SCM. What the firm could not have known was that a case like Ruth's was precisely the reason Walker had invested wisely to run a pro bono practice. He not only had the resources to fight, but he also enjoyed the battle. Besides, he didn't think he'd end up denting his savings. If FLDS could afford to keep pricey legal help like SCM on retainer, there was a money pot somewhere. At the moment, he couldn't imagine a group more worthy of being relieved of the money allowing them to stay in business. All of it.

In late January 2002, Walker made the 130-mile drive from Tucson to Phoenix to meet his client. Ruth's case had already become personal for Walker, but after he met the young mother, it became a cause. "I don't think I've ever had a client who always told the truth like Ruth did," he said, frowning at the rarity of honesty. "People always shade things to make their behavior more positive, but Ruth told the truth whether it helped or hurt her. Even when I'd say, 'Well, it would help us if such and such happened,' if it hadn't gone down that way, she'd say, 'That's not what happened.' I never had to worry about going into court with bad facts because Ruth always told the truth." He smiled grimly. "Even when it killed us."

Walker was also charmed by Ruth's ready, effervescent smile and the way she tried to put the best spin on things. Free to resume her journal writing without humiliating discovery, Ruth recorded her first month of freedom with the enthusiasm of a child running amok in Disney World: barbecues, lawn parties, any movie she wanted, and a mall shopping trip in which Ruth reckoned she was more enchanted by the kaleidoscope of colorful stores than two-year-old Maranda, who, unlike other FLDS kids who might have cried into their mothers' skirts, wasn't scared at all. Ruth's satisfaction was great. Her plan for freeing her kids was already working, but her own progress was choppier than she realized.

Reflecting her schedule of the past three years, Ruth's journal entries began with exact times. *At 2:15 P.M. I did the laundry. At 7:05 P.M. I played a fun game with my kids.* The time obsession concerned Pennie, who knew firsthand the enormous difficulty of shedding a religion hammered into your head from birth with no outside contact to contradict or even question the information presented as inviolate gospel. Pennie was glad Ruth was having fun, but Ruth needed to buckle down and face what had to be obtained in the real world: a job, a house, a car—all items Ruth was used to being given or directed to perform. Pennie watched her sister's progress warily, hoping there'd be no backsliding from the affidavit she'd completed to gain a temporary custody order Pennie helped her obtain from Maricopa County Superior Court judge Richard Trujillo on December 19, 2001—only ten days after her escape.

"Incest is common," Ruth's affidavit stated in part.

> Wives are required to submit fully to the husband, to the extent that permission had to be granted for every move,

including trips to the grocery store and doctor. Punishment is severe for all who are disobedient, including beating, shunning and expulsion to a community in Canada for retraining. . . .

My "husband" has threatened to take my children back to be raised with the other 18 children by his 2 other wives. He has also suggested that we give the children to the "Prophet," Warren Jeffs to raise. It is not uncommon for children to be taken from their mothers by a "Prophet" and transported to Salt Lake City for placement with more "deserving" families. I fear that should my "husband" be given custody or unsupervised parenting time with the children they will be injured or otherwise harmed or that he will abscond with them and I will never see them again.

While Pennie fretted about Ruth's ignorance of electric bills, Walker was glummer about Ruth's bent on forgiveness. Now that she was free, Ruth didn't want to damage FLDS or Rod Holm. Specifically, she did not want Holm to lose his job. With everything Ruth Stubbs had to worry about, Walker was confounded that she was worried about Holm's *job*, for Christ's sake. Walker planned on losses for Holm far exceeding employment, which he should have lost years ago. Did Ruth not understand it was against the law for a policeman to sleep with a sixteen-year-old girl? Why wasn't she angry, enraged even? It was fuel for Walker's growing apprehension. Given their opponent's money, expertise, and home court advantage, a Holm indictment was their strongest card, but the fact that no judge could award custody to a man who'd been indicted for underage sex crimes was not sinking in for Ruth. Wrapped up in her own euphoria, Ruth seemed to believe that no one who knew her would wish her harm and everything would work out for the best.

Walker needed for Ruth to get back in an affidavit frame of mind, but in the meantime, the custody order meant kidnapping charges could be levied against anyone snatching Ruth's kids without her permission, both a state and federal crime enhanced if the children were taken across state lines into Utah. However, Pennie wanted more insurance to deter the dark vans of FLDS.

On January 14, 2002, Pennie had arranged the formal taped interview between Ruth and Arizona Attorney General's Office investigators Ron

Gibson and Patty Rustenburg, who left Ruth with the cell numbers of state investigators should the vans appear anyway. Walker was particularly glad for this interview, in which Ruth clearly told the state cops that Rod Holm was a policeman certified in both Utah and Arizona. Investigator Gibson clearly knew his purpose, directing his questions to discover dates and locations of Holm's sexual liaisons with Ruth in Arizona, specifics required for any indictment. Ruth remembered the dates as well as the romantic Arizona locale Holm selected—the toolshed on his brother Gregg's property made available because, at the time, Holm was trying to convince his two other jealous wives he was not favoring Ruth with his "visits."

The forthcoming Arizona indictment would circumvent Ruth's annoying impulses to protect the man who'd enslaved her, relieving Walker of the uncomfortable chore of guiding a resistant client toward the correct decision. It was all good, and yet he could not shake a sense of unease over the time that had elapsed between contacts with Gibson. Keeping the probe of a police officer for statutory rape quiet until an indictment was ready was quite normal, but Walker felt Gibson should have made contact with his complaining witness's attorney of record by now. Polygamy might be a twitchy subject for the attorney general in Mormon Utah, but Walker could think of no good reason why Arizona attorney general Janet Napolitano would not act on clear evidence that a cop in her jurisdiction had engaged in systematic underage sex, among other crimes. He made a mental note in Ruth's file to call Gibson and feel him out, maybe wheedle a date out of him.

For the moment, the legal arrows Pennie let fly had persuaded FLDS to withdraw from the now dangerous Arizona border. With the unauthorized retrieval of Ruth's kids rendered untenable, FLDS relied upon the tried-and-true method of alternately soothing and threatening phone calls to Ruth. Pennie thought it was worse than unfortunate that Ruth had made that part very easy for them. Against the advice of everyone, Ruth decided she could not deprive her children of a father's love. She'd agreed to give Holm visitation, producing a barrage of phone calls to Ruth from Short Creek under the guise of setting schedules.

It was soon abundantly evident to everyone except Ruth that her tender mercies were misplaced and that Holm would have gladly sacrificed the fatherly visitation honors for a little peace of mind. For Holm, the day Ruth disappeared had been the most sickening of his life. Ruth had pulled the wool over his eyes, pretending to love the whole second honeymoon thing, abusing his relaxed supervision by taking off. Holm had thought he'd faint dead away when he was informed. There was nothing in FLDS that said "unworthy and weak" like having your prized third wife run off with the kids. But then a funny thing happened. Once the shock wore off, Holm's depression gave way to something unexpected and wonderful, but he could hardly tell anyone: Ruth's departure made him feel, well, *liberated*.

No doubt Ruth was gorgeous and sexy, but the truth was, he'd always been afraid of her. She was just *irrepressible*. He'd tried everything to get her high-maintenance, selfish habits under control, but the diet, the strict time schedule, and the ban (on penalty of her salvation) from talking to virtually anyone outside the house had failed to produce the kind of obedience required for his serenity. His other ladies were always up in arms about Ruth, wreaking havoc and forcing him into corners. He was in the *priesthood*. He didn't have time for these worldly problems.

Then there was Ruth's surprising allegiance to her kids. Children were a blessing and all, but Wendy had just given birth again, bringing the number of his kids to twenty-three, not counting the one he now knew Ruth carried. Finding that out had been another zinger, but in truth, all those kids could damage your calm. It was a lot of noise and trouble, and it was expensive, even with the "lying for the Lord" welfare applications Susie so ably executed. Susie said Ruth's kids were brats anyway, and Ruth kept whining about introducing them to her family. Ruth *knew* that was impossible! Her family were apostates! She was trying to jeopardize the salvation of the whole house by even *talking* about them. At least Susie and Wendy understood about how *he* held the priesthood and how *he* could make or break them in the afterlife, but Ruth had just never seemed to get that. Well, what could you expect from a former apostate who'd gone right back to Satan despite everything he'd given her? Oh, there was no doubt about it. Ruth was bad trouble, and by now the kids were tainted, too.

In his heart he knew it was delusional, but for a while, Holm had entertained the possibility that Warren Jeffs would embrace these obvious facts and simply say "good riddance." It would have all been for the best, because Holm was not so wrapped up in Short Creek that he didn't understand what the outside world would think of a thirty-two-year-old policeman sleeping with a sixteen-year-old girl. Holm had given unquestioning service to the prophets he served, even participating in the gang beating of a twelve-year-old boy who'd displeased elders by smiling at a girl on whom the prophet already had designs.* He really hoped Uncle Warren would weigh the possibility of criminal indictment of a faithful priesthood member against the recovery of an ungrateful, selfish apostate, no matter how nicely she was packaged.

Summoned to Uncle Warren's presence soon after Ruth's escape, Holm knew his secret hopes were toast. "We do not give up our women and children," Jeffs informed him with a chilly, hateful glare. From that moment on, Rod Holm and FLDS became synonymous. It would have been easy to settle Ruth's case. From the start, she'd asked only for custody, her only condition concerning liberal visitation that it not occur in Holm's polygamous home. Holm would have jumped at it, especially since the words "child support" were not mentioned, but the decision about his own life had never been in his hands. If Holm harbored any illusions that Warren Jeffs would reward his loyalty or be humbled by the fact that Holm was risking his livelihood and very freedom to do Warren's bidding, he was tragically mistaken. In thousands of pages of personal dictations recorded during the time, Warren Jeffs mentions Holm exactly twice. One entry was a phone call he took from Holm in which he advised his distraught follower, "These things take time. Keep sweet," ironically the same lame advice Holm doled out to his warring wives.

Before the ink on Ruth's Arizona custody order was dry, longtime SCM attorney Rod Parker was representing Rod Holm, and by extension FLDS, in Utah's Fifth District Court, the legal domicile for the children where the case was automatically transferred for final resolution. Located in St. George, Utah, the Fifth District had been historically sympathetic to polygamists, but it was still a public arena with records anyone could see. Initially, Holm had been primarily worried about keeping his job, but now he was unnerved by the prospect of a prison cell only he seemed to understand. Hoping to avoid what would be inevitable public revelations, Holm tripled his efforts to talk Ruth back in, enlisting Susie and Wendy to make plaintive phone calls reminding Ruth of all the good times and of course her salvation, which might yet be reclaimed if she returned.

Pennie worried her little sister might still be vulnerable to the gibberish, but her fears proved to be unjustified. Throughout hours of cajoling, Ruth

---

* Rod Holm admitted the beating, which involved other Hildale police officers, in taped phone calls and in a deposition taken for the custody hearing. He said he "regretted" the incident, but he failed to mention that roughing up the boy wasn't his only transgression. The recent memoirs of several ex-FLDS members identify Holm as a member of the feared God squad, the hand-selected group of spies and enforcers for the prophet's will.

never budged from her position. She stoutly told her former family that she didn't remember any good times and she didn't believe her salvation was in jeopardy because she was doing what was right for her children. Again and again she rebuffed offers for forgiveness, saying she didn't need any. She laughed at Holm's threats and contradicted his lame efforts to convince her she'd been eighteen when they'd had sex in Arizona.

As Rod Holm's nerves frayed, Warren Jeffs hardened his position, refusing to negotiate any outcome that did not include giving full custody of Ruth's children to Holm. Even more than women, children are literally considered FLDS priesthood property. Once born, mothers are understood to have no further claim on their babies, and indeed, Warren Jeffs would soon take up the habit of reassigning children willy-nilly to families of his selection, informing the biological mothers that they would never see their kids again. Jeffs was unconcerned with any visitation negotiations for Ruth. It was expected that Ruth would return with them, but if she didn't, the children would be permanently physically removed from her reach no matter what was promised in a settlement. The priesthood must at least reclaim the souls of the babies, especially the female baby.

No attorney in the country could bring more passion or have a deeper understanding for Warren Jeffs's position than Rod Parker, the sect's lead attorney for nearly twenty years. Tall and fair-skinned with reddish-blond hair, Parker is a former Catholic with a frank, easygoing demeanor and a startling array of cuss words, *fucking* being the most popular, introduced into normal conversation with a stranger without blush or restraint. He is married with five children whose photographs and mementos dot the spacious office on a key card–secured floor at the exclusive Ten Exchange Place address in downtown Salt Lake.

An intelligent and insightful conversationalist, Parker's wholesale dedication to FLDS is a puzzle to his colleagues in the legal community, who understand the millions of dollars FLDS has paid to Parker's firm but not his ferocious advocacy for indefensible FLDS practices nor why he is apparently willing to act as the sect's chief media and public relations spokesman. At times during conversations, Parker seemed puzzled himself, admitting that his intense affiliation with FLDS most probably contributed to major career setbacks. He speculated that his iron links to FLDS factored when he was passed over for a judge appointment for which he'd lobbied hard and called in favors, but after frowning at that memory for a half minute, Parker shrugged off the bad feelings.

"They were looking for someone younger, mainly," he reassured himself. Asked if his media statements defending FLDS stray from the legal to the dogmatic, a relaxed Parker replied: "Everyone is entitled to a vigorous defense. These folks are crazy, but they're good people—the very best people trying to live their beliefs—and they deserve my all. It's their religion, and it's constitutionally protected."

The remark brought a derisive snort from Bill Walker. "Just think about that," he said hotly. "A guy raking in millions advocating the constitutional rights of men to systemically rape young girls. It's bullshit, and it's disgusting."

FLDS turned the 1953 raid photographs to their favor, but as a general rule, publicity FLDS cannot control bites the sect hard. Parker may be the first call reporters place when seeking FLDS reaction to any dustup, but Parker keeps no media abreast of FLDS movements if he can help it. With Ruth Stubbs, the idea was to get in and out of court quietly, get the kids back to their "rightful" family, and let Ruth return or fade into obscurity like all the other upstart women.

Walker wanted to get out quickly, but quietly didn't aid that goal. More appalled by FLDS every day and convinced that the courts in St. George were insurmountably biased in favor of FLDS, he wanted the whole country to share his enlightenment, turning public sympathy toward his young client in the process. In late January 2002, Walker allowed persistent television reporter Mike Watkiss of KTVK in Phoenix to interview Ruth for the evening news.

In the post-1953 climate in which media had been largely complicit in shielding FLDS from outside scrutiny, Mike Watkiss was a standout, one of only a handful of reporters consistently battling news directors skittish about being cast as religious persecutors by the FLDS attorneys.* For twenty years, Watkiss battled the tide, refusing to paint FLDS as some misunderstood version of the Amish, convinced that public exposure could literally save lives. Watkiss could be described as a crusader, and Walker's client was the sort of interview he'd hoped for for years. Apple cheeked and freshly scrubbed, her young face makeup free, blond-banged hair pulled back in

---

* Thin, incomplete, or apologetic reporting on FLDS has contributed to the general public unawareness of the group's core tenets, and reporters who consistently reveal the illegal practices within FLDS continue to be a rarity. In addition to Watkiss, they include former Phoenix *New Times* reporter John Dougherty; Salt Lake City ABC 4's Brent Hunsaker; and Ben Winslow, formerly of the LDS newspaper the *Deseret News*, currently reporting for Salt Lake City's KSTU news.

a ponytail, and just a tad chubby with pregnancy, Ruth looked more like an older sister to the tow-headed toddlers scampering about her legs than a seasoned mother. The dichotomy was as stunning as Watkiss's shocking questions, answered with Ruth's characteristic forthright bluntness.

The first-ever interview with an actual FLDS child bride running for her life was a sensation seen coast to coast. As editors from New York to Los Angeles squinted at maps trying to locate St. George, Utah, Ruth appeared on nightly news shows across the West to the horror of Rod Holm, who apparently heard the coffin being lowered to the grave.

Although FLDS spokesmen and Holm himself would assert to the end that they did not know about any underage sex laws, a panicked Holm in fact called Ruth (who was taping her phone calls from FLDS) on February 9, alternately professing his love, calling her names, denying they'd had sex in Arizona before she was eighteen, and ultimately laying his inevitable wrack and ruin at her feet. The television interview, he predicted, this staggering evidence of her self-centered wickedness, would do him in:

> It's too late! And I'll tell ya why. . . . There's absolutely noth-ing you can do about it, even if you was to go and try and find that Mike Watkiss guy and say, "'Kay, don't do anything else." . . . They won't even listen to you now. I mean, it's out of your hands. . . .
>
> Well, Ruth, I'm certainly concerned, but isn't it interesting how you, you inflict all the pain and suffering and a want to be selfish, and now you're concerned after. . . . Is the potential there that you're gonna have to tell your children that you put their father in jail?

In reality, Rod Holm's prison possibilities were never Ruth's call. She would have settled the case without even a demand for child support. It was Warren Jeffs's unbending demand that she unconditionally surrender her children to the sect that sent *Holm v. Stubbs* into open court and Ruth Stubbs before Watkiss's cameras. The Stubbs interviews were a crowbar jammed under a teetering mountain boulder. FLDS lay directly in its path.

4

JUDGE SHUMATE

I say, rather than that apostates should flourish here, I will unsheathe my bowie knife,
and conquer or die [Great commotion in the congregation, and a simultaneous burst
of feeling assenting to the declaration]. Now you nasty apostates, clear out, or judg-
ment will be put to the line and righteousness to the plummet. [Voices, generally "Go
it! Go it!"] If you say it is right, raise your hands. [All hands up] Let us call upon the
Lord to assist us in this, and in every good work.
> —Brigham Young, *Journal of Discourses*, Vol. 1, March 27, 1853

Every day is a miracle. Every day we exist as a people and as families. . . . We are
facing the final scenes. . . . The Lord is about to clean house. He is about to sweep
the wicked off this land.
> —Warren Jeffs Sunday School lesson, November 3, 2002

The theocratic empire Brigham Young envisioned would have included Nevada, Texas, Arizona, Utah, Southern California, and sizeable portions of six other states, but a jaded Congress had other ideas. Once the United States acquired the territories, Young could do nothing to stop the government from chiseling Deseret down in increments. When it was granted territorial status in 1850, Congress even rejected Young's chosen name, electing instead to acknowledge the resident Indians with "Utah."*

Undeterred, Young continued plans for an isolated, self-sufficient country of Deseret masquerading as a state. To accomplish this, he drafted sometimes reluctant settlers already established in one place to relocate, erecting

---

* Several of the land cuts followed the discovery of precious metals, wealth Congress may have wished to remove from Brigham Young's control. The final cut occurred during the administration of Abraham Lincoln, who checked *The Book of Mormon* out of the Library of Congress and famously compared Mormons to the proverbial stubborn tree stump farmers should plow around to conserve energy. However, Lincoln signed the tough Morill Anti-Bigamy Act into law, refused Young's demands to appoint Mormons to territorial positions, and observed that Utah was "probably" in a state of insurrection.

new towns from scratch in wilderness surveyed as suitable for the production of commodities specific to self-containment. Total isolation was the
goal, but when the Civil War broke out in 1861, the Utah Territory Young
insisted on calling Deseret wasn't there yet. Fearing the loss of Southern
state cotton, which the Mormons still needed to make clothes, Young gave
three hundred loyal Mormon families one month to pull up stakes and get
their backsides to the region now known as Washington County, Utah, to
grow cotton in the unexpectedly moderate climate.

The directive earned the settlement a nickname it still carries, "Utah's
Dixie," and the pioneers Young selected for this mission were not some
foot-dragging draftees casting longing backward glances at their hard-built
properties that Young usurped or gave to other men. The families sent to
Dixie were among Mormonism's most inspired devotees. In some parts of
Utah, only about 10 percent of the population practiced polygamy, but in
southern Utah the figure was upward of 40 percent. The territory's main
town of St. George was named for apostle George A. Smith, cousin to the
slain prophet and a popular firebrand speaker known for whipping settlements into religious frenzies during the 1856 Mormon Reformation.*

Despite a willing spirit, Utah's cotton colony never really took off. The
population remained sedentary, and southern Utah became as close to
Young's ideal of insular living as the state could get, making it very attractive
for polygamists when pressure from the mainstream church turned serious
during the Smoot hearings. Certain that LDS was now irredeemably apostated, disgusted polygamists began filtering into what is called the Arizona
strip some fifty miles east of St. George, founding a community called The
Work. It would evolve into FLDS. Sect members still refer to The Work, just
as they continue to call the twin cities of Colorado City and Hildale "Short
Creek," or simply "The Crick," an area geographically isolated by natural
barriers like the Grand Canyon, which effectively severs the community
from the rest of Arizona.

---

*   Although he tried valiantly to wriggle out of it, George A. Smith was a major player in the
Mountain Meadows Massacre. Days before the massacre, Smith, who held the rank of general
in the Nauvoo legion, made a swing through southern Utah, inflaming the faithful with hellfire
sermons. In his memoirs, John D. Lee, the only man Young sacrificed to the authorities for the
massacre, said Smith then met with Indian tribes, reminding them of the "Americrats'" deadly
intentions, adding that an army of Americrats were coming their way. "I have always believed,
since that day," Lee wrote, "that General George A. Smith was then visiting Southern Utah to
prepare the people for the work of exterminating Captain Fancher's train of emigrants, and I
now believe he was sent for that purpose by the direct command of Brigham Young."

This, and the low population in southern Utah, would cloak FLDS in practical invisibility for nearly one hundred years. The '53 raid shattered the calm for a year or so, but everyone arrested in that action returned to Short Creek to resume their lives uninterrupted by further police action. In 1950, St. George had only forty-five hundred residents and a decade later had added only five hundred to the roster. The five thousand overwhelmingly Mormon families in the sleepy village were only a few generations removed from the Mormons sent there in 1861. Virtually everyone in St. George and the surrounding hamlets had some polygamy in their family trees, a normal fact of life for folks who were neither shocked nor unhappy about the burgeoning polygamist population east of their city.

In 1990, forty years after the raid, there were still only twenty-eight thousand people in St. George, but seismic change was imminent. Bordered by the stunning Pine Valley Mountains, the beguiling Mohave Desert, and the pristine Zion National Park, word spread that the St. George area was a wonderland of natural beauty for outdoors sports enthusiasts, who began trekking to the overlooked area in droves. Golden sunsets, serene vistas, and a climate more like sunny Arizona than frozen Salt Lake City made St. George the new top destination for retirees as well. In 2010, St. George had been ranked as one of the top three—if not the number one—fastest growing cities in America for the previous five years, surpassing even Las Vegas during the boom years preceding the economic crash of 2009. But unlike Las Vegas, growth in St. George was not paused by economic downturn.

Destined for St. George, buses outfitted to carry kayaks, mountain bikes, water or snow skis, fishing gear, and anything else that will fit on a plane line the curb at Las Vegas's McCarran International Airport. Vacationers, sightseers, and potential homebuyers don't even glance at the slot machines or showgirls before boarding for the scenic 110-mile trip to the upbeat town embracing its future with lovely new homes, comfortable hotels, and a cache of superior restaurants offering international cuisine.

Now the polar opposite of Young's ideal of isolation, a half-dozen languages might be overheard in the upscale shops prettily encased in the restored buildings of the pioneers. No longer the staging areas for apostle George A. Smith's incendiary calls to arms, the gleaming white Mormon temples are today photographed by curious tourists. Even a decent portion of the local population is uncertain about the tenets of the faith the buildings represent. With a population pushing one hundred thousand,

St. George has grown up in such a hurry that the relationship between the new normal and a past not yet ancient history is still in flux.

Before the city's transformation, FLDS prairie dresses and plain shirts were a common sight on St. George's streets. The Crick was never a self-contained community. FLDS members shopped at the Wal-Mart and strip malls that erupted miles outside the town, and they came into St. George regularly for supplies. More so than in the cosmopolitan metropolises like Salt Lake City, the sect was accepted, even protected, in St. George as a part of the greater community, as well as a critical piece of the Mormon heritage LDS leaders were striving to erase. Pregnant teenage girls were nobody's business, and the Short Creek police were likely to get good cooperation from St. George authorities when needed, which was especially helpful for the retrieval of escaping girls who beat the odds by making it as far as Dixie's capital.

FLDS members still visit St. George, but they are primarily the less conspicuously attired men. They haven't included pregnant teenagers in their excursions for a very long time, as a big chunk of new St. George residents probably wouldn't understand. Although FLDS women may still patronize the big-box discount stores well outside of town, even these venues are no longer considered safe for pregnant underage girls. "You just don't see pregnant teenagers waiting outside Taco Bell or even way out there at Wal-Mart anymore," said Washington County attorney Brock Belnap, an intelligent, soft-spoken man who saw FLDS members on St. George's streets regularly as a kid. "Everybody kind of knew who they were, and we just didn't think much about it," he explained. "But today they [FLDS] know there's a strong likelihood that a pregnant fourteen-year-old in a grocery store aisle is going to be reported, and there's no doubt we'd investigate. If there are any underage pregnant girls out there now, they're being kept out of sight. I feel fairly confident I'd have heard about it if these girls were walking around town. Public awareness has changed."

MANY OF ST. GEORGE'S current residents have never seen an FLDS prairie dress on the streets of their city, but Utah Fifth District judge James Shumate wasn't one of them. A southern Utah native, Shumate served as county attorney in neighboring Iron County from 1979 to 1982, long before St. George's transformation. After some years in private practice, Shumate was appointed to the bench in 1992. Like Belnap, he was accustomed to and accepting of the FLDS presence. Unlike Belnap, Shumate appeared to be on the fence about both the legality and appropriateness of FLDS practices, specifically polygamy, when he was assigned Ruth's custody battle in early 2002.

"While we don't know for certain," Bill Walker's Utah co-counsel, former Utah attorney general Jan Graham, e-mailed a journalist, "there is indication of a curious disinterest in the fundamental problems of raising children in polygamous homes on the part of the judge, the guardian *ad litem* and the psychological evaluator."

From the start, the only condition Ruth put on Holm's visitation with Winston and Maranda was that it not occur in the Hildale, Utah, home where the children had been physically abused and where polygamy was not only practiced but taught against their mother's wishes as a religious requirement for the children's salvation. Ruth's Arizona court order specified that Holm must exercise any unsupervised visitation in Maricopa County, but after the Utah case was filed, Holm disregarded this order along with one ordering him to pay $200 a month in child support.* Saying that they "meant more to him than her," Holm refused to relinquish desperately needed items like Winston's crib and "diaper genie," along with the wedding dress over which Ruth was inexplicably sentimental. Even when he had the children, Holm often left them in the care of others—including Susie and Wendy—while he attended to business or marathon priesthood meetings. On one occasion, Winston was returned with an untreated head injury Holm said he'd received falling out of a parked pickup truck.

Holm began a series of strange rebellions against the visitation arrangements. On one occasion, Ruth brought the kids with her from Phoenix to St. George for her court-ordered evaluation to spare Holm a pick-up trip, but Holm refused to take the children because Ruth would not hand them over to Susie. Ruth drove back to Phoenix with the kids, followed by Holm. But Holm also refused to set foot anywhere near the home of one of FLDS's most deadly apostates— Pennie Petersen.

The increasingly complicated machinations were stressful and difficult for the seven-months-pregnant Ruth, whose unabated spirit of goodwill caused her to reject her supporters' observations that the escalating resistance was a tactic—part of an overall FLDS plan to undermine and wear her down.

---

*   Despite Holm's ongoing complaints that he was spending more on Ruth's children than the other eighteen combined, Ruth maintains she received only about one hundred dollars from Holm in the ten months after her defection. Since that time, Ruth states that Holm has not complied with any child support orders and has not requested or exercised visitation for the past three years.

Evidence of FLDS lawyer Rod Parker's perplexing role as more than just a lawyer to the sect was on display in a May 10 letter that he wrote to Walker after one of the confusingly botched visitations. "Both as a matter of Utah law and of good parenting," the tart missive concluded, "it would have been appropriate for Ruth to have made arrangements for the children's father to care for them today rather than leave them in surrogate care. Similarly, Ruth should be encouraging as long a visit as possible tomorrow, rather than simply getting by with minimum compliance."

Walker responded curtly: "Thank you for your cooperation in getting the visitation scheduled. The excess verbiage was not necessary."

The exchange was emblematic of where Walker thought Ruth's fight was heading: downhill fast. One of Walker's witnesses disappeared into thin air. Lydia Cook, Ruth's FLDS married sister, was never located after Walker filed notice he'd be taking her deposition regarding the child abuse she'd witnessed in the Holm household. Walker had a bad feeling about everything, including Judge Shumate's sympathies, fears confirmed when the psychologist Shumate appointed for initial parenting evaluations turned in her reports in mid-May 2002, only a few weeks before the major June 3 custody hearing scheduled in Shumate's courtroom.

While court-appointed psychologists are not required to verify facts, Dr. Christina Durham's report on Ruth was nonetheless checkered with errors about her history, apparently furnished by Susie Holm. Durham's conclusions jibed with Susie and Wendy's previously vocal condemnations of Ruth's character as selfish and self-centered, immature qualities that made her parenting skills suspect. For two hours each on consecutive days, Durham administered a handful of psychological tests leading her to conclude that Ruth had "limited verbal communications skills" and fell into "a borderline range of intelligence." Durham was particularly unnerved that Ruth bought a Nintendo game for the two-and-a-half-year-old Maranda, twice referring to the purchase as evidence that Ruth didn't understand parenting, in part because her mental and emotional development was little better than a child's herself.

"People with similar profiles tend to be self-involved or self-oriented," the report stated. "They tend to have an inflated or faulty sense of self, seeing themselves as better, smarter, or more clever than others. This sense is often based on imaginary rather than real achievements or personal qualities. A person with this presentation often needs repeated reinforcement from others to maintain their self-image. When others do not fulfill this need, the person is more likely to become angry or more demanding. The profile suggests the person is more likely to take advantage of others to get their needs met, with limited concern about their impact on others."

There were several tests Durham felt Ruth was incapable of under-standing, but for those tests she did, the theme was always the same. Of the Rorschach test she concluded: "Responses suggest a tendency to self-focus or to be self-centered, with the likelihood of over valuing personal worth. This type of presentation is common among children, but tends to disappear in early adolescence. When it does persist through adulthood the inflated sense of self often effects [sic] perceptions, decision making and behaviors."

Impulsive, immature, narcissistic, dumb, delusional, demanding, and pissed off, with poor verbal and no job skills, Ruth might be OK with her kids in their early years, Durham felt, "but beyond that is likely to struggle." Durham recommended what amounted to a full personality makeover for Ruth, including individual therapy to correct her fanciful notions of self-esteem and intensive parenting classes that might be helpful if there were "hands-on instruction and mentoring."

In contrast, Durham couldn't find much wrong with Rod Holm at all, save the fact he'd been saddled with a pack of trouble like Ruth, producing the stress one might expect. Evidently oblivious to the criminal implications, Durham characterized Holm's "marriage" to a teenager as a deep-seated tes-tament to his unassailable faith and duty to God and his prophet. Polygamy (and statutory rape) in the Holm household was as normal as dinnertime, and so was Rod Holm, with Durham's report concluding: "At this time, Mr. Holm appears to be functioning well in all areas and did not appear to be in need of services at this time."

Durham was similarly sympathetic to Susie Holm's untenable circum-stances as the troublesome Ruth's older sister and rape facilitator. Although Susie did admit that she'd hit, slapped, scratched, and kicked the children, Durham felt the behaviors were honest mistakes. Almost as an afterthought, Durham suggested that Susie might find a class outlining various disciplin-ary options to physical beatings useful, but Durham implied that the rest of Susie's anxieties were explained by the Ruth Stubbs problem. In fact, Ruth's behavior had been so destructive that Susie might herself require "support-ive counseling" down the road to help her overcome the damage.

Once again, Walker felt like he'd tumbled down the rabbit hole. Here was a girl who, at sixteen years of age, had been "given" to a thirty-two-year-old policeman with two other wives and eighteen children, kept continuously pregnant, forced to ask permission for her movements and food intake, and made to work fourteen-hour shifts without pay while her children were being hit and punched at home. Walker couldn't believe that in the United States of America, in a real courtroom, there was a serious question as to whether this young woman or her abusive "husband" deserved custody of their children. A judge, a guardian *ad litem*, and a court-appointed psychologist saw nothing especially askew in that picture, and now Walker held a report in his hands concluding the policeman was a well-adjusted guy and one of the self-admitted abusive wives might be the one needing help down the line to recover from her ungrateful victims.

Although Parker had scoffed at Walker's notices to depose Susie and Wendy Holm, Walker had questioned the women and Rod Holm under oath two weeks before the court hearing. Susie Holm denied most of the statements she had made to both Durham and the guardian *ad litem* Angela Adams, to whom Susie had also confessed abusing children, and went so far as to say Adams and Durham would be lying if they testified that Susie had admitted the abuse to the court experts. Rod Holm denied knowledge of any laws against underage sex or bigamy, taking the fifth or refusing to answer questions with a sexual bent.

The depositions were a poor showing for Parker's clients, who would look like liars or fools before a jury. In her journal, an elated Ruth exclaimed: "I think we have our case won! There were so many lies we caught them in!" In any other circumstance, Walker would have agreed the depositions were a deal clincher. In southern Utah, he was no longer sure that hitting little kids in the back of the head with heavy books wasn't excused by constitutionally protected religious beliefs.

When Walker rolled into St. George for the June 3 hearing, he was delighted to find a first-rate steakhouse across the street from his hotel. But in the morning, he was again left to wonder who had spiked the drinking water. The continuing swirl of national attention, instead of producing the clarifying effect Walker had anticipated, only encouraged Judge Shumate, who seemed to have mistaken it for applause for his religious tolerance. In the videotaped hearing, Shumate issued unbidden, folksy homilies about the honor of family, suggesting from the bench that definition of family was certainly flexible enough to include people from Short Creek like Rod Holm's family. Without even addressing the child abuse, Shumate seemed to imply that Ruth's decision to reject the rock of stability provided by Holm's different but still *Leave It to Beaver*–esque, wholesome family demonstrated a certain instability of character. Nodding in approval, Parker did not have to say much at all while Walker did his best to tiptoe around Shumate's apparent predispositions, trying to make what seemed like obvious arguments without disturbing the judge's inexplicable sensibilities.

In the end, Shumate issued temporary orders in which Ruth retained custody but Holm's visitation was allowed to occur in his Hildale home against Ruth's wishes. It was a major blow, but more ominous was Shumate's decision to appoint Christina Durham for the final parental evaluations over Walker's vociferous objections and in contradiction to judicial rules, which instruct the court to choose an evaluator acceptable to both parties, appointing his own only if the parties cannot agree. In this case, both Parker and Walker had agreed upon an evaluator in Salt Lake City, but Shumate chose Durham, whose views on Ruth were already known, in spite of the agreement.

As Walker's incredulity blurred into worry, he was forced to accept the case might be lost. He would naturally appeal, but appeals could take years. If Shumate gave Ruth's children to Rod Holm, she would probably go with them. "Pennie told me, 'If that happens, we'll never find her again,'" Bill remembered. "She said they'd move her around to all kinds of places and an army of private investigators wouldn't be able to find her. It was a really chilling thought I knew was true." Bill needed an indictment on Rod Holm to turn back the tides. He couldn't imagine why, six months after interviewing Ruth, an indictment had not been forthcoming from the Arizona Attorney General's Office, and he wasn't alone.

The Holm case had piqued the interest of an Arizona print journalist, investigative reporter John Dougherty of the alternative Phoenix weekly *New Times*. The news magazine began an interest in the FLDS-controlled public schools in August 2000. But in what would become a relentless campaign, Dougherty picked up coverage during Ruth's custody case with a story that would be only the beginning of Arizona attorney general Janet Napolitano's FLDS nightmare. Dougherty's opening salvo began, "Napolitano's office is covering up information documenting extensive and ongoing criminal activity including rape, incest, assault, kidnapping, forced marriages of underage girls, weapons violations, and welfare fraud that is rampant in the remote polygamous community of Colorado City, state records obtained by *New Times* have revealed."

The paper fortified the resolve of Mohave County supervisor Buster Johnson, who along with Dougherty would become a crusader against FLDS in the coming decade. A former Los Angeles sheriff's deputy who'd transplanted to Arizona four years earlier, Johnson had been stupefied by the commonly known practices in Short Creek and the state's lack of response. Johnson told Dougherty he'd been conducting his own investigation, hoping to persuade Napolitano to act, but the attorney general had so far asserted there was not enough documentation to bring charges. Napolitano's actual fears concerning FLDS—that it was a career breaker and a violent Waco, Texas, waiting to happen—would become public in a few years, but for now Bill could get no good answers from investigator Ron Gibson and his office as to why an Arizona cop was not even being fired for "marrying" a sixteen-year-old girl.

Back in Phoenix, Ruth managed to scrape together money for a junker car she alternately cajoled and threatened her brothers into repairing. She qualified for a roach-infested, 700-square-foot apartment she knew was terrible, but although poor, the neighborhood was relatively safe, and she wasn't afraid of this little bit of cleaning. Rod Holm had once ordered her to clean a house occupied by twenty-four people, most of them rambunctious children, three days after giving birth to Maranda, so the roaches and black grime and stink of only a four-room apartment didn't faze her.

Donning rubber gloves, coveralls, and a medical mask, she scrubbed the place down with bleach for three days, making friends with her neighbors in the process. With their help and Pennie's, Ruth hit the secondhand stores, and even a few dumpsters, securing broken-down furniture she reglued, varnished, or painted with bright, happy colors. She sewed her own curtains and patched together quilts and throws to cover the grimmer aspects of the furniture. Her new neighbors even babysat the kids so Ruth could attend job training seminars in preparation for working after her baby was born. In the end, she was quite proud of what she considered a good start toward a free life.

Meanwhile, emboldened by the scent of a court victory, Holm's calls over the months had become harassing, abusive, and studded with yelling and name-calling. Winston was returned from one visit to Short Creek with a mangled, freakish haircut, with chunks of hair slashed too close to the scalp for comfort. The tearful boy reported that an angry Susie—who he was instructed to call "mother" against Ruth's wishes—pinned the toddler to the ground, going after his head with snapping scissors. Ruth had concerns about Maranda's distant silences after visiting her father, and Winston was increasingly weepy while in Short Creek, crying and begging to come home when he was put on the phone with Ruth, infuriating Rod Holm.

Shortly after the June hearing, when Ruth was eight months pregnant, Holm violated court orders by appearing at her Phoenix apartment at 5:00 A.M., flying fists pounding the thin wood until the walls rattled. A frightened Ruth scrunched into the corner of her bed, knees clasped to her chest, rocking as she waited for Holm to leave, but the terrible racket continued unabated. Scared the children would awake in terror or she'd lose the apartment or—she didn't know what—Ruth wrapped herself in a defensive blanket, padding out to crack the front door a few inches. She ordered Holm to leave, but he forced his way into the home, refusing to leave without the children.

Ruth considered it a miracle they hadn't already been woken up. Keeping them unaware of this unnerving potential for violence now seemed like the most important thing she could do for their sense of well-being. The situation had to be de-escalated, but Ruth could not think of a way to get the agitated Holm to leave the tiny apartment. Switching tacks, she coolly offered him her blanket, mildly suggesting the children would be less cranky if they were allowed to complete their night's sleep. Grunting his acquiescence, Holm took the blanket and laid down on the living room floor, blocking the only exit. Ruth returned to her bedroom in a cold sweat, her own breath rattling her ears for hours, straining to detect the faint, familiar sounds of her children stirring in their beds. After she got them washed and dressed, Ruth could not think of a way to prevent Holm from taking the children away. Having been raised in Short Creek, where the prophet controlled the police, the idea of calling them to enforce a court order and protect her from an intruder never occurred to her.

But the incident did take the shine off Ruth's relentless goodwill. In late June, she allowed Walker to file an order to show cause, asking that Holm be enjoined from calling her except to arrange visitation, that from here out the children should be collected at Pennie's house, that Holm stop exercising visitation in Short Creek, and that Holm start paying $205 per month in child support. Walker was also in negotiations with *Dateline NBC*, a national television news magazine interested in doing a segment on Ruth and FLDS, but he didn't think either the order or the press would be enough to save Ruth's skin. All the bad polygamy press so far had not inspired officers of the St. George courts to reevaluate their sympathies for the practice, and the show wouldn't air in time anyway. As for Ruth, she had to go further than an order to show cause. Much further. She had to swear a criminal complaint against Rod Holm.

By July, Walker thought he had the whole dark picture on an Arizona attorney general too cowardly or politically ambitious to move on the sect that had blown up the careers of her predecessors. Janet Napolitano intended to run for governor, and though investigator Ron Gibson was politically diplomatic in their conversations, Walker could hear between the lines. Everyone thought FLDS was awful. Everybody thought they were breaking the law. Everybody thought Rod Holm should be charged. Nobody was going to do it. Janet Napolitano thought the Short Creek scenario spelled violence that would derail her plans. That was it.

Given the fact that Utah was in essence a Mormon state, *that* attorney general seemed like a laughable long shot. Bill knew very little about Utah's recently elected AG, a young, relative newcomer to politics. Mark Shurtleff was a Republican, of course. Most everybody in Utah was, and Shurtleff was also a Mormon, but Walker didn't know if those two things would necessarily work against him. Liberals were more likely to support FLDS's "religious freedom" battle cries, usually without knowing what the "freedoms" were, but nevertheless, it was conservative Republicans who were more inclined to be offended by FLDS's gross flauting of laws. Walker decided to give it a shot, but first he had to motivate Ruth by crushing some of that wonderful, ebullient spirit.

Walker laid it out for her. "Read the depositions, Ruth. They'll testify you were always pawning your children off on others and that you just wanted to please yourself and party. They'll say you hit your kids and dropped Maranda from a table in her car seat. They've got a psych evaluation saying you're not equipped to parent. Ruth," he told her evenly, "they'll testify under oath that you are a *bad mother*." The time for histrionics would have been then. Ruth was not proud of all that much in her life. She had little education and few achievements, but there was one aspect of her life of which she was proud. She was a good mother, and her children were good kids.

"It's not true, 'kay?" she told him softly. "None of it's true. Rod *said* I was a good mother. It's in the phone calls." She shifted, niggling her bottom lip. Walker shook his head impatiently.

"They're going to *lie*, Ruth. You have to understand that people will get up on that stand and *lie* to get the result they want. Maybe not you, but a lot of people. Are you willing to bet your kids' futures the lies won't be believed?" Walker waited. A dark frown smeared Ruth's normally cheerful features as she studied her unadorned, bitten-down fingernails, turning them this way and that as if imagining a manicure. Sighing, she returned her eyes to him, clear, blue eyes with a total absence of guile he always found slightly unnerving.

"I'm not a bad mother," she repeated with flat determination. "What do I need to do?"

That same month, Ruth gave birth to her third child, naming the baby girl Carly, after her lost love, Carl Cook. The relentlessly optimistic Ruth had tracked Carl down after her escape, gaining a phone number and the sweet hope he would come back to her and their dreams of the blue ranch house. But Jeffs had excommunicated and banished Cook from the community after Ruth had been married off to Holm, one more male who'd dared to harbor hopes for a wife and family "handled," as Jeffs called his exiling of men. Carl told Ruth he wanted nothing more to do with her, ordering her to stop calling his home.

Ruth admits that, in a painfully sad attempt to regain what had been stolen from her, she called Carl's house up to five times a day, drinking in his voice on the answering machine before hanging up. "I just dreamed a little when I did it," she would explain years later, smiling but with a little sheepishness in her bright, blue eyes. "I'd never seen myself with anyone but him."

5

THE NEW SHERIFF

When you tell me that father Adam was made as we make adobies from the earth, you tell me what I deem an idle tale. . . . There is no such thing in all the eternities where the Gods dwell. Mankind are here because they are the offspring of parents who were first brought here from another planet, and power was given them to propagate their species, and they were commanded to multiply and replenish the earth.
    —Brigham Young, *Journal of Discourses*, Vol. 7, October 9, 1859

It has been shown to me that those who continue to go out among the wicked for pleasure and entertainment will go down with the wicked. . . . We are here to redeem Zion by redeeming ourselves, saving ourselves from this wicked and fallen world, for our God has a controversy with the nations, and He is about to stretch forth His hand and sweep the wicked off this land. You say you have heard this all your lives. Beware. Unbelief is as simple as being slow in your preparation.
    —Warren Jeffs, General Meeting Address, November 17, 2002

From his office window, Utah attorney Mark Shurtleff can see the tawny mountain foothill upon which Brigham Young stood 160 years earlier, surveying the breathtaking but parched Valley of the Great Salt Lake. It was a belligerent land from which his Saints would have to strangle a living, but when Young selected the spot, its hostility was among its best selling points. Who else would want such a place so far from the safe boundaries of the United States? Here, the Mormons could practice polygamy, and all their tenets went unmolested. "This is the place," Young is said to have announced simply.

Today, the "This Is the Place" hilltop is a lavish monument and tourist destination overlooking a sweeping metropolis of 1.3 million souls, the thirty-fifth largest U.S. city, pushing impatiently against a ring of soaring mountain ranges. Mark Shurtleff has visited the spot many times, remembering that his ancestors were among the first of the seventy thousand mostly Mormon pioneers who passed the landmark to settle the valley between 1847 and 1869, when the transcontinental railroad was completed.

Although Mark doesn't think about his ancestors every day or week or month, he does think about them. In LDS and FLDS alike, families and family trees are integral to the Mormon concept of heavenly afterlife, in which family members will recognize each other, reuniting to populate their own celestial kingdoms into perpetuity. In both LDS and FLDS, worldly events must be recorded in this life in order to be acknowledged in the next. Joseph Smith urged all his converts to keep punctilious personal journals, which helped make the settling of the Salt Lake Valley one of the most documented events in American history. Journal writing remains a widespread habit among mainstream Mormons and ex-Mormons.

The journals are important, but both LDS and FLDS believe meticulous records of births, deaths, marriages, and the like are critical to keeping good order in the afterlife. FLDS accepts no converts in this life or the next, but there are fifty thousand LDS missionaries rapping on doors on any given day, and the church is said to have the most extensive genealogy resources in the world to assist members wishing to locate far-flung relatives, living or dead, for baptism. Many Mormons have a good knowledge of their ancestries, and Mark Shurtleff is no exception, although separating the ancestral threads tangled by polygamous marriages can be challenging. Not all Mormons hail from polygamous backgrounds, but many do, and like Shurtleff, the matter is discussed without reticence, as a simple matter of fact. There may even be some enthusiasm for the curious novelty of it all and certainly pride in the hardships overcome by their determined and resourceful forbearers.

Mark Shurtleff is tickled, impressed, and eager to claim colorful pioneer hit man "Wild Bill" Hickman as an ancestor. "You've never heard of Wild Bill Hickman?" Shurtleff demanded gleefully. "Oh, *man*," he laughed, shaking his head happily. "You've *got* to read his book!"

Hickman was a member of Young's band of "destroying angels," a shadowy group of enforcers whose existence LDS-approved historians downplay or deny, but Shurtleff harbors no such squeamishness. Like Joseph Smith's Danites before them, the destroying angels were rough men, converts to the faith who were unruffled by any form of rank violence. Uninhibited precursors of the goon or God squads operating in Short Creek today, destroying angels muscled and sometimes murdered early church detractors who would not go away quietly. In Utah, Hickman doesn't have the modern-day name recognition of Joseph Smith's still-famous sociopath assassin Porter Rockwell (who also worked for Young), but Hickman was a legend in the mid-1800s and no one you'd want interested in your whereabouts.

After a nasty falling-out with Young—a not uncommon occurrence for Young confederates—Hickman penned a surprisingly literate and entertaining biography detailing the nine men he "used up" on Young's orders, along with a few others who just deserved it and one madman who thought he could steal Hickman's prized "French horse" and get away with it. A horse-worshiper like Rockwell, Hickman discovered his horse with "a glorious mane hanging to his knees" had gone missing through a manmade hole in his fence and set out immediately, methodically tracking the thief for three days through five-foot snowdrifts. Not knowing who Hickman was, the horse thief rode right up to him in the wilderness, buoyant with relief that he'd found a fellow traveler in the forbidding terrain, whereupon Hickman shot him in the face without a word of response or the least bit of interest in his identity. "I was both tired and mad," Hickman explained. "I felt too indignant to speak."

Hickman seems to have written *Brigham's Destroying Angel: Being the Life, Confession; and Startling Disclosures of the Notorious Bill Hickman, the Danite Chief of Utah* in part as an explanation for his behavior to the children of his ten wives, especially one daughter whose estrangement particularly pained him. The killings, he explained, were nothing personal. Although Hickman's opinion of Brigham Young deteriorated over time, Hickman emphasized Young was a prophet of God when he ordered the murders as part of church business. The reasons were between Young and the Almighty, no business of Hickman's, an assertion Shurtleff accepts good-naturedly. "He was a *destroying angel*," Mark enthused, his eyes shining. "I mean, how cool is *that*?"

Despite his occupation, Wild Bill comes across in his book as a man of some wit and intelligence who loved his children, if not his wives, dearly. Mark can claim some of Hickman's better attributes, but as cool as Wild Bill was, the Utah attorney general is probably more like a less notorious forebearer who spelled his name slightly differently. The journals of the young Mormon pioneer Lewis Shurtliff reveal an insightful, analytical young man with the heart of a poet and a revulsion for political or religious extremism, even when it came from his own church. It is a testament to Lewis's diplomatic skills that he was able to stay on the blood atonement–approving Brigham Young's good side, even though Lewis criticized the prophet's merciless purges during the Mormon Reformation and thought Young's openly seditious political stances ill advised. Mark even looks like Lewis, whose full-page, slightly self-conscious photograph of a very tall young man in a rounded black pioneer hat holding a rifle and lariat kicks off David L. Bigler's *Fort Limhi; The Mormon Adventure in Oregon Territory, 1855–1858.*

Like his ancestor, Mark Shurtleff is a giant. A meaty six feet five inches tall, Shurtleff is the guy everyone sees as soon as he enters the restaurant, but he keeps your attention for other reasons. He has an easy, athletic confidence, not elegant exactly, but composed and, more importantly, approachable. With dark hair and deeply blue eyes, he does not have movie star looks, but his face is open, interesting, and intelligent. He can—and does—make some of his points by quoting entire Kipling, Shelley, and Keats poems from memory. He is a lively conversationalist, quick on his feet, with an unguarded, guileless style that drives his political handlers crazy. "It's terrifying," confided Shurtleff's former Senate campaign manager Jason Powers. "Mark will talk to anyone who wants to talk to him. He throws carefully prepared scripts away, he ignores talking points, and he wings entire speeches. It's like, every time you take him somewhere you have no idea if he's going to say something that will mean political death in the morning's headlines."

Shurtleff's 2010 stab at the U.S. Senate seat held by Bob Bennett didn't make it to the Utah Republican primaries. Three of Shurtleff's five children were adopted at birth with drug addictions, courtesy of their mothers. When one of them—then seventeen years old—began losing her own fight with drugs, Shurtleff suspended his campaign to help his daughter succeed in a residential treatment program she might not have elected to complete in another year when she'd be eighteen and legally beyond Shurtleff's reach. "I can always run for the senate," Shurtleff said. "She was only going to be seventeen for another year."

But there were certainly other concerns. A declared fiscal, constitutional, and social conservative with a Triple-A rating from the National Rifle Association, Shurtleff nevertheless favors a path to citizenship for undocumented workers as part of overall immigration reform, as well as civil rights for gays. He tried, unsuccessfully, to get a hate crimes law through a state legislature with one of the lowest diversity ratios in the nation, a body that proposed eliminating the pesky twelfth grade as a cost-saving measure.

Though the "tea party" types were gearing up to portray Shurtleff as a white man–hating sodomist, Shurtleff remained as philosophical as his ancestor, convinced that extremism would not impress the American public in the long run. He also objects to political extremists who play fast and loose with facts. Mark spent three years researching a historical fiction, *Am I Not a Man? The Dred Scott Story*, about the slave at the center of one of the U.S. Supreme Court's most infamous decisions declaring black men to be subhuman property. "I've always found that case so deeply disturbing," Shurtleff says earnestly. "I researched it down to the dialects—down to the words people used for, say, *pants*. I wasn't going to have one historian or critic say, 'Well, Shurtleff didn't put in the work.'"

During the 2008 presidential primaries, he became John McCain's Utah campaign chairman while the Mormon, Mitt Romney, was still the Republican favorite, angering both Republicans and probably LDS, though Shurtleff denies the latter with uncharacteristic umbrage. "Mark is as devout a Mormon as they come," advised one of his staffers—an ex-Mormon—somberly. "He doesn't wear it on his sleeve, but he is." In fact, Shurtleff sacrificed an appointment to West Point to accommodate LDS's requirement for all young people to go on a two-year stint as missionaries for the faith. Shurtleff's family was neither wealthy nor connected, and the young military enthusiast had worked his brains out to get the assignment to the only school he'd ever wanted to attend, but he went instead to the jungles of Peru, where he was the only white man for a hundred miles among a small-statured population who didn't have furniture to fit Mark's flabbergasting size.

Remembering West Point, a shadow of regret flickered across his eyes, but Mark quickly recovered with tales of his hilarious jungle adventures. He still speaks Spanish with pride, but the Peru mission also put him on a collision course with another of Mormonism's founding tenets: the condemnation of African Americans as actively evil, unsaveable souls whose black skin was the mark of Cain, a curse of God. Black men could not be admitted to the Mormon priesthood. The mortified young Shurtleff was forced to confront the human meaning of such dogma when he was obliged to inform stunned black Peruvians of their irredeemable, subhuman status. "I will never forget the looks on their faces," a subdued Shurtleff said.

After the civil rights movement took hold in the United States, LDS's blistering rhetoric and discriminatory policies regarding African Americans came under social and political pressure, capped off when Mormon universities and colleges were excluded from national competitions, including sporting competitions. LDS resisted the pressures until 1978, when the prohibition of blacks from holding the priesthood was reversed, in time for Shurtleff to return to some of the black Peruvians who'd expressed interest with the offer of baptism. "It was a bad time, and I'm glad it's over," Mark said of LDS's history with African Americans. But so-called fundamentalist Mormon groups practicing polygamy do not accept the 1978 change.

Groups like FLDS still actively portray dark-skinned people as evil and call African Americans "niggers," a fact that makes Shurtleff wince.

His self-described "perfect childhood" included interactions with polygamists. Like many Utahans, Shurtleff was aware of the polygamist families in his neighborhood, people who didn't advertise the lifestyle but were known to practice "celestial marriage." In school, Mark played with children from polygamous households. "I don't think there was acceptance nor nonacceptance," he considered with a pensive frown. "It was more like, 'Well, they're polygamists.' It just was. Of course, everyone knew there had been polygamy in Utah before. I think it was just viewed as a curious holdover from days gone by. I didn't think about it at all then."

AS RUTH STUBBS steadied herself for flight in December 2001, Mark Shurtleff was a newly elected attorney general whose only previous political experience was a term as Salt Lake County Commissioner. The forty-four year-old Shurtleff returned to his native city with his wife, M'Liss, and their children after completing a four-year stint as a defense attorney in the Navy JAG corps in San Diego, followed by three years of private practice. At one time, Mark saw himself involved in politics only as a West Point grad who'd make it to the Joint Chiefs of Staff. Now he entered one of Utah's iconic buildings set high and visible from anywhere in the city. One of his main priorities was protecting young people from predators, but Mark was concentrating on a good system for catching Internet predators, not the FLDS.

In late summer 2002, Shurtleff's chief criminal deputy Kirt Torgensen and investigator Ron Barton entered his office wearing somber expressions. Having packed his schedule with meetings and appearances from dawn till past dusk, Shurtleff hoped it wouldn't take long to explain whatever was casting the funereal pall over his men. Barton began, saying he'd been contacted by an Arizona attorney named Bill Walker about a custody dispute down in St. George, which, as far as Shurtleff could tell, wouldn't have a thing to do with the chief criminal deputy much less the Attorney General's Office. As Mark waited impatiently for illumination, an uncomfortable Torgensen explained that Walker's co-counsel, the former attorney general of Utah, had subsequently lunched with assistant attorney general Kris Knowlton, currently a juvenile sex crimes prosecutor, who reported that she believed charges should be brought against an FLDS polygamous Hildale, Utah, police officer who'd taken a sixteen-year-old girl as a third wife. They'd had two children, with one more on the way, when the girl ran, and now the sect was trying to get her kids back into Short Creek with a custody challenge by the policeman. There was a lot of press on it, a lot of heat. As Torgensen took a breath, Shurtleff blinked a few times.

"*What?*" he demanded, louder than he'd intended. "*A policeman?*"

It is estimated that there are thirty thousand polygamists in the Salt Lake Valley alone, running the spectrum from members of violent sects to discreet independents or what Mormons sometimes call "freelancers." Utah has two statutes addressing bigamy, having added a cohabitation law to reinforce the state's commitment to ending polygamy, but Shurtleff prefers to sidestep social commentary when addressing the touchy issue of prosecution. Because there are rarely complaining witnesses, the crime is notoriously difficult to prosecute, but even if it weren't, Shurtleff insists that prosecuting polygamy as policy would bankrupt the state, which doesn't have a fraction of the prison space needed to incarcerate the guilty. "We've got six thousand jail cells in this state," he said, shrugging his palms upward. "You do the math." Without extenuating circumstances, even well-known polygamists have a slim chance of arrest, but Shurtleff felt that bar had been satisfied when Juab County attorney David Leavitt went after fifty-three-year-old freelance polygamist Tom Green in 2001.

Leavitt, younger brother of governor Mike Leavitt, generally agreed with Shurtleff's position regarding polygamy prosecutions. Like Shurtleff, Leavitt was descended from polygamy and, growing up, knew classmates from polygamous homes. Even though he'd known about Green's extremely isolated compound of decrepit trailers parked in wilderness near the Nevada line, the prosecutor had not seen a reason to invade Greenhaven, as it was called, until he switched on his television one night and was thunderstruck to find Green on *Dateline NBC* boasting about his thirteen-year-old wives and the wily welfare fraud system he'd devised for supporting seven women and thirty kids. It seemed the formerly invisible Green had developed a voracious appetite for the public spotlight, making television appearances on more salacious but still national shows like *The Jerry Springer Show, Sally Jessy Raphael*, and *Queen Latifah*, crowing away about his welfare-soaking ways and marrying his own stepdaughters. Seven of the ten women Green "married" were daughters of his wives, all under sixteen and one who was thirteen years old when they were introduced to Green's matrimonial bed.

Green's insufferable bragging about child rape and welfare fraud couldn't have come at a more inconvenient time for Utah. In 2001, Salt Lake City was slicking up for its world stage debut hosting the 2002 Winter Olympics. After all the work scrubbing the taint of polygamy off the state, LDS and Utah would have preferred a hole in the head to the snarky headlines and rude cartoons generated by Green's appearances from South Africa to Europe. And for Leavitt, polygamy was one thing, sex with thirteen-year-olds quite another. Nevertheless, Leavitt knew the difficulty of prosecuting these cases was too rich for his county's coffers. When he asked the new attorney general for help, Shurtleff didn't hesitate. "He didn't have witnesses to take the stand, and he knew the county couldn't afford the kind of investigation required to win the case," Shurtleff stated. "I knew he was right, and when he asked for help I didn't think twice about it. Of course we were going to help."

One hundred thousand dollars later, AG investigators had pulled together birth and other records supporting bigamy charges. They also determined that Green's family had raked in $647,000 in state and federal welfare between 1989 and 1999, including $300,000 in medical and dental expenses. Had they been given access to the records, the investigators estimated Green received around $1 million in welfare since 1985. In August 2002, Leavitt secured a jury conviction on four counts of bigamy and one count of criminal nonsupport, for which Green was sentenced to five years and nearly $79,000 restitution. A year later, Leavitt brought the more serious charge of child rape, which could have earned Green life in prison. Leavitt and others were disappointed when Green received the minimum sentence of five years to life, concurrent with the first penalty. In the end, Green served six years.*

The Green case and the nebulous neighbors of his childhood were the sum total of Mark's experience with polygamists until learning about officer Rodney Holm and Ruth Stubbs. He insists he'd never heard of FLDS until Torgensen and Barton explained the situation in Short Creek. "Of course I knew there were polygamists," said an exasperated Shurtleff, as if everybody knows at least one polygamist. "But I didn't know there were that kind of polygamists."

Antipolygamist groups who'd been trying to flag attention to FLDS for years are dubious of the claim. "For heaven's sake," exclaimed Elaine Tyler, founder of Hope Organization in St. George. "How is it possible that Mark wouldn't have heard of ten thousand polygamists controlling a city in his

---

* Leavitt lost a subsequent reelection bid, a defeat many attribute to a backlash against the Green prosecution.

state?" A Utah transplant, Tyler became aware of FLDS when she and her husband decided to renovate their new home in St. George. She didn't know it at the time, but the contracting firm doing the work was FLDS owned. The ages of the boys climbing around her roof, handling dangerous electric saws, and pounding nails from dawn till dusk surprised her. "Some of them were ten years old," she said, getting angry all over again. "And at first I thought, 'How nice that their fathers are doing a bring-your-kid-to-work thing.' But they were there day after day, and then somebody told me, 'No, no. Those men aren't their fathers. Those boys are FLDS. They work *full-time* for these companies.'" Slapping a hand to her forehead she exclaimed: "It just blew my mind! I had to *do* something."

Tyler is among many who suspect the devout Shurtleff is influenced by LDS elders who would prefer to keep publicity around polygamists that both embarrass and frustrate the church to a minimum. It's a proposition Shurtleff instantly and vehemently denies.

"The truth is," he said evenly, "I went to them [LDS] to tell them what I was going to do. I said, 'Hey, I'm prosecuting this guy for child rape.' Just like a heads-up thing. Nobody ever told me, 'You can't do that,' or 'Stay out of that,' or anything like that. They said I had to do what I thought was right, thanked me for the courtesy of coming by, and that was that."

Shurtleff knew he was going to prosecute Holm before his meeting with Torgensen and Barton ended. How he was going to do it was another matter. Unlike the Green prosecution a few years earlier, he had assurances Ruth would testify against Rod Holm, but one witness did not constitute a conclusive investigation. "We have a three-quarters rule in this office," he explained gravely. "If you're not three-fourths *sure* you're going to get a conviction, we don't bring the case. The power of the state is awesome, and I won't wield it, risk ruining someone's life, unless I'm *sure*." To bolster the case against Holm, the Attorney General's Office issued subpoenas for birth and marriage records as well as DNA swabs. Shurtleff dispatched a handful of his own investigators into Short Creek to collect what amounted to routine evidence, but there was nothing routine about what happened that day.

It is a four-hour drive from Salt Lake City to the FLDS border stronghold, and today the boisterous growth around St. George camouflages the searing isolation of the place. Even in 2002, the sensory uneasiness experienced when you cross into an unstable third world country may not have penetrated until the investigators began their ascent on Hurricane Hill, just outside the village of Hurricane. The climb on a snaking two-lane blacktop switchbacking over sheer drops is raw, heart-stopping, and unforgiving of attention lapses. On top, the road levels off, a straight line bordered on both sides by distant mountains and ancient mesas showing eons of exposed layers of glowing geological rock of mesmerizing colors changing under the ethereal desert light.

After twenty miles there are more houses off the road, but they don't feel right. A window is out; a door dangles off one hinge; a room is exposed; a front portion is covered in a tattered, flapping tarp, the only sound from anywhere. There are swing sets but no children. Parked cars but no people. Entering the twin cities comprising Short Creek, there is no one on the street. There are no traffic lights, only a stop sign at the main junction anchored by the convenience store where Ruth Stubbs worked, the Mark Twain Inn, and some storefront offices for FLDS businesses. With similar facial features resulting from decades of intrafamily marriages,* dressed alike in plain shirts and jeans, the few men on the store's steps go as motionless as Stepford drones, staring at the unfamiliar car before pulling out cell phones to raise the general alarm in an atmosphere already thick with paranoia.

As the strange car turns into the half-paved, half-dirt residential streets, any sprinkling of prairie-dressed women caught unawares will bolt in a dead run toward unfinished houses, fleeing with an unabashed panic that transfers to the terrified children they herd before them into the structures, slamming doors with frame-rattling force as if Satan's smoking fingers were grasping at their long hems, which is exactly what they believe. Within fifteen minutes of any unknown car's entrance, the streets of Short Creek go empty and silent, the eerie, crazy quilts of half-finished houses like some science fiction scene in which an entire population is sucked away by Borgs in the middle of eating lunch.

---

*   Generational inbreeding, escalated under Rulon and Warren Jeffs, has produced a population that looks remarkably alike as well as a number of genetic disorders within the FLDS membership. For example, in 2006 there were twenty-five known cases of the ultrarare Fumarase Deficiency in Short Creek, yet there were only about thirteen additional known cases in the entire world. The genetic disorder is among the severest forms of mental retardation. Among other effects, Fumarase children, who may have an IQ of around twenty-five, have no muscle coordination, cannot direct their bodies, and are subject to epileptic seizures. Retired neurosurgeon Dr. Theodore Tarby accepted state contracts over twenty years to work in clinics near Short Creek, in part to study the disorder. Tarby, now affiliated with St. Joseph's Hospital's Children's Rehabilitative Services in Phoenix, said that he and others made the FLDS population aware that the genetic condition was avoidable but could not persuade members to cease marriages between closely related individuals or those known to carry the defective gene. "Their attitude was, 'It's our religion, and this is just a part of it,'" Tarby said.

For Shurtleff's investigators, the scene was not amusing. Uncomfortable and edgy, the men parked in front of the ghostly city hall to serve their subpoenas. Nothing stirred in the building before them, but as they exited their vehicles they were glad they had guns. Pickup trucks and vans converged from several directions, surrounding their car and cutting off any exit. Resisting the urge to unsnap his holster, one investigator drew out his camera instead. Shurtleff's men were quickly surrounded by an aggressive pack of FLDS men clearly familiar with bullying and physical intimidation.

The officers' badges mattered not a bit to the FLDS men, who closed within inches of their targets, demanding they leave the "private property" of the tax-maintained city hall. The officer with the camera was shocked when it was ripped from his hands. Jostling and yelling escalated. The cops feared their weapons would be confiscated next but were reluctant to draw them in the volatile mix. How to explain a shooting during a routine paper service? Shurtleff's men withdrew, feeling shaken and angry, the long return drive to Salt Lake affording plenty of time to contemplate the unenviable prospect of telling "the general," as Shurtleff is affectionately called, that they'd failed to collect public records open to anyone.

When Shurtleff heard about the incident, he was dumbfounded with shock. "I was just . . ." he stammered about it later, searching for words. "'What are you *talking* about? Didn't those people know these guys were *cops*?'" Shaking his head, eyes wide in continuing disbelief, Shurtleff's voice became uncharacteristically loud. "They put their *hands* on them!" he exclaimed of the FLDS men who accosted his men. "They took a camera out of a *cop's hands*! Did these people think they had their own *country*? Well, that was it. I wasn't putting up with *that*."

A few days after the town hall scuffle, Shurtleff drove at the head of a caravan of ominous black SUVs that entered Short Creek as a kaleidoscope of flashing, blazing lights, slow as a funeral procession to give everyone time to get the picture. As some of the vehicles peeled away for a second visit to City Hall, Shurtleff pulled up to one of Short Creek's two restaurants known for refusing service to bewildered travelers and anyone else who was not a sect member. As his giant form filled the doorway, he noticed a few prairie-dressed women fleeing through the kitchen and out the back door, leaving only a handful of motionless, darkly angry FLDS men.

"I'd be lying if I said I wasn't a little nervous," Shurtleff acknowledged. "I had no idea what these people were capable of, but I wasn't leaving until they understood I meant business." He doesn't remember which restaurant he entered—he thinks it was the Vermillion Candy Shop—but he remembers the place was silent as a tomb, even after he introduced himself. When no one moved, he seated himself by a window in view of his men in the parking lot, nonchalantly allowing his suit jacket to fall open and fully display the badge and big black semiautomatic pistol on his belt. Shurtleff could almost hear his watch ticking as the standoff dragged on. He was not going to leave without being served, but just seconds before he intended to announce the penalties for discrimination, one of the sullen men approached, eyeing Shurtleff's gun as he plunked a menu on the table and fled.

Shurtleff got his lunch, his men got their paperwork and swabs, and in October 2002, Rodney Holm got the indictment for bigamy and child rape he'd been dreading. The charges jolted Short Creek to the bone and made headlines across the country. If Rod Parker had anticipated this turn of events, it wasn't evident in his actions. Having protected FLDS from every scrutiny for fifteen years, FLDS attorney Parker was obliged to prepare a defense for the first criminal action against the sect since the 1953 raid. In this light, Ruth Stubbs seemed to lose some of her significance. Within a month of his indictment, Holm signed a custody arrangement with Ruth agreeing to everything she'd asked for at the start.

With her kids secure, Ruth lost the angry edge sharpened by Holm's invasion of her apartment, returning to her original insistence that Holm not go to jail. That was disconcerting enough for Bill Walker, but when Ruth refused to sue FLDS for damages, he was downright deflated. He'd put $15,000 of his own, now unrecoverable money into Ruth's battle, but that wasn't the deepest cut. Walker's life work was a crusade for humanity, and over the past eleven months, he'd been convinced FLDS needed to be taken apart at the seams. Taking the prophet's money and land would end his power, but without Ruth, Walker couldn't do a thing but go home to Tucson. "She said she wanted to put it behind her, take her kids, and get on with her life, and I had to respect that," he concluded without conviction. "She's the client. I have to do what she says."

Thinking that Ruth would need extra motivation to see the criminal case through, Walker kept in touch with the Utah Attorney General's Office, urging investigators to call him if there were any bumps in the road, which, unfortunately, there were. Ruth failed to appear for the preliminary hearing, raising serious doubts about her stability in prosecutors Kris Knowlton's mind. Shurtleff was comforted that the evidence he'd collected against Holm would stand with or without Ruth's testimony, though she did appear to testify against him at his St. George jury trial before Fifth District Court judge G. Rand Beacham.

In August 2003, Holm was convicted of one count of bigamy and two counts of child rape, but Beacham's attitude toward the verdict was old St. George. The judge suspended a five-year prison term, saying that no punishment could deter Holm's religious convictions, nor should any governmental agency attempt to do so. Ruth added to Knowlton's problems by writing a sentencing letter supporting Holm. "My eyes tear up as I think about how this will affect my children," Ruth wrote. "While I don't want to be his wife, he is still an awesome and loving father."

Holm would eventually spend only a year in jail on work release, but he did lose his job before returning to his Short Creek, where his awesome parenting skills left something to be desired. He rarely exercised visitation with Maranda and Winston and paid little to nothing in child support. In early 2010, Ruth reported he had not sought visitation or paid any support for the previous three years and had indicated amenability to having the kids adopted by another man if it would release him from court-ordered parental responsibilities.

Like Leavitt, Shurtleff asserted the prosecution had nothing to do with religion and everything to do with child rape, but Ruth's poor showing when the rubber met the road caused him to rethink further criminal charges. "Warren [Jeffs] performed the marriage, so-called, and was therefore a facilitator," he said firmly. "If we'd felt more confident about Ruth Stubbs, we would have charged Warren right then."

The remark drew a red-hot poker reaction from Bill Walker, who said he was never contacted by the Utah AG's office despite his numerous offers to help with Ruth. "Anyone who has any experience with these girls knows they require a lot of reinforcement," he said angrily. "They're brainwashed from birth to believe they're going to hell if they go against the religion. They're put under enormous pressure from the community to retract any accusations. You just can't leave them out there. They need support and reinforcement to break the cycle."

Years after Walker had left the Ruth Stubbs case, Ruth again demonstrated the precarious nature of an escaped FLDS girl's emotional stability. Arizona had gotten around to indicting Rod Holm but was forced to drop the case in 2009 when FLDS spokesmen revealed that Ruth's brothers, apparently with her knowledge, had attempted to extort hundreds of thousands of dollars from the sect in exchange for Ruth's amnesia about the criminal charges facing Holm in Arizona. Ruth admitted that she had regretted her decision not to sue FLDS and that her brothers had come to her with a plan to have FLDS pay $500,000 for a land parcel worth half that much, but she claimed she didn't believe they'd go through with it and denied having knowledge that they had.

Whether Ruth knew or not, her track record and a clandestinely recorded tape of the extortion attempt placed her credibility as a witness beyond redemption. But the troubling gaffe was not enough to stop the landslide on the horizon. The respite Warren Jeffs and FLDS would enjoy after the Holm affair died down was a brief lull in the storm. The teetering boulder Ruth had pushed off its center was rolling downhill, knocking loose others like pool balls at the break.

6

DAN FISCHER
AND THE LOST BOYS

What man or woman on earth, what spirit in the spirit world can say truthfully that I ever gave a wrong word of counsel or a word of advice that could not be sanctioned by the heavens? The success which has attended me in my presidency is owing to the blessings of the Almighty.
                    —Brigham Young, *Journal of Discourses, Vol. 12*

There were some young men who wrote some letters on their jacket, had some discs— music discs—in their possession, and it was AC/DC—Anti-Christ, Devil's Child. When this was brought before our prophet, he was alarmed that there was devil worship among us. . . .

Father said: "That is too much" and he cast them out. . . . We are in the final scenes, the last great struggles. Even the evil powers know the redemption of Zion must come through a people choosing to repent and become clean before the Lord.
        —Warren Jeffs, Morning Meeting Address, September 16, 2002

I asked about how his new wife, Annette Jessop, formerly Allen Steed's wife, is doing. He described how she defends her wayward children. . . . I told Kendall Johnson to warn his wife Annette that she is guilty of the sin of Eli of old when she protects her children in their wrong doing and she will lose her place if she continues to do this.
            —Warren Jeffs dictation, April 19, 2005, Place of Refuge R17,
                                                    Eldorado, Texas

About twenty miles south of the regal, copper-domed Capitol Building where Mark Shurtleff does business lies the Salt Lake City suburb of South Jordan and the kingdom of Ultradent, a multimillion-dollar world-wide supplier of breakthrough dental products first imagined by ex-FLDS member Dr. Dan Fischer at his kitchen table. Born and raised in the Salt Lake City branch of FLDS, the slender, silver-haired Fischer had never expected to become a professional man, let alone a doctor. Like most FLDS boys born and raised in FLDS, he expected without complaint a life of back-breaking work in FLDS construction firms. But Fischer came of age in a different kind of FLDS.

For one thing, the oldest of thirty-six children in his father's household of three wives attended public high school, graduating in 1967 with exceptional grades. Today, Fischer's quick mind and hardy curiosity wouldn't be tolerated in Short Creek, the boy's interest in all subjects a flag for expulsion. But when Fischer graduated high school, Leroy Johnson was the FLDS prophet. It had occurred to Johnson that his flock could do with a dentist. You could have knocked Dan Fischer over with a feather when he was summoned before the prophet to receive the assignment. It is a ridiculous thought today, but in 1967, FLDS put Dan Fischer through college and medical school.*

As a child of polygamy, Fischer felt a little out of place in Utah's public schools, but he'd not been obliged to conceal his background in a state that ignored such things. His classmates and teachers all knew what his home life was. Once he began his medical education in Loma Linda, California, however, the aspiring dentist lived under a cloud of anxiety, fearful that he'd be unable to graduate if either the authorities or the university discovered the multiple wives that Johnson kept awarding Fischer without his—or their—consent. To his great surprise, Fischer did not find the arrangement a fulfilling one.

It wasn't only the strain of keeping his illegal polygamous lifestyle a secret. Fischer understood that he was being blessed into the celestial kingdom with his three wives, two of them sisters, but he didn't feel the joy he thought he should have. Guiltily, he found himself wishing he could have finished school before marrying. In truth, he found the whole responsibility of juggling the needs of three women he hadn't asked for, didn't know, and certainly didn't love to be stressful. Years later, Fischer would come to fall in love with his second wife, but at the time, each new wife the prophet

---

* Johnson (1888–1986) was the last FLDS prophet to allow some semblance of a normal curriculum including history, math, liberal arts, and some sciences to be taught to FLDS children. Besides Fischer, Johnson selected a number of young FLDS men for higher education to provide the sect with doctors, veterinarians, and other necessary specialists. Although Johnson ended the FLDS quasidemocracy by instituting one-man rule, he is remembered as a benevolent leader, once famously remarking that he did not himself believe that men had landed on the moon but did not care if others believed it because he'd been known to make mistakes, an admission of fallibility that his successors would reject.

Johnson bestowed on him left Fischer feeling burdened, uncomfortable, and vaguely angry.

It would take decades for the questions bubbling around Fischer's soul to punch through a lifetime of FLDS indoctrination. At the time, he simply sucked it up, finished school, and returned to Salt Lake City as a dentist to ten thousand men, women, and children. Fischer didn't just want to fill their cavities. He wanted to bring the wonders of modern dentistry—advances he believed could improve lives—to his own people. With a workload like that, there wasn't enough of him to do both, so Fischer took to his barn, experimenting with new tools, designing new products, and inventing new dental techniques and compounds that would allow him to treat more people in less time with better results.

Today, Fischer's inventions generate global sales of $75 million a year, creating steady paychecks for six hundred well-compensated employees. "I have a 'give everybody a hand up, not a handout' philosophy," Fischer said. "People who work hard and apply themselves deserve to be treated with dignity. I'm willing to help anyone with disadvantages overcome those challenges, but they must work for it." Fischer doesn't believe in outsourcing. He doesn't scrimp on employee benefits to increase profits. And to create a serene work environment some call beautiful, he sank huge sums into the six-story office building he erected next to a lush nature preserve.

Fischer explained his nonprofitable investment this way: "When we realized the location was available, I just felt like we'd been handed a marvelous gift. The sanctuary is protected by law, so it will always be there. Every day, we can be reminded of how beautiful life really is, how diverse and resilient and what a wonder and treasure it is to be alive and part of it all. I can look out my office window and find peace watching a six-point buck make his way to water. I hope everybody who comes into the building can share that." Ultradent employees do appear to share that, as well as a genuine admiration for a corporate CEO who sometimes gets in the cafeteria line with everybody else. When Fischer walks in, he is beset by workers eager to tell him of a child's accomplishment or a spouse's recovery from an illness. He knows all of their names. A little hard of hearing, he takes their extended hands, cupping them as he bends forward to hear the reports, his dark blue eyes focused with interest. "Dr. Fischer is a wonderful boss and a great man," said Robyn Drown, Fischer's executive assistant. Lowering her voice, she added confidentially, "It's a disgrace what they do to him."

Drown was referring to FLDS. Dan Fischer is the man FLDS considers its most wicked archnemesis, a man so evil that FLDS lawyers routinely pepper their court documents with Fischer-based conspiracies against the sect. On their best days, Pennie Petersen and Mark Shurtleff combined couldn't draw the hateful vitriol FLDS reserves for Dan Fischer. Nor does anyone sustain the legal and public relations attacks FLDS is escalating against their former dentist, aided by the *Salt Lake Tribune*, whose coverage is widely acknowledged to be FLDS sympathetic.

On the landscape of FLDS media coverage, Utah's paper of record is the antithesis of work produced by Watkiss, Dougherty, and others. Although the *Tribune* was founded in 1870 by businessmen who objected to the Mormon theocracy, it is now owned by MediaNews Group and distributed by the same company as the LDS daily, *Deseret News*. Until 2010, former *Deseret News* staffer Brooke Adams was the *Tribune*'s full-time polygamy reporter. In the tumultuous years following the Holm case, the *Tribune* and Adams's blog *The Polygamy File*, formerly *The Plural Life*, frequently portrayed FLDS as an outgunned, besieged religion to Salt Lake City residents.

Like FLDS, Adams is no fan of Dan Fischer. After Fischer testified against FLDS at a U.S. Senate hearing in 2008, Adams ran a news story based on affidavits from FLDS members who opined that Fischer was a drunkard, a wife and child beater, maybe a drug addict, and a guy who tried to lure teenage boys into his lair with booze before stealing their souls. As Fischer was not given the opportunity to respond to the charges, he was obliged to issue a formal statement to the newspaper refuting the charges that began, "I woke up this morning to read a statement in the *Salt Lake Tribune* saying that I have been trying to hide my life. Anyone who knows me knows that nothing could be further from the truth."*

Fueling the attacks on Fischer is the hatred FLDS harbors for the entrepreneur's Diversity Foundation, a nonprofit organization Fischer established to, quite simply, promote tolerance for humankind's diversity. Headed by the tough-minded and outspoken Shannon Price, the foundation produces such evil wares as the Scrapyard Detectives comic book series in which children of all races and backgrounds, with disabilities and without, band together to solve thorny neighborhood mysteries by learning from one another and working in harmony.

---

* The *Tribune* printed Fischer's full rebuttal on Adams's blog and then provided a link to the fifty-eight pages of angry FLDS affidavits submitted after he'd testified before the Senate.

The comic books would be offensive to FLDS merely because they include interaction with a race Warren Jeffs calls "niggers," but presumably, FLDS is more concerned about the grants and loans Diversity makes to young people who wish to further their educations and the shelter it provides for people in desperate financial straights. This includes young people who have fled FLDS, including hosts of "lost boys," the subject of the beer-luring accusation.* Diversity had helped hundreds of lost boys ejected from the FLDS community to cull the herd of marriagable men. Worse, Fischer has helped women with children and prized young girls fleeing FLDS, providing food, shelter, and education.**

Hysterical FLDS claims that a venomous Dan Fischer is using his fortune to destroy the sect stem from the simple fact that Diversity Foundation paid for attorneys pursuing the now-famous lost boys suit and another that followed it filed by an escaped child bride. Because those suits went forward, FLDS property would end up under court control, unleashing one of the largest lawsuits in Utah history. In reality, the sect produced its own negative results independent of Dan Fischer. Fischer's foundation only made a grant to lawyers representing teenage boys whose lives FLDS had tossed in the trash. Warren Jeffs abandoned Short Creek, knowing he would lose everything there, when he declined to answer the suits, but that would never be discussed in the avalanche of legal pleadings on the horizon. "When I left [FLDS], I never intended to do any of this," Fischer stated wearily. "It just got to the point where somebody had to speak out. It had gone too far. People had to know what was happening out there."

Indeed, after Fischer returned from California to become the FLDS dentist, leaving the sect was nowhere in his thoughts. He admitted he always felt uncomfortable with the FLDS intolerance for others and outright bigotry against races, but the real trouble started when he began enrolling his children in FLDS's Alta Academy, located on the Jeffses' Salt Lake City

---

*   Fischer does not drink but does keep beer and wine in his home for secular dinner guests. At a dinner Fischer hosted to introduce author Jon Krakauer to a group of lost boys, beer was served.

**   When she fled FLDS with her eight children in 2003, Fischer provided shelter and security for Carolyn Jessop, who feared she or her children would be kidnapped off the street. In 2007, Jessop published *Escape*, her best-selling account of her life in FLDS and flight from Short Creek. In addition to hundreds of lost boys, Diversity has helped fifty-eight FLDS girls get on their feet after fleeing the sect. Because they have received virtually no education, all FLDS children need help getting up to speed before they can succeed in accredited schools, but all the Diversity girls have gone on to college.

compound. When Rulon Jeffs installed his sulking son Warren as principal, education as Fischer understood it disappeared. Fischer had always been suspicious of the obsequious Warren. Bad stories swirled around the man Fischer just tried to avoid, but once Warren Jeffs had control of his children's education, evasion was not an option.

Fischer's first concern became Warren's eradication of actual learning. Instead of history, reading, math, or social studies, FLDS children were subjected to hours of droning religious tapes recorded by Warren Jeffs, who inserted himself in the children's lives as their only concern. Fischer's children returned from school innocently spewing vile racial slurs, their knees ulcerated from hours of kneeling and their little bodies bearing the purple bruises of Warren's sadistic discipline.

To demonstrate the level of "sweetness" Warren Jeffs expected, he brought one of his wives before classrooms, twisting her long braid around and around his hand, forcing the pitiful young girl lower and lower until she came to a kneeling position, silent tears of stabbing pain streaking a face he demanded remain emotionless. "This is what keeping sweet is," he'd warn with a lipless smile and a final vicious yank before releasing the braid, allowing the girl to collapse on the floor as he left the room without a word.

Alarmed by Warren Jeffs's growing influence within FLDS, Fischer spoke up at priesthood meetings, but the days of Leroy Johnson were long gone. If Fischer hadn't fully understood the new FLDS order before, the icy condemnations of his protests drove it home. It was only a matter of time before Warren Jeffs threw him out. Dan Fischer decided to leave before allowing him that pleasure. Fischer's second wife, and eventually six of his children, went with him. The remaining wives and children were reassigned. The two reassigned women poison-penned affidavits after his 2008 Senate testimony. Fischer has not seen the children who had stayed in the sect for thirteen years, a pain that still produces large tears. "I think about them every single day," he said, struggling against open sobbing. "I cannot imagine what has happened to them."*

But Fischer would soon find out what was happening to other children, particularly boys. From afar, Fischer watched the destruction of men and

---

* Warren Jeffs was not content with Fischer's departure. In 1999, he broke up Fischer's father's family, reassigning all the elderly man's wives and children. Fischer's brother, Shem, was removed from an innovative design and construction company he'd developed. Shem Fischer elected to sue FLDS. He won his case but could not remain in the sect. He now works for his brother in Ultradent's development arm.

families escalate, while detecting a vicious and revolting new trend: boys as young as thirteen were being discarded on the sides of roads like garbage, left to die for all anyone in FLDS cared, for Jeffs told everyone these boys were as good as dead and better off that way in any event—blood atonement without the actual murder.

Rulon Jeffs began the policy of tossing boys away, but when Rulon died in 2002, Warren Jeffs escalated the practice to near genocidal proportions. As Rodney Holm faced trial in 2003, Jeffs was evicting dozens of boys on a regular basis. Sometimes he gave a reason, however transparent, sometimes not, and sometimes he announced he'd dreamed the boy was going to fall into Satan's hands in the future, so better deal with it now. It's difficult to understand how parents could drive their child into the desert, or Las Vegas, or St. George, and dump him without a cent. Their final words would not be of encouragement or love but a rain of curses upon the child they said was already in hell. FLDS parents followed the prophet's orders without hesitation and would never see their boys again.

Through word of mouth, some of the boys learned there was an ex-FLDS member willing to help them. They began showing up on Dan Fischer's doorstep. Soon, Fischer had converted unused office space into makeshift dormitories for the homeless boys, helping them prepare for jobs, feeding them, clothing them, offering them help with education. The numbers were staggering. Dozens and dozens of boys with only the clothes on their backs materialized. The stories of desperation they brought broke Fischer's heart. He and one of his brothers, Shem, began actively looking for the boys who might be living under bridges or abandoned toolsheds, contemplating suicide.

Then, in 2004, Dan Fischer met Brent Jeffs.

"Sometimes the mom might stick some bread or something into her son's pockets," a stony-faced Brent Jeffs, now twenty-eight, said during a dinner at one of South Jordan's Market Street restaurants, "but yeah, that was it. They put 'em out of the car and said, 'So long, son. Sorry you're going to hell. Don't come back around, ever.'" Brent shook his head, fighting angry tears. "Did you want to kill yourself? Hey, it was the first thing that came to your mind. Everybody thought about doing it." He pauses, conquering the anger. "Some of 'em succeeded," he continued. "There wasn't even anyone to bury them."

Brent Jeffs is Warren Jeffs's nephew, which makes him Rulon Jeffs's grandson. He was born in 1983, a year after Ruth. Ruth's family was old

FLDS, but Brent's had been elevated to royalty, even though Rulon Jeffs had not converted to fundamentalist polygamy until the 1940s, when he was in his thirties. The Jeffses had a polygamist pedigree going back to the tawny hill visible from Mark Shurtleff's office. A branch of the Jeffs tree had crested that hill when Brigham Young announced, "This is the place," and a good thing, too.

Today, FLDS does not accept converts, but the sect wasn't always so rigid. Although Rulon Jeffs began life in the apostated LDS church and entered into a monogamous marriage, his independent study of Mormon theology and polygamy had persuaded him that LDS had committed a grave error when it had abandoned the practice. Jeffs had earned an accounting degree from Brigham Young University, which he'd parlayed into considerable wealth, the sort of wealth to which the prophet Leroy Johnson thought FLDS should aspire. Johnson needed a sharp accountant, and Jeffs had enough polygamist credentials in his ancestry to fudge the facts of his early life so that he might be admitted with limited explanation. His anguished wife, unable to reconcile herself to plural wifery, divorced him. But like Brigham Young, Rulon recovered quickly. No one is certain how many wives he had at the time of his death, but it was more than forty, taking the last fourteen-year-old bride when he was eighty-six. Brent Jeffs's father, Ward, was among an equally uncertain number of children, commonly put at sixty-seven or more.

Although he was now the FLDS accountant in charge of a host of profitable businesses, Rulon did not move to Short Creek, a decision some "Crickers" felt high handed. "He thought we were a bunch of hicks," remembered Ruth Stubbs, and why not? The Crickers were descended from poor farmers living in shacks. At the time, there was a substantial FLDS population in Salt Lake, and Jeffs built a swanky family compound with a trout pond, wine cellars, and swimming pools between 40,000-square-foot homes equipped with tunnels and escape hatches for imagined raids. To facilitate the order that no FLDS member mix with the apostate city's population, Rulon also built a school. Alta Academy was a sex-segregated K–12 school where all FLDS children were educated unmolested by science, history, or geography classes but not by Warren Jeffs. Rulon had placed his unstable favorite son in charge of the Alta Academy, despite the fact that Warren had no education beyond high school and had begun manifesting sadistic and cruel behavior as a boy.

Brent Jeffs grew up in the Salt Lake compound with his father, his father's three wives, and some thirty siblings. Brent's mother, Susan, was Ward

Jeffs's first wife of unusual circumstances. When Susan was young, women were still able to approach the prophet with their own ideas about who they should marry, even though their opinions carried no weight in the final decision.* Susan, then seventeen, had her eye on Ward Jeffs, an eighteen-year-old on his way to the jungles of Vietnam. (His enlistment was unusual; military service is another aberration for FLDS members.) Fortunately for Susan, Johnson was amenable to the match, and Susan was willing to wait for Ward. The couple was married upon his return from a terrible war that Ward wouldn't discuss but that often left him in impenetrable moods. Brent now thinks his father suffers from post–traumatic stress syndrome, but he also thinks his father's time out in the world broadened an already intelligent mind and a soul sensitive to the humanity of others—exactly the kind of individual Ward's father, Rulon, and brother, Warren, could not tolerate.

In his 2009 book, *Lost Boy*, Brent described childhood in a home not unlike the Holm household Ruth describes. Brent recalled fishing trips as the happiest gems in his life, but those were like quicksilver disappearing through his fingers in a flash, eclipsed by the skin-splitting beatings he and his full brothers endured from Ward's envious, bitterly jealous second and third wives. Like Holm's wives, two of Ward's women—Susan and Felicia—were rival sisters, although as Ward's first and legal wife, Susan technically held the upper hand.

And like Rod Holm, Ward Jeffs was a distant taskmaster, unwilling or unable to engage with the warring wives as he struggled to keep the "visitation" schedule equitable, a chore that seemed to suck the life from him. As priesthood head in charge of everyone's salvation, however, Ward could at least demand blissful oblivion of the problems. No matter what chaos of screaming, beating, and sobbing reigned in the home during the day, when Ward returned from work the wives were instantly sweet, putting supper on the enormous table in front of thirty kids who dared not speak.

The beatings and bedlam took a toll on Brent's adored oldest brother, Clayne, who seemed to snap when he was twelve. Brent, a toddler at the

---

*   The practice of allowing women to participate in choosing their husbands ended shortly after the 1953 raid, when Leroy Johnson noticed that girls tended to select partners their own age. A forthright Johnson announced the math wasn't working out to allow older men to acquire the requisite wives for the celestial kingdom. When he decided that the prophet would make marriage assignments from then on, Johnson apparently didn't look down the field far enough to realize that practice would only intensify the girl/boy ratio problem. Nevertheless, Johnson sometimes bent his own rules, allowing girls so moved to express their marital preferences without fear but with the understanding that their desires would not figure into the decision.

time, was under attack from the belt-wielding third wife, Vera, when Clayne suddenly, audaciously intervened, shielding little Brent from the raining blows with his own body as he backed him into the kitchen. Now cornered, Clayne grasped desperately at a utility drawer, hurling its wooden and slat spoons at the advancing Vera one by one as Brent cowered behind him, clutching his older brother for dear life. Clayne emptied several drawers before Vera retreated from the unprecedented counterattack for which there would be hell to pay.

For Brent, Clayne's actions that day were liberating, so influential he still refers to the event as "the great utensil fight," but Clayne's psyche would not be so positively affected. By sixteen he was heavily involved with alcohol and drugs, a condition Brent's father tried to shield from the general Jeffs compound by placing Clayne in various treatment facilities when his son should have been kicked to the curb.

But Ward Jeffs loved his children and could not bring himself to do such a thing. His Vietnam War experience had left him empathetic to emotional disturbance he knew had nothing to do with Satan, and so he kept looking for solutions to Clayne's problems, but nothing stuck. Eventually, five of Brent's brothers would be evicted or leave FLDS, but Clayne was the first to depart, landing in a crummy Salt Lake City apartment where his downward spiral continued unabated. Soon, Brent's older brothers, David and Brandon, would join Clayne in a foggy world devoid of guiding light. As Ruth had discovered, throwing off the yolk of a cruel religion was only a beginning. If nothing else, the harsh black-and-white rules in which the brothers had been raised provided direction, however misguided, for their lives. That lost direction had to be replaced with new principles and goals, but unlike Ruth, the Jeffs brothers did not have the support for tackling that monumental job.

Though it was forbidden to speak to apostates, Ward and Susan Jeffs kept in contact with their disintegrating sons, hoping against hope for a breakthrough. They thought they had one when Clayne fathered a child, a daughter named Cheyenne who became the light of his life and a reason for sobriety. When Cheyenne was taken by sudden infant death syndrome at seven months, Clayne could not afford a proper service, wake, and burial, and Ward had no stomach for turning a son devastated by grief away. Fourteen at the time, Brent remembers his father's stoic eyes upon the ominous caravan of black SUVs with sinisterly dark bulletproof glass gliding slowly by Ward Jeffs's home as the stricken family gathered for food and comfort after Cheyenne's burial. It was, Ward knew, his brother Warren and Warren's collection of bodyguards and thugs, collecting evidence that the personally popular—and therefore threatening—Ward Jeffs was associating with apostates, his own sons. Brent thought his dad looked a little sad but resolute as he guided Brent gently back to the mourners, cautioning his son not to add misery to the gathering by reporting what they'd just seen.

No one is certain when Rulon Jeffs began suffering his debilitating strokes, yielding more and more power to his manipulative son Warren, but only a few days after the funeral the knock on the door Ward had been expecting came. Warren Jeffs did not have the fortitude to face his brother in the flesh, sending instead three enforcers to order Ward Jeffs off the property and "release" his wives and children. Warren didn't seem to know what to do when a defiant Ward refused to leave the home his carpentry skills had built and furnished. Eventually, Warren had his brother's property fenced off from the rest of the compound. Only Susan Jeffs forfeited her salvation to stay with her husband. Fearful of hell, Ward's other wives made haste abandoning the house, taking their children with them.

In a testament to the feral grip the religion has on its members, Brent Jeffs abandoned his parents as well, terrified of losing his priesthood and salvation if he stayed, but that was only an ethereal concern. A more urgent concern for the teenager was the gripping terror of being butchered in the upcoming apocalypse, which every FLDS member knows could happen any day. If he apostated, Brent knew he'd be slashed and stabbed, his guts pulled out while he was still alive, and so much more. The fear of being slaughtered by the FLDS holy people kept him awake at night. He just couldn't stay. "My dad said he understood," Brent later said, trying to beat back tears. "I just didn't know . . ." Losing his struggle to tame a choking voice, Brent was unable to complete the sentence.

It was decided that Brent should be sent to Short Creek to stay with an FLDS family above reproach. He was excited about living in the land of refuge, where the ten thousand or so FLDS people would soon be tasked with killing every human being on earth. The world's six billion desperate apostates were expected to converge on Short Creek in futile attempts to destroy the chosen FLDS people, who would be naturally protected by God. Still, it was an epic job that might take some time. Consequently, the caves and crannies pocking the soaring cliffs behind the town were continuously being stocked with ammunition and nonperishable food items so that the

FLDS warriors could hide during breathers and still eat well.* Soon after Brent arrived in Short Creek, he joined other youngsters for live, somewhat sickening butchery demonstrations from FLDS survivalist Dee Jessop, who seemed to enjoy slitting the throats of various hog-tied farm animals.

Cow throat–slitting came as a bit of an unpleasant shock to Brent, who also soon discovered that his devotion to FLDS was unappreciated. Far from being rewarded for abandoning his apostate parents and brothers, Brent was treated like a leper in the prophet's school and on the streets. It seemed no one wanted to even look at a boy who'd been among apostates, lest they be contaminated. His humiliation, frustration, and confusion were compounded when he found he could not banish his interest in girls. Though it was strictly prohibited, Brent wanted badly to speak with girls or even just be in their presence, desires becoming increasingly risky as Warren Jeffs issued what seemed like daily proclamations separating the sexes further and further. Brent felt sorry for the girls who were now forced to wear two sets of long underwear under their stifling long dresses in the worse kind of summer heat.

After an excruciating year of repression and rejection, Brent's unwanted doubts burst into bloom when he figured out the boy/girl math for himself. At the rate that girls were being snapped up by old guys, Brent would never have a wife. Plus, the prophet kept insisting the world was going to end soon. The only reason it hadn't ended on the prophet's previously identified dates was the foolproof explanation that the people hadn't been pure enough for Jesus and Joseph Smith to come back. Either way, whether it was no wives or the end of the world, Brent was starting to harbor actual regret about his decision to leave his understanding, loving parents. "I mean, what would be the point?" Brent argued. "Without three wives or if the end of the world came, I wouldn't be getting my own celestial kingdom. I'd have to be in someone else's celestial kingdom." He looked up, grinning. "I'd be getting bossed around for eternity."

At the time, Brent didn't comprehend that such a conclusion meant he'd essentially already left FLDS. Instead, he began caving to worldly desires he knew intellectually would land him in hell, but for some reason, the idea of hell had been emasculated by Brent's young logic. Like Ruth, he drank beer and snuck out of the house at night. A good-looking boy with an athletic

---

* In his book, Brent explains that one of his father's many FLDS deficiencies was his failure to stock enough nonperishable foodstuffs to keep the family alive while FLDS members killed the world's population. Ward Jeffs made honest efforts to stockpile food, but there wasn't enough pantry space in the home, and there were so many children the wives had to constantly deplete the Armageddon rations to get dinner on the table.

build, dark hair, and flashy brown eyes, Brent's interest in girls was reciprocated. Lisa, a beautiful blue-eyed blond his own age, now risked her salvation to sneak out of her father's house for rendezvous with Brent at a secret place. "I would wait for her every night," Brent writes in his book. "Sometimes I'd wait an hour before I realized that she hadn't been able to sneak out." When the couple was inevitably discovered, Lisa was sent away to a remote trailer in the desert for behavior modification for months. When she returned, she was not allowed to go anywhere without an FLDS chaperone.

Most boys with or without Brent's background would have been immediately evicted, but Brent was only called into Warren Jeffs's office to be threatened. He believes he knows why, but Warren's threats did not impress the teenager. "One part of me deeply believed everything I was told by the church and believed in hellfire and brimstone," he writes. "The other part insisted that my religion made no sense and that the things I wanted to do were normal. . . . In a split second, I could go back and forth—holding completely opposite positions and not even noticing the contradictions in my thinking or behavior."

With Lisa removed from his life, Brent gave in to the deadly doubts he'd been entertaining and decided to leave Short Creek, returning to his welcoming father and mother in Salt Lake. He managed to get a message to Lisa through one of her sympathetic sisters that included his parents' phone number and a pledge to drive back to Short Creek and bust her out of FLDS if she'd just say the word. "I waited for years for that call," he said, sadly, "but it never came." And soon, Brent wondered if he'd gone from the pan to the fire himself.

"I sat in the school assistant's office shaking uncontrollably," Brent writes of his first ever enrollment in public school. "She was trying to show me where my classes were on a little map of Albion Middle School. I was terrified because I wasn't sure that giving up the church had been the right thing to do. Now here I was, surrounded by gentiles. . . . The sermons I'd heard about how evil and corrupt outsiders were and how apostates like me would burn in hell were running through my mind yet again, even as I tried fruitlessly to concentrate on what she was saying."

Like all FLDS kids, Brent was socially unskilled with nearly insurmountable gaps in his education. He knew nothing of history, government, and literature, and less of science, most of which FLDS teaches is a nefarious government hoax. He didn't know about dinosaurs or the Great Wall of China. Meaner kids sniggered at his "plyg" clothes and ignorance of contemporary music.* Perhaps unsurprisingly, the first group of kids to accept Brent were "stoners" who weren't exercised over class schedules or homework, giving Brent his first opportunity to slip away from his pain in the classroom. His second and final opportunity was provided by his older, FLDS-rejected brothers who'd rented a dive of an apartment and descended into rampant drug abuse. Against his frightened parents' wishes, Brent quit school and moved in with the now five brothers who'd been ejected or left FLDS. "Although I didn't realize it at the time," Brent wrote, "the 'lost boy' label was pretty accurate. Like Peter Pan's sidekicks, we had never really grown up. We'd been trapped in our own sick but also sheltered never-never land and were completely unprepared for what faced us in what now passed for American reality. So we got high."

Days, then weeks, blurred and blended together, a never-ending dream in which Brent lay on the couch watching television through a haze of cigarette and pot smoke, trying to comprehend what he saw on the screen, wondering if life was worth pursuing. He was afraid to leave the apartment by himself, and not because the neighborhood was violent or dangerous. It was, but Brent was still simply terrified of Gentiles and their society. He had no idea if he was going to hell; he couldn't even lift his eyes to look at a girl in the mall, much less speak to one. In this, and all things, Brent looked for guidance to his beloved, idolized brother Clayne.

Clayne knew how to talk to girls at malls. He knew how to dress and what music the brothers should be hearing to stay hip. He was like a lifeline in this alien, unmanageable world. He had many heart-to-hearts with Brent, helping him through the transition. Brent knew that Clayne was a heroin and cocaine addict, but when others in his family gave up, unable to endure the lying, cheating, and thievery of a young man they no longer knew, Brent stayed connected to Clayne. This time, Brent would not abandon his childhood protector.

In 2001, Clayne made another stab at rehab. It was his fifth or sixth attempt—Brent had lost count by then—but this one was different. Voluntarily confined to a hospital psychiatric ward, a desperate Clayne agreed to an untested treatment involving regressive hypnotherapy, a program in which the hypnotized subject is guided through his past in a search for traumas so devastating they might have triggered self-medicating drug

---

*   Underscoring the commonality of polygamy and the children of polygamous unions in Utah, certain slang terms are part of the language heard only in that state. "Plyg" or "plygie" have derogatory connotations intended to hurt or humiliate. Although no one ever hurled the insult at his face, Brent heard it whispered regularly behind his back.

abuse to bury the pain. Susan Jeffs collapsed when Clayne's therapist told her that he believed her son had been molested by his uncle, Warren Jeffs, on numerous occasions in the basement of Alta Academy when the boy was four or five years old. A five-year-old Clayne had been punished on several different occasions when the boy returned from Alta Academy, his pants soiled with bloody stool. It had not occurred to her that something bad might have happened to him. She'd been too busy worrying about the stained clothes that would be needed later for hand-me-downs to ask.

As revolting as Clayne's memories were, his family was hopeful that identifying the terrible trauma would finally allow Clayne to do real, productive work battling his addictions. Though he still had no independent memory of the molestations, Clayne was himself excitedly optimistic at the prospect of resolving an identifiable problem to finally achieve peace. No one saw Clayne's suicide coming. He was twenty-nine, the father of four, when he shot himself in his apartment in January 2002. After receiving a hysterical phone call from Clayne's common-law wife, Brent raced to his brother's apartment, tearing free of police attempting to restrain him to weep over his brother's lifeless body.

A year later, Brent met a girl he loved at first sight. For the second time, he was employed at Ultradent by Dr. Dan Fischer, a friend of his father's who'd given Brent another chance after he'd messed up his first Ultradent job with drug use. Brent's girl, Jody, was a dark-haired, green-eyed beauty Brent wanted to marry in the worst way, but for the moment they were living together as Brent proved he could be a stable husband and good provider for the couple's anticipated children. Everything was coming up roses when the nightmares started.

They were always the same. Brent was four or five years old. He was in the basement of Alta Academy, the FLDS school in Salt Lake where his uncle Warren was principal. Uncle Warren had a death grip on his tiny hand, and Brent was afraid, crying, but his uncle told him they were doing God's will as he led Brent into a small bathroom with an old tub. Two of his other uncles were inside the bathroom. They leaned against the closed door, their weight preventing anyone from opening it as Warren took Brent's pants down, bending the small boy's belly over the edge of the tub. Brent could not see anything but the other side of the tub, but he heard Warren's droning, monotonous voice instructing him to bow to God's will or be damned. After that, there was a rustling of clothes and then searing, white hot pain that felt like it was inside his body. Warren clamped a hand over the tiny mouth to mute the screams. The door-guard uncles helped hold him still if the writhing began interfering with Warren's activities. The five-year-old was threatened with hell if he told.

Unlike Clayne, Brent's dreams produced snatches of independent memories he'd never known before. He'd awake from the nightmares screaming, drenched in sweat. On some nights, Brent was too immersed in the terror to awake at all. Lying beside him, Jody was sometimes roused by Brent's frightening, animalistic growling, clawing at the bedclothes with such intensity she had to slap him in the face, hard and repeatedly, to wake him up. Jody was unnerved by the episodes she considered too persistent, too extreme, to be chalked up to nightmares. Brent knew she questioned his emotional stability, but he worried she'd leave him if he divulged the content of the nightmares. Describing the dreams would require a full explanation of the FLDS upbringing he'd heretofore glossed over. He was fearful Jody would find everything about him too bizarre to handle. After a dozen nightmares, however, it became clear that Jody would think him bizarre if he *didn't* tell her what was happening. Far from recoiling from Brent's full confession, Jody was empathic, supportive, and insistent they go to the authorities.

Brent was now of the opinion that Warren Jeffs was a serial pedophile with a taste for boys four to five years old. There's was no telling how many he'd taken to that bathroom, but Brent was certain of two that he had. There wasn't a doubt in his head that Warren Jeffs was the source of Clayne's addictions, beginning with teenage alcoholism and ending with heroin, cocaine, and a fatal gunshot wound. Because Brent couldn't bring himself to do so, Jody went to Brent's parents with the horrible revelation. Only then was Brent able to sit down with his father. After the tears, both men decided they needed something more than healing. Revenge sounded good.

"Now I really felt I had to do something to stop Warren," Brent wrote in *Lost Boy*. "My anger over what had happened to me and over Clayne's death continued to grow. There had to be something I could do. . . . No one should be able to get away with what he had done. Being a self-proclaimed prophet didn't make him above the law. This was America, not Afghanistan. Finally, I realized that there was someone I knew who might know, someone who might just be willing and able to help."

The man was Dr. Dan Fischer, who in 2004 financed the lawsuit that would begin the deconstruction of FLDS.

7

ROGER HOOLE
AND THE LOST BOYS LAWSUIT

I have never given council that is wrong.
                          —Brigham Young, *Journal of Discourses, Vol. 16*

[Looking at Mother Ora, he said] *You need to know when to write and when to listen. Write when I say write, and listen when I say listen. Generally write, unless I say listen instead. Or write.*
                          —Warren Jeffs, instructions to his scribe, September 20, 2002

Depression, drugs, girls, despair, banking bewilderment, car and school difficulties, traffic tickets that turned into bench warrants because the citation wasn't understood—Dan Fischer was ready for any of these topics common to the lost boys he helped, offering solutions that would have been obvious to anyone except a young man who'd never heard of Catholics or checking accounts, ski resorts or fighter jets, or virtually anything outside of what Warren Jeffs had allowed them to know, boys for whom Salt Lake City's timed intersection crossings were the stuff of alien worlds—too inexplicable and frightening to be navigated.

Dan was rarely surprised by the boys' problems and never at a loss for words, but of all the evil he'd have easily believed of Warren Jeffs, the story Brent Jeffs told in his tranquil office that day in 2003 made him shiver with cold. Listening to Brent, Fischer felt the familiar tendrils of despair and grief that curled about his heart when he wondered what Warren Jeffs might have done to Fischer's own estranged children. Looking at Brent, he thought the boy might have the courage to execute what he was about to propose.

"If you want to do something about this," a somber Fischer told Brent quietly. "You'll have to go public. It will get very bad. They will lie about you. They will try to ruin you. You will have to answer it all in a public court. You'll be cross-examined by their lawyers. Everyone will know everything that has happened to you." Dan thought he might be shaking some, but a clear-eyed Brent did not seem to notice.

"I'm ready," Brent announced steadily, "to do whatever is necessary to expose that man."

Fischer got Brent a psychiatrist for therapy and a lawyer for justice. After researching attorneys, Dan settled on Joanne Suder, a nationally known Baltimore litigator for victims in pedophile and sex abuse cases. Suder made worldwide headlines in 1994 securing a $350 million settlement from the Archdiocese of Baltimore for a dozen victims of the widening Catholic priest sex abuse scandals in the United States. Brent and his father met Suder in a lush, marble-floored hotel where confident masters of the universe floated through the expensive quiet in very good clothes.

The opulence was intimidating, and Brent felt like a sore thumb hayseed in his dumb T-shirt and unintentionally worn-out jeans, and even more so when he met the exquisitely attired Suder with her crisp (to put it politely) East Coast manner. Sternly, Brent reminded himself that he could hardly expect to testify against the FLDS prophet in a public arena if he couldn't raise his eyes to his own attorney. Sufficiently self-motivated, Brent suppressed the shame and dirty feeling he couldn't seem to shake, even though he knew the molestations had not been his fault.

As news of Brent's audacious choice to go public swept the community of lost boys under Diversity's wing, Dan met with other boys emboldened by Brent's decision. These boys told Dan they had not been molested. They had merely been ejected from their homes without warning or cause, abandoned to hell for what they now knew was a design to eliminate competition for young girls. They had struggled with drug addiction, alcoholism, depression, gnawing hunger, endless shame, and stark attacks of terror, day and night, but far worse in the darkness in which they were certain the devil's minions waited. Did Dr. Fischer think they might also have a case in the courts? The boys said they did not want money. They wanted to save others from their fates if they could. Dan understood the boys very well, but taking their cause to court presented challenges.

Damages in civil cases must be quantifiable. Hurt feelings or anger is not sufficient. A plaintiff must prove "actual" losses such as lost income, property, medical bills, or the like. Only if actual damages are established can plaintiffs ask for punitive damages relating to emotional distress. Before damages can even be weighed, civil cases are decided upon a "preponderance of evidence," a far less stringent requirement than the absence of reasonable doubt needed for a criminal conviction, but civil suits must nevertheless charge and prove the defendant's *legally defined* bad behavior, be it negligent, reckless, criminal, civil rights related, or some other legal misstep. Anyone with a few hundred dollars can file a civil suit, but meeting these requirements is considerably more difficult, particularly for teenagers who had no income or property to lose and who would be portrayed as dangerously incorrigible juvenile delinquents ejected from a closed religion whose rules and the consequences for breaking them were common knowledge.

Brent Jeffs alleged an obvious and despicable criminal act around which Suder had tried dozens of cases, but the other boys' charges were legally fuzzy. Their parents might be eligible for child abandonment charges, but, like Ruth, the boys did not want to punish the families who'd cast them into darkness—families they still loved. And they didn't want financial compensation. Like Bill Walker, Joanne Suder found her clients' altruism alarming, but she also delayed the inevitable discussion of grittier details to focus on a winning legal position for a situation so unique there was no precedent.

After six months of preparation, Suder filed Brent's groundbreaking suit in July 2004, followed by what would become famously known as the "lost boy suit" a month later. Suder's ingenious argument in the lost boy suit was a shock to a Utah court system still acclimated to viewing polygamy as more of a "lifestyle" issue, a sometimes politically inconvenient but fundamentally harmless religious choice for eccentric Mormons. For the lost boys' suffering, Suder alleged polygamy as an underlying crime.

The lawsuits that would soon begin the unstoppable avalanche for FLDS asserted the sect was a "predominately criminal enterprise," with legal damages "sustained as a result of the [FLDS] pattern of unlawful activity, fraud, breach of fiduciary duties, breach of assumed duties, alienation of parental affections, inflictions of emotional distress, invasion of privacy, and civil conspiracy which arose from the unconscionable conduct including their [FLDS leaders'] practice of expulsion to further the illegal practice of polygamy." Warren Jeffs and FLDS established the "secret, cruel, abusive, and unlawful practice of reducing the surplus male population by systematically expelling young males from the FLDS communities in which they were raised." The sole purpose of the expulsions was intended to "foster the unlawful and aggressive" practice of plural marriage.

For the local counsel required by Utah law, Dan Fischer selected Roger and Greg Hoole of the Salt Lake firm Hoole and King. The Hooles practice law in a charming but smallish house, an inconspicuous locale for lawyers battling the titanic firm of Snow, Christensen, and Martineau, whose attorneys enjoy private elevators and sweeping views of a bustling city laid at their feet. The view from Roger Hoole's paper-choked office is an embarrassingly overgrown garden, an early casualty of the eternal FLDS court dates. For the Herculean research required of FLDS court proceedings, Roger cannot flick an intercom switch to produce a half-dozen scrubbed, well-heeled underlings eager to accomplish the legwork. Hoole's library is the open law books stacked one over the other in teetering towers, competing for space with similar towers of paper, discs, photographs, and tapes. Roger's army of researchers consists of his brother and his dedicated paralegal/receptionist Jacqueline Meacham, who can see her boss from her own desk.

Roger is not among Utah attorney general Mark Shurtleff's fans, but the Salt Lake City native and Mormon accepts without question Mark's insistence that he did not know what FLDS was when he took office. "It seems impossible to me now that I *didn't* know about FLDS, but I didn't," Shurtleff said gravely. "When Dan came to me with these so-called lost boys . . . well, I just couldn't believe what I was hearing."

Like Bill Walker, Roger Hoole's commitment to his clients quickly transcended the professional. "There aren't words to describe what Warren Jeffs has done to that community," he stated fiercely. "No raid, no government action, no law could have ever inflicted the suffering this one man has brought to thousands. He's a narcissist, and he's power mad, but he's not insane. He enjoys knowing he has the power to force people to live in misery. He's just . . . evil."

Cracks eventually developed between the Hooles and Suder, who'd also incorporated another high-powered Texas firm into the action. Money was the trouble. There wasn't any to go after, at least not as far as Suder could tell. In reality, FLDS controlled dozens of highly profitable businesses bringing tens of millions of dollars into the sect. One of them alone, the specialized tool production plant of Western Precision Inc., brought in millions from U.S. government contracts, but even though profits were funneled into FLDS, the businesses were legally structured to be independent of the sect. Diversity Foundation was paying for bare bones legal expenses, but firms like Suder's were habituated to raking in millions on these multiple-client suits. The Diversity money wasn't going to cut it.

In addition to that, Suder rather unpleasantly discovered that her clients didn't actually want to destroy their oppressors. While Rod Parker railed about the separation of church and state, painting the boys as degenerates who couldn't abide religious life and now wanted to destroy it with greed and hate, nothing could have been further from the truth. The lost boys were adamant that no actions be taken that would harm anyone still inside FLDS.

The Texas law firm withdrew, followed by Suder, but a jackhammer couldn't have pried Roger off the case. "I envy the pro bono work Bill [Walker] does," Roger affirms. "We're a small law firm, but here were these boys, good boys subjected to a torture we can't even imagine. They had no money, but there was no way I was going to let that determine whether they got justice."

Brent Jeffs filed his lawsuit in July 2004, followed by the six young men who filed the lost boys suit in August. Both suits were filed in Salt Lake City's Third Judicial District, far from the warm cradle of polygamy in St. George. In July 2004, Dan Fischer organized a massive press conference on the steps of the Utah Capitol Building, drawing a sea of television trucks from around the country. Best-selling author Jon Krakauer, who'd become profoundly involved with the lost boys while researching *Under the Banner of Heaven*, addressed what had become more of a rally, as did Mark Shurtleff.* "It breaks my heart and keeps me awake at night to know there are hundreds of boys and women who are abused and mistreated in the name of religion," Shurtleff told the crowd, promising to seek legal ways to hold FLDS accountable for its actions.

One by one, lost boys approached the microphones to tell their stories. Richard Gilbert was excommunicated at sixteen for expressing a desire to stay in public schools. Tom Steed was fifteen when he was excommunicated in the dead of winter for seeing part of an episode of *Charlie's Angels*. With nowhere to go, he found an abandoned toolshed to keep the icy winds at bay, stealing food where he could for months. Davis Holm was seventeen when Warren Jeffs's God squad forced him out of Short Creek at gunpoint. He lived under an underpass until making contact with other lost boys, who crammed together in apartments in St. George or Las Vegas, ten to a room, wallowing in drugs and alcohol and stealing food. To

---

*   Krakauer's book *Under the Banner of Heaven: A Story of Violent Faith* is a masterful rendition of early Mormon history and a study of the gruesome murders of a mother and her infant daughter at the hands of her fundamentalist Mormon brother-in-law, who received a blood oath revelation from God to kill her for her opposition to polygamy. Though his book does not concentrate on FLDS or the lost boys, Krakauer was so moved by their situations he offered to adopt one. He remains friendly with Dan Fischer and active in the cause against FLDS and polygamous fundamentalism.

financially support the group, some teenagers who'd never had a discussion about sex became boy prostitutes, catering to the worst clientele in the seedy backstreets of Las Vegas.

To this day, Roger marvels that the boys did not seek retribution, sometimes repeating that fact more than once in the same conversation, as if he does not actually believe it himself. But even if the goal was not profit, he knew FLDS had to be threatened with some kind of spiked financial stick to gain their full attention. Like Walker, Roger reckoned there had to be a money pot somewhere or the attorneys at SCM would not be working for FLDS. When back surgery put him in a hospital, flat on his back for a week, Roger had plenty of miserable free time to consider the possibilities.

It would take FLDS leaders some time to realize it, but what Roger came up with would shatter their power base.

8

SHORT CREEK

The only men who become Gods, even the Sons of God, are those who enter into polygamy.
—Brigham Young, *Journal and Discourses*, Vol. 11, August 9, 1866

I will now say, not only to our delegate to Congress but to the Elders who lead the body of the Church, that he thought that all the cats and kittens were let out of the bag when brother [Orson] Pratt went back last fall, and published the revelation concerning the plurality of wives; it was thought there was no other cat to let out. But allow me to tell you, Elders of Israel and delegates to Congress, you may expect an eternity of cats, and that have not yet escaped from the bag. Bless your souls, there is no end to them, for if there is not one thing, there will always be another.
—Brigham Young, confirming Mormon polygamy, *Journal of Discourses*, Vol. 1, June 19, 1853,

Although nineteenth-century Americans never really bought the um-braged denials, they were nevertheless rocked when Brigham Young publically confirmed the Mormon practice of polygamy. Although Young himself boasted to his confederates of his voluminous marriages, the practice was still piously denied outside of Utah until popular apostle Orson Pratt inadvertently let the cat out of the bag, as Young mischievously characterized it, in a public speech. But Young seemed untroubled by Pratt's blunder, joining with the apostle to cheerfully reveal the content of Article 132 from the podium at an 1852 church assembly in Salt Lake City. As Young's lighthearted confirmation of Mormon polygamy clattered over telegraph wires, the outrage of an internationally appalled public suggests that, once again, Mormon leaders had tin ears.

It is one thing to suspect a lie, quite another to have it cavalierly tossed in your face, and although Young would not live to see the full repercussions of his admission with the Edmonds-Tucker Act and subsequent Supreme Court decisions, there was an immediate, far more devastating reaction he certainly did not expect: his river of European converts desperately needed to populate Deseret dried to a trickle.

That Americans were violently opposed to polygamy was no secret, an inconvenience Young had planned on managing by starting his own country. But that country needed Mormon-converted settlers, and for years, Mormon missionaries had enjoyed enormous success in Europe, particularly in Scandinavia and the British Isles where the Industrial Revolution had impoverished and displaced millions into teeming slums. Mormon missionaries were able to offer the destitute and hopeless more than a planet in the afterlife. In *this* life, they could promise the richest farmland of your choice, a brotherly community that would never let you or yours go hungry again, and free passage to America courtesy of the church's Perpetual Emigration Fund.

It was an attractive alternative for people starving in packed, crime-ridden tenements without even a change of clothes to their name. Six to ten thousand Mormon-converted Europeans a year made the ocean crossing and then the grueling trek across the American frontier, swelling the Mormon population. However, the otherwise helpful Mormon missionaries had apparently failed to inform their eager converts of the polygamy condition, and its companion fact that monogamists would not be entering the celestial kingdom, the whole point of being Mormon. When news of Young's announcement crossed the Atlantic, European emigrants were absolutely horrified, deserting Mormonism in devastating numbers.

That Young's Utah could have prevailed over American jurisprudence in the long run by fortifying its boundaries with a slew of feisty converts is probably wishful thinking, but the dent in a reliable pool of converts was not the first time polygamy had disrupted Mormonism from the inside. Dozens of Smith's earliest supporters, leaders of the new church, could not accept polygamy, and some left to start their own religions. Although he seems to have recovered nicely from his initial shock, even Brigham Young said he'd "yearned for the grave" when he first heard about polygamy. Joseph F. Smith acknowledged that his uncle burned the original polygamy revelation the night before he turned himself over to Illinois authorities, probably to destroy evidence, as he also ordered the burning of minutes from any meetings in which polygamy was discussed.

Even if the destruction of such documents represented moments of legal clarity, there is evidence Smith thought he might have made a giant mistake only a few years after he introduced "the principle." Although Emma Smith's recollections might be colored by her fierce opposition to plural marriage, she goes much further than Young's observation that Smith had wearied of polygamy before his murder. In her only known admission that her husband ever practiced polygamy, Emma told future apostle William McLellin that Smith "told her that the doctrine and practice of polygamy was going to ruin the church" before he burned the dratted revelation.

Polygamy exasperated Young as well, or rather, the Mormon women's reaction to it did. His unsympathetic advice to women who were expected to share their husbands after many years of marriage and children: "But the first wife will say, 'It's hard, for I have lived with my husband twenty years, or thirty, and have raised a family of children for him, and it is a great trial for me for him to have more women.' Then I say it is time that you gave him up to other women who will bear children. If my wife had borne me all the children that she ever would bear, the celestial law would teach me to take young women that would have children. Do you understand this?"

Young opined: "Men will say: 'My wife, though a most excellent woman, has not seen a happy day since I took my second wife.' 'No, not a happy day for a year,' says one and another has not seen a happy day for five years." Saying he would "rid himself of the whiners," Young made an extraordinary offer. In mid-September 1856, Young gave all unhappy women two weeks to leave the territory at his expense.* "I do know there will be a cessation to the everlasting whining of many of the women in this territory," he declared, "but if you stay with me, you shall comply with the law of God, and that too without any murmuring and whining. You must fulfill the law of God in every respect and round up your shoulders to walk up to the mark without any grunting."

Unhappily for Young, so many women lined up to take advantage of a free passage out of Utah he was forced to withdraw the offer, sending most of the whiners back to their unhappy homes. And although Mormon converts continued driving wagon trains into Utah, they frequently passed scraggly, understocked trains of Mormon deserters going the other way. "We've had enough of heaven and will try our luck in hell," the ex-Mormons called out. Nevertheless, the iron Smith may have regretted forging to link polygamy to salvation proved too emotionally and psychologically strong for many Mormons to sever. After his unexpectedly popular 1865

---

* Ever the entrepreneur, Young recouped these expenses by charging the discarded husbands ten dollars ($214 in today's currency) for each deserting wife. It is estimated Young may have taken in more than $300,000 before withdrawing the offer.

offer to malcontented women, Young didn't return to the subject of polygamy's downsides.

The last Mormon prophet to remain unequivocal about polygamy was Young's successor, John Taylor, the father and patron saint of the modern fundamentalist movement. Taylor is the last Mormon prophet accepted as legitimate by LDS and the dozen or more contemporary Mormon fundamentalist sects, each of which developed their own line of prophets as they argued, splintered, and even murdered for their brand of fundamentalism led by their own prophets. More than any prophet save Smith, John Taylor is revered by all modern sects, especially FLDS, whose leaders quote Taylor as much as the faith's founding prophet. Taylor is quoted far more often than Young, whose vision of society and governing style seems like a blueprint for FLDS's Short Creek.

Young did not live long enough to battle the antipolygamist invaders, a cup that passed to Young's successor in the last three years of Taylor's life. Taylor was present when Joseph Smith was murdered in the Carthage jail. Utterly devoted to Joseph Smith and the Mormon Church, Taylor vowed he would "suffer his right hand to be cut off" before abandoning plural marriage. But by 1885, both the Congress and the public were reaching the end of their polygamy patience tether. Around this time, the federal government's so-called cohab hunts were coming into full swing, transforming Utah's prisons into polygamist dormitories. In January 1885, Taylor learned there was a polygamy warrant with his name on it. A few weeks later, Taylor—like Warren Jeffs 150 years later—went into hiding, continuing to accumulate wives.

Meanwhile, Utah was desperate to gain statehood, sending skilled operators into the halls of Congress to lobby for the territory. To cover all the bases, Mormon leaders freed up $20,000, sending apostle Brigham Young Jr. and *Deseret News* editor Charles W. Penrose to place it in the hands of politicians "where it would do the most good." The church also designated $74,000 to ease the consciences of newspapermen printing stories advocating statehood for the Utah Territory, with another $70,000 to be awarded if their silky words bore fruit.* In Congress, church lobbyists were confidently optimistic Utah would be granted statehood, but their cheery outlook seems to have been another example of Mormon tunnel

* Today, the amounts would have been equal to $600,000, $2.2 million, and $2.1 million, respectively.

vision. Nobody had forgotten about the big sticking point of polygamy. The Edmonds Act, making it possible to prosecute the easily proved charge of cohabitation, became law in 1882. Debate on the devastating Edmonds-Tucker Act began in 1886. As soon as it became law a year later, U.S. attorneys filed the suits that would have destroyed the Mormon Church without drastic action from its leaders.

In 1886, LDS president and prophet John Taylor was hiding out in the home of John C. Woolley and his son, Lorin.* In the wee morning hours of September 27, Taylor said he received what would become the most controversial and contested revelation from God in Mormon Church history. Taylor reported that on this night, he'd been favored with a congenial and entertaining visit from Joseph Smith and Jesus Christ, who lingered nearly until dawn. Lorin Woolley would later report that he heard three distinct male voices conversing in Taylor's room and saw an eerie light emanating from under the door. When Taylor emerged, Lorin declared, "We could scarcely look at him on account of the brightness of his personage."

Upon emerging from his room, a lighthearted Taylor told the agog Lorin, "I have had a very pleasant conversation with Brother Joseph." Taylor explained that he'd made a special appeal to the Lord, asking for his thoughts on the current polygamy situation and what to do about it. The Lord didn't hem or haw about it, answering: "Thus saith the Lord. All commandments that I give must be obeyed by those calling themselves by my name unless they are revoked by me or by my authority. . . . I have not revoked this law nor will I for it is everlasting and those who will enter into my glory must obey the conditions thereof, even so. Amen."

Fundamentalists believe Taylor then called ten staunch believers in addition to the Woolleys—the twelve newly minted disciples he ordained with powers to not only perform plural marriages but to transfer those powers to others of their choosing so that "no year passed by without children being born in the principle of Plural Marriage." If FLDS had an Independence Day, it would probably fall on September 27, when Taylor basically created a line of God's anointed representatives on earth outside the mainstream church.

LDS disputes almost every detail of the Taylor revelation and the subsequent eight-hour meeting the mainstream church doubts occurred. Going through his deceased father's things, Taylor's son, John W. Taylor, provided

---

* Both Taylor and Woolley are familiar surnames in present-day Short Creek.

LDS with what he said was his father's handwritten commemoration of the 1886 polygamy revelation, but the document was not accepted with the gravitas the younger Taylor expected. Noting firstly that the handwritten note was unsigned, LDS also complained it had never been authenticated or discussed as required by Mormon procedure. Dismissed as a peculiarity, the note soon disappeared into the massive vaults in Salt Lake City, leaving only an oral history of the revelation that would end up causing so much grief.

After Taylor's death in 1887, his successor, eighty-two-year-old Wilford Woodruff, didn't have nearly enough fingers at his disposal to plug the cracking dam. Modern fundamentalists demonize Woodruff's political capitulation, but when the Supreme Court affirmed the government's right to seize Mormon Church property, the embattled prophet's only remaining choices were to withdraw from polygamy or watch government forces dismantle the territory, piece by piece. Polygamy devotees at the time were able to grudgingly live with Woodruff's choice, in part because it hadn't been truly characterized as a revelation but mostly because LDS winked at the Manifesto from the start. After Joseph Fielding Smith was suitably blistered in Congress, however, things changed.

Not all Mormons thought the church would perish without polygamy, and by 1910 they'd begun wrestling the megaphone away from staunch polygamists. Reed Smoot, the senator who'd been forced to endure thirty months of contentious polygamy hearings before being allowed to take his place on the Senate floor, insisted that "all new [polygamy] cases should be excommunicated from the church and that action should be taken at once." Although the then anti-Mormon *Salt Lake Tribune* ridiculed the church's new policy by digging up evidence of continuing plural marriages, the writing was on the wall. Like so many other projects the church has undertaken, once LDS was fully acclimated to the job, it brought ferocious commitment to its completion.

After the 1904 Manifesto, apostles John W. Taylor, son of prophet John Taylor, and Matthias M. Cowley—both high officials in the church— helped LDS out with Congress by submitting their resignations for their parts in continuing plural marriages after the 1890 Manifesto. The resignations were accepted with assurances the men would be reinstated after the storm blew over, but the *Tribune* stories included both ex-apostles in the list of blatant, post-Manifest polygamists, causing Smoot to declare: "If Taylor and Cowley are brought back . . . nothing will save us from the wrath of the American people."

With the permanent, somewhat poetic, exile of Cowley and the son of the last polygamist prophet, the knitting of a Mormon Church unified in rejecting polygamy started to unravel. Ardent polygamist Joseph W. Musser, a giant thorn in the LDS paw, began organizing dissatisfied Mormons in secret meetings held in private homes. Musser was the son of an LDS church historian and had access to sensitive, vault-guarded archives as he began privately recording the sacrilege of church leaders while gathering testimony from those involved with John Taylor's revelation and subsequent ordination. At the same time, Joseph F. Smith's successor as prophet, Heber J. Grant, appointed the aggressive former advisor to the State Department and Mexican ambassador and legal scholar J. Reuben Clark Jr. to root out and prosecute polygamists on a whole new level. A polygamist himself who had pleaded guilty to violating Utah's cohabitation laws in 1899, Grant's hypocrisy didn't seem to haunt him at all. "We never believed polygamy was wrong, and never will," Grant said.

Despite that, Grant hinted that LDS would be willing to assist in the legal prosecution of Mormon polygamists. Under his rule and Clark's relentless direction, LDS would conduct surveillance on suspected fundamentalists, turning the information over to authorities. LDS would also assist in the 1944 so-called Boyden Crusade in which forty-six Salt Lake City polygamists were arrested and copies of Joseph Musser's irritating fundamentalist periodical *Truth* were confiscated.

But while Musser and his followers were loath to quit Salt Lake, the exodus of other polygamists disgusted by what they saw as the spectacle of a fallen church had commenced decades earlier. Like Brigham Young, they sought out a piece of spectacularly beautiful land in which no one else seemed interested. The land's parched condition was overridden by its major asset—it was four hundred punishing miles from the nearest law. In fact, Young might be credited with opening the land on which today's Short Creek exists when he ordered John D. Lee to establish a primitive ferry station—a tiny, bare-bones shack—on the Colorado River one hundred miles east of the present-day twin cities. The crossing, made on a raft, enabled Mormon settlers to filter into Arizona, a state Young badly wanted to colonize.

IN 1871, BRIGHAM Young dispatched the now elderly, ailing John D. Lee, the man who'd induced the besieged and doomed members of the Fancher wagon train to surrender at Mountain Meadows, to one of the few fordable sections of the Colorado River.* Lee was ordered to establish a ferry and way station just upstream from where the river surges into the Grand Canyon, a river crossing critical for Saints traveling between Utah and Arizona and Mexico. An arrogant, unpopular blowhard of a man with probable sexual deviancies, Lee had been one of Young's most favored, devout, and, most importantly, obedient Saints since the days in Nauvoo. The prophet had taken the unusual and envied step of adopting Lee as a son, sending him on numerous colonizing missions from which Lee became enormously wealthy while acquiring at least nineteen wives, supplemented by a proclivity for purchasing young Indian girls.

By 1871, however, Lee had become a burden. Old and sick, he was the least liked of a half-dozen men the government had managed to identify as perpetrators of the 1857 massacre, and it was becoming increasingly unlikely that Young could protect all of them from arrest. In a less than honorable concession, Young secretly excommunicated Lee, releasing his wives to others, and sent Lee to the barren, empty outpost that would bear his name to this day: Lee's Ferry, Arizona. Young may have been trying to hide Lee, but, beset by health problems, Lee balked at abandoning a stone mansion and farm for a lean-to in the wilderness. His misery was short lived. Lee was the only Mormon man handed over to the U.S. government for the atrocity, and he was executed at the site of the massacre by firing squad in 1877 after delivering a blistering assessment of Brigham Young's character.

Two years after Lee's execution, LDS bought Lee's Ferry for one hundred milk cows from Emma Lee, the only wife who'd stuck with him after the excommunication. Prior to that, however, LDS had recruited another Saint, Warren M. Johnson, to help Emma with the crucial river crossing after Lee's 1874 arrest. Johnson moved his two wives to the north bank of the river where on June 12, 1888, one of them gave birth to a healthy boy, Leroy Sunderland Johnson, who became Uncle Roy, the first prophet, seer, revelator, and president of the Fundamentalist Church of Jesus Christ of Latter-Day Saints.

According to unofficial Short Creek historian and ex-FLDS member

---

*   Although the Mormon age of innocence is eight, Lee wrote that Mormon leaders worried that eight-year-olds would still be able to remember the event. Therefore, only seventeen children under age five were spared in the raid, to be doled out to Mormon families. When the U.S. government sent troops to escort the children home years after the slaughter, the Mormons who'd sheltered them charged the government $3,000 a head ($900,000) for their care. Young also charged the government for the Fancher party's superior-quality livestock, which he claimed he'd been forced to bestow upon restless Indians to keep peace but were undoubtedly divvied up between Mormons.

Ben Bistline, the first Short Creek settler was nonpolygamist rancher John Lauritzen, who moved his extended family to the area in 1914 and success-fully irrigated the valley. (Short Creek was named for the mere three-mile distance from the canyon stream to the lake bed into which it emptied.) Meanwhile, LDS Salt Lake City sentiment against polygamy was gathering steam, inspiring the LDS renegade Joseph Musser to begin publications of his *Truth* pamphlets in 1927. By 1928, Lorin Woolley, son of the man who'd hidden prophet John Taylor for his now controversial meeting with Joseph Smith and Jesus, was the only living eyewitness to Taylor's revelation that polygamy must never be abandoned. Anxious to keep the fundamentalist movement alive, Woolley began recruiting hardcore polygamy supporters, some of whom dreamed of creating a United Order—a sort of commune—for polygamists in an area too isolated to draw attention.

Self-sufficiency via resource pooling was a concept the church played with from its earliest days. Joseph Smith first introduced a vague notion of commu-nal living, though he seemed to treat it more as theory than a substantive plan. In Nauvoo, the commune concept generated quite a bit more enthusiasm among poorer Mormons than those with property and healthy finances, and Smith never promoted the plan futher than words, particularly since Smith was himself prone to usurping prime real estate to be recorded in his own name along with fat bank accounts. Although he insisted upon and received strict tithing, Smith seemed content to leave the commune notion to dangle as a promise, particularly because he drew no lines between religious virtue and unbridled capitalism, of which he taught God heartily approved.

Unsurprisingly, the consummate Yankee organizer Brigham Young was more ferocious about Mormon tithing obligations than the easygoing Smith. Explaining that God wished it done, Young was known to simply confis-cate an individual's cattle, horses, lumber, or similar possessions, ostensibly for the benefit of the larger community. Young, too, toyed with communal property concepts but also seemed to noodle the idea half heartedly, relying instead upon tithing and free labor to build Zion.*

---

*   Young frequently declared he'd never taken a cent from the church to accumulate his per-sonal fortune, but the claim seems absurd on its face. Young admits he was penniless when Smith was murdered in 1844, but thirty years later Young told *New York Herald* editor Horace Greeley he'd accumulated a personal fortune of $285,000—about $500 million in today's currency—while serving full-time as LDS president. Immediately upon his arrival in the Salt Lake Valley, Young owned a self-contained working plantation, continuing to acquire businesses throughout his life. Young's tangled financial affairs became a public embarrassment when his heirs, unwilling to part with their luxurious lifestyles, embarked on a prolonged court battle to prevent LDS from reclaiming riches the church felt Young had reaped in his capacity as church president.

Not all of the new Mormon fundamentalists believed in a United Order, but by 1935 its strongest advocate, John Y. Barlow, was in charge of the collection of leaders calling themselves the Priesthood Council or simply the Group. Barlow favored leaving the increasingly inhospitable environs of Salt Lake, an idea initially supported by Musser. About this time, Leroy Johnson and his brothers approached the Group, offering lands they'd acquired in Short Creek for the new polygamist state. Among those who scouted the land before accepting the offer was Fred Jessop, a man who would become a critical sticking point in FLDS society fifty years later.

The handful of polygamous families who migrated to Short Creek around 1935 was a handful too many for Arizona authorities. Although the nearest sheriff's station was four hundred miles away in Kingman, Arizona, police quickly arrested most of the men on open cohabitation charges. Just as quickly, the charges were dismissed by the local judge and sympathetic Short Creek founder John Lauritzen. Some of the men were jailed in subsequent proceedings, signaling the downfall of the original United Order trust fund, a failed precursor to the FLDS's United Effort Plan. According to Bistline, some were more equal than others in the fund's distribution, with Barlow living the relative high life while the families of the jailed men starved.

Although these circumstances created a fissure between Barlow and Musser, the two tried again in 1944, creating the United Effort Plan with Fred Jessop as its bishop and Marion Hammon as general manager, the basic structure of which remains today. The Short Creek population was caught up in the 1944 Salt Lake City Boyden Crusade sanctioned by LDS, and several Short Creekers, including Musser, served brief jail sentences. The trust survived, but unity in Short Creek did not.

Having suffered stroke and illness, Musser attempted to force the unpopular Rulon Allred upon the Short Creek Priesthood Council, claiming divine revelation. This was rejected, sending the embittered Musser and Allred back to Salt Lake City to found the Apostolic United Bretheren, one of FLDS's chief polygamy sect rivals. While FLDS was battling the fallout of the Hoole suits nearly fifty years later, history was clearly forgotten as the sect resurrected the late Musser as one of its chief prophets and unassailable designator of "sacred temple sites."

John Y. Barlow died in 1949, leaving the son of Lee's Ferry, Leroy Johnson, to become prophet of the new FLDS. Johnson eventually extinguished the one element distinguishing the FLDS in 1950 from the one that exists today: democracy. Up until Johnson's term as prophet, Short Creek had been loosely governed by a council of seven to twelve men who heard grievances and appeals, weighing disputes much as a court of law. Even those subjected to excommunication had a right to petition the council for redress and reconsideration. Although Joseph Smith was a de facto dictator, he had also established avenues for appeal, but Johnson felt such window dressing unnecessary. Disbanding the council, he established the principle of "one-man rule": his.

Today, the late Uncle Roy is remembered as a cherished, benevolent leader loved by all, an idyllic consensus that might have been retroactively shaped by the audacious cruelty of his successor. After discarding his first family in favor of polygamy in the mid-1940s, Rulon Jeffs chose to remain in Salt Lake City, using FLDS private jets to fly in and out of Short Creek to help Uncle Roy with what would become astoundingly successful financial decisions. Under Jeffs's supervision, FLDS moved from a primarily agricultural endeavor into lumber, concrete, and tool production, as well as establishing construction firms underbidding anyone in the nation due to their absence of labor expenses.* Although Leroy Johnson had designated no successor when he died in 1986, part-time Short Creek resident Rulon Jeffs managed to wrest the prophet mantle from an opposition whose spirit was no match for the slashing knife fight Jeffs was willing and able to execute for what had become an empire worth tens of millions of dollars.

Instead of Danites or Destroying Angels, Short Creekers were familiar with a band of spies and ruffians they would call goon squads or God squads, men so loyal to the prophet they'd burst into homes to beat up misbehaving members or search for evidence of moral impurity. Rulon Jeffs made such effective use of the intrusive, frightening God squads that FLDS members may be forgiven for overlooking that the squads were actually established by the sainted Uncle Roy to "clean up the people" and "handle" men, fearsome phrases that harkened back to the days of Brigham Young, when "handling" men was often synonymous with murder. Rulon Jeffs would not go that far, but his brand of "handling" would resurrect feelings of dread not known since pioneer days.

---

*   The legal labyrinth of dozens of FLDS-connected businesses and the exact nature of their financial relationships to the sect is coming under increasing scrutiny as FLDS members convicted of crimes petition the courts for indigent status to obtain tax-paid lawyers for their appeals. Partial results of an FBI investigation into these finances showing millions of dollars in transfers from a single business have been filed in the Texas courts.

The United Effort Plan, established in 1944, guaranteed generational occupancy on properties FLDS members "in good standing"—a phrase that would become important decades later—were encouraged to continuously improve and develop. Everyone contributed to the land purchases, which were then jointly held under the umbrella of the UEP and assigned to families for their perpetual use, provisions made when FLDS was governed with the semblance of democracy compatible with communal living. Roy Johnson's imposition of one-man rule implied cataclysmic changes for the security of FLDS families' homesteads, but only after Johnson's death did anyone comprehend the nature of the devastation. Almost immediately, Rulon Jeffs declared all Short Creek residents to be "tenants at will"—*his* will. With the scythe of one-man rule, Jeffs began "handling" men who displeased him in some way by throwing them out of their homes and snatching their wives and children away.

It was a bridge too far for some FLDS members who'd objected to one-man rule from the start. Led by original Short Creek settlers like Marion Hammon, several hundred FLDS members splintered, resettling in nearby Centennial Park. Others, like Ruth's father, David Stubbs, refused to leave their lives for a man they hadn't much liked to begin with.

In what would become a series of FLDS actions, FLDS attorney Rod Parker began filing eviction notices on the families but lost the effort in 1998 when the Utah Supreme Court held that the families had a right to stay. The court addressed a variety of legal issues—unjust enrichment, color of title, and claimant acts, to name a few—but the conclusion that would reach into the future and bite FLDS was the court's conclusion that the UEP trust was not "charitable" but "private." The legally defined distinction between these categories benefitted the families fighting eviction at the time. In an obvious attempt to prevent this sort of thing in the future, and to circumvent the high court's ruling, Rulon Jeffs immediately revised the UEP charter, switching it back to a "charitable" trust, an act that exploded in FLDS faces a few years later.

Although the switch bore Rulon Jeffs's name, it is just as likely the change was made by his son Warren. Because 1998 also appears to be the year when Rulon suffered the first in a series of progressively crippling strokes, no one is certain how competent the elder Jeffs really was after the first one. It is unclear whether a deteriorating physical condition prompted Rulon to leave Salt Lake for good that year. His son and the future prophet, Warren, later offered the mystifying explanation that the decision had been God's because

Rulon's jet suffered a mechanical problem delaying takeoff one weekend. In any event, Rulon shut down the Salt Lake compound, which was so large it was purchased for use as a school, trout pond and all.

In 2001, Jeffs ordered all FLDS members remaining in Salt Lake to relocate to Short Creek right away. Jeffs informed his wide-eyed Saints that God was using the upcoming 2002 Olympics as a clever ruse to lure a bunch of dark-skinned evil folk and Godless foreigners to one place where they would be destroyed in a festival of gore and natural disaster as a prelude to the end of the world. The end of days was about to begin, and if it didn't, it would at least be the end of the wicked Salt Lake City that an irritated God would destroy for hosting the scandalously sacrilegious event. Either way, there was no time to lose retreating to the safety of the red cliff caves stocked with canned food and ammo to await the flood of Gentiles who would soon be in a jealous clamor for FLDS's destruction.

Members running long-established businesses in the metropolis were instructed to turn all cash assets over to Jeffs and then declare personal bankruptcy to avoid their Godless creditors, a move that Warren later wryly observed was a twofer of prime FLDS's principles: "Lying for the Lord" and "bleeding the beast," even though the beasts in this case were individual Gentile creditors instead of the whole government. Sect members transferred hundreds of thousands, possibly millions, of dollars into Jeffs's pocket without hesitation, well adjusted to the various Armageddon scenarios their prophets announced with stupefying regularity.

No one inside or out of FLDS can testify with confidence to the prophet's mental comprehension between 1998 and his death in 2002, just shy of his ninety-second birthday, or to what degree the whole show was being run by his shadowy son, Warren. Groups of evicted FLDS members, too large and consistent for FLDS attorneys to dismiss as merely vengeful, independently report that Rulon regularly seemed confused by his surroundings and even his identity, routinely failed to recognize people he'd known for decades, and lost track of the subjects under discussion. Brent Jeffs writes that his grandfather was never without a tall glass of clear liquid that Jeffs's followers assumed to be water but was in fact vodka. Others report Rulon suddenly perking up during meetings being channeled by Warren to exclaim: "I want my job back!" Rulon's excommunicated son and Brent's dad, Ward, recalls that his father married so many girls so frequently that Ward could not assess the totality of his siblings, a curious state of affairs given the fact that Rulon reportedly shouted at Warren, "No more wives!" on more than one occasion. No one is sure what Rulon was doing, but everybody is certain that Warren was ultimately in charge. "If you had something to say," Ruth Stubbs observed dryly, "you said it to Warren."

Today, Uncle Rulon is included with Uncle Roy in Short Creek's fond reminiscences of warmhearted prophets past, a testament to the mind-blowing and bizarre savagery the current FLDS prophet Warren Jeffs brought to the job—a roller-coaster ride on the edge of sanity that would finally force somebody to see the polygamous community that had been rendered invisible since the 1953 raid.

9

WARREN JEFFS

Who can tell us of the inhabitants of this little planet that shines of an evening, called the moon? When we view its face, we may see what is termed "the man in the moon" and what some philosophers declare are the shadows of mountains. . . . So it is with regard to the inhabitants of the sun. . . . Do you think there is any life there? No question of it; it was not made in vain. It was made to give light to those who dwell upon it and to other planets; and so will this earth when it is celestialized.
—Brigham Young, *Journal of Discourses*, Vol. 13, July 24, 1870

I was not to leave Albuquerque until I had found the baggy black britches the Lord wanted me to wear. I sent the brethren to go do that. They bought some tight black britches and then went off to buy some baggy ones. I got ready and loaded the car by 11 A.M. and they drove up and had their baggy britches for me. I changed.
—Warren Jeffs, "Record of President Warren Jeffs," p. 241, June 19, 2004

The ladies that were sealed: the former wives of Thomas Barlow were sealed to LeGrande Barlow. I started that ceremony using his name, LeGrande Spencer Barlow, and then I stopped and asked him who his mother was and who she was married to and he is now the son of Richard Allred, his mother being sealed to Richard Allred for time and eternity. So LeGrande Spencer Allred, formerly Barlow, received Fern Luana Shapley and Teri Elissa Shapley. And then Thomas Arden Holm received the former wives of Don Holm, Linda Jessop, and Enid Jessop.
—Warren Jeffs, "Record of President Warren Jeffs," p. 160, April 30, 2004

Although Rulon Jeffs faced opposition when he assumed the prophet's chair, his predecessor had at least elevated him to apostle status before passing on without declaring an heir. The elder Jeffs had also enjoyed the benefits of seniority that, combined with his rank, offered a minimally plausible argument for assuming leadership of FLDS. Warren Jeffs had none of these qualifications. He was merely an "elder." He wasn't even a first-born son. In fact, he wasn't even born to the first wife. People didn't like him. All of this would make the swath of Warren Jeffs's power grab infinitely more sinister than that of his father.

The problem of legitimate succession was compounded by two elements: older elders suspicious of the way Warren handled his father's illness and younger ones who remembered the beatings from Alta Academy and the creepy way Warren lingered over little girls or sneaked up behind them to scare the bejeezus out of them with the demand, "Are you keeping sweet enough?" The six-foot-four-inch, 145-pound Warren, with his anemic complexion and droning, monotone voice described as "talking through a daydream" was a spooky guy even by FLDS standards. When Uncle Roy Johnson died, his goon squads had robotically transferred their feral loyalty from him to Rulon, but it was unclear if the spindly Warren enjoyed this important advantage, even though he'd been the actual commandant of the squads from at least the time he rolled by Brent Jeffs's house during the funeral for the infant Cheyenne.

Warren had received the immediate and unequivocal support of Short Creek old-schooler and sometimes bodyguard/enforcer Wendell Nielsen, who'd made a lot of money with Rulon Jeffs. Rulon had put Nielsen in charge of the 55,000-square-foot specialized tool manufacturing business, Western Precision, which incredibly held millions in contracts from the U.S. government. Apparently deciding to stick with what worked, Nielsen noodled, muscled, cajoled—whatever seemed appropriate—to convince FLDS members of Warren's legitimacy, but it wasn't enough. A number of grumbling FLDS elders had for years been resentful and suspicious of Warren's cloying hovering over the ailing Rulon Jeffs, even speculating that Warren, who took charge of Rulon's prescription drugs, was deliberately overmedicating the old man to keep him in a semistuporous and physically isolated condition. Warren's assertions that the cloistered Rulon was speaking through him were sometimes met with open skepticism rarely seen under one-man rule.

Given his zealously exclusive attendance to the discombobulated Rulon, it seems strange that Warren had been unable to secure irrefutable evidence of his elevation from a man so ill he required assistance to execute his bathroom trips. After Rulon's death on September 8, 2002, Warren was apoplectic when the community did not instantly turn to him for guidance but instead began openly ruminating on the identity of the new prophet, wondering when God would make him known to the people. Warren's name didn't even surface among the four most popular contenders, a field led by

Fred Jessop, the much-beloved elder statesman who first scouted the Short Creek site with Leroy Johnson.*

How Warren Jeffs managed to gain control of his father is the subject of bitter speculation among hundreds of excommunicated FLDS members who rightly suspect they were targeted because the increasingly paranoid Jeffs saw them as a threat to his power. They trace the origin of their shattered lives to Warren's birth. He was the middle son of Rulon's insufferably pious fourth wife, the former Merilyn Steed, who despite her diminutive, deferring stature was the type of political creature well known to Short Creek plural wives forced to compete for attention and favors for themselves and their children. "She was always trying to shame you with her virtue," remembered Brent Jeffs, "and then she'd stick the knife in when your back was turned. She had grandfather wrapped around her little finger, and he never even knew it."

Warren Jeffs was born sickly and premature—brought home in a shoe box, some said—a pitiful little creature whose helplessness and expected death tugged at Rulon's heartstrings. Merilyn knew right away she had something useful and convinced the worried prophet that the boy's survival was an act of God, a heavenly finger pointing right at his favored one. As a result Warren grew up sheltered and babied by an awestruck father and easily slipped into the role of Rulon's gofer, driving away all comers with whisper campaigns and deceit and, when all else failed, urging their ejection from the community. When Rulon fell ill, Warren was right there.

"In Salt Lake City, Warren really got used to the high life, too," sighed Jethro Barlow, grandson of Short Creek founder John Y. Barlow and a man who would soon find himself on the business end of Warren's cutthroat ambition. "Lobster, private planes, five-star restaurants, the finest wine, and of course, women." The soft-spoken, bespectacled Barlow, who lost his home and children in a Warren Jeffs purge, choked on his words as he tried to recover himself. "It was . . . very sick," he concluded.

---

* "Uncle Fred" was not beloved by everyone. In her book, *Church of Lies*, anti-FLDS activist Flora Jessop, Fred's great niece, asserts she was imprisoned and abused in Jessop's house for years after a failed escape attempt; that Fred's wife Lydia performed abortions, including one on Flora to terminate a pregnancy by Flora's father; and that Fred ensured secrecy for the unmarked graveyard for hundreds of infants who died under suspicious circumstances. Elissa Wall, who wrote *Lost Innocence*, was also underwhelmed by Uncle Fred, a man her mother was forced to marry after Elissa's own beloved father was excommunicated. Because Jessop could not have his own children, Wall questioned his role in the excommunication of many men whose children Jessop accumulated. Despite her pleas, Jessop forced Wall into a marriage when she was fourteen, an act the whole sect would come to rue.

But being the spoiled son of God's prophet hadn't erased Warren's business acumen. Well aware of his legitimacy difficulties, trained at his remorseless father's knee, Warren brought a gun to a pillow fight. Likely challengers for the prophet's chair included three descendants of Short Creek founder John Y. Barlow known as the Barlow Boys along with the elderly Fred Jessop, a familiar, if not always comforting, FLDS fixture from its beginnings. Jessop seemed to have had little heart for the fight to begin with, but the Barlow Boys' position on Warren Jeffs was less certain. Characterized as religious zealots, they adored Rulon's predecessor, Roy Johnson, taking enthusiastic charge of his goon squads, a responsibility they also exercised for Rulon. However, the dead prophet had failed to appoint them to the high-ranking priesthood positions they desired, and the Barlows may have been waiting to see if Warren would correct the mistake.

Having no intention of promoting anyone with a pedigree as strong as the Barlow Boys to anything, Warren created his own band of intimidators. Like the Danites and Destroying Angels, Warren's "Sons of Helaman" brought a poetic name to the grim work of muscling their way into FLDS homes, rifling through underwear and desk drawers for evidence of the inhabitant's impurity that could be alternately used for future eviction or to blackmail loyalty oaths and "testimonials" for Warren Jeffs out of the victims.* There was no reason to believe the dead-of-night evictions and family reassignments started by Rulon and endorsed by Fred Jessop and the Barlow Boys would stop with Rulon's death, so most families were amenable to the vaguely threatening cases being presented by anywhere from twelve to fifteen intense Sons of Helaman breathing fire in their living rooms.

But one tactic does not a strategy make, and Warren had other cards to play. At a meeting days after Rulon's death, Warren threatened his would-be followers, "Hands off father's wives!"—a jarring, entirely unnecessary proclamation that simultaneously puzzled and alarmed the membership.**

---

*   Helaman was a prophet in *The Book of Mormon* who was thought to have lived in the Nephite capital of Zarahemla around the first century B.C. His sons were famous missionaries to the Zormanites, and Helaman himself tried to persuade the anti-Nephi Lehites known as Ammonites not to take up arms. In 66 B.C., Helaman led an armed force of two thousand young men known as the Stripling Warriors to recapture critical territories taken by the Lamanites. Warren told sect members he was recapturing a community sliding toward hell.

**   In his September 16, 2002, dictations, Jeffs records his announcement as "Hands off father's family!" However, three excommunicated FLDS members present at the meeting independently remember that Warren specified the wives, a position more consistent with Warren's subsequent actions.

Warren immediately shut his father's wives and his own—anywhere from seventy to one hundred women—up in the Jeffses' lavish Short Creek compound, around which Warren had installed eight-foot walls, security cameras, and locked, key-carded gates shortly after his father's death. Even if they'd wanted to, the women could not leave their luxurious prison.

Press reports often put the number of Rulon Jeffs's wives at around twenty-one, taking his last, fourteen-year-old bride when he was eighty-six years old, but Warren's newly released dictations, seized in a 2008 warrant, reference more than fifty females associated with his father with marriages occurring up until a month prior to his death. In thousands of pages detailing every moment of his life, Warren puts his own wife count at the time of his father's death at twenty-five, a number he felt wholly inadequate. Warren's dictations reveal a petulant resentment over his number of wives, complaining that Rulon kept saying "no" when Warren asked for more "blessings," an FLDS euphemism for new brides.

The dictations all but confirm what many Short Creekers suspected at the time: lacking the revelatory authority to take his own "blessings," Warren had for years been "plucking," as he called it, choice girls from the community whom Warren wanted for himself, marrying them to an old, sick, heavily medicated man not fully cognizant of the situation. At FLDS meetings at which Rulon Jeffs was decreasingly present, he'd been known for spontaneously and incongruously yelling, "No more wives!" before falling back into his rheumy silence. An outburst like that makes better sense if his son was forcing young women upon him, as does the mirthless joke among anti-FLDS activists that Rulon had forty wives and twenty virgins. "Everybody knew Warren was scouting FLDS territories as far as Canada, picking out the prettiest girls," said a disgusted Brent Jeffs, who lost several sisters, age fourteen and under, to Warren Jeffs. "He liked them young. *Real* young. He was looking at girls who were ten, eleven years old. After he got them, the light just went out of their eyes. I felt sick for them."

Under the circumstances, it's possible that many of the girls would have had more contact with Warren than with their husband. A few weeks after Rulon's death, Warren reminded the "ladies" that he had selected many of them, plucking a few from grade school to be with the prophet. "Isn't it interesting, ladies," he told them pointedly, "that I have been training you all these years? I was not surprised. I was delighted, joyful, happy. My love for my father was too deep to treat you young ladies wrong. I only thought of him when I was with you." Warren wanted the ladies to keep this in mind while pondering his next series of selective suggestions. To help solidify his prophet claim, what Warren required of the women were written testimonials. In the testimonials, the girls needed to say that Rulon Jeffs had told them always and often that Warren Jeffs was not only the designated prophet but their future husband as well.

That's what Warren needed, but he understood he couldn't just *order* the girls to do it. Even though they'd been carefully trained from the cradle to obey priesthood men without question, they were still like sheltered children who might be shocked by so sudden a marriage to their stepson. The lying part was problematic, too. Any FLDS girl worth her salt could assume the innocence of a lamb while "lying for the Lord" to Gentiles, but lying to the priesthood was a different animal. *That* kind of lying could earn you beatings, food deprivation, isolation, "behavior modification," and, worse than any of those, loss of salvation. Since Rulon had obviously *not* designated Warren as either his successor or his own wives' future husband, Warren had to somehow make the women believe that he actually *did* make those designations.

To accomplish this, Warren began a campaign of sly suggestions that the ladies had known of Rulon's instructions all along but had simply forgotten. It was not their fault, Warren soothed, because they were, after all, just weak women. And Warren offered the girls another out. There was the good possibility they'd been too girlishly dense to understand what "Father," as the ladies called Rulon, had been "hinting" at them. If they would just think back on conversations in *this* light, Warren encouraged smoothly, they might now be able to detect the succession hints. Finally, for those too girlishly dense to understand the hint process, Warren offered the straight-up amnesia solution: Rulon *had* told them straight-out about the succession and marriages, but the Lord gave the women temporary amnesia, eliminating the tragic possibility that they would spill the beans before the time was ripe.* This was because the weak character of women prevented them from keeping confidences and the Lord didn't want the succession known until Rulon was gone.

---

* The testimonials Warren eventually obtained inadvertently indicated that Rulon's wives called him "Father" or "sir" and practiced the odd ritual of filing into the kitchen like humble house servants in the morning, one by one, for an antiseptic shake of Rulon's hand while they briefly praised his holiness and wished him a good day. For many, it was the only time they ever saw the man.

Warren worked on the girls in groups, driving six to ten at a time around in his fancy, bulletproof SUVs, allowing them into the hallowed prophet's office—a jaw-dropping experience—or taking them on fishing trips to Navajo Lake. In the first weeks after Rulon's death, no appointment was too important for Warren to cancel on behalf of the ladies, though he noted that, if he canceled an appointment for lady training, he preferred it be a group of ladies because one-on-one training diluted precious time.

He took at least one group of thirteen ladies to dinner at the elegant, expensive, five-star Painted Pony gourmet restaurant in St. George, and several women received diamond rings and other jewelry after private dining experiences. Warren summoned a romantic side, taking the ladies out for midnight drives, stopping to dance in the moonlight. For the most part, the ladies responded to the unexpected attention and elite, exclusive outings unavailable to other FLDS women with growing concern for Warren's needs, which they now saw as their salvation. Singing songs, having "family time," and riding around in cars became events to be sought after, even fought over. Jealousies arose as the women jockeyed for position, making conditions good for manipulation. Warren preened, basking in the happiness that came with a bunch of girls fighting over him.

And he was successful. After weeks of carefully applied training and "correcting," Warren's intended brides were slapping their foreheads over how dumb they'd been not to have seen all along that "Father" had appointed Warren to be prophet and their husband. The "testimonials" came fast and furious, but one beautiful girl, the former Naomie Jessop, tumbled to the plan much quicker than the others and with superior comprehension. Never mind Rulon's vague "hints" or a heavenly blackout, Naomie announced in a clear, unwavering voice that "Father" had been quite specific with her about Warren's destiny (and hers) on numerous occasions. Probably selected by Warren himself, Naomie is described in other FLDS memoirs as one of the youngest girls in the group, with a lovely face, good figure, and blond hair down to her knees. Smitten by brains and beauty, Warren glommed on to Naomie early and would eventually go nowhere without her, unless she was being punished for insufficient adoration, and even then he called her hourly and instructed the five or six men assigned as her guards to "never let her out of your sight," even when she went to the bathroom. Warren was in love.

Warren's problems weren't solved, though. There were some balkers among the ladies—some women who just didn't like him and some who experienced nagging ethical qualms about marrying their stepson within a week of their husband's death.* Even with the ladies' testimonies, the intolerable doubts of prominent male FLDS members had not been completely banished either. Something more was required to sway the footdraggers, and Warren introduced a revolutionary concept: Rulon Jeffs was not really dead.

Warren cleverly tied this revelation to Rulon's frequent declarations (when he was alive) that he would live until the second coming. Though Rulon had been sick for years and Warren seemed cognizant of his inevitable death by selecting his future wives, the aspiring prophet seemed to have been caught flatfooted when his father actually died in the hospital before witnesses. Winging it, Warren ordered the hospital group to pray there and then for his father's "renewal." Quite literally, the group expected Rulon to throw off the hospital sheets covering his body, rise, and accompany them all back to Short Creek. When that didn't happen, Warren insisted that if the continuing renewal prayers were more "fervent," Rulon would yet rise. Warren even painted a picture of his father bounding about with the vigor of an eighteen-year old (the age Warren had selected for his own afterlife) with an ethereal glow he'd have absorbed during embrace with the celestial Joseph Smith (or Jesus) during his brief sojourn to heaven.

Everyone in Short Creek had bruised knees from hours of feverish renewal praying, but when the fervency proved insufficient to persuade God to relent, Warren Jeffs was left with a four day-old dead body. It seems odd that a man of Warren's foresight would not have anticipated the problems endemic to raising the dead, especially because the usually foolproof explanation for its failure wasn't yet available to him. Only the prophet could announce that the failure of predicted events to materialize was the fault of the wicked, undeserving FLDS people, and Warren was not the acknowledged prophet. Even in his own voluminous tape-recorded dictations typed by harried "scribes," Warren still referred to himself, however disingenuously, as "Elder Warren Jeffs." The fact that he felt compelled to use the galling lesser title was evidence that Jeffs himself understood the difficulty he faced gaining acceptance as prophet.

Even with the bulk of the wives in place, Warren's other difficulties meant he still needed his father. Warren's concept of "transference" instead of "renewal" seems to have evolved over a few days in late September 2002, but when it all came together, the concept had something for everyone.

---

* At least two of Warren's prospective brides fled Short Creek. Two were excommunicated for refusing his advances, and several more disappeared for months, and in one case years, before reappearing to tell investigators there was absolutely nothing wrong.

While stopping short of claiming that he was *inhabited* by his father, Warren presented a scenario in which Rulon would flit in and out of his mind, while always remaining nearby. By "nearby" Warren meant he could be behind the curtain, in a closet, sitting on his bed, or anywhere in between. Although the physicalities of the feat were a tad sketchy, Warren did explain that Rulon and God were now merged. Bad thoughts would be known to Rulon, who would "transfer" them to Warren, who would from here on know every-thing about everyone.

After delivering this sobering news, Warren offered the remaining reluc-tant ladies a salve for the conscience. When they married Warren, he told them, they wouldn't *really* be marrying Warren. Since Rulon was in "trans-fer," they'd be marrying Rulon all over again, and therefore any resulting children would actually be Rulon's. Fundamentalists marry for "time" or for "time and eternity." Marrying for "time" is strictly temporal and not such a big deal. Marrying for "time and eternity" means the woman belongs to her husband in perpetuity by God's iron will. It's a tricky knot for a prophet who decides to reassign women sealed for "eternity" to dead or banished men, but Warren didn't try to cross that bridge yet. For now, he contented himself with a promise to the ladies they would be sealed to him only in "time," meaning they'd be joining "Father" on his planet in the afterlife, assuming they could ever complete the work Rulon needed to finish up in the closets and laundry rooms of Short Creek to move on.

On October 7, 2002, just a month after Rulon's death, Warren secretly married his first batch of seven of Rulon's widows. After taking them all upstairs for a little dancing and nuptials, the women were promptly sequestered in rooms lacking the compound's intercoms to prevent their blabbing about the marriages to anyone else. Warren knew that marrying his father's women was going to be a community shocker. He probably should have selected as precedent Brigham Young, who married most of Joseph Smith's widows, but Warren instead began comparing himself to Smith in his public speaking engagements. He also began hinting that he wasn't channeling only Rulon but Uncle Roy as well, irrefutable proof that the last two prophets, at least, approved of Warren's ascension.

That left the irritating problem of the living Fred Jessop, the elder whose name was most often whispered as the next, rightful prophet. Though it seemed to pain him to do it, Jeffs knew that he must kiss Jessop's backside. He did so by announcing that he and Jessop were "entwined" and "meshed," correctly gambling that Jessop would be too fearful to contradict Jeffs's characterizations. To his brother, Jeffs complained that Jessop didn't treat him with the proper awe, but he bit the humiliating bullet when he cozied up to Jessop in public. Jeffs knew Jessop was probably the only man in town who could say the word and take half the population with him to Centennial Park. It was critical that the two men be seen as one.

Jessop, however, seemed reluctant to become merged into Uncle Warren's—as he was increasingly called—crowded head of spirits. His tepid "testimonials" indicated only that Rulon had made substantial "investment" in Warren and that Warren was definitely *trying* to do what Uncle Rulon wanted. Jessop even offered some support for the notion that Rulon was still floating about the community, but he always stopped short of endorsing Warren for prophethood or claiming that Rulon had anointed his son.

Resenting every minute of it, Warren worked feverishly to align himself with "Uncle Fred," while pressing the old man hard to seek a "revelation testimonial" from Rulon about Warren's legitimacy. Berating Jessop after yet another mediocre "testimonial" in which Warren was not the star, a cowed Jessop protested weakly: "I don't know how much plainer I can put it." Warren huffed away from a funeral early after deeming Uncle Fred's remarks too lengthy. Riding back to his compound, Warren dropped the "saiths" and "doeths" from the dictation lingo as he told his brother sourly, "He sure has me painted as the little boy in need of teaching."*

Jessop's thick skull forced a frustrated Warren to continue assuring the dubious among his flock that the undead Rulon was actually the one "running the show." Being stuck in prophet limbo was exasperating work that Warren tried to move along by increasing his comparisons to past prophets and escalating threatening rhetoric warning of "impure" or "halfhearted" bad apples infecting the whole barrel. There were dark hints of future purges Warren might be forced to undertake in order to save the faithful, seeds of terror that found fertile ground in a community fearful of hell at every single moment of their lives, and Warren also dragged the old "blood atonement" doctrine out of storage, advocating murder for those whose sins were too great to be overcome by any other means. He added that gangs of assassins were roaming about, trying to kill him, a fantasy some wished were true.

Police chief Sam Roundy, a Warren Jeffs true believer, used his tax-supported resources to spy on the entire community, with special attention

---

*   Oddly, Warren Jeffs had a disconcerting habit of referring to himself as a "little boy" or a "lost little boy" when he was feeling amorous toward his "ladies."

paid to suspected malcontents and boys age thirteen to sixteen who might become eligible for eviction. A zealous Roundy provided nearly daily, sometimes hourly reports on everybody's goings-on, including lists of preposterous crimes being committed by a slew of unsuspecting juvenile males stopping just short of murder. Warren was injecting all the nerve-racking fear and paranoia he could muster, and *still* there were some who weren't hiding. At one Sunday service, a stern Warren advised that any man who did not believe he was channeling Rulon should refrain from taking the sacrament. Refusing the sacrament was the kind of public display of impurity to which no one would aspire, and Warren was astounded when three men, including FLDS accountant Jethro Barlow, took Warren up on his challenge. In another tantrum, Warren stormed from the building, his fawning entourage skittering behind him, awaiting their marching orders.*

After days like this, Warren liked to unwind with a massage. He especially liked foot massages administered by two to three women, but high-stress days required more—up to eight women massaging his whole body while another clutch of girls might be in the room, singing original material, songs of praise for Warren. A little food never hurt either, and Warren liked to have six to twelve ladies prepare individual dishes they thought he might enjoy, serving them to him in a kind of *Top Chef* competition graded in part by how accurately they'd assessed his culinary desires.

By this time, the appalled shock experienced by the community when they'd learned Warren had married most of Rulon's wives had been replaced by an undercurrent of desperate fear and frayed nerves as people wondered if they'd be reported for any evildoing. He still didn't have the title, but Warren was finally in complete control of Short Creek, free to add all the wives he wanted. The number of wives held by Warren Jeffs remains a matter of speculation, but the estimates of ninety-one are certainly low. Myriad ex-FLDS bloggers put the number between two and three hundred. In his dictations, Warren indicates he had almost eighty wives by the end of 2002, and he was just getting started.

---

* Warren followed his father's method of rewarding loyalty with wives. His brothers LeRoy and Isaac had already received several, including some of Rulon's wives, albeit the older ones. Although he does not always name the recipients of these "blessings," Warren's relentless dictations indicate he was formulating and executing dozens of marriages, sidestepping the issue of his authority to do so by pressing an eager Wendell Nielsen and reluctant Fred Jessop into service as "witnesses," i.e., accomplices.

The sense of general unease, paranoia, and fearful anticipation in Short Creek suited Warren. His sudden edicts kept people off balance, bent to his every word. The flock was now prohibited from speaking to any Gentiles or apostated family members on pain of excommunication. One day he declared red to be the color owned by Jesus. Anyone with a speck of red found anywhere in his or her home was subject to immediate exile for aspiring to become Jesus, a pursuit only Warren was allowed. As frantic families scrambled to throw out clothes, drapes, toys—anything with a red thread—Warren decreed that having fun in water was devil's play. No swimming, boating, floating, or wading. The same went for air, though people were trying to figure out exactly what that meant. No kites? It was confusing, but another of Warren's edicts was not. When a young girl was mauled by a stray dog, Warren ordered all the dogs in Short Creek, a community of nearly ten thousand dog owners, to be killed. No selling them or giving them away. The blood from their slashed throats must soak the desert red. Mothers tried to hush their wailing children as Warren's enforcers swept the town with honed knives, cutting the throats of their pets. The mothers were afraid Warren would take the children away for their evil weeping.

Meanwhile, Warren had a lot of real world work to catch up on. Maybe he couldn't be the prophet yet, but he had to get control of the money by becoming president of the state-registered FLDS sole corporation. After badgering the exasperating Fred Jessop for weeks, Warren was able to force the ninety-three year-old's reluctant signature to paperwork declaring Warren the secular president of FLDS. He was now in complete control of all the homes, commercial property, and business assets for the sect worth hundreds of millions of dollars.

All Warren's riding around in cars with girls had also taken his attention off the fact that the FLDS community in Bountiful, British Columbia, Canada, was in full revolt under the leadership of Winston Blackmore. Warren had excommunicated Blackmore after he forgave a young girl fleeing Short Creek with the boy she wanted to marry, allowing the couple to settle in Canada as husband and wife. Authorities on both sides of the border would later investigate claims that Warren had placed a blood atonement sentence on the head of the girl, Veronica Rohbeck, which Blackmore had refused to execute. Warren's breathless Canadian spy, Jim Oler, told an infuriated Warren many of the thousand FLDS members in the Canadian branch didn't accept his prophet claims. There were too many of them to run off. In fact, Warren's supporters were a distinct minority in some danger of being run off themselves. The spectacularly scenic Canadian lands, with an estimated value of $300 million, were part of the FLDS United Effort Plan trust.* Forced to accept Blackmore's victory, Warren pondered a kind of reverse excommunication, instructing the sect's Salt Lake lawyers to discover a way to wrench the land out from under the rebels, but that fell apart when it was discovered Blackmore was a bit of an operator himself. It was probably not legal, but the new head of the Canadian FLDS had placed most of the UEP lands in his name. It would take years of court action to sort out.

There were other businesses to look after as well. Warren's schedule, once burdened with securing "testimonies," picking out jewelry, enjoying ritzy dinners, and attending a few general meetings in which he continued to explain Rulon's omnipresence and his own love for Fred Jessop, shifted to more prophetlike appointments. He dedicated businesses, like the new FLDS potato processing plant under the direction of Stephen Harker. Warren now headed the Monday morning scheduling meetings instead of just attending. He was present for the dedication of a new $10 million school paid for by Arizona taxpayers. "Soon, that building will be ours," he remarked to Wendell Nielsen, a promise he made good on within a year, simply usurping the property under the state of Arizona's nose.

Knowing that every move he made had immortal significance, Warren inducted three of his wives into "scribe" service. Tapping his shirt pocket containing his small tape recorder, Warren sternly advised the scribes that they, like he, were never to be without a fully charged recorder so that every detail of his movements could be recorded for the heavens as well as the world. Warren also put his instrument to work recording the personal sessions of FLDS members unwise enough to confess their sins or unburden themselves of an embarrassing family situation. These sessions were not transcribed but later used for blackmail or excommunication purposes. Trying to stay true to their assignments, however, the lady scribes typed thousands of pages that dutifully recorded every sock change, smile, or grimace, yet only Naomie Jessop Jeffs comprehended that when Jeffs said "record everything," he meant everything that made him look like a clairvoyant seer on a first-name basis with God. Warren relieved his less- talented

---

*   The value of UEP holdings in Short Creek were estimated at $110 million in 2005, but the increasing popularity of St. George as a recreation destination has increased the value of the UEP lands. UEP also holds properties in Colorado, Idaho, Nevada, Texas, New Mexico, and several other states. FLDS land holdings are separate from its businesses.

scribes, assigning them to typing duties only. The lovely Naomie was becoming indispensable to the aspiring prophet.

But Naomie couldn't help him with the law. Warren didn't like to think about the Ruth Stubbs affair very much. The girl had been an unusual case, and she'd received unanticipated assistance from the terrible apostate sister. That should have been the end of it, but in a stunning turn of events, Holm was indicted. Warren still had trouble believing it—he felt like the Utah attorney general would come to his senses. Didn't they remember the 1953 raid? Warren did, or rather he remembered that no one had dared touch FLDS afterward. Warren had even been informed that this Mark Shurtleff heathen had spoken publically about arresting *him*, the prophet Warren Jeffs. It was absurd.

Warren didn't want to take up too much dictation time on ancillary matters like Rod Holm's fifteen-year prison exposure, the new Utah attorney general polygamy investigator, or the fact that Arizona's Mohave County attorney was jumping on the bandwagon with child rape investigations and a lot of questions about Dan Barlow, Colorado City Mayor Don Barlow's son, who'd admitted to using five of his now teenage daughters as "surrogate wives" from the time they were five years old. That matter had been managed when police chief Sam Roundy referred the errant Barlow for priesthood counseling and sent the hysterical seventeen-year-old daughter who'd run to the police station after fleeing the latest attack back to her father's home. FLDS did not condone father/daughter incest, but Barlow was sorry, and that's what counted.

Actually, the whole Barlow matter resolidified Warren's conviction that girls should be impregnated as soon as they were physically able to bear children. Girls with children didn't entertain meandering daydreams or imagine futures beyond what they were intended for: childbearing to build up Zion. A man receiving a newly menstruating girl didn't have to worry if she'd been with anyone else or expect much back talk either. Their minds untangled by education, experience, or hope, young girls with children settled so much more easily into priesthood obedience. It worked out better for everyone, but Warren was not ready to unveil that part of his strategy. Not yet. Because the strategy Warren Jeffs had decided upon was extreme, devastating, cruel, and irresponsible, and it would lay the groundwork for the unthinkable: a court takeover of FLDS property. In the years to come, FLDS lawyers would spend all their time furiously denying that what was about to happen actually did.

Warren Jeffs had decided that he hated Short Creek, and because he hated Short Creek, so did God. It wasn't only that Short Creek was full of "halfhearted" people, traitors, and undiscovered apostates. The Rod Holm indictment and subsequent conviction in 2003 convinced Warren that staying in Utah—or Arizona for that matter—was untenable. The intrusive Utah attorney general was evidence that the protection afforded by the 1953 raid was obviously wearing off. A slew of investigations in both states was proof the Lord had deserted the area and its unworthy people.

Warren began marrying dozens of girls while ejecting the nuisance boys upon whom Sam Roundy had pinned trumped-up charges. More submissive but still excess boys were sent off to work in FLDS businesses, destined to become "eunuchs" like Ruth Stubb's first love, Carl Cook. Bit by bit, the dictations drifted away from Rulon's predilections for whispering in Warren's ear or showing up in the kitchen after breakfast. Less and less often did Warren feel it necessary to insist he was entwined with Fred Jessop.

Everyone should have seen it coming, but Short Creek was still in shock when, in 2003, Warren Jeffs declared himself prophet. After all the drama, the event was startlingly simple. Warren merely had his brother make the ordination, with Jessop and Nielsen standing up as witnesses. Now Warren would repay every slight, snicker, and doubt with vengeful interest.

Stunned Short Creek residents chose to view the ordination as just another of the FLDS "tests" imposed by God nearly every day—tests that are often a sort of heavenly trick in which the Lord makes you think something bad is happening when it really isn't, just to see how you'll react. The daily test concept is a handy tool for FLDS power brokers. If they take your home and children, it's a test to see if you'll rebel and cry "No!" If you pass the test with a dutiful acceptance of the verdict and they still fail to return your home and children, that's a test too, and so forth and so on. The test concept means that anything can be done to an FLDS member and he or she must accept it without a word or the test is failed and salvation lost forever.

And now the tests came fast and furious. Warren had already pulled all children from school. Now he ended all meetings, religious or otherwise. No point in allowing people any opportunity to congregate and commiserate. Warren ordered a treasured monument to the 1953 raid bearing Leroy Johnson's name not just destroyed but pulverized, the powder scattered in the mountains. Jeffs had been annoyed that the monument was erected while he was out of town, scouting for properties to which he would relocate with only his chosen people, abandoning the folks who would actually enjoy the memorial monument.

Jeffs was out of town more than he was in, and even when he was in Short Creek, he made no public appearances. By 2004, most of the membership now confined to their jobs and homes had not seen Jeffs for years, but Jeffs had certainly seen *them*. He had taken to driving around town incognito, slumped in a backseat wearing sunglasses and a hat, to confirm what he already suspected. The town was full of evildoers and assassins who resorted to such wickedness as putting on plays in their unkempt backyards, laughing a lot, and singing songs that weren't about Warren or God. As further evidence of God's dissatisfaction with this Gomorrah, the cops and process servers were starting to crawl all over the place. Mohave County attorney Matt Smith was nosing around the underage sex thing, an Arizona newspaper called *New Times* was relentlessly running child sex and welfare fraud stories, and there was talk of civil lawsuits in the air.

But the most devastating blows came from Mark Shurtleff, his polygamy investigators, and the Rod Holm conviction in August 2003.* If Shurtleff could reach into Short Creek and pluck out an FLDS policeman, what else might be possible? The trumpeters were circling the city, and the walls were falling. Warren knew he could not withstand the kind of legal scrutiny he saw coming his way, especially not with the unreliable support he perceived from certain elements in his flock. Like Brigham Young, Warren knew when it was time to hit the road, building Zion in a less-traveled venue, preferably one where no one had ever heard of FLDS.

In the summer of 2003, the wily Warren camouflaged his dictations so that not even his "scribes" would know he'd made the stunning decision to abandon the FLDS homeland, buying at least a half-dozen remote properties of around two thousand acres in mostly underpopulated Western states. In his dictations, Warren explained, "By August 10, our meetings were stopped. But from that time forth, the Lord directed me to start traveling throughout the United States, naming to me places to go. . . . And He directed me to purchase lands in scattered places against the time when the faithful of His people would be driven. . . . I yearned unto the Lord what this was all about, because our people continued in Short Creek."

---

* After Holm's conviction, Warren Jeffs abandoned the man who'd put his freedom on the line for FLDS, denying legal expenses for Holm's appeal.

· But the only knowledge Warren was yearning for was a method to finance the Nauvoo-style city-state he intended to build for himself in one of those locations, and he didn't yearn for long. As president of FLDS, Warren began surreptitiously and illegally selling off millions in UEP land out from under an unsuspecting FLDS membership. In a few years, the sect would scream bloody murder when Shurtleff assumed temporary control of UEP to prevent the sell-offs, howling that the government was interfering with religiously sacred lands and homesteads that would have assuredly been lost had Jeffs been left unfettered. FLDS members refused to believe that Jeffs's intention was to abandon most of them to abject poverty after he'd liquidated their homes. But first, he delivered a kick to the Short Creek gut so savage it actually made the mainstream press.

On January 10, 2004, Warren Jeffs evicted twenty-one FLDS men with families from their homes and lives in front of thousands of their lifelong neighbors, friends, and relatives who didn't utter a peep of protest. One eyewitness later wrote that you could have heard a pin drop in the cavernous meeting hall as the stunned men were ordered to rise for their concocted public eviscerations. The mass public sentencing was a Neroesque declaration of absolute power by Warren, who'd heretofore poofed men on the down-low, hustling them from their homes after dark when no one was about, leaving it to everyone's imaginations to where, or why, they'd disappeared.

The cruel blow to the community in broad daylight affected dozens of women and hundreds of children. Efficient goon squads at the ready escorted the disgraced men from the meetinghouse to the highway with only the shirts on their backs. Returning to town, the squads fanned out to strip the homes the men had built themselves of all furnishings, silverware, drapes—whatever wasn't nailed down. Women who did not dare to weep toted pathetic garbage bags with the meager clothing they were allowed to keep as their dishes, Crock-Pots, sofas, and sheets they'd embroidered were carted off for Warren's chosen recipients, as were the women themselves. Piled into vans, they were driven away in a state of shock, reassigned by dinnertime for sex with strange men who may or may not have known their names. Their biological children went with them, ripped from full- and half-blooded brothers and sisters to be replaced by a brood of their new father's children, who regarded them with suspicion and scorn. Their mothers strained against the embrace of a man they and their children did not know but whose name they must all assume, a man the children must call

"Father" now that they would never see or even speak their former, excommunicated father's name again.

"Think of the unspeakable trauma," pleaded an anguished Dan Fischer, his face drawn and grim. "These children don't know they're in a cult run by vicious, power-hungry men. They love their fathers like every child loves their father, and then he is gone. Their family is gone. Their mothers are crying, and they can't help. Warren reassigned some of these girls and their children three and four times. The kids changed names so often they didn't even know who they were after a while. Hundreds and hundreds of children who weren't sure of their own names."

For Warren, however, the trauma of others seemed to be a pleasurable experience—fitting proof of his power. On a reassignment subsequent to the January 10 massacre, the prophet decided to "release" four of one woman's eight children from her sight forever, sending them to a more deserving family in another state where, he assured her, she would never see them again. Upon hearing this, the woman collapsed, crumbling to Warren's feet in a momentary loss of consciousness. Unmoved, Warren allowed no one to check the woman's condition, seemingly irked by the delay as he waited for her to come to. When she did, sobbing and groveling on the ground at Warren's feet, the prophet noted with smug superiority that the reaction was the right one for a woman standing in judgment of his perfect knowledge. After the whimpering children had been removed, Warren walked off, leaving the woman face down in the dirt.

With the sinful Short Creek shaking in fear and Mark Shurtleff's investigators in the vicinity, Warren decided it was a good time for a road trip. His first destination was Jackson County, Missouri. Having been evicted from several states, Joseph Smith no doubt thought he'd reached a permanent landing zone when he ended up in Jackson County in 1837, promptly declaring the area to be the original site of Eden and the place where the Saints would live for one thousand years with Jesus after they'd wiped out the world. Since Smith was evicted from Missouri the following year, the logistics of fulfilling Smith's proclamation has been a headache for devout Mormons, fundamentalist or not, ever since. But Warren was certain God would give him a plan for getting back there if he arrived in person.

Warren also wanted advice on temple building. Smith had declared the great Mormon temple would be built before he and Jesus returned, so Warren wanted to know where, exactly, and with what materials. God needed to show him where the marble was, for instance. Taking his scribe,

Naomie, and several carloads of bodyguards and attendants, Warren set out for Missouri. His intention was to get the architectural plans and then build a practice temple in his new "land of refuge." That way, his workers would already know what to do when Armageddon happened and they all moved back to Jackson County.

As he fretted about the location of a marble rock quarry, Warren was oblivious to the storm gathering around his arrogant miscalculations. Brent Jeffs and six other lost boys were no longer afraid of Warren Jeffs. The boys no longer believed they—or anyone else in Short Creek—deserved their banishments. They'd been directed to Roger Hoole, who'd drawn up two lawsuits to be filed in Utah's Third District Court. Following Ruth's example, a fourteen-year-old girl Warren had forced into marriage with her detested first cousin had also successfully escaped Short Creek. In another year, she'd be signing her own lawsuit in Roger Hoole's office.

But perhaps the worst miscalculations overall were Warren's site selection for the new Zion and his decision to lie to the sparsely populated county in which "land of refuge R17" was located. "R17" was the designation Warren gave to the property he'd purchased outside Eldorado in Schleicher County, Texas. His agent, David Allred, told county authorities that R17 would be a hunting lodge for wealthy corporate clients. Warren wasn't much worried about the three thousand local residents, whom he judged to be hillbilly yokels he would soon have outnumbered three to one. But when the "yokels" discovered the subterfuge, they were not amused. Down Texas way, folks don't typically wait fifty years before they arrest people for marrying little girls.

10

TEXAS AT BAT

I have frequently told you, and I will tell you again that the very report of the Church and kingdom of God on Earth is a terror to all nations, wheresoever the sound thereof goeth. The sound of "Mormonism" is a terror to towns, counties, states, the pretended republican governments and to all of the world.
        —Brigham Young, *Journal of Discourses*, Vol. 4, August 31, 1856

The ordinances of the Priesthood are being given. The ordinances will not be restored in Short Creek. The meetings will not be restored in Short Creek. But that work continues among the obedient on the lands of refuge [Texas, Colorado, Idaho]. For oneness to exist, there must be oneness in training. And before you can join the laborers, then you must listen to all the trainings. . . . Will you abide these truths, dear brethren?

RESPONSE: *"Yes, sir."*
        —Warren Jeffs, from typed dictations marked "Copyright 2005 by Warren Jeffs"

For a lot of people in Eldorado, Texas, there was something just not right about David Allred. They didn't hold the guy's vacant personality against him—perhaps he was born with that—but there was something just *furtive* about the man, and what Allred was representing about some seventeen hundred acres of land he'd purchased near the town wasn't adding up.

With its rugged but close-knit population of about eighteen hundred, Eldorado is primarily a ranching and agricultural community with a live-and-let-live streak, unless someone's idea of living breaks laws and spooks the livestock. During his brief stay in town, Allred assured prominent Eldoradoans that the purchased property would become a hunting lodge for corporate fat cats, primarily from Las Vegas, and that sounded fine. Many Schleicher County residents were themselves hunters of the plentiful game in the gently rolling Texas hills. Something as benign as a hunting lodge might even benefit the local economy in some way. The problem was, a lot of Eldoradoans harbored suspicions that Allred's "lodge" wasn't anything near benign.

Ranchers are also businessmen, and businessmen in the oceanic Texas backcountry sometimes use private aircraft to get around, aircraft that passed directly over the lodge property to reach the noncommercial county airport. What the pilots saw from the air didn't look like any hunting lodge they knew about. The pilots saw an anthill of workers of unknown origin erecting three large, two- to three-story hotel-sized buildings at least twenty thousand square feet each, any one of which could have housed two hunting lodges, even in Texas. What upsetting explanation for these buildings justified the fact that Allred paved a highway of inept cover lies right off the bat?

The first spot of trouble appeared on February 26, 2004, when Texas Parks and Wildlife game warden Marco Alvizo entered the property to investigate illegal hunting complaints. Alvizo's lawman radar was activated by the evasive manner and strange clothing of Hildale, Utah, resident William Benjamin Johnson, who was ticketed for hunting without a license. Johnson had trouble with eye contact and his responses to routine questions were needlessly vague, as if he were hiding something . . . but what? Johnson didn't strike Alvizo as anything close to a Las Vegas corporate dandy, but his plain, almost nineteenth-century clothing and evasive manner made him just as alien here. However, bagging a deer without a license wasn't exactly a hair-raising offense in this part of the world. Alvizo withdrew, and Johnson paid his $253 fine promptly and without complaint.

But given the tense speculation about Allred's true intentions, the eerie Alvizo/Johnson encounter interested Eldorado residents, some of whom thought they'd connected some dots when they happened to see a television news show a few days later. On March 4, ABC's *Primetime* aired an interview with anti-FLDS activist Flora Jessop, who had escaped the sect eighteen years earlier and was now dedicated to rescuing other FLDS girls, helping them escape Short Creek via a network of volunteers known as the Colorado City Underground Railroad. The eccentric, some would say wild, Jessop, a vociferous FLDS critic well known to Utah's news media, told a harrowing tale of a cultlike religious group ruled by a mad prophet who used young girls as currency to reward loyal followers and threw young men out of town. Although the program didn't mention anything about Texas, the Eldorado residents were convinced there was a connection between what Jessop described and their new, lying-like-dogs neighbors, so much so that they contacted Flora Jessop themselves, directing her to town leader and intrepid newspaperman, *Eldorado Success* publisher Randy Mankin.

When Warren Jeffs chose to escape Mark Shurtleff to underpopulated Schleicher County, he undoubtedly didn't expect to find somebody like Randy Mankin and his wife, Kathy, in the wilds of Texas, running a newspaper with the steely-eyed commitment of any *New York Times* publisher. Confident, tenacious, and, unfortunately for Warren, a gifted researcher, the stout Mankin did not much care for unsolved mysteries in his town, especially not those produced by furtive strangers who might be members of a dark cult fixated on underage girls. Putting what he already knew together with what Jessop told him, Mankin hit the bricks. Internet, court records, public records, phone calls—there was an avalanche of information on this FLDS, but Randy couldn't even get their lawyer and spokesman, Rod Parker, to return a phone call to answer a few simple questions. Randy didn't want to go to press without firm confirmation that the "lodge" builders were actually members of a Utah sect fleeing prosecution, but he was personally convinced when all of the phone numbers provided by David Allred on state recording documents and on Allred's own, heavily distributed DAVE'S BUILDERS business cards turned out to be out of service.

Well aware of how poorly his constituents might receive news of a child-marrying cult with a self-proclaimed prophet in their midst, Randy's friend and next-door neighbor, Schleicher County sheriff David Doran, downplayed the developments with a police officer's circumspection, reminding Mankin they had no evidence of either lawbreaking or an FLDS connection. Randy sympathized, but whereas Doran was solemnly sworn to protect the public, Randy had taken an oath to inform them, and that's what he intended to do. On March 25, 2004, with the headline "Corporate Retreat or Prophet's Refuge?" Mankin published the first of hundreds of scrupulously researched stories about FLDS, its complete history going back to Joseph Smith and John Taylor, its current legal problems in Utah and Arizona, and the Rod Holm conviction that prompted a shell-shocked Jeffs to flee Utah and build a city of polygamists in their backyard. Randy and Kathy Mankin would become authorities on FLDS and everyone in it, making numerous trips to Short Creek for the relentless coverage that would become the Texas equivalent of the teetering boulder the Rod Holm case had crowbarred over the mountaintop in Utah.

In the weeks after the *Eldorado Success* published its first story, UPS trucks streamed into the Texas community delivering Internet-ordered FLDS-related books and videos to residents appalled by what they learned. They determined that David Allred was one of many sons-in-law of a man named Warren Jeffs, who said he was the prophet of God for a large group of fundamentalist Mormons on the Utah/Arizona border who married little girls off to old men on Jeffs's say-so. Though the sect controlled tens of millions of dollars, the tribal-sized families survived by collecting *welfare*, a word that could curdle milk in Texas. They ran their own country with *tax-supported* institutions and jobs, another Texas skin crawler.*

This FLDS was audacious, in your face with religious persecution charges if anyone breathed on them, which as far as Randy Mankin could tell, nobody did. Furthermore, a major sect tenet was racism, and the man they worshipped as a prophet was beyond bizarre. On the *Success* website, Mankin posted audio of Warren Jeffs droning on and on about things like how the Beatles were agents of the evil black race—"niggers" as Jeffs called them—out to destroy the world. John, Paul, Ringo, and George, Jeffs intoned, were delivering satanic organizational messages through their music.

It took Randy's breath away, as did the sect's next delusional move. In mid-April, FLDS resurrected the elusive David Allred to make the rounds in Schleicher County, insisting to incredulous town leaders that no matter what it looked like, the property was indeed a corporate retreat hunting lodge. The three 21,600-square-foot structures under construction, Allred explained, were intended to house the guests of the guests, or something like that. But in an apparently improvised afterthought, Allred added that, yeah, some heretofore undiscussed families might move permanently into the corporate hunting lodge for Las Vegas captains of industry. If these families did move there, Allred advised, they would only want to be let alone to practice their beliefs. As Brigham Young would say, the cat was out of the bag, whereupon a wearily resigned Sheriff Doran felt obliged to inform Allred of the Texas statutes regarding bigamy and child rape.

It still took a week after this little PR disaster for FLDS attorney Rod Parker to confirm that the property recorded as owned by YFZ Land LLC, was not, in

---

* When Jeffs began moving men to Eldorado, he told a small group that "monies were not in place in the land of refuge." He meant that because FLDS had not gained control of city governments as it had in Short Creek, welfare and other tax-based revenue, such as police and teacher salaries, were not yet available. Almost as soon as the FLDS connection became known, Texas legislators publicly and angrily vowed they would not tolerate a welfare city-state like Short Creek. This combination of factors discouraged the FLDS Texas transplants from obtaining welfare as they had in other states. At the end of 2010, it was unknown if any FLDS members in Texas were on the welfare rolls.

fact, a hunting lodge but "clearly connected" to FLDS. Based on the title of a Jeffs-composed song that Mankin had discovered online, he deduced that YFZ meant "Yearning for Zion." In media reports, Parker refused further details, except to reconfirm with perplexing laissez-faire that his clients were "committed" to the illegal practice of polygamy. "Polygamy is the bedrock of their faith," Parker informed Mankin, as if that settled everything.

The tin ears of polygamists and polygamy sympathizers past and present were again evident just a week after that when David Allred blithely abandoned the lodge story as if it had never happened. When the unrepentant Allred opined that FLDS wanted to be "proactive" about informing authorities of its intentions, the hearts of Eldorado leaders were as cold as those of the bamboozled U.S. senators trying to strangle straight answers from LDS leaders about "the principle" at the turn of the century. Highlighting FLDS's difficulties conceptualizing real time, Allred gave an annoyed Doran only a few hours to gather officials for a take-it-or-leave-it meeting to which the sheriff wanted plenty of witnesses. Allred now informed the officials Doran was able to grab on short notice that they could expect two hundred FLDS members to inhabit the now five hotel-sized buildings under construction. Responding to certain concerns raised by unpleasant news articles in the *Success* (and apparently unaware that Mankin verified his reporting with public records), a pious Allred denied that FLDS members subsisted on welfare. Furthermore, whereas some underage marriages may have unfortunately transpired in the distant past, modern sect members condemn the practice as rigorously as anyone else.*

"I guess they figured we were a whole lot dumber than we looked," says Mankin dryly, who was well acquainted with, among other things, the officer Rod Holm and Ruth Stubbs underage marriage/custody case in St. George. Randy Mankin's trips to Short Creek earned him ongoing relationships with excommunicated FLDS members—some ousted in the infamous mass destruction of families in 2004. Educated about the "lying for the Lord" and "bleeding the beast" FLDS mantras, Mankin learned that when Allred said two hundred folks would be coming, he meant two hundred *men*. Because these were Warren Jeffs's favored men, all would have at least three, and some more than twenty, wives kept continuously pregnant.

---

*   At the time Allred made these representations, Warren Jeffs was presiding over carnivals of underage marriages—as many as eighteen per night in cheap hotel rooms from Flagstaff, Arizona, to Mesquite, Nevada. Dozens of marriages, many of them underage, were conducted at the YFZ ranch.

Depending on the number of men Warren Jeffs eventually intended to favor, the actual number of FLDS members Texas could expect to receive over time might number well into the thousands.

It was a sobering proposition. There were only three thousand people in the entire county that would be overwhelmed by substantial welfare claims, but darker than that was the worry that had nettled Joseph Smith's neighbors more than a century earlier. A large population at the FLDS property meant a voting block that could decide elections. With enough people, FLDS could elect its own officials, take over the county, and turn Eldorado into Short Creek. At their "proactive" meeting with FLDS, Doran did not beat around the bush, bluntly asking Allred if FLDS would use the vote as a club. Allred's answer was a tad on the insidious side. While such secular scheming was beneath them as a rule, Allred said, FLDS members would certainly *register* to exercise their rights as citizens—citizens who happened to agree on just about everything.

As tensions mounted, Doran urged calm on his jittery constituents infuriated by the sect's initial prevarications. No matter how disagreeable Eldoradoans might find FLDS's religious tenets, Doran said, they had broken no laws anyone could prove. In interviews and press conferences, Doran insisted there would be no violations of anyone's civil rights on his watch, a stance that brought a peculiar response from Washington County, Utah, sheriff Kirk Smith, who ostensibly had authority over the FLDS stronghold in Short Creek but had never prosecuted anyone.

Saying he wished to "support" the Texas sheriff's uphill battle for civility, Smith traveled to Eldorado for a town hall meeting with civic leaders, including Randy Mankin, at which he seemed to imply the best way of handling FLDS was to let them alone. Smith proudly told perplexed Eldoradoans he'd been a law enforcement officer with jurisdiction over the FLDS community for thirty-four years without making any significant arrests, a boast for which the Texans had trouble locating merit. Smith assured the Texans that FLDS folk were hardworking, law-abiding, family-values good neighbors whose problems with underage sex were no worse than society's as a whole, a premise met with polite frowns. Were they all still talking about illegal polygamy, child rape, and welfare fraud, or had Smith wandered off into the brush of another subject? "It's all about becoming educated about the group," a diplomatically evasive Doran said of the Smith meeting after the Utah police officer left town. The Texans were certain of one thing. They figured their own educations wouldn't take thirty-four years.

In addition to the bottomless credibility chasm created with the lodge ruse, FLDS leaders could not seem to comprehend the reality that private aircraft flying over the YFZ property could independently assess the veracity of diminutive population and land use claims. Having been so long and blissfully accustomed to deferential invisibility of the sort Kirk Smith had implied his Texas counterparts should adopt, FLDS leaders also might not have considered the prospect that veiled threats upon the jobs of elected officials might backfire, as it did with Jimmy Dan Doyle. J.D., as he was called, owned a Piper Cherokee aircraft he now put to use photographically documenting the actual construction on the FLDS property. Randy published photographs showing large-scale construction that looked to include factories and wastewater treatment facilities as well as large living structures, six intersecting streets, and agricultural areas.

Because FLDS owned everything in Short Creek—water, electricity, waste management—Warren Jeffs may have forgotten about the pesky state regulations of those services, although insiders say that is unlikely. "FLDS does construction work all over the country," advises Roger Hoole. "They have expert understanding of permits and paperwork. They just thought, as usual, that they were above the law and no one would hold them to account. After all, they're usually right about that."

Not this time. A month after game warden Alvizo issued his citation to William Johnson for hunting without a license, unsympathetic investigators for the Texas Commission on Environmental Quality paid a visit to the lodge property with their own ticket books at the ready, informing FLDS leaders that their inadequate generators violated air quality standards with offensive emissions sufficient to shut them down, that the septic tank system was also deficient, and that no permit had been secured for construction related to storm water drainage or the astounding cement factory operating full steam.

Nobody knew it yet, but besides Naomie, the cement factory was the most important thing in Warren Jeffs's life. According to his dictations, Warren was in reception of divine revelations from a God on the brink of providing him a supernatural recipe for concrete that would last into perpetuity. Warren believed government agents from around the globe were stalking him in the hopes of discovering the magical formula God was releasing specifically for temple construction in Texas and, eventually, Jackson County, Missouri. There would literally be hell to pay if the formula got out and wicked governments used it to build indestructible buildings. For

Warren Jeffs, the light planes overhead were not ranchers looking after their business interests but high-tech government spy planes seeking his concrete concoction. So paranoid was he about the cement, he excommunicated at least three men he suspected of blabbing about the ingredients God had disclosed thus far, reassigning their wives and changing the names of their children while instructing them never to mention the men's names again.

Warren Jeffs might have preferred to concentrate on the cement issue, but his construction workers were driving him crazy. The crews FLDS sent around the country on numerous valuable construction contracts couldn't do anything right in Jeffs's eyes, and they certainly weren't getting it done fast enough. Once Warren decided to abandon Short Creek and its "half-hearted" residents, he found he couldn't stand being there, especially after people began deducing that they were being "pruned" from the pure FLDS flock. Only the pure would be selected to live in Texas and achieve an after-life of planetary rule, as Warren had declared Short Creek to be abandoned by God. All Short Creekers were anguished and terrified, watching Warren's every move for a sign they and their families would be moved to YFZ and saved from imminent slaughter and the eternal licking flames of hell.

Their agony was a nuisance for Warren, who was forced to avoid atten-tion by sneaking in and out of town in disguises as he traveled erratically between Texas, as-yet-unknown FLDS compounds in Colorado and Idaho, and Short Creek, conducting marriage sprees in rundown hotels along the way. The marriages came to Jeffs in dreams sent by God, who might reveal the intended unions of twelve to eighteen mostly underage girls at a pop. Typically, Jeffs would have someone phone the girls' families, instructing them to leave immediately for a state, say Colorado. It might be the middle of the night, but the families would scramble into their cars, waiting for radio instructions as to specific hotel destinations. After driving for six, eigh-teen, or thirty hours over specified circuitous routes designed to confuse government spies, the families might drive around a destination city aim-lessly for another three or four hours—no revealing public bathroom stops allowed—until Warren was moved to illuminate their final location.

At one, two, five A.M., as many as eighteen bleary-eyed, bedraggled, food- and sleep-deprived girls as young as twelve years old would be herded into cheesy hotel rooms with some clumsy pink construction paper or cutout hearts slapped on the walls, handed over to men they'd never seen before in their lives. Warren Jeffs ran them through the sealings and then sent them to a room next door to be, quite often, forcibly raped.

Bill Walker's co-counsel in the Ruth Stubbs case and former Utah attorney general Jan Graham once observed in a voice shuddering with disgust, "The older FLDS men in particular are addicted to rape. You have a young girl who has never disrobed before *anyone*, and now a man old enough to be her grandfather is taking off her clothes." Graham paused nearly a full minute before continuing with halting disgust, almost against her will. "The girl is often shaking and crying. She might be pleading for time or a reprieve. Quite simply, the men develop a taste for it—for the power—and like any addiction, it needs feeding. They want more and more girls, younger and younger girls."

FLDS was still committed to the lodge story in November 2003 when Warren Jeffs recorded his own ruminations on the matter of young girls demonstrating one thing for certain: he knew exactly what he was doing. "The Lord is showing me the young girls of this community, those who are pure and righteous will be taken care of at a younger age. *As the government finds out about this*, it will bring great pressure upon us. . . . And I will teach the young people that *there is no such thing as an underage Priesthood marriage. . . .* The Lord will have me do this, *get more young girls married, not only as a test to the parents, but also to test this people to see if they will give the Prophet up.*" [Emphasis added.]

The snapping frenzy to secure young girls from a limited pool was reaching 1856 Mormon Reformation levels. Warren Jeffs's mercurial schedule seems to have been influenced by dramatic new evidence of his prophethood: the heavenly sessions. At first, Warren thought Naomie's "testimonials" would be sufficient proof of these events, in which Warren would usually be lying on his bed when he was "called away" by the Lord, sometimes for hours, usually in the deserted, wee hours of the morning. To the mere mortal Naomie, the sessions would deceptively look as if Warren Jeffs were doing a lot of uncontrollable shaking, shuddering, and writhing on the bed or chair, accompanied by frequently unintelligible verbal revelations.*

---

* Warren Jeffs eventually decided he needed more witnesses to prove his heavenly sessions existed but was frustrated when numerous wives he "trained" to help him through the agony the way Naomie did failed to see the things Naomie saw. Exasperated, Jeffs tried to train Naomie's younger sister, Ida (whom he would also marry), to record the gymnastic sessions, but he became angry when the girl consistently fell asleep during all the thrashing, physical travails. This was, at least, the reason Jeffs offered for Ida's failure to "witness" the sessions, but it's difficult to swallow given the fact that the girl was lying right next to Jeffs as he allegedly levitated with visible angels or writhed uncontrollably with physical punishment. It seems more reasonable that both Ida and Jeffs fell asleep, but in the end, Naomie remained the only person Warren could trust to see things his way.

According to Jeffs, the prophet was experiencing the "all-consuming fire from heaven," having been spiritually transported to a divine dimension for lively interactions with the Lord or his representatives who were not always in the best of moods. The inadequate religious purity and poor construction schedules of the FLDS membership were generally the source of the trouble, and Warren was menaced by flaming sword–wielding angels more than once. Luckily, the Lord would accept a Christlike atonement from the Christlike Jeffs. Like Jesus, Jeffs could suffer intense physical pain courtesy of the Lord to gain forgiveness for his followers, and so the heavenly sessions were sometimes more like a Godly torture.

FLDS prophets have always relied upon the divine source of their revelations to engage terror and shut down dissent, but the heavenly sessions were fine-tuned genius. Because Warren Jeffs claimed he was unconscious during most of his heavenly sessions, the events became an invaluable tool for further terrorizing FLDS members without being tagged personally for the new agonies he was about to impose. The edicts, after all, didn't come *from* Warren but *through* him and without his knowledge. Without his faithful scribe Naomie, Warren wouldn't even remember the terrible directives, so how could he be blamed for their devastating results? Although Jeffs never stated that Short Creek was condemned, he might as well have blared it from a bullhorn when he began using "removal" to the old homeland as a punishment, while assignment to YFZ meant salvation.

A man who didn't meet Jeffs's impossible construction deadlines might be removed to Short Creek, a terrifying disgrace. In turn, the lives of people left in Short Creek were creased with the hourly fear that they would not be removed to YFZ for salvation and the planetary afterlife. On top of that, Jeffs began reassigning homes on a whim, ordering families out of one and into another in a sinister shell game that moved families of sixty from adequate housing into a disintegrating trailer overnight. Warren Jeffs didn't need designated spies anymore. Neighbor informed against neighbor, brother against brother, in attempts to torpedo someone, anyone, and take their seat at the YFZ table. The already precarious daily life in Short Creek became an affair of gross uncertainty permeated with crippling angst with all eyes on the shifting moods of Warren Jeffs.

It was a good vise, but that tool is meant to be tightened. As Randy Mankin tried to get a handle on the FLDS population Eldorado might expect, Warren intensified his dog breeder approach to razing FLDS families, mixing and matching stunned individuals according to "worthy" or "unworthy" bloodlines, "handling" more males as he reassigned dozens of women and hundreds of their emotionally damaged children like a pimp. To this tried-and-true terror tool Warren added another ingenious twist: he began separating families *within* families. Women fainted when a smug Jeffs presided over the removal of half of their tearful children from the home, sending them from Short Creek to YFZ and vice versa, with Warren's declaration that the women would never see them again, in this world or the next.*

The destruction of families and the mass shufflings between Utah and Texas were so severe that Randy Mankin noticed the upheaval from outside the gated compound, commenting on the erratic FLDS population in the "Meanwhile, Back at the Ranch" footnotes concluding some YFZ news stories. Randy, as well as Sheriff Doran, had been notified of a more ominous population change as well. A missing persons report had been filed for ninety-four-year-old FLDS elder statesman Fred Jessop. The notice had of course been filed by FLDS apostates, but apparently the elderly man with the tepid testimonials so irksome to Warren Jeff hadn't been seen or heard from in a year.

As Randy tried to discover who had been cashing Jessop's social security checks, and where and how, he marveled again that it had ever come to this. The failure of Utah authorities to act against a sect with staggering disregard for laws might —might—be understood through historical religious ties, but what was the excuse in Arizona, where the majority of Short Creekers resided? Was the fallout from one lousy raid in the rearview mirror for a half century really worth the lives of countless young girls and boys alike, not to mention the millions Arizona spent on welfare and a city government answering to a "prophet"? Soon, the whole country would be waiting for that answer.

---

* Based in part on the frequency with which he appeared in person for these separations, Warren Jeffs seemed to enjoy the process of taking children from their mothers, more so perhaps because he was able to lambast the women for whatever reaction they displayed. Mothers whose children were going to YFZ were supposed to be rejoicing that they were saved, even if the mother and other siblings weren't. Women whose children were sent to Short Creek were supposed to be rejoicing they'd been relieved of devil spawn. The women received a tongue-lashing and were told they were "selfish" if they expressed any reaction short of joy to losing their children.

11

ARIZONA AT BAT, AGAIN

The Lord is building up Zion and is emptying the earth of wickedness, gathering his people, bringing again Zion, redeeming his Israel, sending forth his work, withdrawing his Spirit from the wicked world and commencing to build up his kingdom. Can this be done without revelation? No. You will not make a move, or do anything—plant corn, build a hall or temple, make a farm or go to the States— no, not a thing toward building up Zion without the power of revelation.
      —Brigham Young, *Journal of Discourses, Vol. 9,* July 28, 1861

I then had the impression to go north toward Chicago and in making our reservations we ended up in a town that was the suburb of Chicago, Warrenville. I was entertained by that. [In a heavenly session God said] *Chicago, and that area will be destroyed by fire, earthquake, and water sitting right along the Great Lake, Lake Michigan.*
      —Warren Jeffs, "Record of President Warren Jeffs," June 9, 2004

O ne of the Arizonans jolted into action after the Ruth Stubbs case was pugnacious Phoenix *New Times* investigative reporter John Dougherty, whose unforgiving FLDS exposés might have provoked then Arizona governor Janet Napolitano to wonder if the publicity following the 1953 raid was really all that bad. Dougherty had written about FLDS prior to Utah's prosecution of Rod Holm, but in March 2003, *New Times* declared war on the sect and the current Secretary of Homeland Security with a seventeen-thousand-word opus, the result of a five-month investigation into FLDS in Colorado City headlined: "Bound by Fear: Polygamy in Arizona. For Decades the State Has Let a Feudal Colony of Fundamentalist Mormons Force Underage Girls into Illegal Polygamous Marriages."

    The article was the start of a six-year hammering. Week after week, year after year, Dougherty and *New Times* punished Arizona legislators with eye-popping accounts of FLDS bad behavior they'd studiously ignored since the 1953 raid. Special cattle prodding was directed at Napolitano,

who'd served as Arizona attorney general before her successful gubernatorial election in 2002. A half century of willful blindness had given the
paper a lot of juice for the barbed jolts Napolitano didn't feel she deserved.
Though Napolitano had been the first to send investigators into the Ruth
Stubbs fray, the assignments had not received the fanfare Mark Shurtleff
generated after sending "polygamy czar" Ron Barton to interview Ruth
Stubbs. Mohave County attorney Matt Smith was indicting FLDS men,
again without much publicity.

The Arizona Attorney General's Office may have despised Dougherty
and *New Times*, but it could be argued that their bitterness was misdirected
and their real beef lay with the rest of Arizona's mainstream media. With
the exception of Dougherty and Mike Watkiss, who'd first aired the Ruth
Stubbs interviews, the entire Arizona press corps cleaved to tried-and-true,
post-'53 raid policy of pretending Colorado City didn't exist, not even in
a sunny *National Geographic* kind of way. The *Arizona Republic*, the state's
paper of record, seemed bored by Dougherty and Watkiss's continuing coverage, including Dougherty's shocking documentation of welfare
fraud and Watkiss's groundbreaking series on Flora Jessop's Colorado City
Underground Railroad. The series documenting volunteers helping young
girls escape FLDS went viral on the Web but was apparently too dull for
Arizona's journalists. Addressing the absence of FLDS press coverage in
Arizona, Watkiss nearly shouted, "It's too *hard* to cover these *complicated*
stories," in a tone dripping with angry sarcasm.

When Arizonans learned that one of their tax-paid policemen was
"marrying" and impregnating sixteen-year-old girls, the seismic shock was
amplified by the fact that the public had no context for FLDS and had largely
been unaware of its existence—this in a state which arguably had bigger
problems with FLDS than Mormon Utah. Most of Short Creek's residents,
as well as most of the public buildings, were located on the Arizona side of
town, which meant Arizona was on the hook for most of the welfare paid
to families and tax-salaried jobs in city government, police departments,
and schools. Arizona paid millions to construction firms to put up public
buildings and then suffered the further indignity of paying FLDS tens of
thousands annually in rent because the buildings were situated on FLDS
lands in the UEP trust. In turn, the public buildings and all of the associated
supplies, such as expensive phone and computer systems, were converted
for the exclusive use of FLDS to promote its business interests and escalate
a frenzy to get every underage girl in the community pregnant.

It should have been an intolerable racket, made sickening by both the human and financial tolls. More than 80 percent of FLDS members were on some kind of welfare. Including state and federal food stamps, Medicaid, aid to dependent children and other family welfare programs, and state and county services and jobs, Short Creek raked in approximately $33 million tax dollars a year for around seven thousand residents, including an estimated $15 million to run the combined Short Creek city governments. Under Rulon Jeffs, the sect learned to tap the federal grant market as well. The tiny Colorado City Fire Department received the third largest Homeland Security grant in the state to stave off terrorists—$350,000. Before the *Salt Lake Tribune* began defending FLDS, it printed an exposé titled "Polygamy on the Dole," revealing that Colorado City raked in $1.8 million from the Department of Housing and Urban Development to pave streets (Hildale got $94,000) and $2.8 million to build an airport used only by the Jeffs, ostensibly to promote tourism in a community that believes outsiders are trying to kill them. The list of federal and state grants of $100,000 and up is long, and it all goes into FLDS bank accounts one way or another.

Using welfare to support exploding families polygamists could otherwise not afford was a solution as old as FLDS itself. At the turn of the century, non-Mormon Arizona cattlemen, angry that their grazing fees were being used to shore up a religion they abhorred, staged protests of near riot proportions. Despite later backpedaling, angry non-Mormon Arizonans pressured governor Howard Pyle relentlessly to take action against FLDS, and non-Mormon members of a cheerleading legislature forked out an astronomical $300,000 in 1953 money to finance the infamous raid before they turned on Pyle after it backfired. However, the operative description for Arizonans opposing FLDS may be that they are not Mormons.

It is not a secret, but it's also not commonly known, that Arizona is home to one of the oldest, largest, and wealthiest Mormon populations in the country, an intensely reliable voting block that has for decades allied itself with the ultra–right wing. Mormon candidates for state office, handsomely financed by Mormon businesses, hold key committee positions in the state legislature as well as up to 20 percent of the elective seats, though Mormons comprise only between 5 and 8 percent of the total population. "They are in a position of influence way out of proportion to their numbers," observed journalist and author Jon Talton, who wrote a column for the *Arizona Republic* for seven years. "There is a revolving door between Mormon businesses and Mormon representatives with sometimes disastrous results for the state."

For illustration, Talton cites the notorious "alt fuel" legislation, which was written by the late Arizona speaker of the house Jeff Groscost's business partners and rammed through in the middle of the night as a ninety-two-page amendment to a clean air bill. Groscost, who was also a pricey natural gas industry consultant, had the idea to reimburse new, cost-is-no-object SUV and truck buyers up to 40 percent if they also installed a useless, easily disconnected propane "fuel converter" sold by his business associate Nathan Learner, who was also a car dealer.

Groscost's career was trampled in the ensuing stampede of car buyers looking for a 40 percent discount on $50,000 vehicles, but so was the state of Arizona, which lost nearly a billion dollars buying its citizens new SUVs and nearly went bankrupt before the legislature could kill Groscost's bill. Writing for Stateline.org, political journalist and former *Arizona Republic* reporter Robbie Sherwood noted: "The fiasco would easily qualify as one of the worst chapters in Arizona's political history if there weren't so many contenders for that dubious honor."*

It is understood (if not always acknowledged) that there is a political gap between the radically conservative Arizona LDS and the merely conservative LDS in Utah that may extend to attitudes about FLDS. Longtime observers of Arizona politics like Talton, himself a fourth-generation Arizonan who grew up in the heavily Mormon city of Mesa, say Arizona Mormons began aligning themselves with the Christian right decades ago, forming a big-money coalition that transformed the state's Republican Party from the party of Barry Goldwater, who plenty of people thought was radical enough, to a party the Arizona icon wouldn't recognize—one of the most extreme, corporate-backed Christian right-wing state governments in the country.

The alliance between conservative Mormons and the Christian right is surprising to say the least. Christian evangelicals do not hide their lights under bushels when attacking Mormonism, jeering at the LDS insistence it is a Christian, Protestant faith, attacking Mormonism as a sinister and dark cult. In 2008, the Christian right was warming up for an ugly campaign against possible Republican presidential nominee Mitt Romney, who avoided a messy tarring only because he failed to win a single primary. But, "you have to make a distinction between federal and state politics," advises Talton. "The corporate Christian right—the Dick Armey and Ralph

---

* Other contenders might be indicted former governors Even Meacham and Fife Symington and the Keating Five bank collapse scandal.

Reed and Heritage Foundation crowds—have been going state by state for years, and in Arizona they found an organized, reliable, substantial group of Mormons willing to put aside differences to achieve a common goal. In an election where 25 percent of the general population might vote, 90 percent of Mormons would turn out. It made all the difference."

How much further right-wing than Utah is Arizona's right wing? In addition to the immigrants-as-scapegoats legislation and worship of business and money, Republican Arizona state representative Sylvia Allen, arguing in favor of "getting the money" by allowing radioactive uranium mining in the state in 2009, enlightened her apprehensive colleagues with the observation that "the earth has been here for six thousand years, long before anyone had environmental laws, and somehow it hasn't been done away with."*

Why Republican Mormons in Arizona have swung so far right might be a matter of unchecked evolution, but one of the earliest Arizona settlement expeditions ordered by Brigham Young did originate in the ferociously devout, reformation-frenzied town of St. George, Utah, where fiery antigovernment sermons ruled the day. Mormons weren't the first settlers in Arizona, but after Mountain Meadows Massacre fugitive John D. Lee established his ferry crossing, Young sent in the Saints quickly and in greater numbers than any other group, settling the eastern portion of the state around St. Johns, Showlow, and Snowflake first, buying up most of the land that wasn't settled.** In 1877, Young dispatched Daniel Webster Jones from St. George to Arizona's center, founding the town of Mesa, which today boasts more LDS members than Salt Lake City, some 470,000 Saints, all of them reliable voters.

Mesa was the first hamlet in what is now the six-million-strong megalopolis of Phoenix, and the Arizona Saints made billions selling their oceanic land holdings off to eager developers who razed the place over the decades before the 2008 economic collapse, when Phoenix was routinely among the top five fastest-growing American cities. Fleeing the inhospitality of the

---

*   Although Allen's declaration was greeted with a smattering of laughter from the gallery, she defended her position with a spirited retort, citing religious texts as evidence of the earth's youth. Scientists were quick to point out the irony in Allen's support of uranium mining, as it is through the radioactive decay of uranium that the earth's age has been determined in the billions of years. Mormonism addresses this kind of dating and matters like the fossil record by saying that God mashed and rolled the earth together from pieces of other, much older planets, meaning the fossil record is the remains of extraterrestrials.

**   John D. Lee's descendants continue to be a force in Arizona politics. The late Mo Udall and his brother Stewart, patriarchs of a Western political dynasty, are Lee's great-grandsons.

new, hot, concrete monument to chaotic, unregulated growth for which Phoenix is known, wealthy Mormons established themselves in the more civilized environs of Chandler and Gilbert. But these towns are considered Phoenix suburbs, all located in Maricopa County. With a population dwarfing the rest of Arizona combined, Maricopa is Arizona's political powerhouse county. Pima County, anchored by the more livable and aesthetic Tucson, remains a Democratic stronghold (with strict environmental and building codes), but Talton asserts that Arizona progressives are no match for the money, organization, and sheer numbers of the Maricopa County conservatives, who have a definite view about how to handle FLDS. "They want them left alone," Talton says.

This may have been on Janet Napolitano's mind when Mike Watkiss and John Dougherty let the horses out of the barn during the Rod Holm affair. A woman with higher political ambitions than state office, Napolitano was already in trouble with powerful right-wing Mormons without doing a thing. She'd entered the stage from the center-left in 1984, when her valedictorian grades and Ninth Circuit Court of Appeals clerking experience landed her a job at the legendary Lewis and Roca law firm in Phoenix, whose founders were themselves from Arizona pioneer stock, albeit the liberal sort. Firm founder Orme Lewis served as president Dwight Eisenhower's assistant secretary of the interior and amassed one of the finest private art collections in the country, a passion the firm still pursues. In 1965, the firm took on pro bono the appeal for accused rapist Ernesto Miranda, arguing before the U.S. Supreme Court that Miranda had not been advised of his rights to have an attorney present during police questioning. On June 13, 1966, chief justice Earl Warren agreed, overturning Miranda's conviction and putting in place the Miranda warnings required today for anyone under arrest. With two hundred attorneys in four states, the renowned firm has become a nursery for future judges and politicians and has been quietly entwined with the Democratic Party for decades.

Three years after she made partner at the firm, Napolitano was tapped to join the legal team assisting law professor Anita Hill, who had accused Supreme Court nominee Clarence Thomas of making crude and unwanted sexual advances when Hill was his employee at two federal agencies.* Republican accusations that Napolitano improperly coached Hill's supporting

---

* Thomas was Hill's boss at the Department of Education and Equal Opportunity Employment Commission. He was eventually confirmed to the court by a margin of four votes.

witnesses may have endeared her to president Bill Clinton, who appointed her U.S. district attorney for Arizona in 1993, launching the quiet, diminutive, five-foot-four-inch Napolitano into politics.* In 1998, she was elected Arizona attorney general on a platform that promised better consumer protection and law enforcement capability—a far cry from addressing the underage sex and welfare fraud in Short Creek. It's a safe bet that taking a mud bath in a political hole like FLDS wasn't even a blip on Napolitano's screen, especially because she seems to have had higher office on her mind from the start. Napolitano, who endured consciousness-threatening pain to speak at the 2000 Democratic National Convention only three weeks after a mastectomy, was on the party's radar for a vice presidential slot. And no matter what, Napolitano intended to run for governor in 2002 after only one term as AG.

With the Maricopa County Mormon coalition forever biting at her electoral heels, the ambitious Napolitano needed the specters of the 1953 raid like a bullet to the brain, and she said so, though not in those terms. She didn't do so often, but when Napolitano commented publicly on FLDS, she invoked the fiery disaster at Waco, Texas, and used words like "casualties" and "armed standoffs." Napolitano admitted that, in varying degrees, FLDS met or exceeded all standardized law enforcement criteria to categorize it as a potentially violent cult along the lines of the Branch Davidians at Waco or the militia types at Ruby Ridge. However, since the 1953 raid, FLDS had coached women and children in the arts of weeping, fainting, or just looking terror-stricken when government authorities and photographers were present at the same time and place, images that didn't interest Napolitano in the least.

Napolitano said she didn't send investigators into Short Creek to look into child abuse and underage sex charges because she feared for their safety. She added that she didn't send uniformed police because she feared for their safety, too, and she also feared their presence might ignite unsightly, casualty-producing gun battles. Many found it baffling that the attorney general would deal with a clear threat to public safety by averting her eyes. Her critics saw Napolitano's anticipatory fears as paralyzing, or maybe a time-gobbling stategy, counting down to the gubernatorial election, and when the Ruth Stubbs matter broke wide open in late 2001, the Arizona attorney general was silent about what fate the state-certified peace officer

---

* Considering Clinton to be one of her mentors, Napolitano supported the president without equivocation, but her loyalties were torn between Hillary Clinton and Barack Obama in the 2008 Democratic primaries. After what could only have been a period of intense pressure, Napolitano endorsed Obama.

Sixteen-year-old Ruth Stubbs and Rodney Holm pose with Rulon Jeffs on their "wedding" day. COURTESY RUTH STUBBS

A typical FLDS family portrait. COURTESY RUTH STUBBS

Ruth Stubbs poses with her new husband and sister wives. From left, Wendy Holm, Rod Holm, Ruth, and Susie Holm. COURTESY RUTH STUBBS

Attorney Bill Walker in his Tucson office. Walker represented Ruth Stubbs pro bono, winning her custody case against police officer Rodney Holm. The attorney currently represents the ex-FLDS Cooke family pro bono in their struggle against the sect. COURTESY WILLIAM G. WALKER

Elissa Wall at age fourteen, just before Warren Jeffs ordered her to be married to a cousin she hated. COURTESY ROGER HOOLE, WITH PERMISSION

From left, attorney Roger Hoole, Elissa Wall (at age twenty-one), and her husband Lamont Barlow leave the courthouse during Warren Jeffs's rape facilitation trial, September 2007. Wall is one of the few ex-FLDS girls or women who have testified against Jeffs. COURTESY ROGER HOOLE, WITH PERMISSION

Attorney Roger Hoole, who sparked an epic FLDS legal battle in Utah, in his Salt Lake City office. Hoole brought civil suits on behalf of both Elissa Wall and the lost boys. COURTESY ROGER HOOLE

Utah attorney general Mark Shurtleff was the first Utah official to prosecute an FLDS member for underage marriage. In 2005, he assumed temporary control of the sect's $110 million land trust fund after FLDS leaders defaulted in several civil actions, raising hopes that the sect's illegal activities could be stopped. COURTESY OF THE UTAH OFFICE OF THE ATTORNEY GENERAL

Texas attorney general Greg Abbott (center) took aggressive action against FLDS after the sect began relocating to Texas. Abbott indicted twelve FLDS men for underage marriages and continues convening grand juries to look into the sect's behavior. COURTESY OF THE TEXAS OFFICE OF THE ATTORNEY GENERAL

Former Arizona attorney general Terry Goddard (speaking at right) disbanded the FLDS Colorado City Unified School District, raided FLDS fire stations for evidence of malfeasance with public funds, and joined Mark Shurtleff in taking temporary control of the sect's land trust. COURTESY TERRY GODDARD

Left: The flamboyant Willie Jessop, also known as Willie the Thug.
Right: Prosecutor Eric Nichols outside the Schleicher County Courthouse during his successful prosecution of sect member Allan Keate. Nichols has a 100 percent conviction rate for FLDS men indicted after the 2008 raid. Texas has named him special prosecutor for the remaining cases and any new ones that may be brought by ongoing grand juries. PHOTOS COURTESY KATHY AND RANDY MANKIN

Bruce Wisan (left) is interrupted by the FLDS mayor of Hildale, David Zitting, during a meeting of the United Effort Plan board of trustees in 2006. Warren Jeffs had put the homes of thousands of FLDS members in jeopardy when he ordered followers not to pay the property taxes Wisan was trying to collect. GEORGE FREY / GETTY IMAGES NEWS

Publishers of the *Eldorado Success*, Kathy and Randy Mankin were instrumental in raising alarms about FLDS throughout Texas. COURTESY KATHY AND RANDY MANKIN

FLDS-controlled utilities have denied Ron and Jinjer Cooke and their three children water and electricity for three years. While they fight the sect in federal court to gain control of a UEP home, they've been living in a tiny trailer. COURTESY RON AND JINJER COOKE

WANTED FUGITIVE

UNLAWFUL FLIGHT TO AVOID PROSECUTION - SEXUAL CONDUCT WITH A MINOR, CONSPIRACY TO COMMIT SEXUAL CONDUCT WITH A MINOR; RAPE AS AN ACCOMPLICE

WARREN STEED JEFFS

This FBI poster ended Jeffs's nearly two-year flight from justice; a Nevada highway patrolman recognized the fugitive during a routine traffic stop. GETTY IMAGES NEWS

Schleicher County sheriff David Doran (far left) and Texas Rangers escort Warren Jeffs to his jail cell. Although Jeffs fought extradition to Texas, he quickly changed his mind about the state, which allowed him to purchase phone cards and spend up to twelve hours a day talking to his supporters. COURTESY KATHY AND RANDY MANKIN

Rod Holm might expect in her state. In fact, Holm was not indicted in Arizona until he had already been convicted in Utah.

Infuriated and offended by Napolitano's ennui, John Dougherty and *New Times* kept hammering her inaction even after she won the governor's mansion in 2002, derisively calling her a "rising Democratic starlet." The paper rarely included her successor, the current attorney general, Terry Goddard, as a culpable partner in Arizona's shameful policy of "Eyes Wide Shut," as one headline accused, but did issue stinging comparisons between Napolitano and Utah attorney general Mark Shurtleff, a Mormon who forsook far better excuses than Napolitano could claim to act against the sect. "While Arizona Authorities Languish, the Utah Attorney General's Office Focuses on the Leader of the Fundamentalist Mormon Church," cried one headline around the time of Rod Holm's conviction. "Governor Napolitano Went to Utah, And All We Got Was Some Lousy Ring Kissing," snorted another.

Without knowing it at the time, *New Times* published the results of an investigation Napolitano *could* get behind, though it would take her years to do it. After spending months pouring through thousands of credit card receipts, purchase orders, travel vouchers, lease agreements, and board minutes, John Dougherty concluded that the Colorado City School District, which received more than $5 million annually from state and federal sources, had for decades been administered as an FLDS slush fund. It was anybody's guess how many millions of tax dollars had disappeared into FLDS pockets, but Dougherty had a few choice specifics.

The FLDS school board members and their families charged tens of thousands of dollars to state credit cards for personal purchases. They bought high-end Ford Excursions, F-350 pickups, and Chevy Suburbans. The district sold off state assets, including supplies and phone systems, pocketing the money and directing the sales of new equipment to relatives. They took entire families on exotic vacations, and had purchased a $225,000 airplane that was apparently flown only by the mayor's unemployed son. The district employed three people for every one student in attendance. After Warren Jeffs pulled all FLDS kids out of the schools in 2000, nearly $5 million in emergency state and federal aid intended to keep districts with catastrophic population loss afloat had simply vanished into the invisible coffers of FLDS, all controlled by Jeffs.

And there was this research from Elaine Tyler, founder of Hope Organization: In the school year 2002–03, when the Colorado City Unified School District boasted about a hundred K–12 students from the FLDS splinter group in nearby Centennial Park, the school board was still controlled by FLDS members. Per Warren Jeffs's orders, all FLDS children had been removed from the schools in 2000, yet the district that year *increased* its bus transportation budget by $145,000, ostensibly to lease two new school buses, money that apparently went into FLDS pockets. In that year, Colorado City channeled $14.5 million in tax dollars through the school district, while the comparable district in Littlefield, Arizona, spent $3.9 million. According to Tyler's figures, it cost $40,000 a year to educate a child from Colorado City, but in Littlefield the number was under $10,000.

It was all there for anyone to see. Left to their own devices for fifty years, the Colorado City School Board was so confident in their invisibility they'd been too smug, or incompetent, to disguise a flagrant conversion of public funds, the kind of debacle that appealed to Napolitano. Looking into this kind of illegality would require only bespectacled clerks performing forensics on lifeless paperwork in a windowless room instead of the heart-stopping statement of a caravan of police entering Short Creek with lights flashing as the Utah attorney general demanded lunch at a sect restaurant to signal things had changed. But for some Arizona authorities, Maricopa County Republicans weren't as scary as what was going on in Short Creek, and paperwork wasn't going to do the trick.

Escalated by the Rod Holm prosecution, Warren Jeffs's sadistic appetite for ripping families asunder while shuffling women around like gambling chits produced a small group of hardcore resisters whose only hope for survival rested with the people they'd been trained to believe were of Satan: Mohave County, Arizona, authorities. With barely a whisper of press coverage, Mohave County law enforcement and courts were dealing with the flood of FLDS lawyers sent to handle the misfits defying Warren Jeffs by refusing to leave their homes after excommunications. Fighting for their homes in the Mohave County courts were Milton and Lenore Holm, banished ten minutes after Lenore changed her mind about submitting her sixteen-year-old daughter to Jeffs for marriage assignment.* Richard Holm refused to leave, as did Ross Chatwin, who was ejected in the mass banishment and braved blood atonement death threats and constant utility cutoffs rather than surrender his home, wife, and children to Warren Jeffs. Chatwin held press conferences decrying FLDS that required the heavy presence of Mohave County deputy sheriffs to ensure his physical safety.

---

* Rather than risk her salvation, Nicole Holm fled her parents' home to humble herself before Jeffs. Lenore Holm did not see her daughter again after she was "married."

On the peripheries circulated men like Isaac Wyler and Jethro Barlow, one of the sect's premiere accountants who would become critical in the years ahead. Wyler, Barlow, and a dozen other men had initially removed themselves from their homes, wives, and children but had never really swallowed the reasoning like some others, returning from exile to settle just outside Short Creek's dangerous (for them) boundaries. The resisters mustered every ounce of courage they could separate from a lifetime of bombastic religious training to help harried Mohave County authorities deal with the onslaught of FLDS attorneys by gathering information. And always, the FLDS insurgents related the awful stories of underage sexual abuse and incest ignored by a police department whose officers reported to the FLDS prophet.

It was never ending, and Mohave County supervisor Buster Johnson was sick of it. So was newly minted county attorney Matt Smith, who was appointed to succeed Bill Eckstrom, the architect of the dumbfounding Barlow plea. A longtime Mohave County prosecutor and FLDS apologist, Eckstrom had been firmly directed toward the tearful conclusion that resignation might spare him further investigation into his chronic failure to prosecute blatant FLDS sex crimes.

Propertywise, Mohave County is the fifth largest in the country. Like St. George's Washington County on its northern border, Mohave is an outdoors paradise with something its neighbor lacks—one thousand miles of stunning freshwater shorelines along four lakes, including Lake Mead and Lake Havasu. The county boasts the west end of the Grand Canyon along with the Grand Canyon Caverns, the pristine Music Mountains, and the Kaibab National Forest. Bordered on the west by California's San Bernardino County, Mohave is a long, long way from Phoenix politics. Unlike Utah's Washington County, Mohave and its seat of Kingman, Arizona, have not become international tourist destinations, with only two hundred thousand residents spread over nearly fourteen thousand square miles, exactly the kind of peace, tranquility, and beauty a hard-nosed, shaved-headed retired cop from Los Angeles was looking for.

Mohave County supervisor Buster Johnson's initial stupefied disbelief had been replaced with unmitigated outrage upon discovering his dream move to spectacular Mohave County would be seasoned by the ominous presence of an outright cult untroubled by human laws. In 1998, he abandoned retirement to do what he could about FLDS by running for the District 3 county supervisor spot, a post he's held ever since. Unfazed by the Maricopa County right-wing Republican coalition, the blunt ex-cop raised hell about the inexplicable absence of law enforcement upon a group of men committing what Johnson considered institutionalized child rape, not to mention fraud. In 2003, Johnson accompanied Flora Jessop to Eldorado for a press conference Flora insisted upon after being contacted by Randy Mankin. Like many others familiar with the volatile Jessop, Johnson confided to Mankin that the anti-FLDS activist could be a tad over the top, but she was "on the side of the angels on this one." Johnson would himself aid in the escapes of eight underage FLDS girls fleeing forced marriages, taking the extraordinary step of helping block their return to the FLDS parents claiming the girls' underage status required their return to their legal guardians.

Johnson was vocal, but more than words he wanted action, and that meant a meaningful law enforcement arm in Short Creek. After the Holm prosecution, Shurtleff and Napolitano had decertified several Short Creek cops in 2003 for practicing polygamy, but they'd simply been replaced by other FLDS members.

With the Colorado City and Hildale police departments wholly owned and operated by Warren Jeffs—with no objection from Utah's Washington County, under the jurisdiction of Kirk Smith, who'd urged Texans to leave FLDS alone—Johnson figured Mohave County was the only hope for meaningful law enforcement in Short Creek. But the settlement was still at least a two-hour drive for any of his deputies. After the Rod Holm conviction, the Mohave County Board of Supervisors and sheriff Tom Sheahan started talking to Mark Shurtleff about a joint substation to be located within walking distance of Short Creek, one that would include investigators from Child Protective Services. As meetings for the proposed $500,000 station progressed, *New Times*'s John Dougherty noted the representatives from Governor Napolitano's office or Arizona Child Protective Services were conspicuously absent.

Meanwhile, county attorney Matt Smith was apparently also unmoved by Maricopa County politics. Shortly after replacing Eckstrom, Smith hired former Bullhead City police officer Gary Engels to investigate FLDS underage sex crimes exclusively. Although he would not be remembered for it, Matt Smith was the first to bring charges against FLDS men and their prophet, Warren Jeffs. Although Jeffs was already in hiding, Smith would turn him into a fugitive, eventually landing on the FBI's Most Wanted List with a $100,000 bounty on his head.

12

ANSWER THEM NOTHING

I say to you brethren, no person, no court, no government, no people on the face of the whole earth has the right or authority to bring God into question what He has his Prophets do in the Celestial Law among his Priesthood people on His consecrated lands. That is what these present lawsuits and attacks are. And so the Lord told me: "Answer them nothing." . . . The Attorney General of Utah has been pushing a court in the so called "Lost Boys" case where the Lord had me answer nothing.
— Warren Jeffs, dictations, April 19, 2004

By spring 2005, Roger Hoole had collected bales of returned court notifications, summons, and subpoenas inked to death with stamps advising the sender he was out of luck. The notices, sent to Short Creek in relation to the Brent Jeffs and "lost boys" lawsuits, were met by FLDS recipients who demonstrated imagination when complying with their prophet's edict to "answer them nothing." Bulging from stuffed cartons and spilling from file cabinets, the undelivered legal documents were smeared with a variety of explanations for their return, ranging from the cryptic but self-explanatory "Returned" or "Refused" to the mysterious "No such address" to the spunky and increasingly popular assertion that "No such person" existed, as if Hoole and the state of Utah had imagined individuals like Warren Jeffs and Wendell Neilsen who, liberated from reality by a postage notice, would now be free to proceed with their nonexistent lives.

Initially, Roger was perplexed by the self-imploding "answer them nothing" scheme, which exposed the entire $110 million UEP trust to forfeiture. Failure to answer a legal complaint within a legally specified time does not make the lawsuit go away anymore than failing to pay a speeding ticket makes it disappear. A judge may issue a bench warrant for the tardy speeder's arrest. Similarly, a jurist may, in a flat minute, order the cases of nonresponsive civil defendants to be lost by default and all their assets available for seizure to satisfy the winner's claims.

Splattered throughout Warren Jeffs's voluminous dictations are his specific statements demonstrating that he understood this legal reality perfectly, an astonishing revelation given that FLDS would later claim the government was illegally seizing religious lands Jeffs would have forfeited or sold off himself. For years and continuing to present day, FLDS attorneys would deny Warren Jeffs said anything like his dictation of January 10, 2005:

> We are fulfilling the directive of the Lord that the Priesthood people will be driven from Short Creek. . . . The court is expected to rule a default judgment to take away our lands and houses on January 12—in two days.*

Jeffs's date for the court supervision of UEP lands was premature and his characterization of that procedure false, but the entry was emblematic of dozens that demonstrated that Jeffs had a perfect grasp on the consequences of his "answer them nothing" strategy. And he didn't seem much overwrought about it. The very next sentence in the entry reads: "Also, the Lord is having me perform marriages before our people are not able to be out and about."

But Jeffs's records hadn't yet been seized in 2005, and nobody could imagine a scenario in which Jeffs and his legion of lawyers would allow a default that would expose $110 million worth of property, including hundreds of homes, to forfeiture. Nobody yet knew that Jeffs was moving people of his choice to Texas and didn't give two shakes about the families left behind. But even if they had known, it made no sense that Jeffs would relinquish such a huge asset just because he didn't feel like filling out some paperwork. Of course, also at that time nobody knew that Jeffs had already sold chunks of UEP to finance his escape hatch in Texas. If the civil plaintiffs didn't liquidate the property, Warren Jeffs would have.

Nobody knew except, perhaps, lead FLDS attorney Rod Parker, whose pricey firm had been fired as part of the "answer them nothing" strategy.

---

* In fact, a default judgment had already been issued for the lost boys case. The event Jeffs describes is the petition from the Utah attorney general to assume control of the lands to prevent them from being seized, an action that would protect UEP beneficiaries, not harm them. As they would throughout the years of litigation to come, the Utah courts bent over backward to accommodate the recalcitrant and uncooperative FLDS leadership. The actual court order for supervision of UEP lands was not issued until May 2005.

Parker wasted no time abandoning two decades of indignant public proclamations defending FLDS as a persecuted religion packed with hardworking, honest family folk. When Parker learned of the "answer them nothing" legal gambit, he promptly withdrew as FLDS counsel and liened FLDS lands against his most recent bill of more than $400,000, placing the FLDS lawyer in the same reception line as Brent Jeffs and the lost boys, an awkward position for the lawyer who was supposed to be fighting those cases in court.

Parker did not stop with the lien, however. Instead of filing a simple notice of withdrawal with the court, Parker took the extraordinary extra step of filing a four-page warning to the judge. In the filing, Parker emphasized that Jeffs's behavior jeopardized thousands of women, children, and men by exposing their homes to court seizure. Thousands of people faced homelessness, and they didn't even know it. The importance of other elements in Parker's filing cannot be understated, because in a few years he would completely reverse positions in what can only be viewed as a grand definition of hypocrisy.

In a few years, Parker would studiously ignore this court filing, but in 2004, he urged the courts to implement a system whereby individual Short Creek residents would be notified of the "lost boy" suit default judgment and potential calamity in the loss of their homes. If *individuals*—a key factor later on—wanted to obtain legal representation, Parker argued they should have the right to find lawyers to fight the default judgment Jeffs had allowed. Better still, Parker urged the court to place the Utah attorney general in charge of the endangered trust as allowed under Utah law. If Mark Shurtleff took over trust management, the potential loss of property would be immediately stopped.

Parker's final critical point, one he would spend most of the coming decade rebuking, was that *non-FLDS* residents, not just FLDS members, deserved notification of the default as well as the right to hire lawyers to protect their homes. Presumably, this included individuals like Ross Chatwin, Richard Holm, and others Parker had once, and would again, try to evict from Short Creek. Nevertheless, as he sat in his office in 2009, after he'd reversed course, Parker remembered Warren Jeffs's rank irresponsibility and possible calamitous consequences for thousands of people with disgust. "I had to do it," a subdued Parker said of his 2004 court filing. "I couldn't walk away without making the court understand what was at stake."

Parker's advisory to the court was gracious, but FLDS's longtime lawyer had never needed to concern himself about the intentions of Brent Jeffs or the six lost boys who'd never been after money. The young men had already lost the services of flashy law firms in Baltimore and Texas, in part because of their rock-solid insistence that they would not liquidate UEP lands even if they received all of them in judgment, not in a million years. Such a move would mean evicting FLDS families from their homes. As any children might, the boys still loved the mothers and fathers who'd driven them into the desert and thrown them away like rotting debris; they still worried about the brothers and sisters who thought their childhood playmates were better off dead. "They didn't—don't—know any better," said a clench-jawed Brent Jeffs, adding with a cracking voice: "People have to understand, it's cradle-to-grave programming. . . . You just don't *know* anything else." He smiled helplessly, fighting the wounded tears again.

In the past, FLDS had never backed away from a court fight. To the contrary, the typical FLDS legal strategy was throwing scads of lawyers and blizzards of pretrial motions, frequently alleging First Amendment or civil rights violations, at judges and opposing counsel who often found themselves overwhelmed by the attack. Small law firms like Hoole's, working on contingencies without the enormous cash reserves of Parker's firm, could simply not afford to keep the lights on *and* deal with a hurricane of legal maneuvers, each one requiring a timely answer no matter how repetitive or irrelevant. Without Diversity Foundation's grants, Hoole would have gone belly-up fighting for the lost boys—a fact that is not lost on the Dan Fischer–hating FLDS leadership even today—but they would soon be able to add another villain to the list of persecutors.

After winding its way through a series of judges, the UEP case ended up before Third District Court judge Denise Posse-Blanco Lindberg. Judge Lindberg was a woman of dry humor, iron patience, and unassailable credentials. Born in Cuba, Lindberg's family escaped the Castro regime in the 1960s, settling first in Puerto Rico and later in New York City, where Lindberg attended high school. Lindberg's three degrees from Brigham Young University were concentrated in psychology, health services, and social work, but after working in these areas for a few years, Lindberg discovered she "liked thinking like a lawyer" and returned to BYU for a law degree. She clerked for the Tenth Circuit Court of Appeals and U.S. Supreme Court justice Sandra Day O'Connor before joining a prestigious Washington, D.C., law firm working on health care issues. She returned to Utah in 1995 when she became in-house counsel for a subsidiary of Aetna Life and Casualty Company, and she was also highly visible in Utah Bar Association committees and professional associations of women attorneys.

Three years after returning to Utah, Lindberg was appointed to the bench by then governor Mike Leavitt, brother of the Juab County attorney David Leavitt, who with Mark Shurtleff's assistance broke Utah's silence on polygamists with the 2001 prosecution of freelance fundamentalist Tom Green. Lindberg became a judge in 1998, Shurtleff won his first race for attorney general in 2000, and in the spring of 2005 the paths taken by the immigrant judge and the descendant of polygamist and Wild West hit man Bill Hickman would intersect for a vicious battle over the future of one of Mormonism's founding tenets: polygamy.

13

THE WHIP COMES DOWN

I could prove to this congregation that I am young; for I could find more girls who would choose me for a husband than any of the young men.
— Brigham Young, *Journal of Discourses, Vol. 5*

I had the Bishop gather up three ladies who were formerly married and their hus-bands are unworthy—Karen Palmer, formerly Dan Wayman's wife; Naomie Holm, formerly Carson Barlow's wife; and Brenda Jessop, Uncle Fred's daughter, formerly Lester Johnson's wife. There were also three other young ladies to be sealed; and circumstances were that either their parents were not there, or I couldn't trust the parents. I had the Bishop pick up one girl, and I called Truman Barlow to have his daughter, Hallie let her daughter Sarah Monique get married and it was all agreed. We arrived at the motel around 10:30 P.M.
— Warren Jeffs, "Record of President Warren Jeffs," May 18, 2004,

Though the hallways are scuffed linoleum and the walls unadorned with fine art, the business end of the Utah Attorney General's Office is also located on a secured, key-carded floor of downtown Salt Lake's Heber Kimball building where a ruthlessly organized Rexine Pitcher is keeper of the burgeoning UEP files threatening to swallow the office whole. The stylish Pitcher is the paralegal to Utah assistant attorney Tim Bodily, Mark Shurtleff's first point man on the trust case, and she's just about the only person who knows how to lay hands on specific documents within several small offices and hallways crammed with exponentially expanding case files. When incoming calls are for Pitcher, the person on the other end is likely one of her harried counterparts in Arizona desperate to get up to speed, frantic that they are missing one item or another.

"I always drop what I'm doing to help Arizona," Pitcher confided with an irrepressible cheeriness that didn't match the depressing workload. "I feel bad for all the work they've got in front of them, because we've never seen anything like this case. I'll bet they haven't either." Pitcher gazed around the hallways cluttered with UEP files and a cubicle, once someone's work space, commandeered to manage some of the overflow. "'Answer them nothing,'" Pitcher said in wistful remembrance of Warren Jeffs's early instructions. "Now *those* were the good old days."

But those days only seemed good in retrospect in 2010, because in 2004 nobody knew how much more miserable things would become. The boxes in the cubicle represented the Utah Attorney General's Office's attempts to notify FLDS leaders and members that Mark Shurtleff was about to take supervisory control of the UEP trust. Because the "answer them nothing" strategy was still in effect, the effort produced the same collection of "No such person" or "Undeliverable" stamped envelopes Roger Hoole had amassed while attempting notice of the "lost boy" suits, but because Shurtleff's office had infinitely more personnel who attempted service for months longer than they were required, Pitchers's collection was infinitely larger than Hoole's.

Some of the notices appeared to have been spat upon or ground contemptuously underfoot, but they were all saved to rebuff possible future claims, however ludicrous, that FLDS had no idea what was happening in the courts. Given the stunning volume of notices sent in 2005, including many posted publicly in a dozen newspapers, no one actually thought FLDS would attempt to claim ignorance of the events about to unfold.

But everyone was wrong. In a few years, everything would be upside down.

Roger Hoole, Brent Jeffs, and the lost boys who filed suits against FLDS had not expected such an effortless win as a default judgment because their complaints went unanswered. In some ways, the win was a letdown, particularly for Brent Jeffs. Brent had hoped his shocking testimony against Warren Jeffs would be something the press couldn't ignore. He thought it might be emotionally freeing, another piece of his recovery from the childhood molestations. More importantly, Brent had wanted to vindicate his dead brother. "I wanted Clayne's suicide to mean something," Brent said thoughtfully. "I thought that exposing Warren in open court would help others."

The lost boys too had been hoping to open the public eye with their testimony. All their energy had been directed toward a trial they hoped would deliver their families from Warren Jeffs's tyrannical whimsy and save other young men from their fates. They didn't want money. Now they were horrified to learn that their swift, unanticipated victory jeopardized the very things they'd sought to protect. All the UEP property, including the homes in which their families lived, were on the block.

It was confusing to say the least. Some of the boys wondered if they could simply get the UEP property upon which their families had built homes as their settlement. If they could secure the property titles for the parents who'd abandoned them with the trash, they could ensure their families, at least, would no longer be subject to Warren Jeffs's cruelty. The selflessness wrenched Roger Hoole's soul, but he was not so sure it would work. For one thing, a court might not so precisely dissect such a settlement. But the biggest obstacles were the FLDS families themselves. There was little doubt in Hoole's mind that they would return any titles they received back over to Warren Jeffs. He would demand it as proof of their purity. These FLDS people who so readily deserted their own children, sending them to scrape out a life on mean streets to prove their devotion to the prophet, would think nothing of giving him a piece of paper they didn't fully understand. The lawsuits would be in vain.

For the first and last time, Hoole agreed with Rod Parker. As Utah's attorney general, Mark Shurtleff should protect the trust's assets by assuming temporary control. The UEP trust was a registered, legal Utah entity subject to Utah law. The UEP trustees—who amounted in real life to Warren Jeffs—had recklessly exposed trust assets to forfeiture and trust beneficiaries to catastrophic loss. When trustees acted against the interest of trust beneficiaries, it violated Utah law, which permitted the Utah attorney general to step in and sort things out. That result required Shurtleff to file a petition with the Utah courts alleging trustee malfeasance, requesting permission of a judge to assume court-supervised control.

If the attorney general took temporary control of the trust, there were a number of possible results. The offending trustees could be removed and replaced. The trust could be restructured. But however it happened, the state would not assume permanent ownership, and that was the liberating fact, the ray of sunshine. The trust assets would have to be rearranged, redistributed, and redesigned before the court took its hand away. What if the UEP lands were divided and titles given to the people living on the parcels as a way of settling the matter? It would be exactly what Hoole's clients wanted from the start. The land would be removed from Jeffs and given to the families living in the homes. Jeffs could never evict anyone again. No one would to need live in fear of losing everything ever again. Hoole was satisfied that he'd at least obtained what his own clients had wanted.

Mark Shurtleff wasn't required to file the petition, however. He had to agree to the proposition, and Hoole didn't know much about this relatively new attorney general. For FLDS activists, there are people who "get it"—that is, they know what FLDS is beyond the *National Geographic* photographs—and those who don't. Even though Shurtleff had OK'd the Rod Holm prosecution, Hoole didn't know into which category he, or judge Denise Lindberg for that matter, fit. Hoole was faced with a difficult choice. Take the sure thing default judgment and get what property he could, or roll the dice on Shurtleff and fulfill his clients' dreams of helping more people than just themselves. Maybe even bring the whole FLDS community into the twenty-first century.

In the end, Judge Lindberg approached Shurtleff about the petition, and as it turned out, she'd caught him at a good time. In a presentation that could have gone better, Shurtleff had testified before the Texas state legislature on April 13, 2005, in support of a bill that would raise the minimum age of girls who could get parental consent to marry from fourteen to sixteen. Standing before the stoic committee on juvenile justice and family matters, Shurtleff found that his passionate discussion of FLDS crimes, along with his heartfelt assertions that he was "ashamed" Utah had done nothing in fifty years to curb the sect now "exported" to Texas, were not met with the empathetic commiseration he might have expected.

"Have you even prosecuted anyone in Utah?" asked one openly skeptical lawmaker before Shurtleff could finish a thought on one of his favorite Dr. Martin Luther King Jr. quotes about injustice anywhere being injustice everywhere. The question forced a detour from his planned remarks to tell his audience that he *had* prosecuted two famous polygamy cases: Tom Green and Rod Holm. "You've probably heard about them," Mark offered casually, and when no one responded, he stuffed the silence with a description of Warren Jeffs's brutal eviction of boys and thirst for young girls. But as shocking as it was, the story again produced the wrong reaction. "Why don't you just go in there and get this guy?" demanded one lawmaker. "Indict him and prosecute him? Is there some reason in Utah why these crimes can't be prosecuted?" Another stated coolly, "We understand that girls who try to leave are returned to the group by [Utah] state authorities, including Child Protective Services." And there was this question: "Is it your testimony that people who escape this group have no recourse in the system?"

While admitting that such dismaying circumstances were part of Utah's past, a somewhat subdued and miffed Shurtleff assured the Texans that the incidents occurred before he was elected. Going on the offensive a little, Shurtleff then decided to cool the lawmakers off with a pointed reminder that their laws allowing fourteen-year-olds to wed with parental consent—the one they were changing—had probably *enticed* Jeffs to Texas to begin with.

The soft needling produced neither embarrassment nor contrition in the Texans, who continued to probe Utah's perceived inactivity as the primary source of their current problems in Eldorado. "How are they making money down there [in Short Creek] besides welfare?" asked another unimpressed Texan. "It seems to me the best way to go after them is at the root—looking into those businesses that aren't paying any taxes." Shurtleff had no sooner made a vague response about initiating RICO (organized crime) investigations when the committee vice chairman, Toby Goodman, seemed ready to wrap things up. "I'd thank you for your [FLDS] export," he told the Utah attorney general amid a chuckling room, "but I don't think it's appropriate."

It happened so fast, Shurtleff had to request additional time to read a Warren Jeffs quote about blood atonement he'd selected to wow the committee, a request grudgingly approved. But his irrepressible spirit could not be doused for long. He later posed for cheery photographs with those who'd testified in support of the bill, including author Jon Krakauer and Roger Hoole's investigator, Sam Brower. Years afterward, he'd dismiss the episode.* "I told them what was going on," he'd say lightly, but his frown suggested an unpalatable memory.

A month after his visit to Texas, Utah assistant attorney general Tim Bodily was getting a temporary restraining order, freezing FLDS's $110 million UEP assets and removing the FLDS figurehead trustees who were completely beholding to Warren Jeffs. Third District Court judge Robert W. Adkins agreed that Warren Jeffs had fraudulently transferred assets from the trust and then negligently abandoned the remaining wealth to the Hoole default judgments obtained in March. For the first time since Leroy Johnson declared "one-man rule" in FLDS in the 1980s, the prophet no longer had a legal right to evict people from their homes, nor could he sell any UEP properties, bought on the backs of beneficiaries, for any reason.

---

* Although Krakauer's best-selling book *Under the Banner of Heaven* did not specifically concern FLDS, Krakauer's extensive research into Mormon fundamentalism included the group, which alarmed him to the point that he adopted a "lost boy" and became an untiring anti-FLDS activist since his book was published in 2004. Krakauer also testified before the Texas committee with mixed results. Giving his disinterested thanks to Krakauer for his appearance, the committee chairman inadvertently called the writer "Mr. Crackhouse." The members seemed most interested in the testimony of private investigator Sam Brower, who they felt had collected evidence that could be used in court.

More monumental than a hundred raids, the decision ripped a substantial chunk of legal power away from the FLDS prophet and his enforcers for the first time, without even displaying a gun or an arrest warrant, and in the beginning, Utah attorney general Mark Shurtleff was all in.

Shurtleff nominated, and the courts accepted, the unflinching, hardboiled, sardonic but highly respected Salt Lake City accountant Bruce Wisan as fiduciary, a public accountant skilled at overseeing the administration of large financial institutions. It was a decision Shurtleff would later backpedal on hard. Along with Wisan, Shurtleff invited Arizona attorney general Terry Goddard, who New Times had gotten around to calling an FLDS "coward" every bit as sickening as Napolitano, into the UEP supervision. Goddard accepted the offer, filing court documents to become a party of legal standing that he held because most of the UEP lands were in Arizona. In a decision they would regret, the lost boys settled their cases with the new UEP fiduciary, confident their lost families' securities were safe with the two attorneys general. Each young man received about three acres of land along with a lump sum of $250,000 to start a foundation to help and educate other lost boys.*

Contrary to what FLDS and their attorneys would later claim, everyone involved in the new UEP structure knocked themselves silly trying to notify FLDS about each step of the proceedings. The cartons stuffed with "refused," "no such address," and "no such person" envelopes Rexine Pitcher hauled around passed for a gym workout. Even when every possible effort had been made to notify FLDS, it was the man who would rival Dan Fischer as FLDS's most hated nemesis who insisted on caution before the old, figurehead FLDS trustees were replaced with new ones appointed by the court. Although FLDS would demonize Bruce Wisan, it was he who pointed out that the only people who'd been nominated for the new positions were FLDS excommunicants. It was Wisan who wanted more time, in an attempt to get people from the FLDS community to participate in their own destinies.

At sixty-two, Bruce Wisan is a bulldog of a man, with a fit physique, bald head, and little patience for fools or scoundrels. He is a Mormon but has no concern for religion where business is concerned. Like other Mormons, he

---

* The foundation was to be funded at $50,000 a year through 2011, when it was hoped the epidemic of ejected young men would have ceased. Hoole's law firm was awarded attorneys' fees and $10,000 a year to feed and clothe young FLDS men who might come to them. For her brief appearance in the matter, Baltimore attorney Joanne Suder received $100,000.

personally knew little of FLDS before he was appointed fiduciary of UEP. Wisan is not a diplomatic man and uses his rapier tongue without much consideration for its slashing effects, but he is not coldhearted. He has a photographic memory for everything under the sun, pulling phone numbers, percentages, and facts of any kind from his head at a finger's snap, no matter how dusty or obscure. He holds his lifetime-earned, above-reproach reputation for honesty, precision, and fairness as a sacred honor, and he didn't appreciate it when FLDS began smearing him in two dozen lawsuits for doing his job.

Speaking about Bruce Wisan in 2009, Mark Shurtleff shook a rueful head. "I told [FLDS] that if they wanted to go after Bruce they were going to have to bring me hard evidence. I told them, 'You're going to lose if you try to go after Wisan without a stack of verifiable facts, because Wisan knows everything. He has complete command of all the evidence, every detail, all the facts, and he will beat you every time because he is that good.'" Mark paused, fingering a pen on his polished conference table. "Of course, they [FLDS] didn't bring me any evidence. That's why I chose Bruce in the first place," he sighed. "He really does have a mind like a steel trap. He's very hard to beat."

Mark chalked up the FLDS leaders' inability to document any scrap of wrongdoing by Wisan to their naïveté about the rules of evidence, but the more likely explanation is that there was no evidence of malfeasance to document in the first place. Despite FLDS's repeated best efforts to oust Wisan as the UEP fiduciary, Wisan remained in the position, a mountain range of unmovable granite obstructing FLDS's increasingly virulent attempts to regain a most critical tool in controlling not just Short Creek but the lives of their followers: the land upon which people live. Without control of the property, FLDS must rely solely on mental indoctrination to control behavior, and that can prove unreliable if just one individual realizes he will *not* lose everything if he fails to comply with unreasonable orders. One man refusing to exile a son or provide an underage daughter to Warren Jeffs and still managing to stay in his home with the support of actual law enforcement could incubate a virus of doubt in others. Anti-FLDS activists like Elaine Tyler believe that if only 30 percent of Short Creek residents elected to keep their own property titles, the community could finally start moving toward the light and opening up to education of children and interaction with society as a whole. "It will never happen overnight," Tyler says. "But if Bruce can accomplish 30 percent, we have a chance."

But in 2005, Warren Jeffs was a long way from realizing what he'd actually lost by failing to defend UEP against the Hoole lawsuits. He was busy
ignoring more than forty Texas Commission on Environmental Quality citations as he whipped construction crews to the breaking point. Meanwhile,
he was crisscrossing the nation, performing marriages and lurking about
various state capitol buildings furtively "shaking the dust off my shoes,"
a kind of voodoo curse robbing the cities of their ability to defend themselves against their imminent annihilation. Hoole's private investigator, Sam
Brower, who was trying to locate Jeffs and was often only a few days behind
him, estimates that the FLDS prophet logged one hundred thousand miles
visiting every capitol in the lower forty-eight so that he might scurry about
the building kicking his shoes against the walls, depositing the dust that
would make life easier for the FLDS people in the very near future. All the
dust shaking was essential to Jeffs's overall plan, making the FLDS people's
(with help from God) vengeful slaughter of the planet's six billion humans
go a little smoother, a little quicker. But Jeffs was about to get popped with
a bunch of problems no amount of shoe dust–shaking was going to solve. It
turned out Terry Goddard was not quite the coward *New Times* had thought.

In May 2005, the same month the UEP assets were frozen, Arizona attorney general Terry Goddard sent state and county police—some wearing
bulletproof vests—into Colorado City, where they spent the better part of a
day carrying out cartons of impounded documents and computers from the
Colorado City Unified School District. Goddard said the district had been
under investigation for about three years, beginning about the time the *New
Times's* John Dougherty published his sensational exposé on the Colorado
City school district. Not coincidentally, the Arizona legislature had managed
to pass a bill effective that August that allowed the state to put mismanaged school districts into receivership, a move for which Goddard advised
he'd already filed paperwork. Given the beginning dates of the investigation (which may have been spurred by Dougherty's article) and the fact that
Napolitano championed the mismanaged school district bill and signed it
into law, it seems likely that Napolitano and Goddard worked in unison to
finally wrench the district's public funds away from FLDS, but *New Times*
was not in a congratulatory mood.

For one thing, FLDS had bankrupted the district by the time Goddard got
there. Teachers' paychecks were bouncing like Ping-Pong balls and millions—
possibly tens of millions—had vanished. Although Goddard never filed any
charges related to the school district collapse and takeover, the state's action

did permanently remove all FLDS members from the school board and teaching positions, a significant dent in the FLDS/Short Creek infrastructure and its cash revenues, more action than Arizona had undertaken since the 1953 raid accomplished, without a single photograph of a wailing child.

Arizona was not finished. A month after the school district raid, Mohave County attorney Matt Smith indicted eight FLDS men for underage sex crimes, including the prophet Warren Jeffs, who was accused of facilitating a crime by arranging the marriage of an unwilling sixteen-year-old named Candy Shapley. The biggest news related to FLDS leadership in fifty years inexplicably raised barely a ripple in the media, but it was big enough to derail interstate plans for capturing Jeffs before he could evaporate into a well-financed underground.

Smith gave police from Utah to Texas a heads-up about the indictment. In Schleicher County, Texas, Sheriff Doran was on alert, ready to enter the YFZ ranch with a warrant for Jeffs's arrest, and deputies from Mohave and Washington Counties stood by near Short Creek. But news of the Jeffs indictment, returned by a Kingman, Arizona, grand jury in March, leaked to the media before Smith could get the legal paperwork into their hands. Doran, who was fairly certain Jeffs was in Texas, was sorely disappointed when he learned that Smith had failed to conceal the grand jury's actions from the public. Doran learned of Jeffs's indictment from a reporter, meaning that everybody now knew and the opportunity to capture the FLDS prophet had certainly been lost. It would not be the first misstep for the well-intentioned Smith, who called the incident "unfortunate" but expressed confidence Jeffs would be apprehended quickly. Though the other indicted FLDS men turned themselves in voluntarily, Jeffs would prove far more elusive, but Smith had transformed the prophet from a simple summons dodger into a criminal fugitive with a $10,000 price placed on his head by the Arizona attorney general, who also called in the FBI.

Mark Shurtleff, who Jeffs had mocked for asserting that Utah would eventually arrest the FLDS prophet, might have been feeling left out, but he was again to cross paths with another FLDS child bride who'd steadied herself for flight and changed everything, again.

14

THE END BEGINS

Monogamy, or restrictions by law to ONE WIFE IS NOT PART OF THE ECONOMY OF HEAVEN AMONG MEN. *Such a system was commenced by the founders of the Roman empire....* *Rome became the mistress of the world, and introduced this order of monogamy wherever her sway was acknowledged. Thus this* MONOGAMIC ORDER OF MARRIAGE *so esteemed by modern Christians as a* HOLY SACRAMENT *and* DIVINE INSTITUTION *is nothing but a system established by a* SET OF ROBBERS.

—Brigham Young, *Deseret News*, August 6, 1862

As of now, the Lord has had me go to every state of the United States on the main land; forty eight states, in kicking the dust of my feet off as a witness against them, and also through prayer, arms to the square. In every state and every major city we passed through, we have delivered that city and state over to the judgments of God in the authority of the Holy Melchizedek Priesthood and by the keys and powers thereof, asking the Lord to remove the spirit and power of protection from those cities.

—Warren Jeffs, "Record of President Warren Jeffs," August 5, 2005

A s Ruth Stubbs planned her escape from Short Creek in 2001, Elissa Wall's FLDS nightmare had just begun. Elissa had grown up outside the Jeffses' Salt Lake City compound before FLDS members were ordered to Short Creek to escape the city's destruction during the Olympics.* In 1999, Elissa was an apple-cheeked thirteen-year-old blond growing up in a house with three wives locked in perpetual combat, more than twenty children, and a father she adored. Despite the problems, Elissa's was not an unhappy childhood until the day Rulon and Warren Jeffs threw her father out of FLDS, "reassigning" her mother, Sharon, and her biological brothers and

---

* Elissa Wall (with Lisa Pulitzer) is the author of the 2008 best-selling book *Stolen Innocence: My Story of Growing Up in a Polygamous Sect, Becoming a Teenage Bride, and Breaking Free of Warren Jeffs*.

sisters to Fred Jessop and his immense Short Creek family of fifteen wives
and dozens of kids acquired through "reassignments."*

Three of Elissa's teenage brothers did not respond to their reassignment
with the appropriate grace. Brad Wall refused to call Fred Jessop "father,"
started skipping "family meetings," wore pullovers instead of button-down
shirts, and, as bad as anything else, had a secret CD collection. Although
most young FLDS men owned an ATV, Fred Jessop confiscated Brad's three-
wheeler, which had been a treasured gift from his "real," now excommunicated, father. Then, one day, a terrorized Elissa watched from the shadows
as a crew of Hildale cops—a goon squad headed by officer Rodney Holm—
burst into her brothers' room, ripping it apart with gratuitous violence in a
search for evidence of the boys' impurities. No one knew what came of the
destructive search, but Elissa's brothers were eventually dropped at the side of
a highway outside of town, banished, their names never to be spoken again.

Like most FLDS girls who cling to their families harder than life itself,
Elissa was devastated. Before her brothers' banishments, Elissa had allowed
herself the daydream belief that her father, Lloyd Wall, would truly be allowed
to "repent from afar," his family and position as an FLDS elder restored and
her family put back the way it should be.** In her head, she was still named
"Wall," not "Jessop." She refused to believe the near-taunting assertions
of Jessop's inhospitable children that her mom would be "resealed" to the
elderly Jessop until the day she walked into her mother's room to find her
putting the finishing touches on a wedding dress. Elissa's shock and pain were
barely assimilated before Warren Jeffs clubbed her with the announcement
that she would marry a nineteen-year-old cousin she detested, Warren's close
relative Allen Steed.

From her earliest memories, Elissa had found Allen Steed creepy, physically repulsive, and sadistic. A pretty girl, Elissa had struggled with "baby
fat" issues for most of her life, a self-consciousness Allen rubbed raw by

---

*   In Short Creek, there was unconfirmed speculation that Fred Jessop could not father the
children he wanted and needed for the celestial kingdom. The reassignment to Fred Jessop
could have meant he was at least as interested in acquiring the children as their mothers.

**   All excommunicated FLDS men are told to "repent from afar," though what "afar" means
is never clear. They are instructed to write letters of confession outlining their sins. Rulon
and Warren Jeffs would then use the letters to make the excommunications permanent. Some
FLDS men continued writing letters for years, expecting a reprieve that was almost never a possibility to begin with. Lloyd Wall, however, was eventually readmitted to FLDS, though he was
forbidden any contact with his "reassigned" children.

calling her "tubby tuna" and other damaging names. Elissa was put off by his obsequious bootlicking to the powerful while he treated the helpless with cruelty. His personal hygiene was offensive, as was his peculiar habit of painting his fingernails with clear nail polish. Only fourteen years old, she nevertheless summoned the courage to question the assigned union, objecting to the marriage immediately and without equivocation. When Warren Jeffs dismissed her concerns, she persisted in her requests to speak to the actual prophet, Warren's father, Rulon, who had supposedly received the divine revelation for her placement with Allen Steed.

Elissa's encounter with Rulon is as good an indicator as any as to just how far gone the elder Jeffs was in 2000. As Warren hovered in the shadows, Elissa knelt at Rulon's dining room chair as he slobbered down a lunch. The old man seemed to realize a young girl was speaking to him, but little more than that. Rulon seemed confused by Elissa's presentation in which she said, among other things, that she felt she was perhaps too young to marry. When Rulon looked lost, Warren Jeffs supplied alarmingly inaccurate translations of Elissa's statements, telling his father that the "young lady" believed she "knew better than the prophet" and his direct revelations from God. The horrified Elissa was too intimidated to contradict Warren, but Rulon seemed to lose interest in the entire event within a few minutes anyway, telling Elissa to "follow your heart" before returning his full attention to the sloppy consumption of lunch.

Elissa was wild with joy. Straight from the prophet's mouth, she'd been told to follow her heart, and her heart said "No!" to marrying Allen Steed. She felt like skipping back to Warren Jeffs's office, but once there, Warren behaved as if the meeting with Rulon had never happened. He told Elissa her "heart was in the wrong place" and the marriage would take place. She made several brave attempts to contradict him, but it was useless. After days of bone-wracking, heaving sobbing, a swollen-faced, weak, and sleep-deprived Elissa Wall had to be physically supported on each side to be loaded into an SUV, driven to the seedy, FLDS-owned Hot Springs Motel outside Caliente, Nevada, for a marriage she equated with living death.*

---

*   Even though the Rod Holm case had not yet been charged, Mark Shurtleff's rhetoric had already made Warren Jeffs nervous about performing underage marriages within Utah or Arizona. The motel in Caliente was owned by FLDS elder Merril Jessop, who would later be prominent in an unflattering FLDS memoir and of great interest to the Texas authorities. Typically, Jessop would clear the motel premises to host a caravan of FLDS SUVs for underage marriages usually performed by Warren Jeffs in room 15.

For a while, the desperate girl was able to evade Steed's demands for sex, even though she'd no idea what sex was. Elissa Wall had never heard the word, had not been naked in front of anyone since she was a small girl, and did not know anything about her body, the bodies of men, or what was involved with making babies. She knew only that she did not want to be touched by Allen Steed anywhere, for any reason. She went to bed fully dressed. She fled the room. She got up early or worked on her ninth grade homework late. She outright refused his advances. After a few weeks, Allen Steed got mad, exposed himself, and ripped her clothes off. Wrapped in a blanket she'd snatched off the bed after warding Steed off, Elissa ran screaming to her mother's room in the enormous Jessop home where the couple lived, but no one would tell her what Steed wanted, only that he had a right to it. When the first rape happened a few days later, Elissa went into a kind of shock during the event she couldn't imagine was sanctioned by anyone and then tried to kill herself by swallowing all the Tylenol and ibuprofen in any medicine cabinet she could find.

Thinking better of the suicide plan, Elissa self-induced vomiting for the rest of the evening. Exhausted and repulsed by what she now knew was expected of her, Elissa accompanied Steed and a large group of FLDS members on a trip to the Canadian branch in Bountiful, where the rapes continued over her sobs and pleas for Steed to stop. During the trip, Elissa finally confided in her sister, Teressa, who'd discovered her alone and weeping on a back porch. The unexpectedly sympathetic Teressa told Elissa that if she felt this bad, something was wrong, and Elissa should return to the prophet for guidance. Elissa didn't know it then, but Teressa's sympathy was rooted in more than sisterly love. Teressa and another of Elissa's sisters who'd been tapped by Warren Jeffs for marriage to his father were secretly planning their own escapes from Short Creek.

When Elissa's group returned to Utah, Short Creek was abuzz over the escape of an underage girl, not Ruth Stubbs but another girl who'd loved a boy her own age but had been forced to marry an older man. Warren Jeffs was said to be beside himself, believing that the girl would go to the increasingly hostile authorities in Salt Lake City or Mohave County, so Elissa postponed her planned visit to his office.* She wanted him calm when she asked for a "release"—the FLDS equivalent of divorce—from Steed.

---

*   The escaped underage girl did not go to the authorities. When Warren Jeffs discovered her location, he sent waves of her relatives to remind her of her fate in hell if she did not return to the community, a technique called "loving them back." With no support system, the girl was beaten down and returned to her "husband."

Three months after her "marriage," a now fifteen-year-old Elissa Wall returned to Warren Jeffs's office to plead for her release from a living hell punctuated with persistent, horrifying rapes. She did not use the word "rape" when describing her bedroom ordeals—she did not know the word at the time—but there wasn't a doubt in her young mind that Jeffs understood what she described. This time, a darkly angry Warren Jeffs didn't allow the facade of chatting with the actual prophet, Rulon. The harsh, frightening Warren ordered Elissa back to her "husband," instructing her in no uncertain terms that she must submit to his every wish, desire, or whim or be damned. The bombastic marching orders were especially disturbing given the fact that Steed had been regaling Elissa with his as-yet-uninflicted but appalling sexual fantasies.

Warren Jeffs made it threateningly clear that Elissa was not to discuss her situation with anyone ever again, and she was not to show her face in his office unless Steed was with her. Steed was her "priesthood head," entitled to every piece of her body, soul, and mind, along with her complete and unquestioning obedience. She was property.

Elissa couldn't do it. She started sleeping in her truck, in the bushes, driving Short Creek's back roads until dawn, anything to stay out of Steed's bedroom. When sex could not be avoided, she checked out by counting cracks in the ceiling, but the rapes still occurred if Elissa pleaded that she was not in the mood, was feeling ill, or had the proverbial headache.

On the day of their one-year anniversary, Elissa reluctantly slipped into the dress she'd sewn for the occasion, only to be called downstairs by her "father," Fred Jessop, before she'd gotten into her shoes. Standing in the foyer of the hotel-sized home was the dreaded Hildale police officer Rod Holm who'd brutalized her brothers. Any visit from Rod Holm was very bad news. Everyone knew what he did and why. When a stoic Fred Jessop ordered her to go with Holm, Elissa went weak and pale with fear. Holm handcuffed the shaking, terrified girl, loaded her into his squad car, and drove her to the police station, her pleas to be told what she'd done wrong met with silence. By the time they reached the station, Elissa was hysterical. Holm went inside, leaving her wailing in the car. He returned in a few minutes, still silent, and drove her to the Mark Twain, where he'd "honeymooned" with Ruth Stubbs. Still in handcuffs, the sobbing Elissa was escorted inside by the prophet's muscle man. In the restaurant stood a beaming Allen Steed and a group of family members, all of them in on the delightful joke Steed had provided his teenage "wife" as a gift for their anniversary meal.

Sometime between that anniversary and Elissa's next stab at freeing herself from the agony of her daily life, some men came to Fred Jessop's house in the middle of the night and dragged away the elderly but healthy bishop in an unrequested ambulance. Elissa's mother and the other Jessop wives spent the rest of the sleepless night wondering what new upheaval awaited them, but no explanation was given. One of Jessop's older sons simply announced he would be the family's new caretaker, and that was that. Fred Jessop was never seen again in Short Creek.

Fred Jessop's abrupt and unexplained disappearance from Short Creek was a jolt to the entire FLDS community. Warren Jeffs's silence on the matter produced a new level of omnipresent, electric fear. If Jeffs could disappear a granite stalwart like Fred Jessop, what could he do to the rest of them? Excommunicated FLDS members speculated about Jessop's fate openly on the Internet. Many entries suggested foul play, Warren's payback for Jessop's perceived foot-dragging at the onset of Jeffs's power plays. For Elissa, the event was troubling, but only in a vague way, because the rest of the sect was upset. Elissa's life was such a daily trauma, she had little energy left over for anything else. Just getting through the nights with Steed required nearly all her strength.

Elissa Wall returned to Warren Jeffs's office one more time, accompanied by her mother, who was taking a significant risk to support her daughter in another request for a "release." The pair was harshly rebuked, with special venom directed at Sharon Wall Jessop for being a "meddlesome mother" directly interfering with the priesthood, a charge that turned Elissa's mother's complexion to ash. Jeffs then restated, more ominously this time, that Elissa was to submit to Alan Steed in all things, in every way. With visions of "behavior modification" dancing in her head, Elissa returned to the new double-wide trailer the couple had been provided, the scene of her most recent, violent rape on an air mattress Steed had thrown on the unfurnished floor.

Jeffs's repeated instructions to Elissa Wall would be the foundation of Utah's criminal prosecution against him, but Elissa would suffer for another two years before gathering the courage to leave, and she would have help. It began one night after Steed had delivered her yet another black eye. Elissa was avoiding him in one of her middle-of-the-night drives through the back country in the frozen cold of mid-November 2003. She got a flat tire as she was suffering her fourth miscarriage, gushing blood as she pulled the truck over to the side of what was little more than a dirt track, wondering again if death weren't preferable to the torment of her life. Staggering from the cab to change the tire, she realized she'd fled the house shoeless. She struggled to the front of the car to survey the damage and collapsed by the fender.

For anyone else in her desperate circumstance, the appearance of oncoming headlights might have produced a well of relief, but for seventeen-year-old Elissa Wall, the lights in feudal Short Creek only meant the terror of the prophet's police force. Perhaps officer Rod Holm was behind the wheel, handcuffs at the ready for real this time. As she stumbled to her feet, Elissa thought her luck had run out. She'd be arrested and hauled before Warren Jeffs for an unimaginable fate. It took a while for her to recognize the gentle young man who refused to accept her heated protestations that she was fine. "You have a black eye," observed Lamont Barlow, whose family included the "Barlow Boys" of Short Creek's founding fame. Eliminating his competition, Warren Jeffs had tossed the three Barlow Boys in a position to challenge him from FLDS during the January 2004 mass expulsion, one of whom was Lamont's grandfather.

Twenty-five-year-old Lamont Barlow's position in the FLDS community was unclear, and Elissa feared he might turn her in, as he insisted on packing her into the cab of her truck while he changed her tire and followed her to her mother's home to make certain she arrived safely. Elissa fairly collapsed into her mom's arms, spending three miserable days in bed recovering from her latest ordeal before going back to work as a waitress at the Mark Twain without informing Steed of the miscarriage. Weeks later, a trembling Elissa hid in the kitchen when Lamont Barlow walked into the restaurant for lunch, but her fear that Barlow would see her and suddenly decide to report the circumstances of their first meeting were baseless. Lamont had, in fact, fallen a little in love with Elissa in the dead of that cold night. Now, he became her friend, confidant, and, within a few months, the first love of Elissa's life. The teenager who'd been reassigned, married off, raped, and beaten, who wondered every day of her life if death were not a better option for her, now could see not just any future but a glorious one.

In late 2004, Warren Jeffs decreed that Elissa Wall needed to be "destroyed"—killed—for entering a relationship with Lamont Barlow that would produce her first full-term pregnancy. Finally, Jeffs dissolved her marriage to Allen, but the result Elissa wanted from the start came with a condition she could not bear. Like Ruth Stubbs, Elissa was devoted beyond measure or understanding to her mother and siblings, and Warren Jeffs now ruled she could no longer speak to them. After weeks of sobbing jags and cruel, second-guessing, "What if they're right?" doubts, Elissa decided to leave Short Creek, settling with Lamont in St. George.

At first, she might as well have been transported to the moon. The couple knew nothing of water bills, rent, or the cost of food. Like all FLDS girls, Elissa's hair had never been cut. Flaxen, thick blond hair hanging below her waist had been the one bit of her beauty Elissa had never doubted. Now, amid all the women with chic pageboys and shoulder-length styles, Elissa's lovely hair made her feel like a freak, painfully reminding her of a life she was trying to put behind her. Still, she could not bring herself to cut her hair, and she couldn't get clear of FLDS. Her mother and two younger sisters who were fast approaching the marriage block of their early teens kept disappearing. Just when Elissa and her other siblings who'd left FLDS were on the verge of filing missing persons reports, FLDS would produce the women for meetings chaperoned by watchful FLDS men in vans with tinted windows. No sooner had Elissa been allowed to see her mom and sisters than they would disappear again.

For years, Elissa had not been in contact with her ex-FLDS sister Rebecca, a girl Warren Jeffs had selected for his father. Upon Rulon's death, realizing she'd be taken by Warren Jeffs, Rebecca fled, an act the devastated Elissa interpreted as cruel abandonment. Now, Rebecca's support was crucial, and for both young women, the worry about their younger sisters was excruciating. The oldest of their young sisters was now thirteen, only a year away from the time Elissa had been plunged into a life of slavery their mother had been unable to prevent and would again allow. But Rebecca knew a way Elissa could save their sisters without their mother: Go to the police. Tell them about her forced underage "marriage" to a man who had raped and beaten her. It would work, Rebecca insisted. The Utah attorney general, Mark Shurtleff, was prosecuting FLDS now. Warren Jeffs was actually indicted in Arizona. For months, Rebecca and other ex-FLDS members worked on Elissa, whose very soul froze at the thought of taking on Warren Jeffs and the FLDS priesthood. She had an infant son now, and she and Lamont were trying to forget what she'd endured for nearly four years. Elissa said no.

Then the bottom fell out. One of the Mohave County cases brought against Warren Jeffs fell apart when FLDS reclaimed one of the young complaining witnesses. To this day and probably forever, the debacle with Candy Shapley is one of Roger Hoole's great regrets in life. Because they often worked together, Hoole's investigator, Sam Brower, and Mohave County investigator Gary Engels brought the fragile sixteen-year-old to Hoole after she came forward, thinking she could benefit from legal counsel and help from Diversity Foundation, but Hoole had only worked so far with ex-FLDS boys. "I don't think anyone fully understood how damaged and vulnerable these young FLDS girls are," Hoole said. "They [FLDS] were able to track her down. They sent waves of the people she loved most, putting tremendous pressure on her. Without a good support system outside, she just fell apart." Fell apart and disappeared. After Candy recanted her accusations and refused to testify at any hearings for Matt Smith, she vanished into FLDS.

Hoole was dismayed he'd not been better protection for Candy Shapley, but Brower and Engels still had jobs to do, and like many who came in close contact with FLDS, the job had become personal. Both men fervently believed Warren Jeffs and FLDS systematically destroyed lives. It had to stop, and the investigators knew about Elissa Wall, a good, solid case, one of the few girls who'd made it out of Short Creek.

Elissa began hearing upsetting rumors that she could be compelled to testify—subpoenaed to tell a bunch of strangers on a Mohave County grand jury what she'd barely been able to tell Lamont in a year. It frightened her, and she feared retribution from the goon squads not just against her but also her remaining sisters and mother. The more Rebecca urged her to speak to Engels, Brower, and finally Hoole, the further she recoiled. This couldn't be happening to her. After all she'd endured, she was reaching for happiness, trying bravely with Lamont to navigate this outside world that was still so weird and unfamiliar. Rebecca had finally talked her into cutting off seventeen inches of her hair in a salon, but what had been intended as a fun, pampering treat became a harrowing experience producing embarrassing, choking tears in public, and even after the cut, her hair still fell to her waist. Elissa couldn't bear any more to be severed. She couldn't possibly take one more straw on her back.

But one day, Elissa changed her mind. When she did, she took control. The courage that had kept her from both self-destruction or capitulation for four brutal years with Allen Steed rumbled up when she phoned Roger Hoole herself, insisting they go forward on her terms. Sensitized by the Candy Shapley debacle, Hoole moved quietly and slowly, gradually introducing Elissa to her options, allowing her to move at her own pace. Eventually, Hoole arranged a meeting with Washington County prosecutor Brock Belnap, the quiet, intelligent St. George native who'd grown up around FLDS and would eventually prosecute Warren Jeffs. They were to meet for lunch in bustling downtown St. George, and Elissa sat with Lamont in their pickup truck outside the restaurant for a half hour, deciding whether to meet with men she'd been taught were trying to kill her.

"We'd pretty much given up on her," remembers Hoole. But Elissa did go in.

In his wildest dreams, Warren Jeffs probably couldn't have imagined that the flea of a nothing girl he'd so callously sentenced to a life of endless pain not once but three times would be the instrument of his destruction. Elissa gained enormous strength from a newfound belief that Belnap, Hoole, Brower, and Engels were actually trying to help her and everyone like her. Once she decided, the meek, cowed girl was transformed into a determined woman loaded for bear.

In December 2005, she filed a civil action against FLDS, Warren Jeffs, and the United Effort Plan. On April 5, 2006, Brock Belnap held a press conference announcing Warren Jeffs's indictment on two counts of rape as a facilitator. Unlike the Arizona indictments, Utah's charges against Jeffs were splashed across global headlines. A few months later, Mark Shurtleff raised the bounty for information as to Jeffs's whereabouts to $100,000 and prevailed upon the FBI to place him on their iconic Most Wanted list, his picture tacked to police bulletin boards across the nation.

Both the civil and criminal charges were filed under the pseudonym "M. J.," but no one harbored illusions that FLDS could not deduce the source of the problem. Having been burned by the Candy Shapley affair, Hoole convinced Elissa and Lamont to accept drastic security measures that included several out-of-state safe houses he rented in the American Northwest, locations known only to Elissa's lawyers and the police officers assigned to guard her from possible physical attack, even murder.

Elissa agreed to the changes, in part because she knew she was susceptible to the emotional siege FLDS laid upon all dissenters. Sure enough, within weeks of the legal action, Elissa's cell phone buzzed and chimed with calls from a mother who'd not spoken to her daughter in eighteen months. It took enormous willpower for Elissa to ignore the calls, yet the messages broke her heart. "We love you, Lesie!" chirped the voices of her beloved little sisters whom she'd been forbidden to see. "We miss you!" Tears streaked her face as Elissa listened to her mother pledge her immortal love, imploring her to return the calls, but Elissa knew she'd be a goner if she did. She'd come to see what she was doing as something bigger than herself—something that might save hundreds of girls from her fate. It was important that she stay focused.

The calls kept coming, but she never returned one. Eventually, Elissa allowed Hoole to change her phone number. Her locations were kept so secret that when she and Lamont married, there were only police and lawyers in attendance. There was nothing left to do but wait for the day when she would face Warren Jeffs, not as a tearful, helpless child but as an adult woman who'd walked through fire to see the day. Mark Shurtleff worried that Jeffs's money and rabid followers could keep him submerged for years, decades even, but in fact, Elissa's day was not far off.

15

FUN ON THE RUN

I have been shown that I must learn the motorcycles so I can go in the Short Creek area in hiding and not be detected. . . . I sought unto the Lord diligently to give me the gift of driving a motorcycle, and that we would not be detected by the people around us, or the police. . . . I have also been told that I would yet stand before this nation and rebuke this nation for its great evils.

—Warren Jeffs, "Record of President Warren Jeffs," August 18, 2005,
Sheriden, Wyoming

I knew that I was to be traveling about, and getting the ladies off to R17 [Texas]. Nephi Jeffs was at Shem Jeffs's house in Colorado City, teaching Nephi's own ladies who were staying there. I was shown that I must go and drop these girls off at one motel and go to a different motel, and name the babies born through father's ladies, then we should leave Colorado and go a northern route around to Las Vegas, Nevada, to perform at least three marriages, and then I would return to the Colorado area to take care of more marriages there among Uncle Fred's family.

—Warren Jeffs, August 20, 2005

The Lord directed that I go to the sun tanning salon and get sun tanned more evenly on their sun tanning beds that have lights, so Naomie and I went and did that in the afternoon. I called Lyle Jeffs that day about what took place on July 21st in the hearing of appointing new trustees for the UEP. He informed me that a new judge was appointed and a hearing was put off until August 4.

—Warren Jeffs, July 29, 2005

Since Warren Jeffs had already established a pattern of skulking, endless travel (he'd not been seen publicly in Short Creek since early 2004), the Arizona and Utah indictments turning him into an FBI Most Wanted fugitive did not necessitate major lifestyle changes. In fact, other than dying his constant companion Naomie's blond hair brown and dressing in casual clothing, Jeffs barely noted the criminal charges development except to add in his dictations new spies and enemies to those already pursuing him.

Although he was aware of the new criminal charges related to Elissa Wall, Jeffs was supremely confident in his own clever talent for evasion and the Lord's willingness to help. Every thunderstorm, road construction project, convenient traffic light, or fluke of nature was recorded as heavenly assistance in evading particularly hairy imagined traps. In deciding his routes, Jeffs had an invisible system by which the Lord "impressed" upon him, through some kind of osmosis, the direction he should head or the way he should turn at a crossroads. The impression method made for erratic traveling. By August 2005, Jeffs himself estimated he'd traveled twenty-six thousand miles, sometimes thirteen hundred miles a day, in under a year. He switched out cars with ease, regularly buying new ones, traveling in motor homes for a while before going back to SUV caravans, and he learned to ride an all-terrain motorcycle so he could scoot in and out of locations without using roads.

One thing that was confounding him, however, was the tactical difficulty of separating his "ladies" into manageable, mobile groups so they could be moved around to various locations for sex and "training" with their absent, now fugitive husband. He put his brother Seth in charge of one group. Wendell Musser, 21, a passionate Jeffs follower whose loyalty was recently rewarded with a young wife, was in charge of coordinating the travel plans of several pods of women, each with their own chaperones, but Jeffs's erratic style of being impressed with the Lord's instructions made this job exhausting. It seems that even God could underestimate Jeffs's cunning opponents, and so vans of women being driven in circuitous routes in Colorado might be suddenly redirected to Idaho or Texas once the Lord discovered traps along the original route. For the keepers of the ladies, it was stressful work. As the construction workers in Texas had discovered, Jeffs didn't suffer schedule failures lightly, even when they were caused by his ceaseless evasive maneuvers.

In reality, the authorities had no good idea where Jeffs was during any of the moments he saw them in the shadows. Investigator Sam Brower logged tens of thousands of miles trailing after Jeffs, but he always missed him, sometimes by only a day or two. Generational secrecy among the closed society of polygamists meant that traditional methods of gathering information through interviews or informants were useless, and people who thought the world could end next Monday weren't enticed by money. A frustrated Terry Goddard stepped on more than a few Texas toes when he publically speculated that maybe Sheriff Doran wasn't keeping a good enough eye peeled on the YFZ ranch, since that's clearly where Jeffs intended to settle. But Mark Shurtleff wasn't so sure. "He had literally thousands of people around the country who would consider it an honor to hide him," Shurtleff observed grimly. "To tell you the truth, we thought he could have been under indefinitely. He had an inexhaustible money supply, and we just didn't know how long it could take."

And Warren Jeffs was throwing around ridiculous amounts of money. Packets of cash between $20,000 and $150,000 routinely passed into his hands from his loyal attendants. Jeffs distributed equally large amounts for building projects at YFZ and elsewhere. He regularly ordered between $10,000 and $50,000 bestowed upon individuals, paid off land loans, and juggled a number of bank accounts with tens of thousands of dollars more. As head of a community in which 80 percent or more of the population subsisted on welfare, Warren Jeffs was a rich man indeed, and he had not forgotten the lessons from his privileged background of wine cellars and private planes. As he had in St. George, he knew how to make his own life comfortable.

In Boston, he took Naomie "from 5:50 to 9:00 P.M. to a restaurant on the 52nd floor of one of the tallest buildings in Boston," probably the Top of the Hub on the fifty-second floor of the Prudential Building. Naomie would have definitely needed a sweet cocktail dress to enter the restaurant offering hard-to-find wines, live jazz, breathtaking views, and an ultragourmet menu from which nobody can escape for under $100, without drinks. Jeffs explained that the Lord had "commanded" the couple "to go mingle with the rich where there was a live band." The Lord also commanded that the evening be topped off with "some dancing bars, lounges, and the saloons." After becoming appropriately revolted by the wickedness they'd been compelled to endure during the extended field trip, Warren and Naomie returned to their hotel whereupon Jeffs called a pod of his ladies currently stashed in Texas for some intensive "training."

Sometimes, Jeffs traveled with up to five of his ladies. In New Orleans, he was commanded to take such a group to witness the evils of Bourbon Street and, later, some racy movies on pay-per-view in the hotel. Jeffs found New Orleans's French Quarter so disgusting he was compelled to visit the city three times with various women, exposing them to the bars, restaurants, and dance halls to further their "training." During this time, Jeffs appears to have become quite the television and movie buff, ordering all manner of films for play in the hotel rooms' DVD players, which Jeffs deduced had been placed there by the Lord for his benefit. The ladies, he noted with satisfaction, were appropriately horrified by the sex and violence he showed them before engaging them in additional "training."*

Jeffs was in St. Louis, Missouri, when Hurricane Katrina hit New Orleans just a few weeks after his last visit, an event that seemed to sadden him even as he recorded his approval and, of course, foreknowledge of the destruction of this den of iniquity that had proven such a useful educational tool. Jeffs could not seem to tear himself away from the news coverage, spending nearly as much energy on the tick-tock dictations of the storm's progress as he did on his other serious matters, of which there were many.

The Texas contingent was trying to keep their prophet apprised of difficulties they were encountering in an area in which they controlled no government, at least not yet, but it was difficult to know what to do when Jeffs's micromanaging made independent thought, let alone decisions, impossible. Texas environmental authorities were finding more and more violations, which nobody from FLDS was answering at the appropriate governmental hearings. It looked like Texas was going to shut the treasured cement factory down, among other things. FLDS wanted their own wastewater facility, and that was being held up. Wastewater would have to be trucked forty miles to San Angelo, Texas. Mark Shurtleff had been down to the Texas legislature, which was going to raise the age of marriage with parental consent, with enhancements attached. The enhancements allowed prosecutors discretion to up the felony level for anyone involved in an underage marriage after the law passed, adding years of extra prison time exposure. Decades of it.

If later videotaped conversations between Jeffs and the men he was instructing are any indicator, the followers seeking direction were left with little to work with. Mostly, these conversations involve a detailed list of subjects requiring attention that Jeffs seems to ignore, instead issuing a set of unrelated directives as his hapless messenger hunches and shrugs, eyes down through a series of submissive "Yes, sir"s and "We love you, sir"s.**

---

*   Although Jeffs never specifies the titles of the movies he watched or rented, the language in the dictations suggests at least some of the films were pornographic. The dictations also suggest occasional group sex or sex witnessed by a group of up to a dozen onlookers. The latter exercise was confirmed by recorded sources other than the dictations.

**   Jeffs's own family members called him "sir," and no wonder. Starting with Ward Jeffs, the prophet excommunicated his own brothers like they were going out of style between 2000 and 2006. Given his tortured path to securing power, it was believed Jeffs viewed his blood relations, particularly his older brothers, as threats even though the community had been fully cowed.

According to his dictations, Jeffs's plan for handling the uncooperative Texas authorities was to let the Lord go ahead and "soften their hearts," though Jeffs offered no guidance about how Texans would transform into bunch of softies as FLDS pointedly ignored their laws.

Having looted and dismissed Short Creek in 2002, it's not hard to understand why Jeffs never seemed to grasp the meaning of Arizona's seizure of the Colorado City school district, a serious cash cow, or the situation with the UEP trust, now under judge Denise Lindberg's control. He may even have confused the two states when he offered a public prayer for God to have "the woman judge in Phoenix" killed. There was no woman judge in Arizona, but Lindberg remained alive and kicking in Utah. Along with fiduciary Bruce Wisan and the attorneys general of Utah and Arizona, she began moving the UEP matter toward an efficient resolution she would apply to any other probate case. She never dreamed that would be impossible.

In those days, Jeffs still thought he could liquidate the UEP assets for the Texas project surreptitiously, well before any government authority that had studiously ignored Short Creek for decades knew what was happening. The only actions Jeffs took to challenge the court-ordered supervision of UEP were illegal. Crews of FLDS men began dismantling UEP assets put under court control exactly to prevent Jeffs from further diminishing UEP wealth ostensibly in place for its beneficiaries—FLDS members. In the course of a few days, the crews dismantled and carted away an 18,000-square-foot warehouse and a 34-by-130-foot building, ripped off its concrete foundations and hauled to unknown locales.* In addition, Wisan discovered several illegal, multimillion-dollar land sales already in progress, pending contracts he went to court to successfully stop.

While Warren Jeffs was smashing the defenses of capital cities with shoe dust–kicking and exposing his ladies to the horrors of five-star restaurants, Judge Lindberg was setting hearings to determine who would become the new trustees of the $110 million trust. Though the hearing dates were heavily noticed with summons and advertised in newspapers, not a single member from FLDS stepped forward to be considered to replace Warren Jeffs and the other ousted trustees.

---

*   By this time, Mohave County investigator Gary Engels and Roger Hoole's investigator, Sam Brower, had established a close working relationship. Together, they gained the trust of non-FLDS residents living in or near Short Creek, people who would call the investigators when they witnessed illegal FLDS activity related to the trust. Consequently, much of the building dismantling was photographed and submitted as evidence in the courts.

Concerned about this, Mark Shurtleff and Terry Goddard made personal appearances in Short Creek, in part to calm baffled and frightened residents and in part to encourage their participation in the courts. Both Lindberg and Wisan postponed appointing replacement trustees five times over six months to make sure no one from FLDS wanted a say in their future. Even Shurtleff, who'd requested the court takeover, asked for and got postponements, because the only people nominated for trustee spots were ex-FLDS members who might have axes to grind.

But the delays couldn't go on forever. Bruce Wisan had to get on with administering what had become the seriously burdensome trust. Like Lindberg, he wanted to dispose of the matter efficiently. His plan was to distribute land titles to beneficiaries who would apply for them in an orderly system. The goal was to give all the land back to the beneficiaries and then get out. In a million years, Wisan wouldn't have imagined that such a routine accounting action would take over his life.

Some educated observers estimated that Jeffs had already drained $50 million from UEP by the time he was stripped of control in June 2005. Whatever UEP operating monies had been in the coffers were long gone, and Wisan didn't embrace pro bono work. He expected to be paid for his services. So did Rod Parker. The FLDS attorney who'd placed liens on FLDS property had presented a $425,000 bill for past services rendered. To set up operating expenses and get rid of Parker, Wisan decided to go through with a land sale already in progress as part of Jeffs's systematic looting schemes before he lost power over the properties.

The $2 million sale of 1,311 acres in Apple Valley, which adjoins Short Creek, is an instructive peek inside FLDS business machinations and served as a warning for the job awaiting Bruce Wisan as he tried to figure out what, exactly, were the UEP assets. Prior to the trust takeover, Jeffs transferred the property to a company called Aspen Management Investments, LLC, a company he controlled. The land was then chopped up and distributed to what Wisan called "a daisy chain" of five FLDS companies in Utah and Nevada.* Aspen Management had agreed to sell 436 of the 1,311 Apple Valley acres to a Utah company, Advantum Inc., with the remainder of the property resting

---

* The companies were: Team Stewart, limited partnership, St. George, Darcy A. Stewart, agent; Boulder Mountain Group, LLC, Las Vegas, Samuel Allred, agent; Northern Star Properties, Ltd., Las Vegas, Nevada First Holdings Inc., agent; DEB Inc., Las Vegas, Nevada First Holdings Inc., agent; and D.C. Saddles and Tack, Inc., Las Vegas, Nevada First Holdings Inc., agent. The last three companies have addresses on Desert Lane in Las Vegas, Nevada.

with the other FLDS businesses, well out of reach of any FLDS beneficiary except Warren Jeffs.

The sale was suspended when Roger Hoole inconveniently filed his lost boys lawsuits against trust assets, but Advantum was still willing to buy after Wisan began supervising the trust. Because the lost boys only wanted their families to receive secure titles to their homes, Hoole was persuaded to release his claims to any proceeds from the Apple Valley sales as helping Bruce Wisan get under way brought his clients closer to their goal. Wisan, however, was only willing to proceed if the tangle of titles was cleared up. In other words, he would sell the 436 acres for $2 million if the remaining 875 acres were handed back to the UEP with clean, uncontested titles. Wisan also agreed to deduct Parker's $425,000 bill from the $2 million, though he did not guarantee that, nor cared if, the money ever found its way into Parker's bank account. "If the money goes for legal services or for a temple in Eldorado, it's not important or that germane," Wisan told reporters at the time.

As Warren Jeffs sat glued to a hotel television, transfixed by Katrina coverage, the land deal went through lickety-split, without muss or fuss. The ease of the transaction may have given everyone involved a false sense of well-being and confidence that, despite the spaghetti bowl of deeds and warranties established by Jeffs, the sale provided enough salary for Wisan to separate the noodle strands and start putting deeds into FLDS beneficiaries' hands. It was a goal complicated—if not rendered hopeless—by the suspended UEP trustees' refusals to comply with court orders compelling them to provide an accounting of assets and to assist Wisan in sorting through the administrative mess Jeffs created, refusals that potentially put them in contempt of court and that continue to this day, so far without consequences.

However, progress was made on other fronts. Judge Lindberg had been struggling for months with the critically important decision that would legally redefine the trust's charter after the offending trustees were removed. There existed a legal option to dismantle UEP, but Lindberg had chosen door number two: restating, reshaping, and redefining UEP. In December 2005, six months after the courts assumed supervision of UEP, Lindberg released her decision, a meticulously worded, thirty-page order lavishly praised for its reasoning and well armored against the relentless attacks it would endure in a few years. In a blackly comedic nutshell, Lindberg agreed with the late prophet Rulon Jeffs, whose trigger-happy attempt to once and for all render FLDS a society closed to the world instead threw open its doors.

After Rulon lost his bid to evict David Stubbs and others in 1998, the vengeful prophet thought he'd pulled a fast one by changing the UEP charter to circumvent the Utah Supreme Court's ruling. The court had ruled that UEP was a "private" as opposed to a "charitable" trust. Before the ink on that decision was dry, an angry Rulon Jeffs had cut a new legal charter specifically defining the trust as "charitable." Seven years later, Lindberg agreed.

For FLDS, this would become the rub: a charitable trust exists for a specific class of individuals, but unlike a private trust, the individuals covered within the specific class are *unlimited*. The UEP trust was ostensibly created to benefit those who had "donated" their "lives, time, talents, or resources" to building and improving the trust, very broad parameters indeed. For instance, anyone who'd improved trust property by, say, putting up a barn; anyone who'd worked a UEP-related job, such as helping with the granaries; anyone who'd helped acquire new trust lands or farmed the old ones, all qualified as beneficiaries. That would include the hundreds of former FLDS members excommunicated by the Jeffses.

The claims of non-FLDS members were doubly fortified by another of Lindberg's legal definitions for the UEP trust: the trust must be "religiously neutral." In other words, religion could play no part in deciding who was entitled to receive benefits. In Utah, the nature of a charitable trust may be historical, humane, or educational. It might even be religious. There's no law against religious trusts, but there *is* a law against historical, humane, educational, or religious trusts that embrace the violation of state and federal law. In her opinion, Lindberg found that FLDS embraced at least two violations of Utah law: polygamy and underage sexual encounters. Ergo, the trust could not be administered by FLDS. The "religiously neutral" designation also included beneficiaries, who for the first time were not required to be FLDS members to be eligible for property leases.

Because he'd fired his platoon of lawyers, Warren Jeffs was informed of these developments by supporters for whom a thorough understanding of American jurisprudence was undoubtedly above their pay grade, yet Jeffs's dictations demonstrate that he understood perfectly the reality of Lindberg's decision. Jeffs frequently discusses the imminent (he thought) dissemination of UEP lands with almost breezy disinterest, an afterthought tagged to his frequent predictions of the end of days. Never once does Jeffs consider the option of challenging the court supervision, let alone the trust reformation defining UEP as religiously neutral. The truth was, Jeffs didn't care. He'd been done with Short Creek for years. His head and heart were in Texas, and because he still thought Short Creek was rife with lurking traitors and the "half hearted," the notion of at least some of its residents suffering the loss of their homes or some other harm may not have kept him up at night.

Of far more interest to Warren Jeffs was the sexual goings-on among his flock, of which he had a lot to keep track. There were girls looking at boys and boys looking at girls, women lusting after men, *married* women lusting after men, and naughty incest situations. Jeffs believed one of his ladies was trying to seduce one of his thirteen-year-old sons, or vice versa, and there were the usual reports of brothers going after sisters and fathers after daughters—Jeffs knew it all. If nothing else, Jeffs's detailed accounts of molestations, infidelity, rape, and incest are evidence that sex crimes were not the unheard-of events FLDS claimed didn't exist inside its fortresses.

Jeffs now wrote frequently about his long-held belief that the secret to controlling sexuality was to snatch young girls off their hopscotch boards and get them married before they ever had a chance to consider the opposite sex in a romantic light. Immediate and continuous pregnancy ensured that the girls would never have time to think about romantic sexuality, while providing men the coveted benefit of a "clean" girl, not only physically but mentally. "Clean" girls, Jeffs noted in his dictations, would mentally imprint on their husbands, sort of the way ducklings imprint their mothers after hatching, forever toddling after them even when they walked into oncoming traffic. Jeffs upped his marriage revelations to a rate even more dizzying than before, performing dozens in a week in batches at 1 A.M., 3 A.M., 5 A.M., in Nevada, Colorado, Idaho, Texas, anywhere he could drag people at a moment's notice for a ten-hour drive.

Between the compulsive traveling, the marriages, and the gymnastic "heavenly sessions," Jeffs was only sleeping a few hours a night, but they were hours well spent with divinely imparted dreams, heavenly puzzles that would spell doom for dozens of men and boys after he finished interpreting the discombobulated images typical of most human dreaming to identify those scheming against him. In one interpreted dream, he led a commando-style group of men lacking only face paint as they sneaked down narrow canals to free the "good ship Zion," a magnificent vessel held captive in "snag harbor" by a black (of course) old-timey sailing schooner and a bunch of cables he severed after magically lifting his team to the besieged ship's deck. In another, he was passing unnoticed through the bodies and activities of nonstop party people in the South Pacific when a giant, flaming planet only he could see hurtled into the revelers full blast, destroying the earth but sparing him; he did not explain what, without an earth to stand upon, he did next.

In his dreams, Jeffs's most dastardly enemies—particularly government agents—are black men or women he calls "niggers." In one dream, a black general seated in a thronelike chair leaps up for the attack with shoe knives—blades protruding from the general's footwear. In another, the assailant is a cooing black woman foolishly attempting to entice the prophet into a brothel. But not all of Jeffs's enemies were so easy to identify. In many of his dreams, his deadly opposition was smiling white men pretending to like him, even inviting him to meals or family outings. Jeffs sometimes needed the Lord's help to identify these fakers, but when he did, the verdict of exile was quick and irrevocable.

"It was . . . quite terrible," remembered a distant, sad, and excommunicated Jethro Barlow, staring out the windows of the Short Creek home he'd been able to reclaim after Bruce Wisan assumed control of the trust. Once one of FLDS's most talented accountants and leading citizens, Barlow was too threatening for Warren Jeffs, who ejected him after a lifetime of service. Today, Barlow works for Bruce Wisan, trying to restore some semblance of sanity to Short Creek by helping potential beneficiaries with the application process, trying to identify trust assets, and generally acting as Wisan's eyes and ears.

It is a difficult life. Barlow is shunned, practically invisible every day to the only people he's known for his entire life. In grocery stores, at the post office, or on the street, FLDS members stare past him. If he speaks, they do not respond. "It's quite . . . difficult to believe that Warren would ruin lives over *dreams*. If a man were taller than Warren was his *dream*, Warren interpreted that to mean the man was trying to take his place." Barlow offered a rare smile. "I guess it's a good thing Warren was so tall."

Not even the cherished Naomie was safe from Jeffs's caprice. When Naomie persisted in a line of mild questioning about health care plans for her mentally ill mother, Jeffs took it as rebellion. In a "heavenly session" transcribed by Naomie, the Lord ordered her "removed" to Short Creek for the affront. Since Jeffs claimed to have no independent memory of the session, he was able to share Naomi's anguish over the harsh penalty he'd supposedly had nothing to do with, but not for long. Jeffs's separation anxiety was so great he assigned four men to guard Naomie, instructing them not to let her out of their sight, even for bathroom trips. As the men were driving Naomie away from the YFZ ranch, a panicked Jeffs stormed up to the top floor, throwing open a window like Omar Sharif in *Doctor Zhivago* to watch the car disappear from sight. Racing back downstairs, he phoned Naomie within minutes of her departure and continued phoning five or six times a day for the next three days until the anxiety became too overwhelming. Within a week, the Lord had reversed the decision to ban Naomie in another heavenly session.

Which is not to say Warren didn't keep up relations with others; on one occasion, he had his brother Seth bring nineteen of Warren's ladies to a far-flung hideout. But all the strict guarding and shuffling of women and girls was taking a toll on Seth. In November 2005, he was arrested outside Pueblo, Colorado, with his cousin Nathan Allred, both of them drunk in the car Seth drove while transporting $142,000 in sealed envelopes addressed to "the prophet" and thousands of dollars in prepaid cell phones. Apparently confused about what would get the pair *out* of trouble, Allred told the cops that Seth had just paid him $5,000 to have sex.

Once they discovered Seth Jeffs's identity, a federal charge of harboring a fugitive was added to the slate, and the U.S. attorney's office in Denver took over. But it didn't get anyone closer to Warren Jeffs.

Meanwhile, judge Denise Lindberg signed the final order for the court supervision and restatement of the UEP trust on October 26, 2006. From the time of the Utah attorney general's petition to assume oversight in May 2005, Lindberg, Wisan, Shurtleff, and Goddard had postponed deadline after deadline in deference to FLDS, giving the sect an extraordinary seventeen months to respond to multiple court hearings. Not a whisper had been raised.

The October 2006 order was final, the end of the road. But American law is born of an abundance of caution for individual rights. Even though FLDS had already been given so much time to get involved with its future, the sect had another thirty days after the final October order to challenge its validity. After that, Lindberg's order would become law. If they chose, FLDS could bring the process back to day one. Like any other American recipient of so much as a speeding ticket, the sect had time to speak up, but if they did not, they were obliged under law to forever hold their peace.

They did not say a word, but then again, FLDS had always considered itself above the law.

16

COPS AND TAXES

In Lyle Jeffs yesterday's report, he talked about the woman judge and this man named Wisan, the so-called protector of the UEP now wanting to be friendly toward our people. And this morning the Lord gave me a very vivid dream. . . . It was as though I saw many people going into a black woman's business and house where she promoted happiness in an immoral way. . . . I observed how filled with flattery and kindness, kind gestures toward any of our people and I repulsed and walked away. . . .

I turned to her and said, "I despise you and I will have nothing to do with you." And as I walked out of where she was, she followed me saying, "I despise me to [sic] I am just a niger [sic] . . . and she tried to touch me and she gathered more of her black helpers and they tried to touch me as I was sitting down and the Lord showed me that I stood up and rose right above them, though they were there to destroy me and I walked away swiftly rising higher and higher above them. . . .

And yet I saw others giving into this, and I have been yearning all morning. The Lord has shown me this much, that this woman judge and the man, named Wyson [sic] are now claiming to protect the rights of the followers of Warren Jeffs and the FLDS Church. And the flattery has already begun—where our people feel like he and this judge will be kind and will allow us our rights and protect us. . . . And the Lord has shown me this is of the Devil. I thank the Lord for this warning and we must continue to answer them nothing.

—Warren Jeffs, "Record of President Warren Jeffs," August 6, 2005

On the 2006 New Year's holiday weekend, Mohave County investigator Gary Engels was working. Engels and Hoole's investigator, Sam Brower, had become friendly warriors, bonded by their mutual convictions that Warren Jeffs was a criminal of the cruelest nature and FLDS a barbarous institution an informed American public would never excuse as a legitimate religion. The men had formed an unofficial alliance to make certain that information got out, and that meant neither man designated any day as a day off work. For Engels, the commitment was especially serious. County attorney Matt Smith had managed to pry some funds loose to pay Engels's meager salary, but the appropriation was a shoestring and subject to termination at any time. Engels's commitment to ending what he believed to be rampant child abuse inside FLDS outweighed his precarious financial situation. He dedicated himself fully to his mission, working out of a triple-wide trailer as close as he dared to Short Creek, where his gun was never far from reach.* Engels knew how to use the gun. In another life, when Engels was a Bullhead City, Arizona, police officer responding to a domestic violence call, the offending husband, who was attacking his wife when the cops arrived, shot Engels in the hip. Engels returned fire, killing the man.

When the courts assumed control of the UEP trust, a growing segment of FLDS outcasts dared to imagine that their lives could be salvaged. Men like Jethro Barlow, Isaac Wyler, Ross Chatwin, Richard Holm, Andrew Chatwin, and others resolved to stay put and fight alongside whichever family members chose to remain with them. Engels's brazen proximity to the FLDS stronghold infused a dash of courage into resistors who'd never entertained a hope of outside help, enough to cautiously funnel information to the authorities they'd been raised to loath, fear, and deceive by rote. During the daylight hours of New Year's Eve, Engels was tipped that there was mischief afoot at the Four Square Feed Store in Colorado City. He arrived to find a crew with a crane dismantling a grain elevator, another UEP asset under court control. Engels snapped pictures as he called Bruce Wisan, who was about to get a rude preview of the next four years.

Wisan happened to be in Mesquite, Nevada, not too far from Short Creek, when he got Engels's call. He was heading to Colorado City when Engels called back, saying the crane operators and workers had evaporated. Believing that the task of dismantling the elevator had been wisely reconsidered, Engels left, but niggling suspicion drove him back to the feed store on New Year's Day morning to discover the elevator gone. The crews had simply waited in other buildings' nooks and crannies until Engels, his camera, and his phone left the scene. Then they scampered back to complete the removal in what was only three hours of remaining daylight.

---

*   Although some of the principals involved in the UEP and other FLDS-related cases declined to speak on the record about concerns for their personal safety, almost all of them either armed themselves or hired security eventually, as Warren Jeffs's blood atonement rhetoric escalated. Mark Shurtleff admits that he placed weapons strategically throughout his home and vehicles and was always personally armed. "You just couldn't be sure if some dedicated Jeffs follower might decide to do a favor for the prophet," Shurtleff said.

Wisan didn't know for sure if the grain elevator per se belonged to the trust or was private property simply located on trust property, so he asked the Colorado City police to investigate the matter. That's when he learned the nature of Short Creek's police force: all the members were FLDS members who practiced polygamy or wanted to, and all swore allegiance to Warren Jeffs over any other authority, a fact the police chief put in a soon-to-be-confiscated letter. Nobody who knew anything about Short Creek would be surprised at the letter or the polygamist cops, but Wisan was new to the game and, like Shurtleff and Hoole, had barely heard of FLDS before the UEP case landed on his desk.

Wisan's alarm over the state of Short Creek law enforcement was well placed. In order to successfully and honorably complete the task of distributing the UEP assets, Wisan needed calm law enforcement dedicated to their oaths, the constitution, and the courts—not the mad dictator who'd created the problem. To understand Wisan's shock, it's useful to go back to 1992, when the Arizona Law Enforcement Officer Advisory Council (ALEOAC) moved to decertify Colorado City deputy marshal Sam Barlow, who'd already been denied peace officer status in Utah because the FLDS member had three wives. Incredibly, Barlow had been an Arizona cop for twenty years before ALEOAC noticed the little illegal polygamy problem, but far from being red-faced and contrite about his personal law breaking, which Barlow openly admitted, the newly scrutinized marshal launched an aggressive counterattack on the board, going to court with religious persecution charges.

Barlow swamped the board's hearings with close to one hundred witnesses from his FLDS community, all of whom swore he was a swell fellow and fine officer, despite the fact that in two decades, Barlow had only arrested FLDS dissenters. While continuing to work as a cop, Barlow pursued his religious persecution case for five years before Arizona, in an astonishing display of gutlessness, dismissed its complaint against him, a complete and total victory for polygamist cops everywhere.

The ALEOAC's inexplicable withdrawal of any threat of enforcing police standards afforded the FLDS polygamist cops—and judges—in Short Creek the same kind of invisible shield the 1953 raid had handed the community as a whole. Law enforcement standard boards in Utah and Arizona went cross-eyed from their earnest dedication to looking the other way until 2003, when Hildale officer and Warren Jeffs strongman Rod Holm entered the stage with a bang nobody could ignore.

Educated to the reality that Holm was not the only polygamist cop in Utah, an infuriated Mark Shurtleff initiated a decertification hearing for the entire Hildale Police Department, to be conducted by Utah's Peace Officer Standards and Training (POST) division, a board of which Shurtleff was a member. A full eighteen months later, POST managed to decertify Colorado City marshal Sam Roundy and deputy Vince Barlow on the Utah side of things, but it took another seven months for Arizona to wake up and follow suit. Noting that Roundy freely admitted he'd never investigated, prosecuted, or reported any of the charges brought by rape and incest victims who'd managed to straggle into his office, a feat in itself, Mohave County sheriff Tom Sheahan announced that his office would take over sex crimes investigations in Short Creek.

But nothing really changed. There was nothing in place to preclude the FLDS city governments from replacing the fired polygamist police with more polygamist police, which is exactly what happened. Roundy and Barlow were replaced with Fred and Preston Barlow, both FLDS members. The five polygamist officers *not* removed with Roundy and Barlow would remain in investigation limbo for years to come, the motions to finally decertify them always tabled.

The interest in the polygamist police did make it difficult for the Utah judiciary to keep ignoring the openly polygamist jurist, Hildale justice Walter Steed, who was removed after a mere four months of investigation following his open admission that he had been a polygamist for twenty-five years and had three wives. Investigators concluded that Steed might be breaking the law enough to disqualify him from making rulings on whether or not other people had broken the law. Steed (represented by Rod Parker), Roundy, and Barlow all fought their terminations on religious persecution grounds, but the fact that the appeals were unsuccessful didn't help Wisan one bit, not by a long shot. Unbeknownst to Wisan, Judge Lindberg, and others charged with overseeing the UEP trust, the Short Creek police force had already declared war upon them.

FLDS crews illegally dismantling a warehouse was just weird, but when they took the grain elevator Wisan saw an emerging bad pattern stitched with subterfuge, obstruction, theft, and deceit. He hoped to nip it in the bud by demanding, and getting, an outside investigation of the emblematic grain elevator by both Utah and Arizona authorities. In April, four months after the elevator disappeared, lawyers for Wisan and Washington and Mohave Counties began writing up summonses for cops in Hildale and Colorado

City, inviting them to various depositions and grand jury proceedings. It didn't take long to find out what sort of party the FLDS cops had in mind for the duration.

In a small town where the appearance of a single unfamiliar vehicle was radioed around the community like news of the black plague, it wasn't hard to keep Short Creek's roughly thirteen police officers apprised of the movements of process servers. The cops elected to perform various forms of childish evasion for a bit, barricading themselves inside the locked, tax-financed town hall, refusing to acknowledge the knocking on the doors or tapping at windows. Or they'd lock themselves *out* of the building, placing chains on the door to discourage return visits while they burrowed into hiding places of their choice. Eventually, though, most of them were cornered, the papers pressed into their hostile hands, not that it did any good.

In depositions, the Short Creekers followed the "answer them nothing" edict to a T, dodging the simplest of questions like surly schoolboys. They feigned ignorance of next-door neighbors they'd known all their lives, drew blanks over town leaders, and had no interest or information about UEP property lines. Short Creek police maintained their stubborn and bored indifference through hours of deposition questioning, but they weren't at all apathetic about FLDS dissidents emboldened to stay in town under Wisan's hoped for protection. Short Creek cops arrested and harassed these people like it was their full-time job.

Cops badged in Utah and Arizona barged into Ross Chatwin's home, arresting him for trespassing in his own living room. They arrested Truman Barlow for allegedly helping a young girl escape the city limits. In harrowing, regular events, FLDS dissidents were run off the unstable, sandy roads by SUVs with identity-concealing darkened windows, often when terrified young children were riding in the targeted vehicles, screaming as their helpless parents tried desperately to keep control of their cars. Excommunicants' property and cars were vandalized. The apostates were physically menaced by groups of men who'd ambush resistors as they brought home groceries, surrounding them on their own property and refusing to allow the defectors to escape to the safety of their homes.

In one despicable incident, Andrew and Michelle Chatwin's toddler fell desperately ill, struggling to breathe and turning blue. They were turned away from the FLDS-staffed but tax-built and -financed clinic put there by the state of Arizona. FLDS had erected a wall around the public clinic, outfitting it with security cameras at the gate so that non-FLDS sick people could be turned away. Not knowing if their child would live or die, Andrew and Michelle were forced to scream down the highway to St. George at unsafe speeds. Their child was saved, but there were no repercussions for FLDS. To all of the complaints, the Short Creek police departments refused to respond, refused to write reports, and refused to investigate or make arrests, and in many of the incidents, the dissidents believed the police were participants, if not organizers.

In response to this organized, state-sanctioned campaign of terror, and noting Wisan's increasing complaints about the refusal of the Short Creek police to comply with court orders to assist him in legal duties, the states of Arizona and Utah wrote "letters of caution" to the Short Creek police, advising them that if they continued to be so naughty they could be in danger of being investigated or maybe losing their jobs or something . . . possibly. Unsurprisingly, the letters had no effect on the FLDS-staffed police force that, along with every other FLDS leader, was well acquainted with both states' absence of resolve.

Arizona showed a little spunk when prosecutors tossed officer Micah Barlow in jail for ignoring a subpoena to testify before a federal grand jury in Phoenix convened to hear evidence about Warren Jeffs. As an aside, both Shurtleff and Goddard had been beating their brains out trying to get the federal government involved in the FLDS matter. Shurtleff made numerous personal trips to the U.S. attorney's office in Salt Lake City, practically begging for help, but none was forthcoming. Shurtleff's ultraconservative dedication to "states' rights" may have precluded such a conclusion, but Goddard was especially convinced that the law enforcement situation in Short Creek could only be resolved by placing federal agents in charge of the area. Since he had to deal with Arizona's Maricopa County Republicans in September 2005, Goddard skipped the state step, writing directly to then U.S. attorney Alberto Gonzales, asking for a federal civil rights investigation into the escalating housing discrimination and harassment of non-FLDS members, but he received the cold shoulder.

No actions were taken against Jeffs as a result of the federal grand jury in Phoenix either, but Micah Barlow ended up cooling his heels in the seriously unpleasant detention center in Florence, Arizona, for five months for his refusal to testify. Although both the Arizona and Utah POST boards spent the five months (with no end in sight) "investigating" whether Barlow's grand jury no-show constituted breach of duty, the worn-out Barlow saved them the trouble of pretense by turning in his badge shortly after his release.

Other Short Creek cops were not so obliging. Using FLDS attorney Peter Stirba, a handful of the cops filed court challenges to the depositions sought by Wisan for the UEP case, asking judge Denise Lindberg to limit areas the fiduciary could probe to name, rank, and serial number. The request was denied, with the court effectively ordering the cops to answer all questions. But so what? For the FLDS-staffed police force, no court order superseded Warren Jeffs's instructions to "answer them nothing." Nobody knew it yet, but Fred Barlow, the marshal who replaced polygamist marshal Sam Roundy, had written a letter to the fugitive Warren Jeffs, proof that if Fred Barlow didn't personally know Jeffs's whereabouts, he certainly knew the person who did. "Dear Uncle Warren," began a letter that went on to boast about the Short Creek cops' noncompliance with any court order under the sun. "I fill [sic] that without priesthood I am nothing. I do not know exactly what we have ahead of us but I do know that I and all of the other officers have expressed our desire to stand with you and the priesthood." Barlow continued, "I love you and acknowledge you as my priesthood head. And I know that you have the right to rule in all aspects of my live [sic]. I yearn to hear from you." The letter is signed: "Your servant, Fred J. Barlow."

This is the briar patch of law enforcement affairs Bruce Wisan stumbled into when he arrived in Short Creek to determine which properties belonged to the trust and who was entitled to them. For a strictly by-the-book, by-the-numbers guy like Wisan, the surreal nature of a tax-sustained police force taking orders from a self-proclaimed prophet obsessed with little girls was difficult to comprehend, and now there was a brand-new crisis requiring law enforcement assistance: property taxes in the amount of $1.3 million for hundreds of homes, businesses, and land were overdue. Wisan was going to collect it despite the lame illegal fences FLDS was erecting around certain houses in the delusional belief the barriers would make the dwellings more "private" or somehow unconnected to the UEP trust.

Unfortunately for FLDS leaders, Bruce Wisan did not believe in letters of caution.

17

SATAN'S ACCOUNTANT

Suppose you found your brother in bed with your wife, and put a javelin through both of them, you would be justified, and they would atone for their sins and be received into the kingdom of God. I would at once do so in such a case; and under such circumstances, I have no wife whom I love so well that I would not put a javelin through her heart, and I would do it with clean hands.

—Brigham Young, Journal of Discourses, Vol. 3

From 10 P.M. 'til 11:30 P.M., I proofread my dictation for April, only reading part of it, making corrections. I had a few ladies in the room until after midnight.

—Warren Jeffs, April 19, 2005

In the past, the UEP trust had paid all property taxes for FLDS members, but in April 2006 Warren Jeffs stripped bare the UEP cupboards, leaving the membership he'd abandoned to come up with the cash. Wisan tried on several occasions to break through to FLDS leaders, hoping to explain what he intended to do and how in addition to discussing solutions to the tax problem. A month in advance, he asked for time to address the FLDS Colorado City Council, which, like the police departments, was merely another group of FLDS men receiving millions in public money. The request was ignored, but Wisan showed up anyway, hoping to present his plan during the public comments portion of the meeting, which allows individuals three minutes to speak.

As FLDS leaders and their attorneys knew it would be, Wisan's work was rendered nearly impossible by the sect's continued defiance (without consequences) of repeated court orders to turn over records identifying UEP assets. Without them, Wisan was flying blind as he tried to discover property lines or who had been awarded what parcels for homes or businesses. Unlike every other municipality in the industrialized world, the twin cities of Short Creek had not been subdivided and zoned and the results made available for public inspection. In desperation, Wisan hired the engineering firm Bush and Gudgell, Inc., to attempt a survey of Short Creek with what scant information *was* available, trying to make sense of the mishmash of properties that prophets had been allocating according to whim, reward, or punishment for decades.* Wisan also wanted to talk about the process he'd developed through which residents could apply for property benefits, eligibility standards, and, finally, taxes.

Shrill FLDS representatives bombarded the press and scared their membership witless with images of a sinister government evicting thousands and stealing their homes, but the truth about Wisan's plan was exactly the opposite and therefore even more horrifying for Warren Jeffs and his inner circle. From day one, the fiduciary's only goal was to *return* the property to the people actually living on it in the form of legal titles. Instead of Jeffs tucking a family's security in his hip pocket, the family would now be able to keep their futures in their own desks. It dawned on sect leaders almost immediately that making people safe in their own homes would remove a critical tool for scaring people into submission. However, at the time Wisan still thought he could break the ice at city council meetings the leaders were still operating under the "answer them nothing" directive.

Cognizant that the solutions to all the problems associated with the UEP trust affected the future well-being of more than ten thousand people, Wisan had slaved over possible solutions for more than a year. But the FLDS Colorado City Council had neither interest in nor intent to cooperate with what lay ahead. Because Wisan had shown up at what was technically a public government meeting, the FLDS council had little choice but to allow him to speak, but when the three-minute buzzer went off, Wisan was rudely stopped in mid-sentence, not allowed to say one more word. "We have been more than fair with your time," a haughty Mayor Pro Tem Terrell Johnson declared.

Wisan had better luck at the Hildale City Council, which allowed him to explain his plan, albeit to men who had no intention of complying with anything. After his shocking education about the surreal nature of the Short Creek police departments, perhaps he shouldn't have been surprised by the

---

* Hiring the survey firm was the beginning of many expenditures Wisan was forced to make in response to FLDS tactics. The survey firm, lawyers, and accountants Wisan was obliged to hire had to be paid from UEP monies, and the trust that had formerly been solvent began acquiring debt. The *Salt Lake Tribune* in particular began portraying Wisan as a greedy wild spender making a fortune off the backs of low-income FLDS members, without explaining that the deliberate actions of FLDS leaders necessitated the unforeseen expenses.

makeup of the city governments. However, if FLDS thought they could beat Wisan back with sulky noncompliance and accusations of persecution, it had another thing coming. A ferocious competitor, he wasn't about to sacrifice the thirty years he'd put in building an unassailable reputation for honorable and superior work to a bunch of people who thought they ran their own country. They didn't, and Wisan meant to enforce the laws. "Everybody has to pay property taxes, and these people are no different," Wisan told increasing numbers of television news crews. The penalty for nonpayment of taxes was eviction—a process that could take as little as ten days. Would Wisan use police to evict the prairie-dressed children from their homes for nonpayment? If he did, the ensuing press coverage could be 1953 all over again.

The usual way of informing people their taxes were due—sending notices by mail—resulted in the notices suffering the same fate as court summons and subpoenas. They were returned, unopened, with the usual assortment of loopy postal stamps explaining their nondeliverable status. Wisan's representatives found the floor of the Short Creek post office coated with unopened tax notices the FLDS postal workers had decided were not only too much trouble to deliver but also too much trouble to stamp and return. In news stories printed as far away as Johannesburg, South Africa, an angry Mark Shurtleff vowed again to investigate FLDS as an organized crime entity, using RICO statutes to bring charges. Bruce Wisan, meanwhile, kept on keeping on.

Despite the coarse treatment he received in a community whose members called him Satan's Accountant to his face, Wisan hosted regular town hall–style meetings in Short Creek with the trust's newly appointed trustees, all available to explain what was happening and how FLDS members could receive their shares of the trust. Nobody ever came, but Bruce kept holding the meetings because it was his job. He'd started warning FLDS leaders about the tax situation in January. Now it was June, and he'd learned that Warren Jeffs, in another wild fit of irresponsibility, had specifically instructed Short Creek residents *not* to pay any taxes. It was as if Jeffs *wanted* Short Creek residents to suffer and lose their homes while he jazzed around the country with hundreds of thousands of dollars at his disposal.

By now, Wisan didn't deny that he viewed Short Creek as Crackpot City, but he was not without sympathy for the vast majority of FLDS members who'd been raised to blindly follow one man's directions, regardless of if those instructions would deprive them of their homes and livelihoods.

Wisan's blunt demeanor, tart sarcasm, and ill-advised comments had widened the negotiation chasm, if that were even possible. But it was his (and Shurtleff's) belief that these families were not accomplices of Warren Jeffs but his innocent victims. It was Wisan's hope—no, his conviction—that these victims were capable of understanding that Jeffs was ruining their lives if they were given the tools.

A conservative with a conservative's reverence for capitalism, Wisan could think of no better tool than ownership of real property, the safety and protection of owning the home in which your family is sheltered, to defeat the Warren Jeffs virus and encourage individuals to assume some control of their own lives. Bestowing free-and-clear property titles upon the people who'd built the homes they occupied was the best way of executing his fiduciary duties, but it also happily opened a path for real reform in feudal Short Creek.

"I'm a realist," an earnest Wisan said. "I know that a lot of these people will just turn around and give that deed right back to Warren Jeffs." With a laser eye lock, Wisan leaned forward, his closed fists bumping his polished conference table to emphasize the magnitude of the other possibility. "But if only 30 percent of them say, 'No, I think I'll keep my home and my family safe,' we will have changed the population out there to the point where we might be able to start addressing this other lawlessness. The underage marriages. The fraud. All of it. And with no raids, no police, and no arrests."

No arrests maybe, but evictions were a distinct possibility, and drooling television producers everywhere correctly deduced police might be required to accomplish that. Not just any police, either. It was unlikely all the "letters of caution" would persuade Short Creek police to evict residents. Mark Shurtleff would have to send in state cops armed to the eyeballs to drag women and children trained to faint, wail, and weep before cameras that the '53 raid proved to be FLDS's best and most fortuitous friends. "Whew!" said Shurtleff about the tax standoff. "Don't misunderstand me. I would have done it, but *that* wasn't going to be a pretty picture." FLDS leaders relished the notion of turning back the clock with stony-faced police evictions, but Wisan wasn't a fool.

He wasn't a weak-kneed bureaucrat either. Figuring that FLDS leaders wouldn't enjoy the sort of personal loss and devastation they expected of their followers, Wisan targeted them first. Lyle Jeffs, Warren's brother, was the bishop thought to be running the show in Short Creek, receiving instructions directly from his underground brother. He owed $14,000 on the sixty-four acres and 9,000-square-foot mansion, the largest of several homes on the property. Wendell Nielsen, the enforcer enriched by Rulon Jeffs and who got behind Warren Jeffs from the start, was now thought to be FLDS's "first counselor." Together with property held by Seth Jeffs, Mayor Pro Tem Terrell Johnson, and former Colorado City School Board chairman Alvin Barlow, $64,000 was owed on five parcels. Wisan also targeted former UEP trustee James Zitting and Colorado City councilman Bill Shapley, who was also on the board of the soon-to-be-embattled Twin Cities Utility Company.

In all, twelve to fourteen individuals were targeted for eviction, and Wisan wasn't going to fall into the trap of a mass eviction. He was going to cut each man from the herd, isolating each to take the fall alone, one at a time. Without a shield of prairie skirts and kids, Wisan didn't reckon the FLDS leaders possessed the intestinal fortitude to lose their homes all alone.

Since FLDS postal workers weren't delivering the tax notices, Wisan decided to avoid future misunderstandings by hand-tacking the eviction notices to the proper doors, and for this he needed on-site workers. In addition to excommunicated accountant Jethro Barlow, Wisan had employed another Jeffs victim, Isaac Wyler, as a kind of liaison for the fiduciary in Salt Lake City. Wyler and excommunicated-but-sticking-to-his-house Andrew Chatwin were up for the tax notice job. In fact, they relished the opportunity.

FLDS interpreted Wisan's use of sect excommunicants enthused about the prospect of reclaiming their homes as an act of war, and the FLDS city governments would soon target Wisan employees like the boisterous Isaac Wyler for retaliation. Like many of those Jeffs excommunicated, Wyler still considers himself to be in the FLDS religion. He believes Jeffs is the apostate fraud, with Jeffs's inner circle nothing more than thugs who are victimizing the rest of the FLDS membership. He regards his work with Wisan identifying vacant properties as potential homesteads for those Jeffs banished as an effort to restore FLDS, not end it.

Before Jeffs came on the scene, Wyler's vocal independent streak, epitomized by his flamboyant cowboy garb, was accepted good-naturedly within FLDS leadership; the irritation of his occasional dissenting outbursts far outweighed by Wyler's unquestioned dedication to FLDS tenets. But dissent infuriated Warren Jeffs, as did Wyler's apparent devotion to a single wife. "I loved my wife a lot," Wyler explained. "I wasn't *against* polygamy," he added emphatically. "I just loved my wife."

Wyler loved his daughters too, and that may have been his undoing. As Warren Jeffs wedged himself into power, Wyler was inclined to say something, but his wife convinced him to keep his tongue in his head and his body out of Warren's way. For a while, Wyler contented himself to stay on his large farm busying himself with his horses and livestock. "She [his wife] told me she would stay with me if I didn't oppose Warren, and I tried. I really tried, but . . ." But Warren Jeffs's behavior became so ridiculous Wyler could not help slipping anonymous tips to reporters who'd been nosing around. As far as he knew, no one in FLDS leadership ever discovered his Deep Throat role, though he was forced to deny his suspicious wife's accusations that he was the source of some printed news items. He was skating on thin ice with that, and the ice finally cracked when Wyler announced he would not submit his daughters for underage marriage. "I said, 'Over my dead body,'" a defiant Wyler said, shoulders thrown back. "I'd say it again."

Wyler was given no warning. One day, in the blink of an eye, his life was gone. Warren Jeffs had him escorted out of the city, his wife was reassigned, and his children were gone. Devastated, anchorless, aching from every inch of his soul, Wyler first attempted to complete the "repent from afar" routine, withdrawing to a dumpy hotel to write letter after letter detailing his sins and crimes—everything he could remember from the time he was a child. He was desperate to get his wife back, but after months passed with no sound from Short Creek, he was forced to accept what he already knew in his heart: it was all gone. Warren Jeffs had taken everything from him and would be giving nothing back.

It sometimes takes years for FLDS men to realize that, despite what the prophet said, there had never been any hope of regaining their families, but not everyone clings to that hope for long, despite overwhelming evidence to the contrary. Excommunicant Richard Holm, ejected during the 2004 mass banishments, spent six weeks in the Mark Twain Hotel going through dozens of paper pads, emptying ink cartridges by the dozen to detail his crimes, real or imagined, for Warren Jeffs's perusal. Then Richard accidentally bumped into his own brother, who hadn't spoken to him since his ejection, on the street, who told him he'd married two of Richard's wives and one of them was pregnant with Richard's brother's baby. "My own *brother*," Richard would repeat in wonder years after the event.

Some FLDS men, like the three Barlow Boys also thrown out in 2004, limp off to waste away, dying alone and impoverished, but not Wyler, Holm, and an ever-increasing number of others. Holm actually stormed from the Mark Twain Hotel, striding down Short Creek's streets to retake his vacant home, and he stayed there despite the constant menacing from FLDS enforcement squads. With Wisan's help, Wyler was able to obtain an occupancy agreement from the UEP trust and a job to help with the bills to boot. For hundreds, maybe thousands of men like Wyler and Holm, the court takeover of UEP headed by the unexpectedly fierce Wisan was a godsend. To be honest again, Wyler saw his job partly as sweet vengeance. It couldn't replace his wife, but part of Isaac's duties included helping other excommunicants get titles to their properties.

In his quieter moments, Wyler admits that his new life brought fear as a constant companion. When his phone rings in the dead of night, it is another death threat from a disembodied voice. Anytime he goes to his truck, he must steel himself for the possibility of another mutilated animal carcass. The blast of a backfiring car sends him sprawling to earth, defensively hugging the ground. Several of Wyler's beloved horses were killed when all of the gates fencing his livestock were mysteriously opened and the frightened animals shooed into traffic. He is never really safe, never sure that he will make it through the day without injury or worse or that his home will be standing even if he does. Sitting in a cathedral-sized great room in Colorado City with a dozen other excommunicants gathered for an interview, the infectious smile is gone from Wyler's perpetually cheerful face as he gazes sorrowfully at the floor, remembering his own losses as others describe theirs. "It's hard sometimes," he admitted, but it is Wisan's good fortune that Wyler doesn't succumb to fear or depression. And FLDS leaders are undoubtedly not amused that Wyler sometimes allows press to accompany him as he carries out court orders in Short Creek, as he did on a day he was delivering tax notices.

"I'm not gonna chase after ya," Wyler yelled cheerfully after a group of prairie-dressed women fleeing his approach, herding their unnecessarily terrified children before them as they beat a hysterical retreat into a nearby home. He and Andrew Chatwin, who often videotapes Wyler's movements to avoid future unfortunate mischaracterizations of the events in court, were going door-to-door with the notices. Wyler knocked on the door the women had slammed and dead bolted, but his only answer was the heartbreaking sobs of the children who were told he was there to murder them. As he began taping the notice to the door, his pent-up pain and frustration were freed by the sight of a man trying to escape down a flight of back porch stairs. "Show some guts!" Wyler shouted after the escaping male. "Take yer papers!"

Very few of Isaac's papers were actually placed in their recipients' hostile hands, but FLDS leaders would have probably remained unimpressed if they had. With very rare exceptions, their experience with edicts from the states of either Utah or Arizona did not leave them quaking in their boots. Rodney Holm had been convicted, but outside of that, the sect had never been touched. Anyone who even got close had been beaten back with threats about religious persecution and reminders of the aftermath of the 1953 raid. Why should a nuisance like unpaid taxes be any different? Bruce Wisan was, everyone could see, a tenacious and stubborn man, but so what? He was playing chicken with FLDS now, and in America, charges of religious persecution always trump any card.

But as Wisan's tax deadline for the targeted FLDS leaders approached, visions of the successful Holm prosecution may have started dancing in their heads. Lyle Jeffs was first in line for eviction, and as the days ticked down to his deadline, there was only silence from the fiduciary in Salt Lake City. Wisan had not tried to reason or negotiate with Lyle Jeffs or any of the other dozen FLDS leaders. There hadn't even been an offer to reduce the bill.

A week became four days, then two days, before Lyle Jeffs would presumably be escorted from his home by Mohave County sheriff's deputies. Maybe even Gary Engels would be with them. Perhaps the television crews would come, but there would not be any gut-wrenching scene to photograph, only the brother of a fugitive on the FBI's Most Wanted list being justly led away for failing to pay his rightful share of taxes. A day before Lyle Jeffs's scheduled eviction, the owed $14,000 was paid. Within a week, hundreds of thousands of dollars were also ponied up anonymously for all the "well-heeled" houses, as Wisan's attorney, Jeffrey Shields, called them.

But that still left the not-so-well-heeled houses, homes belonging to the average FLDS members who were, as usual, left twisting in the wind by their leadership. No one paid the average resident's taxes with suitcases of anonymous cash. Instead, the leadership dragged wheelbarrows into church services, rolling them up and down the aisles, exhorting and embarrassing the fearful congregation into putting every last coin in their pockets into the pot.

It's unknown how much was collected this way, but all the Short Creek taxes were paid, including penalties. However, Wisan and others suspected the wheelbarrows were also part of the "pennies for the prophet" campaign, in which FLDS families who were already eating nothing but

milk-soaked bread for supper were expected to give every last penny over
to support Warren Jeffs's high-flying fugitive lifestyle along with the construction of the new Zion in Texas, a salvation in which most of them
would not be included.

Wisan wasn't sure about the wheelbarrows' role in propping up Warren
Jeffs, but he was dead certain the attempted liquidation of assets in Canada
were meant for Jeffs. The FLDS outpost in Bountiful had split off when
Warren Jeffs took power in the United States. Most of the FLDS Canadians
went with Winston Blackmore, a gregarious if equally power-driven leader
with more than nineteen wives who'd once been a UEP trustee and ally
of Rulon Jeffs. It was Blackmore who'd protected sixteen-year-old Rebecca
Rohbeck from Warren Jeffs's alleged blood atonement order in 2001, openly
defying Jeffs's claims of legitimacy, convincing most of the Canadian population to side with him.

But Warren Jeffs still had a clutch of Canadian followers who walled
themselves off from the Blackmore sect under the leadership of Jeffs's spy
Jim Oler. Incredibly, this segment had control of the tax-financed Canadian
school system, just as FLDS had in Colorado City. In addition to the build-
ings, equipment, and supplies, the Bountiful Elementary-Secondary School
Society (BESS) received $650,000 a year from the Canadian government,
even though the number of children in school was questionable. As in
Colorado City, that money could have gone directly to Warren Jeffs, but
Wisan had now learned that Oler was attempting to duplicate the Colorado
City example by selling off BESS assets.

Wisan filed suit in Canada, and Mark Shurtleff flew out personally to chat
with his Canadian counterpart, Wally Opel. The planned sell-off was halted.

Wisan also filed suit against Warren Jeffs and all former trustees of the
UEP trust for illegally draining its assets, and the resolved tax problems in
Short Creek had been replaced by new ones. Wisan's astounding successes in
the twin cities, as FLDS began calling the community, had impressed newspapers across the country who crowed that the feisty fiduciary was "batting
a thousand." But Short Creek had become a ghost town by day. The streets
were empty, houses locked, curtains drawn, stores shuttered, and even the
public buildings abandoned, doors fastened with chains. FLDS apparently perceived they could only escape Wisan's powerful sunshine with a nocturnal
lifestyle, burrowing underground by day, creeping out cautiously at night.

Isaac Wyler reported that the town's business was now conducted after
dark, including illegal building projects. When UEP was placed under court

supervision, all land transfers or new construction had to be approved by the fiduciary. FLDS leadership apparently thought that proceeding as if there were no fiduciary would go unnoticed if it happened at night. It was a bizarre premise Wisan was nonetheless compelled to address, heaping staff and expense upon the already bankrupt trust.

There were Dan Fischer and Mark Shurtleff and Pennie Petersen and Flora Jessop and even Ruth Stubbs, but for the FLDS, Wisan was the ultimate fiend capable of unspeakable acts. Members of the sect's hatred of the man who'd stood up to them and won was so pure it became supernatural. In 2006, Wisan knew he'd never seen a mess like the UEP trust before and would never again, but he had no idea how bad things would get in a few short months when FLDS changed tactics.

18

NAILED

Uncle Warren is a tall man; he is nearly six feet four,
He sometimes has to duck a bit when coming through a door;
But never is he known to flee or duck responsibility.
Uncle Warren is a slender man; but he's so kind to all,
It's a wonder such a great big heart could fit a frame that small.
And every time I shake his hand, I feel my own little heart expand.
(Chorus)
Uncle Warren is a perfect Priesthood man;
To the Prophet he is loyal through and through,
And he's so full of love for our Father above,
You just can't help but love him, too.

—Song required of FLDS first and second graders

This afternoon, I wrote Paula Jeffs, my wife, a note of correction, teaching her that
she needs to be more fervent in seeking the Lord's will, and not just judging what she
thinks will beautify the Lord's house, as the Lord has rejected the materials for the
upstairs sheers and drapes. I told her the Lord will accept the drapes out of the pres-
ent materials temporarily, but after the dedication of the temple, we will replace the
drapes made out of materials that do not have a grain in it or a pattern in the mate-
rial. She has informed me that some other sheers may have a grain or pattern to them.
We are learning. We are learning. We are learning.

—Warren Jeffs, "Record of President Warren Jeffs," April 22, 2005

While the panicked FLDS membership scrounged for eleventh-hour wheelbarrow pennies to save their homes from the delinquent taxes Warren Jeffs had ordered them not to pay, the prophet was breaking in the massive temple built in Texas from their looted UEP trust. As Wendell Nielsen articulated during one of the supersecret, oil-anointing ordination ceremonies Jeffs was performing, only a "little group" of FLDS people would ever be invited to Texas, much less allowed inside the temple, which had an estimated tax value of $8 million.

Warren Jeffs had received every detail of the enormous structure, which can be seen forty miles away in San Angelo, via dreams from the Lord. Color schemes that vary from floor to floor, turrets, stair rails, and moldings—Jeffs went through an excruciating process interpreting and extracting hints from the Lord over months and months of dreams. Of course, the supernatural cement recipe had never come together, not that Jeffs blamed the Lord for that. The Lord had revealed a half-dozen rocks to be crushed in the YFZ ranch's illegal cement plant that kept getting shut down for environmental violations, which was a bother but not the real problem.

No, the real problem was that the concoctions Jeffs ordered his crews to mix kept falling apart like sand castles. It was his workers' incompetence, he believed, and although he publicly punished the failures, he was still privately nagged that the Lord was coyly holding out on him, failing to disclose a mystery ingredient for reasons certainly tied to the "halfhearted" in his flock. More men required "handling," that was for sure, and more women needed reassigning, not to mention more girls needed to be married. Finally, Jeffs got the dream that showed the critical element that would make his concrete impervious to time or atom bombs: white sand from the Gulf of Mexico.

Jeffs had spent a lot of time in New Orleans and a lot of time in tanning salons, but he'd never actually gotten tan on a Gulf of Mexico beach *near* New Orleans. That's one reason he knew that, when the Lord showed him a dream of him and Naomie romping on a white sand beach, he had his answer. He dispatched crews to the gulf to gather up truckloads of the stuff, but his workers failed him again. The mixture would not set, and with the end of days just around the corner, Jeffs decided to bite the bullet and mix the concrete the sect had always used to build the temple that would be covered with a blinding white limestone.

Along with the giddy escalation in marriages, these were the problems Warren Jeffs was dealing with as Bruce Wisan began warning Short Creek residents they would soon lose their homes if their taxes were not paid. It was a problem never faced by FLDS Texas residents, whose estimated tax bill for the entire ranch was $450,000 annually and was always promptly paid. By June 2006, around the time the tax problem in Short Creek was resolved, Randy Mankin noted that the temple appeared complete, surrounded by a white, twelve-foot fence to keep out the riffraff who'd built it. Apparently, Jeffs used the temple exclusively to perform rituals upon a select group within the select group he'd moved to Texas, a state that continued its refusal to ignore FLDS malfeasance.

Texas environmental agencies had levied a total of $50,000 in fines as the Yearning for Zion ranch added septic equipment, a dairy, a cheese factory, machinist shops, large-scale agricultural plots, and various other endeavors that could transform it into a self-contained community of which Brigham Young would heartily approve. Although Jeffs's dictations indicate he was aware of the sect's difficulties with state agencies, he seemed to regard the persistent run-ins as persecutions the Lord would fix by softening Texan hearts. The newly softened hearts would be created by something like a spell under which Texas authorities would abandon their permits and construction codes and forget about the complaints already in the system. As evidence that the heart-softening process was under way, Jeffs cited a satisfactory interaction between Eldorado hospital personnel and an injured FLDS child rushed into the emergency room after an accident.

Mingling with the locals might have been a good step toward softer hearts, but Jeffs had taken the opposite tack, ordering that no interaction occur, particularly not with the women and girls. And not every FLDS member was fortunate enough to be rushed to the hospital in life-threatening circumstance. A sixteen-year-old girl nearly lost her life in a difficult childbirth because Jeffs would not allow her to be taken to the hospital. After the girl had been in labor for two days, anxious FLDS midwives were able to persuade men in high positions to contact the elusive Jeffs for permission to get her real medical attention, but after considering the matter at his leisure, Jeffs decided the girl's age would invite too many unwanted inquiries. Her underage status might open her "husband," Raymond Merril Jessop, to arrest, and so the writhing, bleeding, agonized girl stayed in the busy FLDS "birthing center" to either make it or not. The girl survived, barely.

Warren Jeffs became increasingly hard to reach when he was in the promised land of Texas. Apparently, Jeffs did not trust the "pruned" and pure population in Texas anymore than the "halfhearted" one in Short Creek, and the completion of the Lord's first FLDS temple had not salved Jeffs's thirst for the open road. He continued a frenetic schedule of travel between Idaho, Colorado, Texas, and Short Creek, but by 2006 he was sneaking in and out of the YFZ ranch under cover of darkness and with disguises, the same as he'd done in Short Creek since 2003. Jeffs hadn't been seen out in the open at YFZ for a year, and even when he was present, he kept himself stashed inside his walled-in mansion with select "ladies," often in disguise.

By the summer of 2006, it almost seemed as if Jeffs found the open road a happier, safer haven than any of his heavily fortified residences in four states, including an opulent chalet in the resort ski city of Durango, Colorado. The constant car swaps and buys exposed him to the danger of eye-catching temporary license plates, and he recorded several impotent traffic stops during his time on the FBI Most Wanted list. In at least one of them, he couldn't produce a car registration or proof of insurance, yet the officer still let him go with a friendly warning. Jeffs interpreted the break as the Lord's divine protection, along with every thunderstorm to mask his passing or unexpectedly vacant hotel suite large enough to accommodate the mass weddings. In fact, he seemed certain of his heavenly invincibility so long as he was in motion, a protection he sourly noted had not been extended to his brother, Seth.

Warren was disgusted by Seth's arrest in Colorado, but more than the drunkenness and this loss of nearly $200,000 in cash and prepaid phones and credit cards, Seth's misfortune was evidence that the Lord didn't like him much. He had to be "handled," along with the hapless Wendell Musser, who'd also been arrested for drunk driving while he and his wife were minding nineteen of Warren Jeffs's women. After spending two days in jail, Musser returned to the "safe house" to find it abandoned by everyone, including his wife and infant son, who'd been immediately reassigned after Musser's instant excommunication.*

Because the Lord was directing everyone's travels, Warren did not take Seth's arrest as a signal that they should be more careful. Together with his heavenly protection, Warren felt his erratic, unpredictable routes and his other nifty countersurveillance measures were foolproof. He preened especially over his cunning idea that he and Naomie would never ride in the first car of the caravans in which he traveled. He stumbled on this ingenious evasive maneuver during one of the close-call stops, when his car was pulled over for a hair-raising interrogation but those behind him just cruised on by.

---

* Warren did not hesitate to excommunicate his own family members, especially brothers he saw as competition. Although Seth was not a perceived threat, Warren had excommunicated upward of a half dozen of his brothers he thought were threats by the summer of 2006 and very nearly had to punish a few of their reassigned wives. The wife of his excommunicated brother David began crying during her reassignment wedding, blasphemously questioning the prophet when she asked if she couldn't have a little more time to see if David could redeem himself and come home. Sternly informed that this was not a possibility, the tearful woman still could not look her new husband in the eye or take his hand for the ceremony. She did, however, get in the car and drive away with him, which Warren observed was lucky for her.

Warren reasoned that if he rode in the *second* caravan car, he'd be the one sailing innocently around the unfortunates in the first car dealing with the police, invisible as air.

The chink in this armor would lead to the biggest problem of Jeffs's life so far, because nobody informed Nevada highway patrolman Eddie Dutchover which of the many vehicles traveling Highway 15 in late August comprised Warren's caravan, much less which one was out front. On August 28, some eighty miles outside of Las Vegas, Officer Dutchover's attention was drawn to a red Cadillac Escalade with a temporary paper license plate obscured by mud or some other substance. Dutchover couldn't read the Cadillac's plate and initiated the stop. Warren Jeffs's confidence in the open road had lulled him into violating a cardinal rule for savvy fugitives: drive a legal car and *never* give police a simple reason, like speeding or muddy license plates, to pull you over.

For Dutchover, it was a routine stop. He only wanted to warn the car's occupants of the plate's condition and even help them dust it off. Inside the Cadillac, driven by Warren's brother and painted red, the color over which Jeffs had destroyed men's lives, the air was thick with fear. With Naomie in her subservient spot in the far backseat of the SUV, Warren had been about to dig into a fast food takeout salad when a cordial Dutchover popped his head inside the car. The Nevada trooper thought it very odd that the spindly, anemic-looking guy in the backseat started robotically shoveling forkful after forkful of salad into his mouth, staring straight ahead and not responding to questions as he kept up the mechanical chewing, like he'd been possessed. "It worried me," Dutchover admitted later. "I even asked him, 'Are you OK?'"

When he didn't get an answer and nobody in the car could even manage to look at him, Dutchover asked the men to exit the vehicle, asking them separately where they were headed. Contradictory answers of "Denver" and "Texas" put Dutchover on full alert. He allowed the men back into the car, where the guy with the salad resumed his demonic chewing, the carotid artery in his neck throbbing with such force Dutchover worried his man might be verging on passing out.

For identification, the salad guy had only been able to produce an eyeglass prescription in the name of John Findley, but looking at him closer now, Dutchover put his finger on something else that had been bothering him since the beginning of the stop. This agitated guy looked familiar. In fact, he looked exactly like the individual whose photograph graced the top of the FBI Most Wanted poster in his office. And that, as they say, was all she wrote.

As Dutchover waited for backup, a handcuffed Jeffs continued to deny his true identity, but once the FBI arrived, Jeffs gave up. "You know who I am," he told the gathering swarm of state and federal cops. In the flash-lighted photograph taken at the side of the highway that Monday night, a handcuffed Warren Jeffs wears a borderline haughty expression and a white Mountain Outfitters T-shirt, baggy green cargo shorts, and black socks and shoes. A handcuffed Naomie, who along with Warren's brother was later released without being charged, wears a T-shirt and jeans, her hair still dyed brown, eyes like a wounded deer, and wearing a goofy half-smile that might have been a product of shock.

From inside the new $70,000 Cadillac, police confiscated mostly hundred-dollar bills totaling nearly $60,000 in cash, ten sets of keys to high-end vehicles, tens of thousands in prepaid credit cards and phones, a number of comput-ers, a number of GPS systems, police scanners, a list of safe houses, wigs, makeup, and a large pile of literally tear-stained letters from excommunicated men begging to return to their families. The letters were in one bag, and in another were checks bearing the stricken men's signatures. Warren Jeffs had extracted the money the anguished men continued to send like clockwork before consigning the brokenhearted pleas for mercy to the trash.

CNN and other television news outlets interrupted broadcasts to break news of Jeffs's arrest, which also made international headlines. Jeffs would later blame his capture on his failure to don one of the three wigs in the car that night, though it is doubtful the sharp-eyed Dutchover would have overlooked one of the Halloweenish-quality hairpieces anymore than he did Jeffs's pulsating artery. Jeffs was taken to a Nevada jail to await extradition to Utah, which he did not contest. On September 6, he appeared in a St. George courtroom under heavy guard and was held without bail. Mohave County investigator Gary Engels was on hand for the event and managed to speak with the man he'd been tracking for years. "I wanted to put a human face to the name," he told a throng of press. "He was decent. I told him he looked thin. He said, 'I always look this way.'"

Not for long. At the aptly named Purgatory facility outside St. George, Jeffs became an immediate headache for jailers forced to protect the FLDS prophet from his own health-threatening fasts and hours of catatonic prayer that left his knees raw, ulcerous, and sometimes infected. Jeffs's weight would drop to as low as 130 pounds on his six-foot-four-inch frame. He sometimes had to be force-fed, and his mental health was often in question, with reports of compulsive masturbation from which Jeffs had to be restrained. In some videotaped jail visits with family members, Jeffs does not seem wholly aware of his circumstances, fingering the cord of the telephone device in odd silences that last up to thirteen minutes between disjointed, droning thoughts.

Skeptics wondered if Jeffs's weird behavior was only the calculating groundwork for a cynical insanity bargain that could land him in a hospital instead of a prison, though his subsequent actions undermine that theory. Whatever Jeffs's actions around his worried jailers, his dictations at the beginning of January 2007 suggest organized thinking, if not a clear head.

In between railing against his enemies in government and traitors within his family and flock, Warren Jeffs had a funeral to plan—Naomie's. In the past, Warren had found more than a few days separation from Naomie unendurable. Now that he'd been incarcerated for eighteen weeks, her death was apparently the only way to salve the pain, a solution the Lord had "whispered with a witness of burning peace." The Lord had been good enough to show Jeffs "how Naomie would be taken and when. He showed me the record that she has with her will be preserved, and that she would go quickly and without blood being shed, and without a police investigation."

It is not known if Naomie Jeffs was actually in danger of being murdered to end Warren's jealous separation anxiety, but no one could have helped her if he had in fact instructed someone to kill her. It was suspected, though not proven, that his dictations and other sensitive papers were being transported in and out of prison by attorneys the sect hired to defend the criminal charges. On Thursday, January 18, Warren entered one of his thrashing "heavenly sessions," which went unobserved by his constant suicide-watch guards but during which the Lord showed him that Naomie "had been taken" and was happily ensconced in heaven, well removed from devising men.

"He [the Lord] allowed me to hear her voice how happy she is . . . and that the record she had with her was hidden in the lining of her luggage." Furthermore, Naomie was not one bit upset about her early demise but advised Warren she'd be waiting for him in "the fullness of Zion." With the Lord's help, Warren planned elaborate public and private services to take place Sunday, designating who would speak at each before her burial in Texas. He even began arrangements so that he could make a call to one of the services from prison.

But if Warren actually asked someone to put a quick, bloodless, and uninvestigated end to Naomie's life, that person didn't go through with it. Sunday came and went without any funerals, and Warren never mentioned her death again, though he continued to be gripped with a rage expressed in visions of bloodshed and mutilation. "The Lord told me that some of my family would be taken and offered as human sacrifice in Satan worship by my enemies," he wrote. Among many other horrors, the Lord told Warren he'd be publically beaten, slashed with knives, and "unsexed" for the pleasure of howling Gentile crowds, but in the end God would restore him while tearing his enemies limb from limb, this time for Warren's pleasure.

Jeffs's flailing hatred is perhaps understandable from a man recently incarcerated. He indulged it with abandon, but his concern over whatever documents Naomie was safeguarding in her luggage lining indicated he was still concerned with running FLDS. After Jeffs's arrest, Mark Shurtleff, Terry Goddard, Matt Smith, Roger Hoole, and a dozen others expressed hope that FLDS members freed from the prophet's immediate vise might be able to reevaluate their position as his victims and chumps, perhaps even cooperating with authorities trying to sort out the UEP mess. Only Bruce Wisan provided a view of grimmer reality. "He controlled things while he was on the run, and he'll control things while he is behind bars," a stoic Wisan said. "Just like a mob boss."

And indeed, wedged between Jeffs's violent "revelations" and dreams of a blood-soaked future were the same micromanaging orders governing his membership's every movement, delivered by family members and high-ranking FLDS visitors to the jail. From the letters and directives given to individuals, it is clear that Jeffs's spy network remained undisrupted by the arrest. Jeffs admonishes women for specific gossiping, tardiness to kitchen tasks, poor disciplinary decisions with children—all details that would have had to have been reported to him.

In Short Creek, the atmosphere was somber, unchanged by the arrest. A national ABC news crew discovered firsthand what law enforcement in the twin cities really meant. After the crew was menaced and nearly assaulted on the street by a mob of hostile FLDS residents, the Colorado City police arrived to threaten the news crew with arrest, herding them from a town from which the working journalists were grateful to escape without injury. In Texas, the streets of the YFZ ranch were deserted as people kept indoors, praying and fasting for Warren Jeffs.

What happened over the next four months was veiled in secrecy, known only to a few of Jeffs's top generals, attorneys hired by the sect to defend the criminal charges, and some court personnel. Considering the crush of national and international press flitting around Utah after Jeffs's arrest, the total information blackout on the shocking developments inside the Purgatory jail and out was an enormous feat.

At the heart of it were videotapes of Warren Jeffs so numbing that his supporters would claim the government hired actors for a rented movie set to fake the tapes. As Jeffs's trial date approached, those videotapes were among the world's best-kept secrets and would restore a phalanx of FLDS attorneys to their former glory.

19

CONVICTION

I say to all grunters, grumblers, whiners, hypocrites, and sycophants, who snivel, crouch, and crawl around the most contemptible of all creatures for a slight favor, should it enter my mind to dig down the Twin Peaks, and I set men to work to do so, it is none of your business. . . . I am not to be called into question as to what I do with my funds, whether I build high walls or low walls, garden walls or city walls, and if I please, it is my right to pull down my walls tomorrow. If anyone wishes to apostatize upon such grounds, the quicker he does so the better.

—Brigham Young, after his order to wall off his mansions (as Jeffs did) was questioned, March 3, 1860

13) I recommend a "tent city" be prepared for R17 [Texas] making "camp sites" east of the new duplexes east of the meeting house, spread out in the trees. Every few camp sites would have a small building with bathroom stalls, showers, and tubs, laundry facilities, and storage room for supplies. Then clear ground and even have many camp stoves and portable tables to give each camp site, and have many tents on hand to put up, in case we have many people suddenly needing refuge.

—Warren Jeffs, instructions from Purgatory jail for temporary housing for his final selections of transplants from Short Creek to Texas, April 30, 2007

Unlike Gary Engels, UEP fiduciary Bruce Wisan had no particular desire to put a face with Warren Jeffs's name, let alone talk to the man he considered a multilayered criminal, but the fiduciary felt he could leave no stone—however immovable—untouched in his duty to sort out the catastrophic mess that was the UEP trust. To imagine that Jeffs would shed light on the trust's missing millions, illegal land sales and transfers, or current property boundaries and assets would be a fool's fantasy. Jeffs was himself legally culpable for the mess and had personally instructed the old trustees not to cooperate, but Wisan submitted numerous written requests for interviews with Jeffs all the same. Predictably, they were all ignored.

Wisan was not surprised when his attempts to visit Jeffs in jail or communicate with him by letter failed, but something had to be done about the trust's cash fluidity crisis. Trying to punch through the sect's obfuscation with surveying firms and attorneys had proved expensive. Wisan's firm was owed $100,000, and the firm of his attorney, Jeffrey Shields, was owed about a half million. Despite court orders, the trust's former FLDS trustees were still refusing to turn over any UEP records and actively obstructing Wisan's attempts to determine the exact nature of the trust independently. In light of the fact that Wisan didn't know himself what the trust was worth, he was unsurprisingly having little luck persuading banks to offer bridge loans to cover administrative expenses. The cash crunch meant one thing: Wisan was going to have to sell UEP property to pay the UEP bills.

Meanwhile, Wisan had opened up the application process for beneficiaries to make claims on the trust based upon their contributions, regardless of whether they currently were FLDS members. This provision was what FLDS leaders feared the most. Warren Jeffs had personally ejected hundreds of FLDS men and boys, his father hundreds more. There could be thousands of FLDS "apostates" drifting around the country, any of them eligible to claim land in Short Creek for contributions made to the sect before they were thrown out.

Wisan knew that, even if he got property titles into the hands of current FLDS members, there was a chance they'd be terrified enough to simply return the deeds to Warren Jeffs. Unlike these people, excommunicated members coming home from exile would *never* consider returning their property deeds to the jailed prophet, leaving FLDS leaders to contemplate their possible demise on two fronts. If some members kept their homes and a good percentage of exiled members returned, FLDS leaders would lose control of the community.

For ex-FLDS activists, a loosening of the leadership's grip on members was all they'd sought. The presence of individuals who did not feel too frightened to question dubious practices could not help but influence the direction of the twin cities as a whole. No one understood this better than FLDS leaders, who in the past had fought tooth and nail to prevent a single non-FLDS believer from infiltrating Short Creek's boundaries.

At the beginning of 2007, however, the FLDS legal strategy was still cruising on "answer them nothing," except, of course, where Warren Jeffs's skin was concerned. The sect had no money to keep UEP afloat, but there was plenty for Jeffs's three criminal lawyers, Walter "Wally" Bugdon Jr. and

Tara Isaacson of Salt Lake City and Richard Wright of Las Vegas. After their client was arraigned and tucked in jail, the defense lawyers turned their skills upon the August 28 stop of the Cadillac Escalade, which they claimed was illegal; the subsequent search of the vehicle, also claimed to be illegal; and the confiscated cash, electronic gear, credit cards, wigs, and the rest, which Warren Jeffs demanded returned to him forthwith.

Challenging arrests, searches, and confiscation of property is standard for any criminal case, and Jeffs's attorneys would not have been doing their jobs if they hadn't tried to negate the search, but there was a little more at stake here than usual. Any number of people wanted access to the material seized from the Cadillac for present and future investigations, especially any documents or records that might be on the three laptops. Interested parties included Mark Shurtleff, who was looking at RICO charges, Terry Goddard and Matt Smith in Arizona, Roger Hoole, and, naturally, Bruce Wisan. No sooner was the search ruled legitimate than Jeffs's lawyers had to get into court staving off challenges from everyone who wanted access to the confiscated material. As it turned out, that would be the least of their problems.

From January 2007 until nearly the end of Jeffs's trial eleven months later, the public had no idea that Jeffs had renounced his position as prophet, declaring himself "the wickedest man in the world" who'd taken power for greedy, selfish reasons, performed illegal marriages, and excommunicated people who didn't deserve it. Though he continued insisting for months that he was an imposter, only a few people knew it, and they weren't talking.

The trouble began shortly after Naomie's funeral failed to materialize and a St. George judge refused to dismiss any of the charges against Jeffs, another standard challenge brought by his attorneys. On January 24, about a week after Naomie didn't die, Jeffs began calling people in for jail visits one by one to admit he was a fraud.

"I am not the prophet. I was never the prophet, and I have been deceived by the powers of evil, and Brother William E. Jessop has been the prophet since father's passing, since the passing of my father. And I have been the most wicked man in this dispensation, in the eyes of God," Jeffs declared. Over two days, Jeffs told a dozen people that what he was telling them was the truth—he specifically and repeatedly emphasized that his confessions were *not* another in the endless series of tests from God. He added that he was not only an imposter but an incestuous pedophile "who committed immoral acts with a sister and a daughter," activities he apparently undertook early on.

"I haven't held the priesthood since I was twenty," he said. He admitted that he took control of FLDS out of selfish greed and released all women and girls from their unsanctioned marriages. He asserted that all the men whose lives he ruined with excommunication did not deserve their ejections. Steps should be taken immediately to bring them back and undo the orgy of marriages and reassignments of women and children.

Not only did Jeffs repeat his crimes over and over again, verbatim, to a number of high-ranking FLDS men, he insisted that his fidgeting, tearful brother Nephi make Warren's January 25 confessional videotape public, displayed to anyone "who wished to see it, so they can see it is me saying it." He wrote out his confession in duplicate, handing it to FLDS leaders with instructions that they show it to the FLDS membership, reminding them his abdication was not a test.

"Well, you can imagine the bind they [FLDS leadership] were in," said Hoole with a Cheshire cat smile. "Wendell Nielsen, or others who might want to be prophet, had utterly no authority, and besides, there cannot be a new prophet unless the old one is dead. It was terrible for them. They couldn't keep control of FLDS without Warren, and Warren was losing it."

No one followed Jeffs's instructions to release his confession. Five days later, Jeffs made the first of several suicide attempts, although when the prison doctor was asked if any of them were serious he responded, "Not really." On one occasion, Jeffs began body-slamming himself against his cell walls, and on another, he banged only his head. An attempt, perhaps less thought through, involved Jeffs wrapping his jail clothes around his neck, trying to manually strangle himself by tugging the ends with his own hands. Only the head-butting effort was rewarded with a hospital visit. Overall, the most serious threat Jeffs posed to himself was his constant fasting and praying, which guards said did not appear to be linked to any death wish.

Although none of Jeffs's confederates released his tape, which would not be unsealed by court order until November 2007, the public did get some advance notice after a strange pretrial hearing before Ruth Stubbs's old judge, James Shumate, in late March. At the end of the hearing, Jeffs told the judge that he wanted to talk to him to "take care of something." As Jeffs tried to approach the alarmed Shumate, he extended a legal-sized sheet of paper covered with handwriting. As Shumate prepared to flee the bench, a photographer for the *Deseret News* snapped a photograph of the interaction. "I want to take care of this now," Jeffs protested, as his attorneys pulled him back and the hearing ended.

When *Deseret News* staff enlarged the photograph, they could clearly read Jeffs's confession that "I am not the prophet and have never been the prophet." Four months after being thwarted by his family and generals, Jeffs had attempted to get the news out by giving it directly to Judge Shumate, but this determined effort would fail too. Soon after the *Deseret News* splashed its discovery over the news wires, Jeffs's attorneys filed a heretofore uncontemplated request that their client's sanity be established.

In his motion, Wally Bugdon pointed to Jeffs's drastic weight loss and asserted that his client drooled and nodded off during meetings at which he appeared uncomprehending and dazed. Shumate went ahead and ordered the exam. In the meantime, Jeffs's visitors became more of the high-ranking FLDS leaders like Wendell Nielsen and the sect's doctor, Larry Barlow, and less of the squirming, hangdog family members like Nephi Jeffs. "Were the big guys in there arguing him out of his position?" queried Hoole. "I don't think there's any question. They had to make him change his mind, or it was game over."

A competency exam completed in late April concluded that Jeffs suffered "a substantial mental illness" identified as depression but was otherwise competent. By this time, the uproar created by the *Deseret News* article had passed, as had Jeffs's remorse. After insisting for months that his confession was not a test, he now reversed course. Not only was what he would describe as his "overanxious statements" a test, it was a test *within* a test his generals had passed with flying colors.

That double-test concept was never fully explained, but by May, Jeffs was his old self again. The distraught Wendell Musser, whose wife and infant son Jeffs had reassigned to another man, had sued the prophet in an effort to discover his child's whereabouts. Musser wanted to see his son and have a chance to speak with his wife. But despite a court order, Jeffs refused to allow anyone to tell Musser where his family had been moved. Only after Jeffs was threatened with added jail time for contempt did he arrange for Musser to see his wife and son for five minutes on a street corner. Musser's wife would not allow him to hold the child.

The tape of Warren Jeffs's recantation of prophethood may have been a double test for his followers, but his lawyers still had to fight to keep it away from a jury in his upcoming trial for facilitating the rapes of Elissa Wall. In a harbinger of what was to come, defense counsel presented months of exhausting motions challenging anything and everything the prosecution intended to present at trial. Defense attorneys even wanted to exclude Jeffs's use of the word "amen" during recorded meetings, saying it falsely implied his consent to topics under discussion. Judge Shumate closed arguments about the admission of the jailhouse tapes to the press and public, but he was apparently swayed by Jeffs's attorneys when they insisted that the prejudicial impact Jeffs would suffer by allowing a jury to know that he'd recanted his authority outweighed all other concerns. In suppressing the tapes Shumate added that they were "very, very inflammatory" and he would "not feel confident picking a jury anywhere in the state of Utah" were they admitted.

After three wearying months, Warren Jeffs's trial began under a surreal swirl of sharpshooters, SWAT teams, and media satellite trucks clogging blocks of St. George's picturesque streets. Shackled in waistband handcuffs and coated in Kevlar, Jeffs was shuffled to the courtroom each day in a cocoon of state troopers as wary police snipers kept their eyes peeled from roofs and nearby hills. Even the press got into the spirit, with some television reporters filing stories while wearing bulletproof vests. "I thought anything was possible," says Mark Shurtleff of the extensive security he ordered for the trial. "There were plenty of people who hated Warren, but I also thought somebody from his own group might want to kill him. There's so many hills around there—so many good vantage points—and I wasn't going to have the guy shot on my watch."

Jethro Barlow and Richard Holm testified about Warren Jeffs's increasingly bizarre rule in Short Creek. Prosecutors introduced Jeffs's droning taped sermons people were expected to listen to through earphones all day long—enough tapes that, if they were played end to end, would go on for eighteen days and nights. After more than a year of safe houses, uncertainty, and fear, now twenty-one-year-old Elissa Wall, who was still known to the public only as "M.J.," summoned all of her courage to walk through the courtroom mobbed with strangers and face the man who ruled her nightmares. Her treasured blond hair finally cut to a fashionable shoulder length, Elissa told her story to a hushed room in a voice calm and clear, steady even when tears rolled over her cheeks. When she was finished, Elissa politely declined the protected rear door that had been prepared for her discreet exit. Instead, she strode resolutely out of the front, into the brilliant autumn sunshine, where a sea of microphones glittered at the base of the courthouse steps. "My name is Elissa Wall," she began confidently and with a voice loud enough to be heard all the way in the back.

Utah's Washington County attorney Brock Belnap was no career politician and would have happily lived out a tranquil life in lovely St. George as a dedicated family man and public servant. He'd been aware of FLDS his whole life and never thought the sect would be at the center of international interest, but when it happened, he accepted his role coolly and without prejudice. Later, with characteristic unruffled understatement, Belnap remembered the Jeffs uproar as an "interesting experience," but to him fell the unenviable task of convincing a jury that a man who was nowhere near the scene of a rape when it occurred could still be responsible for the crime.

Belnap approached the task as he did all thorny issues, methodically and with thorough research. Belnap's jury argument for convicting Warren Jeffs of rape facilitation is legally complex, but the upshot is this: Utah law bestows added legal responsibilities on people who hold "special influence" over others. A priest, a cop, a teacher, and a legal guardian are all individuals whose instructions or advice might lay exceptional influence on the person they are directing. As Elissa Wall's "spiritual guide," Warren Jeffs's repeated orders for her to submit to Allen Steed or lose her salvation (as well as his orders to Steed to demand sexual intercourse) rendered Jeffs legally responsible for the resulting rapes under Utah law.

As the jury retired after a two-week trial, *Time* magazine wrote about the jury what nobody would say out loud. Would the traditionally polygamy-sympathetic St. George panel take the road they'd traveled in the past and let Jeffs go? Or had the population shifts of the past few years placed in the jury box individuals who'd never heard of FLDS and would recoil at what they'd heard? After two days, the jury appeared deadlocked on at least one of the two counts against Jeffs, but after a female juror was removed for undisclosed reasons, it took the panel only three hours to accept Belnap's argument, convicting Jeffs on two counts of rape facilitation on September 25, 2007.

Despite shaky evidence for such a conclusion, the Jeffs verdict was heralded as a sea change for Utah's past hands-off-polygamy stance. Judge Shumate seemed to agree, abandoning the "polygamists as misunderstood *Leave It to Beaver* families" theory he'd assumed during the Stubbs custody battle, and he threw the book at Jeffs on November 20. Shumate took the unusual step of ordering each of Jeffs's two five-years-to-life sentences to be served consecutively, meaning the prophet would have to serve a minimum of ten years before becoming eligible for any kind of parole.

Without knowing a thing about FLDS, a range of unlikely allies from civil libertarians to right-wing talk show hosts condemned the verdict as religious persecution. Mark Shurtleff was drawn into a near shouting match with conservative television personality Tucker Carlson, who sneeringly addressed the Utah attorney general as "pal" and "self-righteous" while ridiculing Jeffs's placement on the FBI's Most Wanted list during an MSNBC broadcast of *Scarborough Country*. "Do you want to learn something, or do you just want to talk?" spat an irate Shurtleff. "This isn't about their religion. It's never been about their religion. It's about a man who has committed serious crimes involving thousands of people."

A smirking Carlson remained unpersuaded, but the FLDS leaders hoping for a 1953-style tsunami of religious persecution sympathy were to be disappointed. This time, Carlson's views did not have legs, especially because Judge Shumate had unsealed Jeffs's jailhouse confession tapes and competency evaluation prior to sentencing. The tape of Jeffs enlightening his squirming brother, Nephi, was a YouTube Internet sensation, as were Texas "wedding" photographs of Jeffs snuggling with a dark-haired, exceptionally pretty twelve-year-old girl released about the same time as the tapes. Eventually, both the photographs and tapes penetrated the walls of Short Creek and the YFZ ranch, shocking the residents.*

"Just try to imagine the position they were in," urged Roger Hoole. "They had literally bet the farm on the belief that Warren Jeffs was the prophet of God, the only man who held the keys to their salvation. Think of everything they'd sacrificed to this man. Sons, daughters, husbands, their entire life's work. If Warren was an imposter, their whole existence had been a lie. I honestly do not believe these people could have accepted that and kept their sanity. These folks simply didn't have the tools to deal with this." The tools FLDS members fell back on were the tried-and-true belief in government conspiracies against them and religious "tests." For FLDS people, Jeffs's statements were either a trial to reveal who would desert him or a hoax.

But for Jeffs, the trial's aftermath brought a much bigger problem into sharp focus. After he'd recovered from his fit of repentant honesty, Jeffs realized his lofty "answer them nothing" technique had destroyed his best money pot—the UEP trust—as well as threatened his biggest stick by removing the property from his control. While he'd been futzing with concrete and ensuring the pregnancies of thirteen-year-old girls, Bruce Wisan had taken

---

* In what would seem a counterintuitive move for Jeffs, he'd encouraged FLDS members to purchase iPods and iPhones to facilitate listening to his sermons and "training" tapes. In fact, in June 2007, hundreds of FLDS members camped overnight outside AT&T stores in Las Vegas and Flagstaff, Arizona, to snap up all the available iPhones, leaving store managers to deal with the slew of angry customers who arrived after the polygamists.

firm control of $110 million with no resistance. In March, Judge Lindberg awarded Wisan an $8.8 million judgment in his suit on behalf of the UEP trust against Warren Jeffs and the sect's former trustees, who Wisan accused of looting the trust prior to the court takeover. For the first time in history, Wisan had sold a home to kicked-out FLDS member Kevin Wyler, who said it was "good to be home" when he received the property deed FLDS leaders could do nothing about.

While Jeffs was anticipating Naomie's touching funeral services, Wisan had met his administrative and legal costs by auctioning off a second piece of UEP property for $1.65 million, and not just any old property either. The enormous Western Precision building, only five years old and offering spectacular views from three landscaped acres, was considered the crown jewel of FLDS businesses, a state-of-the-art specialized tool manufacturing plant that had netted millions in contracts—including U.S. government contracts. It had been sold without a peep of protest. Its loss knocked the wind out of Short Creek residents increasingly panicky about their futures.

As devastating as the Western Precision loss and other Wisan developments were, they didn't compare to the colossal legal blunders Jeffs made when he failed not only to answer the lost boys suit but also to challenge in court the takeover of UEP in a timely manner. "When you get a speeding ticket and you don't pay the fine or contest the thing in court, they put a warrant out for you," observed Roger Hoole. "You don't get to go back after the court date and say, 'Oh, I forgot. Let's start over from before the stop was made.'" Hoole shook a sorrowful head. "You'd be laughed out of court while they slapped the cuffs on you. But FLDS has no experience being held to the same laws the rest of us have to follow."

Those were Warren Jeffs's sentiments precisely. Jeffs couldn't have cared less about Wisan's $8.8 million judgment, and as for Kevin Wyler, Jeffs would make sure the man's life was a living hell to make him move out of Short Creek. The main thing now was the UEP trust. As Jeffs was packed off to Arizona to face charges there, he decided it was time to call Rod Parker, pay the guy whatever he wanted, and get his piggy bank back.

20

TEXAS PULLS THE PLUG

God Almighty will give the United States a pill that will puke them to death, and that is worse than lobelia. I am prophet enough to prophesy the down fall of the government that has driven us out. . . . Woe to the United States! . . . I see them greedy after death and destruction.

—Brigham Young, August 26, 1849

And now I am prepared to say by the authority of Jesus Christ, that not many years shall pass away before the United States shall present such a scene of bloodshed as has not a parallel in the history of our nation: <u>Pestilence, hail, famine, and earthquake will sweep the wicked of this generation from off the face of the land, to open and prepare the way for the return of the lost tribes of Israel from the north country.</u>

—Warren Jeffs, May 3, 2007

In Texas, Randy Mankin followed the Jeffs trial at least as closely as his Utah counterparts and the activities of FLDS in other states far closer than any press. In fact, it was Mankin who discovered that Texas was not the only state in which Jeffs had purchased property after deciding to abandon ship in Utah. Broadening his public records research, Mankin discovered that David Allred had purchased land for other "hunting lodges" in Colorado and South Dakota, duly reporting the property locations in his newspaper. When sheriff Phil Hespen of Custer County, South Dakota, complained about the subsequent "media hype," Mankin fired back in an editorial titled, "Media hype—What a lazy cop calls it when he's not doing his job."

Although Jeffs ultimately settled on Texas as the location for the new Zion, he isolated many of his "wives" in the utterly remote South Dakota location. This may not have concerned Sheriff Hespen, but the sheriffs of Montezuma, Mancos, and Pueblo Counties in Colorado were more than happy to be informed of the true nature of the "hunting lodges" being erected in their jurisdictions. Like Schleicher County folks three years earlier, the afflicted Colorado residents kept UPS busy delivering books and videos about FLDS. The sheriffs themselves invited anti-FLDS activists to speak at packed evening meetings in the high school's gym. The sheriffs assured their constituents they'd watch the fence-enclosed developments like hawks, arresting the first person who even sneezed wrong, much less brought in underage brides. Prior to all the publicity, Jeffs had dispatched a smattering of FLDS construction crews to the other states, but these melted away under scrutiny from the incensed populations.

Not so in Eldorado, where construction projects continued at a frenetic pace. Every time Jeffs suffered a personal setback, Eldoradoans breathed a secret sigh of hope that the YFZ ranch would be abandoned, but it didn't happen. In fact, construction seemed to accelerate in tandem with Jeffs's problems. After Jeffs's conviction in Utah, YFZ construction crews were "building buildings as fast as they could get them up," said Mankin. Although the sect's plans for a wastewater plant were still stalled by environmental citations and fines FLDS leaders studiously ignored, FLDS did not—as it had in Short Creek— allow Texas members to walk the plank for nonpayment of property taxes, which the sect paid early to gain a discount.

Large tracts of land were under cultivation. New streets were bulldozed what seemed like every other day. In addition to the cheese factory, dairy, warehouses, and machine shops, FLDS had added what looked like a sugar refinery plant to J. D. Doyle, who continued his fact-finding flights over the ranch, posting the aerial photographs he snapped on the Internet. "All the stuff they're doing now is commercial stuff," he told Mankin. "They're doing something to either make money or for other reasons." To the moneymaking end, FLDS members like Samuel Fischer were transporting their businesses from Utah and Arizona to Texas towns near Eldorado, such as Lockney and Floydada, whose residents were less than thrilled with the newcomers, even though Fischer's manufacturing plant might provide desperately needed jobs in counties on the first wave of the economic collapse.

Samuel Fischer would later dramatically charge that a power-drunk Bruce Wisan ran him and his business out of Short Creek and seized his million-dollar home in Hildale, but he told Lockney residents a different story when met with an overflow crowd of concerned town leaders and citizens.* In a letter submitted prior to the question-and-answer portion of the evening, Fischer said he'd chosen Lockney because he'd been smitten by the area after taking refuge there when a storm hit as he was returning to Utah from a business trip to North Carolina. "This is an area in the lives of our young people today that we parents need to focus our intention on to instill into our children the values of good work ethic," Fischer explained somewhat disjointedly. "The challenge our society faces today is idleness among our youth, which leads to juvenile delinquency."

Lockneyites were unaware of any juvenile delinquency epidemics in their community of 2,056, and Fischer admitted to having two "ladies" and twenty-three children, but he promised to hire local workers for his modular cabinet-making business, an offer that looked good to a town suffering population loss from a withering economy. Fischer bought his plant, made good on his word, and brought no FLDS population explosion or construction with him, so little more was said about Fischer's or any of the other satellite FLDS businesses that brought no other concerns to their new communities.

FLDS fears in neighboring counties may have quieted, but in Eldorado the pot still simmered. Instead of seeking to comply with Texas regulations, FLDS spokesmen began hinting the group would use its superior numbers in the voting booth to take over city and county governments. Eldorado civic leaders had been troubled by this unacceptable prospect from the moment they'd realized that Jeffs intended to eventually import more people to the YFZ ranch than populated all of Schleicher County. County officials were ready with changes to election rules that would make it impossible for FLDS to gain control of the government by sheer numbers, but even though the possibility of lopsided voting had been anticipated, the threat to run roughshod over the locals was nevertheless shocking and more than a little enraging.

When an FLDS-inspired bill sponsored by state representative Harvey Hilderbran raising the age of marital eligibility with parental consent from

---

* As he executed his staggered plan for abandoning Short Creek, Warren Jeffs warned his inner circle that "the monies were not in place" in Texas, meaning that FLDS did not have control of state government branches such as school districts from which they could bleed tax money. Consequently, Jeffs ordered profitable businesses as well as people to relocate away from Short Creek. Relocating FLDS members simply abandoned their properties in Short Creek, an exodus even the media noticed and reported. The vacant properties posed additional problems for Wisan as he attempted to identify trust assets, but Wisan evicted no businesses from the twin cities. It is more likely that Fischer abandoned his properties on a directive from Warren Jeffs.

fourteen to sixteen stalled in the Texas legislature, Mankin issued an editorial call to arms, berating the state's wrongheaded lawmakers and demanding: "Is there a Texan alive who doesn't know what's going on down here?" If they hadn't before, Texas's elected officials, including governor Rick Perry, got an earful. The bill, which also substantially increased penalties for under-age marriages, passed.

Warren Jeffs judged Short Creekers unfervent, but he'd be hard-pressed to find fault with the fervency with which Texans hoped FLDS would leave their state. Texas had been unable to stop the building explosion at the YFZ ranch with disregarded construction citations, and its residents were losing patience with the community they considered nothing less than a cult grounded in the sexual appetites of old men for little girls. It had been five long years since David Allred got off to a bad start with his "hunting lodge" lie. Enough was enough. "Is Eldorado the next Waco?" wondered an ABC news reporter in a dispatch about Texas tensions. It was a question that exactly echoed the comparison Arizona governor Janet Napolitano had sometimes drawn as a reason—or excuse—to avoid the Short Creek stronghold, an utter failure to act not lost on the Texans who'd vowed to neither repeat Napolitano's mistakes nor assume her bewildering ennui. Texas had had a bellyful of FLDS, and they weren't going to take it anymore.

In what Sheriff Doran would later characterize as basic foresight and prudent planning, Texas had long ago drawn up "worst case scenario" logistical plans should law enforcement be compelled to invade the YFZ ranch with a force that could have subdued a small country. What really happened in the three days or so preceding April 3, 2008, will be litigated for years and may never be fully understood. But on that morning, up to one hundred Texas Rangers, Department of Safety troopers, Schleicher County deputies, Child Protective Service investigators, parks and game investigators, and supporting personnel aided by helicopters, a SWAT team with snipers, and an unmanned drone plane sealed off the YFZ ranch and parked an armored personnel carrier at the bolted, guard-towered front gate as an exclamation point. They had a warrant signed by Fifty-First District judge Barbara Walther authorizing a search of the entire property in an effort to locate a sixteen-year-old girl. She'd called an abuse hotline, identifying herself as "Sarah," an FLDS girl being held against her will at YFZ after being forced to marry a fifty-year-old man named Dan Barlow, a union of rape and beatings that had produced a child.

In an atmosphere thick with the tension often associated with armed personnel carriers at a gate, sheriff David Doran aided negotiations during the three-hour standoff. Doran was eventually able to convince the FLDS leaders barring entry to the YFZ property that forcing a bunch of aggravated SWAT guys to come through the gates was not in anyone's interest. Under increasingly beefed-up security, police and investigators from a variety of agencies were eventually admitted to the ranch for what would become six days of searching, confiscating, and questioning. On that first day, however, their progress was impeded in part because the sect kept moving terrified children, who were told the police had come to murder them, from house to house in a shell game to prevent authorities from interviewing them. In all the confusion, FLDS neglected to hide half a dozen visibly pregnant underage girls whose "husbands" could be overheard instructing the thirteen- to seventeen-year-olds to call them "uncle" and state that they were eighteen years old. The pregnancies were evidence a crime had occurred, to wit, sex with minors. Based on the discovery, authorities went back to Judge Walther for another warrant, inviting the FBI to the dance to look into suspicions of underage interstate transport.

Walther's amended warrant allowed for a search of any and all buildings for *any* evidence of child abuse against any child. With the ranch still sealed, FLDS could get none of the pregnant girls or other frightened children off the premises, and FLDS could not hide them forever. As the week dragged on, news of the raid ignited a global media wildfire. An international army of trucks with satellite dishes poured into Schleicher County as Texas authorities repeated the mistakes of the past, herding some four hundred children and dozens of women and girls into a surreal convoy of buses, subsequently mobbed by television crews who captured all the tears, wails, and terror on the faces of fresh-scrubbed girls being separated from their mothers or, in some cases, children they were instructed not to acknowledge because the mothers were minors.

Texas Child Protective Services explained that so many were removed because all were in danger. All but four or five of the minor girls observed at the ranch that day were either pregnant or had their own infants and toddlers in tow, leading investigators to conclude that nearly every underage girl at YFZ had been raped under Texas law, and the others were in imminent danger of the same fate. In addition, CPS was interested in evidence of more mundane child abuse in the forms of visible bruising and broken bones. Because no FLDS member would cooperate by answering routine questions about family relationships, CPS concluded the best way to ensure no child was left with an abuser was to take them all and collect DNA swabs to determine who belonged where.

Of course, the DNA swabs would also be very handy for possible criminal charges, nailing down which FLDS men had fathered children with underage girls. The FLDS lawyers eventually gathered to answer the Texas raid would charge that the authorities had never been as interested in abused children as they were in procuring secret FLDS membership and financial documents, as well as DNA evidence with which to prosecute FLDS men. The lawyers accused Texas authorities of using phony abuse evidence as a ruse to get into YFZ and collect evidence for which they otherwise could not have obtained a legal warrant.*

If the Texans were concerned about their warrants, they didn't show it. CPS first had to deal with the monster they'd created by removing hundreds of women, children, and young girls into a completely inadequate shelter system. As they had been in 1953, women and girls had to be bussed into surrounding cities, crammed into gyms and coliseums hastily equipped with cots and bunk beds. Tearful, bewildered children who'd been promised from birth that the Gentiles meant to kill them were separated from their families and placed in foster homes all over the state with the aforementioned Gentiles.

Although the foster families pressed into service overwhelmingly embraced their young charges with kindness, generosity, and sympathy, they could never have been prepared for the mental and emotional conditions of children who might as well have landed on the moon. FLDS children had no educations. They'd never been anywhere outside of the FLDS cocoon. If the culture shock wasn't jarring enough, many also believed they were about to be murdered.

Some families coaxed the children out of their restrictive clothing and into newly purchased, fashion-forward jeans or T-shirts, without

---

* The vast majority of search warrants limit police searches to specific areas to obtain specific items. To obtain a warrant, an "affiant," usually a police officer, submits to a judge in writing his or her "probable cause" reasons to believe a crime has occurred, listing specific evidence he or she believes to be located in specific areas on the targeted premises. Unless tangential evidence of other crimes not listed on the warrant is lying "in plain sight," the officer cannot seize that evidence and must return to the judge for another warrant. The boundaries are in place to prevent police from targeting people they find merely suspicious and ransacking their homes. In the YFZ case, the original warrant allowed for a more general search because the property was deemed communal. When the pregnant teenage girls were observed in plain sight, the officers could return to Judge Walther for a broader warrant.

understanding that FLDS garments are tied to salvation and cannot be removed. Restaurateurs donated generously from their menus. "The poor little things didn't even know what steak fingers were," one eatery owner told the *Success*, but this kindness also would have been interpreted as murderous intent. Under Warren Jeffs, the types of food FLDS members were allowed to eat had been drastically curtailed and involved specific preparation, or the temple of one's body would be ruined for the afterlife. Steak fingers were most definitely not a food the children could eat without suffering acute anxiety.

The foster home, gym, and coliseum uproar was followed by the unmitigated pandemonium of hundreds of lawyers appointed to represent all the removed FLDS members individually. They too were pressed into service from around the state, converging on Judge Walther's small rural courthouse for hearings on the forced removals required by Texas law to take place in fourteen days. Like a scene out of a grotesque Fellini movie, hundreds of sweaty, confused lawyers with no good ideas about why they were in the Texas wilderness, who their clients were, or what they were supposed to do for those clients once they were identified, milled around shouting objections aimlessly as they grappled with baffling DNA paperwork that meant nothing to them.

Judge Walther tried to impose sanity on the bedlam by setting up conference cameras in the sweltering courtrooms adjoining hers, herding some of the loudly complaining attorneys into those rooms so that most people could survive the experience without suffocating. With humor and nearly superhuman dignity, Walther managed to persuade the ego-inflated, champing-at-the-bit lawyers not to shriek out their demands indiscriminately, particularly if they'd not yet determined the identities of their clients (many had not) or what the legal goals for said clients might be. In the end, only a handful of attorneys bussed in for what became wincingly known as "the fourteen-day hearing" ever realized what it had really been about. Most never understood they were dealing with FLDS, and if they did, they did not know what the sect represented.*

The cartoonish circus of lawyers was abbreviated when the Texas Court of Appeals, and later the Texas Supreme Court, both ruled in favor of FLDS, whose lawyers had appealed the wholesale removal of the children, women,

---

* One attorney who would become converted to nearly full-time anti-FLDS activism as a result of the fourteen-day hearing was Natalie Malonis, who represented Warren Jeffs's fourteen-year-old daughter, Teresa.

and girls from the YFZ ranch. Both courts found that Child Protective Services had overstepped its legal authority by removing so many with little specific evidence for each case. By June, most of the children had been returned to YFZ, but the fight over the warrant that had launched the raid was just getting started. FLDS lawyers found it highly suspicious that Texas authorities showed up to serve a child abuse warrant with trucks and dollies suitable for carrying off files, computers, and safes and then spent days loading exactly those items into the vans. What they contained was nothing short of devastating for FLDS. If FLDS and Warren Jeffs expected to survive, the lawyers simply had to get that search warrant—and the evidence it yielded—thrown out of court.

There was a lot for FLDS to talk about. For starters, the April 2008 distress call foundational to the grounds for the search was proven to be a hoax, the alleged perpetrator of the rape and beatings of a sixteen-year-old girl called "Sarah" completely innocent. After months of investigation, the "Sarah" call was traced to a Colorado woman named Rozita Swinton, who had pulled such stunts in the past with other police departments. Although the connection is murky, Swinton is alleged to have had a vague link to anti-FLDS activist Flora Jessop, which, if true, had a bad smell to it.

But the legal question was: what did the officers who swore the affidavit for the warrant believe at the time the call came in? If they believed a teenaged girl and others like her were in imminent danger, then exigent circumstances existed, the warrants were sworn in good faith, and the warrant was valid. It is the duty of any defense attorney to turn evidence presented by the overwhelming power of government inside out. An attorney who does not vigorously challenge state evidence is not worth his fee, but FLDS lawyers had to be careful when they challenged the search. Although they may have toyed with the idea, it would have probably been unwise, even for audacious FLDS attorneys to publicly accuse Texas Rangers of knowingly conspiring with a hoaxer and lying to a judge (who might have been in on it) to obtain a warrant under false pretenses.

Instead, FLDS attacked the police investigation of the phone call after it came in, alleging that Texas Ranger Brooks Long and Sheriff Doran "knew or should have known" the call was fake and the alleged perpetrator wasn't anywhere near the YFZ ranch. The urgency for getting the warrant thrown out could not be overstated. Authorities had removed thousands of evidence cartons from the ranch, obtaining critical family records and, later, DNA samples. The federal search warrant, executed on April 10, was based in part on the pregnant teenage girls officers observed after serving the first warrant. In other words, the failure of the first warrant would jeopardize the second one as "fruit of the poisonous tree."

FLDS was particularly unnerved by the seizures of Warren Jeffs's personal dictations. Among the more devastating entries were Jeffs's clearly enunciated, specific plans to abandon Short Creek and the UEP trust and all the family homes in it, as "it was condemned by the Lord." Combined with entries proving Jeffs was regularly updated on all legal activities concerning FLDS and UEP and still chose to "answer them nothing," the dictations undermined every FLDS challenge to Bruce Wisan in the Utah courts.

The YFZ raid warrants were challenged as vigorously in Arizona, where Jeffs was in jail awaiting trial, as they were in Texas, where attorneys for ten indicted FLDS men filed three thousand pages of legal motions and exhibits. "I think that warrant would make it on anyone's top ten most illegal list," snorts Mike Picaretta, one of Jeffs's Arizona attorneys, whose aggressive pursuit of state witnesses against Jeffs would land him on anti-FLDS activists' list of most detested FLDS lawyers. In court filings, Picaretta referred to the warrant as "just a lie" and his difficulties getting Texans to answer questions about their investigation into the call a "Texas two-step."

But the critical legal finding for any judge remained a decision about what the Texas officers honestly *believed* when they submitted their affidavits, and judge Barbara Walther wasn't buying FLDS arguments that Long and Doran had misled the court or harbored any reason to think that the "Sarah" call was a hoax or that her abuser wasn't even in the state. In fact, given what the men knew about the compound, the opposite might have been true. "The Court finds no credible evidence that the officers executing the Arrest and Search Warrant M-08-001-S knew that or should have known that Dale Evans Barlow was not on the ranch at the time of the search," Walther wrote in a lengthy decision.

Since she'd approved the search to begin with, Walther's decision was hardly a surprise, but it could still turn a criminal defense attorney's blood to ice. The warrant's affirmation cleared truckloads of the most damning evidence for use in potential trials. That included all the DNA evidence obtained from the women, girls, and children taken into protective custody after the raid and processed by the FBI. The combination of warrants was unusually sweeping, allowing investigators who searched YFZ for six days in April to collect anything they thought *might* lead to evidence of child abuse.

As it turned out, law enforcement was not flying blind. In a startling disclosure later confirmed by Mark Shurtleff, it became known that authorities had an informant or two *inside* FLDS who had provided general ideas about where the sect kept its most sensitive records, including Jeffs's "priesthood records," "bishop's records," which included marriage and birth records, and the like.* As a result, the Texans had an idea of which individuals' computers would bear fruit or which offices contained safes and secret vaults. By midweek of the raid, FBI agents had obtained their own federal warrants that would allow that agency to eventually process all the DNA evidence in their labs, but everybody agreed the mother lode of evidence they wanted would be found in the most sensitive and difficult point of entry: the gigantic temple.

Almost immediately after police drove through YFZ's front gates, between fifty and seventy-five FLDS men stationed themselves around the massive building to prevent Texas authorities from entering, warrant or not. The sect believed the temple's sanctity would be destroyed and the building rendered useless for all time if a single nonbeliever stepped on any part of the structure, much less rummaged around inside. For two days, the cops indulged the temple's guardians, making no move to enter as negotiators tried to reason with Merril Jessop and other FLDS leaders, explaining that they would indeed eventually get into the place but they'd like to avoid the kind of damage the edifice might suffer without cooperation, not to mention the potential for human injury if the FLDS men resisted the cops' lawful entry.

Their pleas fell on deaf ears, and on April 5 several ambulances were stationed outside the temple in case push came to shove. It didn't. The FLDS men stepped aside, allowing police into the temple, but still refused to provide keys to locked rooms and vaults or combinations for safes. A locksmith was able to open the temple vaults, but in the print shop annex, which included a secret vault, "Jaws of Life" equipment and jackhammers were among the tools necessary to breach the thick walls concealing rows of banklike safety deposit boxes along with a concrete vault. The outer wall was so thick that it required hours of jackhammering before one of the

---

* Mark Shurtleff would later confirm the presence of informants within FLDS, giving some credence to Warren Jeffs's pervasive paranoia about "traitors." Although he would not identify or describe the informants, who were probably women, Shurtleff said his agents, at least, may have proceeded with an excess of caution on some occasions over concerns for the informants' safety.

smaller of the Texas Rangers could wriggle through the opening. The treasure trove of documents would soon become like raw meat before hungry
lions, fought over by authorities in Utah and Arizona who wanted access
for their own cases. But the most dreadful surprise for Texans searching the
temple was yet to come.

Warren Jeffs's divine dreams had dictated the color schemes on each
level of the building, which roughly represented the Mormon levels of
heaven. In the basement was a baptismal area suitable for full immersion.
The first, "telestial" level was done in earth tones while the second, "terrestrial" level was sky blue and white. The third, "celestial" level to which
everyone aspired was a complete, blinding white. Everything was an eye-
hurting white, including an elevated altar accessed by steps. Although the
cavernous room was weirdly disorienting, a temple with an altar room was
to be expected. What police did not expect was the bed adjoining the altar,
with collapsible kneeling pads, suggesting an audience with close contact
to whatever transpired upon the mattress, and upon which investigators
discovered strands of very long hair, long enough to have come from the
heads of girls and women whose FLDS religion provided that females
never cut their hair.

Even the hard-bitten Texas rangers were shocked by the implications of
the bed. They were deeply disgusted upon discovering Warren Jeffs's May
2005 dictations giving excruciating carpentry instructions for constructing
the altar bed. "If you're going to read it [the bed-making instructions],"
said one Texan, "you might want to keep a plastic bag handy because you
could suddenly puke imagining what had happened to young girls on that
bed, in that room, in front of whoever." Jeffs's instructions regarding the
bed read in part:

> There is a table, but it should be made so it can be a table or
> it can be a bed. It should be made so the table top can come
> off. It will be on wheels. It will have a bench you can kneel on
> that will be cushioned and upholstered. When the mattress is
> in place, this bench will be to the right side the bed. This will
> be made so that it may be taken apart and stored in a closet
> where no one can see it.
>
> It will be made of hardwood that is very strong and will
> not rattle when it is shaken. . . . It will be covered with a sheet,

but it will have a plastic cover to protect the mattress from what will happen on it.

It will be the same pattern as the tables I have in my dining room, the underneath part. . . . It must be very strong. And the bed needs some padded sides that can pull up that can hold me in place as the Lord does his work with me.

This last suggests Jeffs also planned to endure his "heavenly sessions" on the table/bed device, which was reserved for his use. Jeffs repeatedly emphasized that the device was to be closeted, kept out of sight when it was not in use. But when police found the bed in 2008, Jeffs had already been imprisoned for two years. Its presence next to the altar on the day of the search would seem to confirm that it was used by others and had been in continuous use despite Jeffs's absence. Weeks later, Doran confirmed Randy Mankin's information that the investigators had actually found two table/beds, one of them out of sight as Jeffs's instructed, but the Texas sheriff found the subject so distasteful he would not elaborate.

As much as they might have preferred to remain blissfully ignorant, authorities didn't have to speculate about what happened on the bed. Among the evidence seized from the red Cadillac Escalade when Jeffs was arrested in Nevada was a tape of Jeffs "breaking in" one of his twelve-year-old "brides" on the bed, a rape performed before up to twenty observers.* Other material in the Cadillac indicated Jeffs kept the tape handy to share with FLDS elders, ostensibly for religious or "training" purposes. Police who were all too familiar with pedophilia did not rule out the probability that Jeffs might have just enjoyed reliving the moment by himself.

It is not known if the tape was made available to the Schleicher County grand jury that was convened shortly after the raid under the direction of Texas assistant attorney general Eric Nichols. Nichols, who would shortly join the pantheon of most hated FLDS persecutors, did have at his disposal DNA evidence connecting FLDS men to the children of underage girls along with the sect's own internal records of underage marriages. Texas attorney general Greg Abbott made the trip from Austin to Eldorado to be on hand as a Schleicher grand jury began spitting out indictments in July

---

* Although authorities acknowledge the existence of the so-called rape tape, they will not elaborate on its form, format, or specific content. It is expected to be used against Jeffs in future criminal trials.

2008. In all, the grand jurors indicted twelve of FLDS's most prominent men, including Merril Jessop, Wendell Nielsen, and the imprisoned prophet himself, Warren Jeffs.

Jeffs's indictment carried exposure to a sentence that meant he could spend the rest of his life in a Texas prison. He was charged in connection to his "marriages" to two underage girls on the ranch, one of them around twelve years old. Pictures of Jeffs snuggling the fresh-faced little girls were posted on the Internet. In one set, Jeffs only caressed a smiling, dark-haired girl in front of a heart-shaped cutout with the couple's names. In another, Jeffs carries a small, red-haired girl in his arms, kissing her with unsettling force.

Perhaps believing they could turn the Texas raid into 1953 publicity gold, FLDS provided a new spokesman for the sect, which had previously directed media inquiries to Rod Parker. Even within FLDS, known goon squad member Willie Jessop was nicknamed Willie the Thug. The swaggering Jessop was brash, aggressive, folksy, rude, and given to wild hyperbole in his curiously entertaining demagoguery. He was nothing like what anyone familiar with FLDS expected. Far from running from strange cars and microphones, he strode out to greet all comers like a bull moose relishing the rut. He was FLDS born and raised, but his exceptional services as an enforcer had been rewarded with the suspension of certain FLDS rules. He had a satellite dish for television, listened to forbidden radio stations in his car, and joked around with non-FLDS people with impunity.

After the Texas raid, Jessop came out guns a-blazin'. He wrote letters of protest to the president, the governor, and the newspapers. He barked at reporters scribbling down every outlandish, rash, unsupportable, but imminently quotable remark.* He showed up at Schleicher County Board of Supervisors meetings, declaring that he wasn't trying to threaten anybody even as he introduced a hunching, miserable-looking ex–American Civil Liberties Union lawyer he had in tow. Then Willie further threatened the unamused, stony-faced supervisors by announcing that the YFZ

---

* In his column, "Over the Back Fence," Randy Mankin described the press attention afforded Willie Jessop with disdain, mocking reporters who "eagerly transcribed" every word and "passed it off as research," with one notable exception. Mankin gave an imaginary award to reporter Mike Watkiss of Phoenix, who gathered his camera crews and walked away from Willie's press conferences. "He had a deadline just like everybody else," Mankin noted, "but he walked away rather than give any credence to Willie Jessop's false statements and went off to find some real facts." Watkiss's friendship with Kathy and Randy Mankin remains close to this day.

ranch—one of the county's biggest taxpayers—was a little tired of "taxation without representation," implying that FLDS would now start their own voting revolution.

When asked about the new face of FLDS, Rod Parker tried unsuccessfully to suppress a wince. "Willie is . . . a character," Parker finally decided. "He's . . . just *Willie*." As Warren Jeffs prepared to reverse course from prison, Willie Jessop would become his sledgehammer.

21

THE COURTS

I have many a time, in this stand, dared the world to produce as mean devils as we can; we can beat them at anything. We have the greatest and smoothest liars in the world, the cunningest and most adroit thieves and any other shade of character that you can mention. We can pick out Elders in Israel right here who can beat the world at gambling, who can handle the cards, cut and shuffle them with the smartest rogue on the face of God's foot stool. I can produce Elders here who can shave their smartest shavers, and take their money from them. We can beat the world at any game.
— Brigham Young, *Journal of Discourses*, Vol. 4, November 9, 1856

The Lord told me that some of my family would be taken and offered as human sacrifice in Satan worship by my enemies, and that they would then be swept off the earth. The Lord told me there will be attempts on my life, and I will need to be in perfect oneness to survive.
— Warren Jeffs, dictating from prison, January 19, 2007

A t first, the Texas raid seemed to produce good results for Bruce Wisan. FLDS leaders had expected that photographs from the raid beamed around the world would produce the same groundswell of sympathy and outrage as the 1953 raid, but it hadn't happened. Willie Jessop did his part with vitriolic press conferences, referencing the '53 raid early and often, though his hyperactive language might have hurt more than it helped. And while there was sympathy for the women and children removed in the raid, along with questions about whether Texas authorities had acted too hastily, public unease with the Texas raid never approached the levels seen in 1953.

The difference may have been subtle shifts in coverage from media that remembered that the FLDS prophet had been on the FBI's Most Wanted list for having sex with little girls. Jeffs's arrest in a flashy Cadillac with unseemly gobs of cash and seedy disguises had been major breaking news. His lurid trial had been covered gavel to gavel just six months prior to the raid, nationally televised on CourtTV. Though Willie Jessop went before the cameras frequently to emphasize FLDS's status as a persecuted religion, reporters felt obliged to at least mention the Warren Jeffs conviction, and Texas authorities did not cede the publicity generator to Jessop. Despite a gag order issued by Judge Walther, Texans knew how to dribble the right sort of information about the sealed results of their searches into the media's hands. A bed with long blond hair next to an altar wasn't too appealing to mainstream Americans, nor were tapes of Jeffs's racist rants or nutty visions.

From the FLDS point of view, the Texas raid was a serious public relations flop, forgotten and abandoned by the national news media within weeks. Confused by the public's failure to respond to government troops ripping babes from their mothers' arms, subdued Short Creek residents huddled in small groups they hoped would go undetected by Jeffs's spies. Jeffs had years ago forbidden activities such as church services that would allow large groups to congregate and share information, but no one in Short Creek could ignore the exodus of people and businesses, the abandoned properties, and the general sense of doom pervading a town where even laughter was interpreted as disobedience. Dark rumors that Jeffs was secretly selecting people for a Texas salvation, leaving the rest to twist in Satan's wind, terrified FLDS members who'd not been tapped for the move. Wisan hoped the disenfranchised members would understand that he was offering them the security of their homes.

Part of Wisan's effort to get a handle on the UEP property was requiring Short Creek residents to sign "occupancy agreements" with the fiduciary, so that Wisan would know who was living in what house and which homes were vacant and therefore available for lease or sale to applying beneficiaries. Like every other court order, FLDS had been ignoring the occupancy agreements as well as the one-hundred-dollar-a-month residency fee Wisan had imposed to help the trust pay its bills. After the Texas raid, anxious Short Creekers defied Jeffs's orders, signing more than fifty occupancy agreements and paying the residency fees.

The most critical element of Wisan's plan to get property deeds into the hands of the people who'd actually built their homes was getting the UEP lands surveyed, mapped, and subdivided. Historically, FLDS members who acquired land deeded it to the UEP trust, after which the prophet would dole it out willy-nilly without regard to property lines. Rulon Jeffs began an even more haphazard system of using the land as a club, assigning and reassigning already occupied property to reward or punish. But it was Warren Jeffs who turned that practice into a tornado of confusion, shuffling families around properties like a demented chess player until nobody was certain where one yard ended and another began.

With their prophet in jail and no lawyers to direct them, the FLDS city councils in Short Creek had eventually agreed to subdivide the land, a step Wisan called "a very big deal." It was. With occupancy agreements getting signed and the surveying on track, Wisan was as happy as any crusty, sarcastic guy could be expected to be. "What really attracted me to the [UEP] situation is that it's so unique," an upbeat, surprisingly benevolent Wisan told the Associated Press. "It sounded like something where I could make a difference. How many times in your life can you make a difference to a lot of people?"

But it was all about to fall apart, plunging Utah and Arizona into one of the most vicious and protracted cases in either state's history. After Warren Jeffs recovered from his bout of self-awareness in June 2007, he brought back the FLDS lawyers with a vengeance in 2008. Their strategy was simple: bury the courts in a never-ending avalanche of legal action brought by an inexhaustible supply of FLDS plaintiffs, all challenging what amounted to settled law over and over again, as if the past three years hadn't happened. When the lower courts upheld previous rulings, FLDS would mire the less-FLDS-knowledgeable higher courts in a blizzard of emergency writs and appeals, hoping to wrench control of the UEP trust away from Judge Lindberg, Wisan, Shurtleff, and Goddard. In short, the FLDS lawyers would try to turn back time, and the Utah courts, at least, would indulge the tactic for years.

Jeffs's dictations do not specifically address the reason that he reversed the "answer them nothing" course, but as he kept tabs on YFZ ranch construction from prison, he became increasingly concerned that the Texas settlement would not be ready to house all his chosen ones in the time frame he'd hoped. Several times in the dictations, Jeffs stated that he'd instructed the attorneys to essentially stall any legal proceedings involving Short Creek, as Jeffs still needed the twin cities for housing as well as a tool for threatening his followers.

Bruce Wisan wouldn't have characterized his own performance this way, but Jeffs was also startled by what he saw as the fiduciary's alarming success in placing non-FLDS members in residences within Short Creek. The families that had rebelled with David Stubbs a decade earlier had done so halfheartedly. They'd kept a low profile, and some had returned to the fold. The families placed through Wisan were stubborn, openly combative toward the FLDS leadership, and eager to educate their former friends and neighbors to the fact that Warren Jeffs could no longer legally take away their homes.

This Jeffs could not allow, as property control was at the core of his temporeal power. Through his representatives, including his attorneys, Jeffs began a successful campaign to convince the FLDS membership that the wicked government they'd been taught to fear from birth had wrenched their homes away with an eye toward guiding them all to hell. To this day, the general membership believes that the government has assumed owner-ship of their homes, when the opposite is true. Any FLDS member who can hold a pen could walk into Bruce Wisan's office, answer some questions, and get a legal title to their own home that no one could take from them without their consent.

"Why is the FLDS leadership so afraid of giving people their own prop-erty?" Wisan perpetually demanded in court documents. The question always clunked to the floor with an unanswered thud, because the answer isn't pretty.

The authorities had long suspected that Jeffs continued governing FLDS from prison by smuggling secret directives to his underlings, but in the fall of 2007 they were able to actually intercept one. In a November 9, 2007, letter from prison designated to "brother Merril *only*," Jeffs also demonstrated that he could be a sly tactician when it suited him. "Have Willie retain an attor-ney to represent many of our people," he wrote, "as a group of individuals demanding the protection of their rights, *without bringing in the authorities of the Church* [emphasis added]. . . . Be careful and do not include those who are disaffected. Everyone does not have to be included. Just have him choose between thirty and forty Elders who will stand united and demand their rights as citizens."

Like Brigham Young before him, Jeffs's view of citizenship included only entitlements. To ensure none of these were overlooked, Jeffs didn't limit him-self to one lawyer. He hired twenty-one of them from five top-dollar firms, and those were just the lawyers who signed the court papers. The number doesn't include the myriad lesser attorneys and paralegals working for each attorney. Parker's firm, Snow, Christensen, and Martineau, sometimes appeared on fil-ings not as individuals but as the entire building of lawyers.

There were around a dozen lawyers on the other side too, but they were spread over three entities: the Arizona attorney general, Terry Goddard; the Utah attorney general, Mark Shurtleff; the fiduciary, Bruce Wisan; and Judge Lindberg, who was forced to hire her own attorney when FLDS sued her for bias after they lost a few early skirmishes. It turns out FLDS practiced poor sportsmanship as ferociously as anything else. It is no small thing to

accuse a sitting judge of bias, malfeasance, and religious or civil discrimination—all charges that are against the law as well as against the ethics of the
bench. Like accusing the president of the United States of treason, it has the
potential to tar the accuser as well as the target, and most lawyers will steer
clear of such shocking charges unless they have a videotape and signed confession, and even then they will think twice. But after Lindberg ruled against
FLDS a few times, citing "black letter law" (law so established as to be free
from doubt or dispute) reasons, FLDS attorneys coolly smeared the judge
with bias accusations in three courts.

Over the next two years, FLDS attorneys would flood five courts with a
relentless barrage of action from at least sixteen separate lawsuits, bombard-
ing their opposition (and judges) with identical claims from mix 'n' match
combinations of the same plaintiffs. Meanwhile, the leadership and membership in Short Creek ignored all court orders as if they'd never happened.
While FLDS law firms could zero in on about four suits, each cranking out
flash floods of legal motions, the attorneys general, Wisan, and Lindberg
were forced to juggle all sixteen suits at once, each of them liberally salted
with demands for emergency hearings and petitions for extraordinary writs.
In November 2008 alone, there were twenty-six pleadings filed in four
courts, as many as seven in a single day as a result of FLDS lawsuits.

Overwhelming the opposition with expensive, depressingly time-
consuming paperwork is a well-worn tactic for law firms that can afford
the manpower hours required to crank it out, but for all their mild varia-
tions, the FLDS lawsuits had a few audacious themes in common. The
suits all ignored the fact that the trust had been legally reformed. They
ignored Lindberg and Wisan's authority. And none of the suits on behalf
of FLDS ever mentioned polygamy or underage marriage as tenets of
the religious beliefs supposedly under attack. For all the judges in receipt
of the paperwork knew, Mark Shurtleff had dragged the Pope out of his
Vatican bed and kicked him into a homeless shelter.*

The first shot across Wisan's bow came in July 2008, when Hildale/
Colorado City attorney Peter Stirba filed a motion for a temporary
restraining order against Wisan in St. George, seeking to strip him of his

---

* Curiously, only Roger Hoole's responses to FLDS pleadings emphasized the illegal
aspects of FLDS religious conviction, but unlike the FLDS attorneys, Hoole understood that
he represented individuals who had no legal standing in the administration of the UEP trust.
Judge Lindberg admitted Hoole's pleadings as a courtesy and advisory condition only, a status Hoole accepted.

fiduciary powers. Filing legal actions to disqualify Wisan and Lindberg or vacate their orders would become a popular FLDS attorney pastime, filed again and again under different actions with slightly different clients, but Stirba was specifically concerned with Wisan's attempt to evict Guy and Ilene Steed from a UEP trailer in which they'd resided since 2000 and claimed as a family heirloom.*

The Steeds were typical FLDS residents who'd refused to sign the court-ordered occupancy agreements or pay the $100 monthly residential fees required to administer the trust, even as they were reportedly giving $1,000 a month to Warren Jeffs to sue the trust, thereby draining its assets. In effect, the Steeds and all who would follow them were suing themselves, paying both the lawyers who were attacking the trust and those defending it. The *Salt Lake Tribune* consistently portrayed Wisan and his lawyers as leeches whose bills were bankrupting the trust, but the lion's share of Wisan's legal expenses billed to the trust were those incurred defending the onslaught of repetitive legal attacks brought by FLDS lawyers, who were being allowed to proceed as if the trust reformation and subsequent beneficiary assignments had never happened at all. FLDS members were convinced that Wisan, especially, had popped up from nowhere to seize their peaceful lands for no reason because the government was trying to destroy their religion. Whipped by blowhards like Willie Jessop and the FLDS attorneys' increasingly vitriolic language, the panic of the FLDS membership surged.

Although Wisan made valiant efforts to countermessage with mailings no one opened and town hall meetings no one attended, his own blunt and sardonic personality played into the hands of Willie Jessop and the lawyers. FLDS attorney Rod Parker's thorough research had turned up a notation made by Wisan's lawyer, Jeffrey Shields, detailing a phone conversation he had with Wisan shortly after Warren Jeffs's renunciation of his prophethood. Shields and Wisan were discussing how the seismic event might be beneficially used in their uphill battle to win over the FLDS membership when Wisan uttered the phrase he would probably now trade an appendage to retract. Shields's notes indicated that Wisan wondered "how to use the

---

* The Steeds' suit exemplified the schizophrenic position taken be FLDS members who, on Jeffs's orders, refused to sign occupancy agreements or seek title to their own homes. At the same time they asserted their property belonged to Warren Jeffs and FLDS, they argued it was theirs individually. To argue against themselves, they relied on some of the same legal arguments, such as life title expectations and unjust enrichment, that David Stubbs used a decade earlier in his successful suit against Rulon Jeffs's claims that there was no individual ownership.

[jailhouse] DVD in the sociological and psychological war with the beneficiaries of the trust."

"Meaningful supervision of the fiduciary's perceived 'sociological and
psychological war with the beneficiaries' is essential," Parker advised sternly,
and he wasn't kidding. Two dozen FLDS attorneys would include the "psychological war" comment in nearly every document they filed for the next
five years—sometimes more than once—as evidence that Wisan was a sinister monster.

Apparently caught off guard, Shields tried to defend the comment in a
stumbling phone interview with the *Deseret News.* "We didn't start the war,"
he protested. "Warren started the war. We're defending the war." But the
diplomacy-challenged Wisan stepped in it again when was he was caught on
tape referring to himself as the "State Ordained Bishop"—SOB for short—
which probably didn't sound nearly as clever when FLDS began gleefully
pairing that remark with the other one.* Soon, nearly every FLDS pleading
would inform any court that would listen that Wisan had declared psychological and social warfare on their clients and had appointed himself the
SOB in charge.

Wisan's unpopularity in Short Creek emboldened Stirba to issue a semihys-
terical "press release" when he sued Wisan twice for the same case in Utah's
Fifth District Court, asking for, among other things, a restraining order to
prevent the eviction of his two clients, Guy and Ilene Steed. The press release
presented a different scenario. "Court Appointed Special Fiduciary Attempts
Mass Eviction of Hildale, Utah and Colorado City, AZ Citizens" was the headline for a two-page open letter in which Stirba gave an accurate account of
how the trust got where it was but asserted that Wisan had "overstepped his
bounds," even though the bounds were clearly enunciated in court orders.
Stirba also complained that Wisan was mean. The FLDS lawyer was offended
that Wisan employed ex-FLDS members to help him. Never mind that actual
FLDS members *refused* to help Wisan; everybody knew that ex-FLDS people
weren't appreciated in Short Creek. Stirba continued with a cavalier claim that
Wisan was driving away local residents and businesses when, in fact, Warren
Jeffs had himself relocated those people and businesses to Texas.

Although Stirba's suit was one of the few FLDS actions that would not
drag on for years, it embraced a number of troubling themes that would

*   Before he wised up, Wisan was also known to whistle the theme music for *The Twilight Zone*
when he entered Short Creek.

be standard in all the FLDS suits to follow. It assumed that Wisan had no authority or that his authority (and by extension Judge Lindberg's authority) was illegitimate. It assumed that the conditions of the UEP trust prior to October 26, 2006, were still in effect, as if Warren Jeffs had never left town, let alone been imprisoned. It assumed that Short Creek was in effect its own country, with a piety of religion that superseded the laws of the states, enabling those "in good standing" to determine who will live there or not and which laws will be followed or ignored.

Finally, and most perplexing to the Salt Lake legal community at large, Stirba and his colleagues would file pleadings that strained the limits of civility, while presenting incomplete, misleading, or flat-out unsupportable facts. All litigators arrange facts to put their clients in the best light, and advocating a specific point of view is a lawyer's job, but most respect a common situational reality in the process. FLDS litigators threw factual caution to the wind and tossed serious charges about like confetti, using volatile, demeaning, and aggressive language. "It's like they get possessed when they get on board with FLDS," marveled Hoole in a sentiment repeated by a dozen others who didn't wish to come to the litigation-happy FLDS attorneys' attention anytime soon. "The things they *say*. The things they *write*. You talk to them at a Christmas party or something and you'd never believe the nice guy talking to you actually accused you of some of these really vile things."

Stirba's disingenuous claims that Wisan was driving away businesses when Warren Jeffs was relocating them was a harbinger of what would become a pattern of half truths, selective facts, sins of omission, and muddled storytelling in FLDS legal motions more pronounced than what is usual for litigators. "They just lie," stated an unconcerned Bill Walker, Ruth Stubbs's former attorney and a man who did not care whose attention he drew. In another few years, a curious twist of circumstance would find Walker again representing an ex-FLDS family, this time in league with the Arizona Attorney General's Office.

But before that happened, a whiteout blizzard of FLDS legal paper would hit courts in Utah and Arizona. As FLDS leaders spit and clawed to regain their kingdom, nobody had seen nothin' yet.

22

EMERGENCY WARS

I could refer you to plenty of instances where men, have been righteously slain, to atone for their sins. . . . I have known a great many men who have left this Church for whom there is no chance whatever for exaltation, but if their blood had been spilled, it would have been better for them. The wickedness and ignorance of the nations forbid this principle's being in full force, but the time will come when the law of God will be in full force.

—Brigham Young, *Journal of Discourses, Vol. 4*

The Lord gave me a vision during the heavenly session. . . . He showed me that I would be taken and scourged and tortured by the officials of the government, and that I would be unsexed and be beaten and starved, to stand as a witness against this generation of their wickedness and abominations; and that I would be taken by my enemies and made to watch my own family ravished and killed before my eyes. They would then put me in prison and hold me there to die. The Lord showed me that I would be healed and renewed. . . . He showed me that I would call down the judgments of God upon my enemies and the Lord would sweep them off the earth.

—Warren Jeffs, dictation from jail, January 20, 2007

In August 2008, three years after Mark Shurtleff filed his petition and two years after the final court order reforming the UEP trust became law, the first of four separate suits with interchangeable combinations of FLDS members and corporations arrived. Each suit used different wording to lob the same complaints with the same goal of wrenching the UEP trust back into Warren Jeffs's hands, come hell or high water. Represented by Rod Parker, Willie Jessop was joined by FLDS members Dan Johnson and Merlin Jessop, appearing in Judge Lindberg's courtroom and declaring themselves to be representatives of FLDS "members in good standing," a religious credential that they felt trumped legal deadlines and superseded narrow definitions of legal standing to challenge a settled court order. The first "movants" wanted permission to intervene in the 2005 UEP trust case in Third District Court.* They also wanted Judge Lindberg to disqualify herself for bias and malfeasance and religious discrimination, and they wanted Lindberg to throw Wisan out for the same reasons.

Later that month, Parker filed a second suit against Bruce Wisan, also in Third District Court, which sought to set aside the two-year-old, $8.8 million default judgment Wisan had won against Warren Jeffs and the trust's former trustees for defrauding the trust. Parker's motion concentrated on accusing Wisan of misrepresentations and outright lies when he documented Jeffs's illegal liquidation of UEP assets as he forsook Short Creek for Texas. In bringing such serious charges, Parker was undeterred by the fact that—like the UEP case—Wisan's case against Jeffs went unchallenged at the time and became settled law after nobody appealed the final default order.

Parker's second filing in as many weeks did get Wisan to thinking, though. Was it kosher for the lawyer who had represented the UEP trust for seventeen years to now be suing that entity? Wisan didn't think so. Turning the tables, Wisan made a motion that Lindberg disqualify *Parker* from future attacks on his former UEP client, now represented by Wisan. While he was at it, Wisan also subpoenaed any records Parker or his firm might have that would help Wisan's efforts to untangle the actual UEP assets, efforts still obstructed by the trust's former trustees who had refused to comply with, or ignored, court orders to shed light on the matter, so far without any repercussions.

Lindberg declined Parker's nasty invitation to withdraw herself, but she properly forwarded the matter to Third District presiding judge Robert K. Hilder to get his take. While she waited for Hilder's verdict on her performance, Lindberg reserved judgment on the Wisan ejection, since it would be moot if Hilder tossed her from the case, but she did reject the FLDS movants' other arguments. Lindberg found that the men did not have legal standing to interfere with the UEP trust and were too late to do so even if they did have it.

---

*   Although its parameters may vary depending on the type of lawsuit, "legal standing" is basically the ability to demonstrate a specific connection, legally protected interest, or possibility of injury directly related to the matter before the court. A fisherman in Oregon, for instance, would not have standing to sue an oil company for damages from a spill in the Gulf of Mexico. Most of the FLDS claims for standing had roots in the argument that the trust had been created by FLDS for FLDS religious purposes. However, because some of FLDS religious tenets were illegal, Lindberg had removed religion from the equation, and the trust had always stood as a single legal entity independent of FLDS and its two registered corporations. This left Wisan and the attorneys general to argue neither FLDS nor its corporations had standing to challenge the administration of UEP on either an ownership or religious basis.

In a few months, Hilder would refuse to remove Lindberg. The presiding judge observed that feeling blue about a court decision that didn't go your way wasn't proof the judge was an unethical religious bigot. As daintily as he could, Hilder also addressed what he hoped weren't FLDS's true motives for the unsupportable attack against the judge, admonishing that "[I]n the absence of any credible evidence of actual bias, claims of appearance [of bias] can become nothing more than a tool for judge shopping."

But with its rigid evidentiary requirements, judge shopping may have never been in the FLDS playbooks. Just as filing an intervener's suit in the court where the original case is being heard is necessary before one can appeal anything, asking the district court to disqualify the trial judge is just a technical step required to get the FLDS lawyers where they really wanted to be—away from a judge who knew the facts of the UEP case and into the appeals courts. The sect's lawyers wanted to sidestep Lindberg and head to the Supreme Court, where the justices were unfamiliar with the facts surrounding the UEP trust. It probably didn't hurt that one of the FLDS lawyers—Michael Zimmerman—had been chief justice of the Utah Supreme Court from 1994 to 1998 and a regular justice until 2000, when he stepped down to join the Salt Lake City law firm of Snell and Wilmer. From now on, FLDS would employ emergency writs, petitions, and rules to springboard from Lindberg's unsatisfactory rulings into the Utah Supreme Court.

The overuse, even abuse, of various emergency rules and other measures in place only for drastic circumstances effectively paralyzed Lindberg—and by extension Wisan—as the Supreme Court entertained surge after surge of FLDS motions, ruling on the purported "emergencies" but never answering the bottom-line questions that Lindberg, the attorneys general of Utah and Arizona, and Wisan posed in their opposition briefs. Did the movants miss the appeal deadline or not? Did they have any legal right to be there at all? Because if they didn't, everything else they were talking about went out the window. With motions from twenty-one FLDS lawyers and four government agencies running into hundreds of pages each, the answers to those questions could have saved a forest. Without knowing whether the waves of FLDS movants had standing, both Lindberg and Wisan were out there with one hand tied behind their backs.

FLDS attorneys had certainly considered the very real possibility that they *would* lose the legal standing fight, and so they put in place a safety net. In October 2008, FLDS lawyers filed a massive suit in U.S. District Court alleging religious persecution and constitutional civil rights violations. Like every other FLDS lawsuit, the federal brief didn't discuss polygamy or under-age marriage or identify the illegal nature of any tenet FLDS members wish to practice but merely claimed they have a constitutional right to act on whatever they believe. The suit sought to nullify parts of Utah's bigamy laws along with 150 years of American law holding that an individual's religion does not excuse criminal conduct.*

"In the last few years, our communities and our faith have come under sustained and systemic attack by the state of Utah," Willie Jessop wrote in a suspiciously articulate affidavit filed with the motion. "The principal means by which that attack has been carried out is the state's takeover of a sacred Trust and appointment of a self-proclaimed 'State-Ordained Bishop' to administer the trust."

FLDS would use the federal suit to launch one emergency petition before allowing the matter to fall dormant in a stay order. Though paused, the federal suit could be resurrected if or when FLDS lost its battle for standing in the state courts. If that happened, FLDS could start all over again from square one in the federal courts.

With a host of lesser lawsuits orbiting the UEP matter, FLDS waded into its first major battle against Wisan, Shurtleff, Goddard, and Lindberg in August 2008, with the proposed sale of an empty, arid piece of property known as Berry Knoll Farm, a fight that would set the gold standard for over-the-top legal assault. Wisan had proposed the sale to pay the cash-strapped trust's $2 million debts accumulated in the never-ending struggle to sort out UEP lands for return to trust beneficiaries. To get the land identified and sub-divided, Wisan had been obliged to sue several recalcitrant FLDS businesses and governmental agencies, in addition to the derelict trustees, and now was defending numerous other lawsuits and countersuits lobbed at the trust.

Lindberg had agreed that selling the property was the best of bad choices to keep the trust afloat, specifically noting that Wisan was incurring ridiculous expenses trying to punch through the sandbags FLDS had erected around all information. When Wisan first proposed the sale of unoccupied Berry Knoll Farm to pay legal bills months earlier, not an eyebrow had been raised. But that was then, and this was now. Now, Berry Knoll Farm was a "sacred site," the location of a long-ago prophesied FLDS temple. In volu-minous court filings and indignant press conferences, FLDS lawyers aided

---

*   Ironically, the landmark case prosecutors still cite when individuals attempt to defend crim-inal behavior on religious grounds is the 1878 U.S. Supreme Court case *United States v. Reynolds*, the case against polygamy practiced by Utah's pioneer Mormons.

by Willie Jessop told a bewitching tale of bloodsucking lawyers directed by the villainous government agent Bruce Wisan ripping the hearts from defenseless religious folk who just wanted to worship and milk their cows in peace. FLDS attorneys also asserted that Berry Knoll was the FLDS farming "breadbasket," and its loss would produce food shortages and hunger. The media didn't seem as fond of the imminent starvation story line as the sacred site imagery, so that's where Willie Jessop directed his efforts.

"Sacred temple site" proved an irresistible buzz phrase, especially to the *Tribune*'s Brooke Adams, who deluged readers with tales of peaceful, bread-baking kinfolk fighting valiantly for their lives against a siege by greedy Wisan's money-grubbing lawyers out to suck their heritage dry. Adams did not wonder where FLDS obtained the millions to pay its own lawyers to sue its own trust. Although Lindberg spelled it out in every order, the *Tribune*, Utah's paper of record, continued to blame the trust's financial problems on Wisan and his lawyers instead of apprising the public that the bulk of Wisan's bills were directly related to the failure of FLDS to obey court orders as well as their legal attacks. In Salt Lake City, the public had the impression that Wisan's lawyers dined on lobster and caviar, laughing all the way to the bank as they destituted the trust and savaged a pitifully poor, pious religious community weeping over the loss of their sacred temple site that, at the time, had not even been court *approved* for a sale, let alone lost.

The Berry Knoll Farm battle bears further scrutiny because it so richly illustrates the dubious lengths to which the sect, with its apparently unlimited resources, was prepared to stretch. FLDS lawyers supported their questionable position that Berry Knoll was a temple site in part with equally questionable evidence. They pointed to an excerpted sentence from a 1952 diary, an old hymn, and a paragraph from unofficial Short Creek historian Ben Bistline's book *The Polygamists*.

In the 1930s, Short Creek was founded by landowner Leroy Johnson and a contingent of Mormon fundamentalists in Salt Lake City. That contingent included Joseph Musser, who published the sensational, fundamentalist, polygamy-advocating pamphlets *Truth* and was at the time the biggest infected thorn in mainstream Mormon Church's paw. It was the beloved Musser, FLDS attorneys proclaimed, who had prophesied the Berry Knoll Farm land as the site of a magnificent temple FLDS members intended to build. Someday.

In fact, Short Creek residents might have been completely unaware of the sacred temple site, and not because Musser's prophecy was a bit dusty.

The paragraph from Ben Bistline's book cited by FLDS attorneys described Musser walking past an area where two fundamentalist Mormon pioneers had been slain by Indians, a spot now part of Berry Knoll Farm. After pausing to reflect upon the tragedy, Musser remarks, almost as afterthought, that the spot should be a future temple site. The temple is never mentioned again, not in Bistline's book or by any subsequent FLDS prophets, including Warren Jeffs, who specifically abandoned the area and chose to build a temple in Texas.

FLDS legal pleadings do not account for this lapse, nor do they acknowledge another important fact: Joseph Musser was disgraced, stripped of his authority, and kicked out of Short Creek and FLDS in 1951. At that time, FLDS was still governed by a quasidemocratic leadership that probably wasn't embracing Musser's prophetic powers when it branded him "mentally unstable." Like Rulon Jeffs, Musser had suffered a debilitating stroke, but that was only cover for the uncharitable judgment. Against the FLDS leadership's wishes, Musser had tried to strong-arm an unacceptable Salt Lake City fundamentalist named Rulon Allred into an FLDS apostle slot. When Musser met resistance, he autocratically disbanded the FLDS hierarchy. The dictator move would be standard today, but in the semidemocratic environs of 1951, Musser's high-handed presumption was very annoying.

Musser and Allred were both ejected from FLDS. Allred then formed a rival fundamentalist group called the Apostolic United Brethren, which, until the Centennial Park group broke away in the 1980s, was FLDS's most hated competitor.* Some Short Creek residents may have been surprised to learn of Musser's suddenly exalted status, because until recently, being called a "Musserite" was a slur and possible grounds for excommunication.**

The FLDS court pleadings ignore the inconvenient fact that the four FLDS prophets to date had not blueprinted any temple for Berry Knoll Farm, and Warren Jeffs specifically rejected the area as "not of God." Instead of Berry Knoll, Warren Jeffs spent millions on his temple in Texas. In thousands of seized dictation pages from 2002 to 2007, Jeffs never mentioned

---

*   Rulon Allred was murdered by a rival fundamentalist group led by the violent LeBaron family in 1997. Although Allred was shot in broad daylight in his homeopathic medicine and chiropractic office, his killers, wives of one of a trio of notorious LeBaron brothers, were acquitted.

**   Musser was also a strong Adolph Hitler supporter and Nazi sympathizer during World War II, though it is unclear if this sentiment is tied to the derogatory FLDS associations with his name or the slur is only theological. Contradicting FLDS practice, Musser was also staunchly opposed to underage marriage.

Berry Knoll Farm as a temple site. And neither did the FLDS lawyers themselves. In a motion opposing FLDS efforts to stop hearings on a land sale
proposal, Arizona assistant attorney general Bill Richards, Terry Goddard's
point man, wryly noted that the FLDS attorneys were themselves new to
the "sacred temple site" idea, having never mentioned it in pleadings filed
immediately after Wisan suggested the sale of Berry Knoll.

And there was this: in an ignored court filing, Roger Hoole filed portions of a deposition with former UEP trustee and breakaway Canadian
FLDS leader Winston Blackmore, in which Blackmore asserts that the
Berry Knoll Farm was specifically rejected as a site for anything—including
farming—by Warren Jeffs's father, Rulon Jeffs.* This claim was supported
by aerial photographs of the property published in the *Tribune*. Prior to
2000, the pictures show verdant crop fields, but by 2005, the Berry Knoll
property was a brown dust bowl. Because the land was prohibitively expensive to irrigate, Blackmore recalled that a penny-pinching Rulon, furious
over the latest water bills for the unproductive acres, ordered that "not one
more dime" would be allocated to Berry Knoll, directing that it be abandoned. As an FLDS renegade now cooperating with Wisan, Blackmore was
tainted goods, his testimony suspect except for the facts that not one more
dime *was* put into the property and it *was* abandoned in the time period
Blackmore references.

Of course, abandoning poor agricultural prospects didn't prove that
Warren Jeffs didn't intend to spend more millions on a Berry Knoll temple, even though he'd looted and abandoned the UEP trust to build one
in Texas. Very soon after FLDS decided to retake UEP, Willie Jessop and
FLDS attorneys had the FLDS faithful convinced that the sale of Berry Knoll
Farm would deprive them of a glorious religious future. The heretofore
unplanned and unmentioned temple was as real as the sunrise to thousands
of FLDS men, women, and children who would be bussed into Salt Lake
City to hold circle prayers and demonstrate outside various courthouses
FLDS attorneys had carpet-bombed with a slew of "emergency" petitions.
FLDS attorneys were not trying to stop the sale of Berry Knoll. They were
trying to stop *hearings* about the *proposal* for the sale, though no one could
have grasped that from print media reports, which continued portraying the

---

* Like all the FLDS "movants," Roger Hoole's clients did not have legal standing in the UEP
trust case, either. In an unusually generous gesture, Lindberg allowed parties without legal
standing to submit opinions to the court, but because he was not a participant, Hoole's filings
were not scrutinized with the same intensity as others.

action as a battle for hallowed ground being plowed under by Wisan's cadre of greedy lawyers.

In an unusually generous gesture for an overbooked district court judge, Lindberg had allowed input in the UEP matter from any interested parties. Willie Jessop appeared at an August hearing with a chip on his shoulder and an attitude that would set the tone for future interactions, such as they were, between FLDS members and the courts. Affecting an odd combination of hayseed innocence and undisguised contempt, Willie professed to be in the dark about three years of UEP rules and regulations, a condition he implied was deliberately inflicted despite dozens of meetings hosted by Wisan and a pressroom full of literature mailed to residents.

When Lindberg reminded Jessop that he'd just filed a suit challenging those procedures and explained the procedures to him again, Jessop stubbornly stuck to his illogical guns. "That's what I'm saying," he insisted. "Nobody has given us access." When Lindberg inquired why no FLDS member had come forward to take one of their two permanently reserved chairs on the UEP advisory board, Willie brushed the question away with a coy suggestion that he just might, someday, think about applying for a seat on the board, but then again, maybe not. "All we're asking for is some clarification on your ideas about FLDS owning property," Jessop told Lindberg piously.*

But the court's "ideas" about FLDS owning property were not only clear, they were the point of Willie Jessop's trek to the courthouse. FLDS, be it a church, a corporation of the president, a corporation of presiding bishops, or an "informal association of individuals," did not own *any* property. In fact, there were no property owners of any kind but only beneficiaries who could use the court-ordered process to claim property. Jessop made it sound as though wounded FLDS members were simply being excluded from a process they really wanted to join, but it is doubtful that FLDS was ever much concerned about one provision or two or three or a thousand. From the beginning, FLDS attorneys made it plain the sect would not stop until every court action taken since 2005 was reversed, non-FLDS people were removed

---

* At the August 14 hearing, Willie Jessop raised a point that did produce changes. Jessop complained that even if FLDS members received home titles, they would not, under present procedures, be allowed to give the property back to FLDS. "I look at that as a direct attack on my religion," Jessop said, and the court later agreed. To the horror of FLDS activists, the rules were changed, allowing anyone who received property to return it to Warren Jeffs if they desired.

from Short Creek, and the trust was safely back in Warren Jeffs's worthy hands. FLDS leaders wanted their old lives back, and nothing else would do.

On October 8, Lindberg agreed with Wisan that Rod Parker had many and obvious conflicts of interest worthy of getting him kicked off the UEP case. She reminded Parker he had a duty to provide Wisan with any enlightening documents his firm might possess regarding the assets and makeup of the UEP trust, an order he was resisting. Parker's ejection produced a mighty howl from the FLDS camp, who shrieked that Lindberg was depriving them of trusted counsel of two decades and ordering disclosure of privileged attorney/client communications. FLDS claimed they would be lost babes in the woods, thrown to the wolves without Parker to defend them, but in fact other attorneys had already appeared at hearings on FLDS's behalf, and the sect had hired seven law firms in addition to Parker's Snow, Christensen, and Martineau.* Even Parker's dismissal from the case was theoretical. He appealed immediately and never left the field. In November 2008, all the firms set about earning some money.

Although she didn't have to, Judge Lindberg had set November 14 for the date on which anybody could weigh in on the proposal to sell Berry Knoll. To further accommodate FLDS, she agreed to hold the hearing in St. George. It seemed there was nothing to complain about. Everyone seemed amenable to the date and venue, but once again, FLDS had been playing possum.

Just days before the St. George hearing was supposed to take place, FLDS attorneys filed simultaneous emergency petitions in three courts to stop the hearing. The petitions, to which everyone had to drop everything to respond, were filed in Mohave County (Arizona) Superior Court, where a selection of "movants" had filed suit against Lindberg and Wisan a few days earlier; in the Utah Supreme Court, which was now in possession of numerous appeals from Lindberg's court; and in U.S. District Court, where the safety net religious persecution suit had been filed in October.

The sheer scope of the attack took the responding parties' breaths away. Opposing the federal action, Wisan attorney Zachary Shields (brother of attorney Jeffrey Shields) wrote: "The present TRO [temporary restraining order] motion is a part of a full-scale assault of abusive, vexatious litigation which the plaintiffs have inflicted upon the fiduciary in recent weeks. Such assault is part of an improper scheme to pound the trust into submission

---

*   The list of eight firms does not include the criminal attorneys hired to defend Jeffs in Utah, Arizona, and Texas, or the lawyers for the other eleven FLDS men indicted with Jeffs in Schleicher County.

with overwhelming, meritless litigation attacks while starving the trust of the funds which are so desperately needed in order to defend itself."

In his opposition brief's introduction, Utah assistant attorney general Jerrold Jensen came to the point: "The FLDS church has *never owned* the farm, is *not a beneficiary* [emphasis added] of the UEP trust, yet is seeking a TRO to block the sales of the property. Does the FLDS church have standing to block the sale of property?" Jensen added that nobody had any idea who the FLDS plaintiffs actually represented at this point. "Is Mr. Jeffs still the president of the Church but not the prophet? Is Willie Jessop, who has filed an affidavit in this case, speaking for the Warren Jeffs faction of the FLDS Church, officers of the church excluding Mr. Jeffs, or another faction?" Finally, Jensen addressed the FLDS claims that their UEP connection by religious conviction gave them standing to bring the action. Setting aside the unaddressed FLDS missed deadline issue for the moment, Jensen wrote, "Essentially, the plaintiff asks this Court to favor their religion over that of others. . . . In other words, plaintiff asks this Court to disavow the Utah State Court's principal of religious neutrality in favor of a standard that requires the Court to choose sides upon religious preferences."

Jensen's summation of the FLDS claims for standing may be simple, but it does capture the essence of the FLDS arguments for legal standing to initiate a do-over of the 2006 order. Writing for FLDS in the federal appeal, attorneys Kenneth Okazaki, Stephen Clark, and Ryan Harris provided the court an exhaustive FLDS history lesson going back to the 1830s and Joseph Smith, with special attention given to the Christian principles of sacred consecration. Without mentioning polygamy or underage marriage, the FLDS attorneys argue that their clients are being deprived of constitutional and First Amendment rights to practice their religion in peace and that Judge Lindberg erred when she reformed the trust to mandate religious neutrality.*

Speaking about their clients, described here as "plaintiff Association members," the FLDS lawyers wrote: "Their purpose is to maintain the status quo and forestall the transfer of economically and spiritually significant real property until this Court has an opportunity to fully consider

---

* FLDS attorneys were sometimes compelled to be creative in their citations of legal precedent. In this case, they cited a federal law prohibiting undue restrictions on the ability of incarcerated inmates to practice their religions in prison. In other instances, although homosexuality was considered an unpardonable sin, FLDS attorneys would align themselves with gay rights activists in their attempts to legalize gay marriage, believing it would open the door to legal arguments for other types of marriage.

the serious and substantial legal questions raised by the state of Utah's decision to secularize what is, at its core, a religious institution. . . . The Berry Knoll Farm is not only central to the economic life of the community whose just wants and needs the trust was formed to provide, but also and more importantly it is central to the spiritual community the trust was created to build." The attorneys add that the loss of the alleged temple site FLDS had never owned would also constitute "a substantial infringement of their [FLDS's] First Amendment Freedoms."

"The central institution of a religious community's economic and spiritual strivings for the Kingdom of God has been defiled, replaced by a secular bureaucracy focused solely on what State functionaries determine, in their unfettered discretion, to be the material benefit of trust beneficiaries. The nature and extent of this intrusion into the internal affairs of a religious institution is literally unprecedented," the FLDS lawyers wrote.

"Movant's motion is another collateral attack on the Court's 2006 Trust Reformation," wrote Arizona assistant attorney general Bill Richards. It was a line Richards and Wisan's attorney, Jeffrey Shields, would eventually be able to recite in a coma as the movants went on to file more requests for injunctions, more requests to remove the judge and fiduciary, and more emergency writs in any available court, new suits with the same complaints from different combinations of movants.

Hundreds of FLDS members were bussed from Short Creek to Salt Lake City for the emergency hearing in U.S. District Court, milling outside the courthouse or praying for the rolling television cameras. As a frustrated Shields tried to enlighten the court to the legal tardiness and questionable standing of the petitioners, FLDS took a more existential road. "What's literally at stake is the preservation of the faith itself," declared another FLDS attorney, Stephen C. Clark. U.S. district judge Dee Benson may not have known that the "faith" required the consentless "marriages" of underage girls and the abandonment of teenage boys, but he did know there was no emergency surrounding the "emergency hearing" about land—sacred or not—that had only been proposed for a sale. "There doesn't seem to be anything of really imminent harm," Benson observed, declining to issue a temporary restraining order to stop the November 14 hearing. "Bulldozers aren't moving in."

Similarly, the Utah Supreme Court declined to halt the Lindberg hearing, but the court did temporarily suspend the two-month-old Lindberg order disqualifying Rod Parker and his firm from participating in the burst of FLDS challenges. For that, the Utah Supreme Court would hold another hearing. In what Parker called a "nice victory," the Utah Supreme Court had now—intentionally or not—entered the UEP case as a kind of shadow court FLDS would use as a lateral "trier of fact."* In their petitions, FLDS attorneys begged the high justices to "retain jurisdiction" over the entire UEP case, confirming speculation that the FLDS strategy rested upon getting the UEP case away from Judge Lindberg.

After exhausting all the parties with failed emergency petitions, FLDS proceeded to overwhelm the diminutive St. George courthouse on November 14, bussing in more than a thousand FLDS members amid a whirl of national media. A rattled Lindberg abruptly halted the hearing, grasping at a lifeline offered by Mark Shurtleff. To the dismay of FLDS activists, Shurtleff, who'd been seriously angered by Wisan's verbal indiscretions, had been holding private, some said secret, meetings with FLDS leaders, including Willie Jessop. Shurtleff advised Lindberg that he thought he could negotiate a UEP settlement out of court, which at this point would be the judge's manna from heaven.

Shurtleff's surprising confidence that a deal could be struck had arisen from the Texas raid, which the Utah attorney general considered ill advised and heavy handed. When Willie Jessop rose from the debris, Shurtleff was intrigued. He knew about Jessop's shady background and unflattering nickname, but the new FLDS spokesman at least seemed familiar with the twenty-first century. Shurtleff devised a sort of character test to determine if the flamboyant Jessop could summon the even temperament and smarts essential for good-faith settlement talks, which would naturally require give-and-take on both sides. If Jessop was just going to stomp around the negotiating table the way he did at press conferences, Shurtleff didn't want to waste his own time.

So the Utah attorney general invited Willie Jessop to dinner, but not just any dinner. Shurtleff chose a sushi restaurant serving fancy raw fish from which he expected Jessop to recoil. "I figured he'd never been exposed to something like this and would think it was . . . I don't know . . . maybe a sissy thing," Shurtleff said. "He puts himself out there as a macho guy, and I wanted to see what he'd do, how he'd handle it." Jessop's muted reaction

---

* The original trial court is considered the "trier of facts," meaning that the first court, in this case Judge Lindberg's, sorts through and confirms the facts of the lawsuit. When a case is appealed, the higher court generally accepts the lower court's conclusions about the evidence, deciding only whether the trial judge properly applied the law to those settled facts.

to sushi impressed the attorney general. "He didn't order any sushi," Mark remembered, "he ordered something else, but he *did* order and he *didn't* make any remarks. He looked uncomfortable, but he sucked it up and went through with the whole dinner." Shurtleff considered the memory for a moment. "I had to hand it to him for that," he said. "The guy was faced with something unexpected and probably repugnant to him, and he just did it." Nodding his approval, he concluded, "I respected that."

Even Wisan set aside his considerable suspicions about FLDS's good faith. He was a little tired of being sued, and if a settlement could be reached, he was all in, but he had conditions. For Wisan, any settlement involving the wholesale return of UEP property to FLDS was out of the question. Even if FLDS members decided to individually return their property to the trust, Wisan would insist on first putting the deeds in their individual hands.

"There's something about handling that piece of paper," Wisan argued fervently, "something *American*. Home ownership. A piece of paper that equals security. You hold it in your hands, and it hits you: This home is *mine*. I worked hard for it, and nobody can take it away from me. I would be derelict in my duty as fiduciary if I didn't at least give people that chance, no matter what they decided to do afterward," he concluded resolutely.

But Roger Hoole never believed that FLDS would agree to any settlement that didn't award them 100 percent of their goals. "FLDS has infinite resources," Hoole lamented. "I think they plan on just wearing everyone out, getting their way in the long run. They always have. With nobody ever telling them 'no,' they might be right."

23

UTAH FADES

My senses tell me that the children of Zion should forsake every needless fashion and custom which they now practise [sic]. *My wives dress very plainly, but I sometimes ask them the utility of some of the stripes and puffs which I see on their dresses. I remember asking a lady this question once, and enquired if they kept the bed bugs and flies away. Well, if they do that they are very useful; but if they do not, now what use are they? None whatever. Now, some ladies will buy a cheap dress, say a cheap calico, and they will spend from five to fifteen dollars worth of time in making it up, which is wasting so much of the substance which God has given them on the lust of the eye, and which should be devoted to a better purpose.*

     —Brigham Young, *Journal of Discourses*, Vol. 18

4). Please have Isaac get suitcases for the new ones [people] who came to the land at R17. . . . We are to exert the faith to <u>stay</u> and to <u>succeed</u>; but have their suitcases in readiness. At least seeing the suitcases should wake everyone up to see how real the attacks are, and how real and grand and great are the protections of heaven.

5). Send me a list of the older, unmarried daughters of Brother Merril Jessop and Brother Wendell Nielsen and who their mothers are and their exact ages.

6). Remind me any marriages the Lord appointed in the record that have not been done, including Uncle Roy's ladies at houses in hiding. I also named two to be given to William E. Jessop; naming the father of the two girls but not knowing the girls' names. See if you or Patricia or Kate remember the father's name.

     —Warren Jeffs, partial list of instructions from jail, May 6, 2007

Utah assistant attorney general Tim Bodily sat in a conference room on the secured sixth floor of Salt Lake's downtown Heber Wells building, submitting wearily to an interview. There was the distinct feeling that Bodily, Shurtleff's FLDS point man, would have rather been spending the time sticking pins in his eyeballs than discussing the sect. He looked sucked dry, lifeless, and exhausted in a white shirt with permanent sweat stains at the armpits. Every now and then he offered a thin smile, but it was sardonically drawn, with no good humor at all.

"The first time I heard about them [FLDS]," he managed, "I was a tax attorney. We had a repossession issue, and I called my usual guy to go get the items, which were located in Short Creek. My guy refused to go there, and I thought, 'Well, that's weird. Maybe I won't use him anymore.'" Remembering those carefree days of ignorant bliss, Bodily shook his head, clasping his hands behind his neck. "So I called the cops. That's what you do when it's a tax issue, you call the police. And *they* refused to go into Short Creek." The mirthless smile appeared. "I couldn't believe it. Who would? And I thought, 'What on earth is going on here? Who are these people?' I informed the police that they had a legal duty to get the items. I had to tell the *cops* about their legal duties. But I still couldn't get them to go."

Bodily didn't know how much more of the UEP case he could stand. It had taken over his life. His children were growing up without him. "They [FLDS] spent *two million dollars* litigating the playground/park issue. They didn't want apostates in their park, playground, whatever." The barbed smile materialized behind a face smeared with incredulity. "*Two million dollars!*" he repeated hotly, offended by the waste. "It took forever. They could have built a state-of-the-art park with a lighted ball field and anything else you could think of. A pool! A gym! You name it, they could have had it for two million dollars but instead . . ." He trailed off, looking away and wincing in what seemed like pain. "Reasonable? That's not in play here."

After the November 2008 round of Berry Knoll emergency writs failed in the upper courts, FLDS agreed to the mediation talks and presumably to the litigation "stand down" order Lindberg issued verbally. The order meant that neither side was to file any additional pleadings, period. Having described the FLDS legal assault as a "never ending flood of litigation" in previous orders, Lindberg thought everyone needed a break, not least of all Bruce Wisan, the target of most of the ongoing attacks.* Wisan and his attorneys had not been paid in over a year. They were defending and administering the

---

* Examples of the ongoing legal skirmishes outside major issues like Berry Knoll included new motions to disqualify Lindberg and Wisan and a motion to force Lindberg to hold hearings on any proposed land sales. Although she was in no way obligated to hold such hearings, Lindberg voluntarily ordered Wisan to seek her permission before selling property and agreed to hold hearings, essentially granting the motion even though it was brought without standing. After Lindberg gave FLDS what it wanted, the sect reversed course, asking a federal judge to overrule both decisions they'd asked for to begin with.

UEP trust basically on IOU notes. The holdup on the Berry Knoll sale meant there was no money on the immediate horizon.

As Wisan looked for short-term solutions to keep the lights on, Mark Shurtleff tried to foster a little goodwill. In December 2008, a month into negotiations, Shurtleff spent two full days getting the royal treatment in Short Creek, chaperoned by FLDS leaders increasingly persuaded the Utah attorney general was leaning their way.* Shurtleff toured the town and engaged in what the media called "historic" meetings, as if meetings with FLDS leaders constituted an international diplomatic coup.

The trip may not have received Shurtleff's undivided attention. He was still recovering from a devastating motorcycle crash that had shredded his left leg a year earlier, twisting it under the Harley Davidson he was riding in a charity event and breaking the leg in seven places. The pain from the accident was excruciating but nowhere close to the agony he experienced during the rehabilitation process, under way at the time of the Short Creek trip. "I was *begging* my doctors to cut it off, the pain was so unbearable," Shurtleff remembered. "I said, 'Just give me one of those springy thingies [prosthesis] and let me get on with my life.'"

And his life encompassed what he freely admitted were more important elements than the complaints of a religious sect. Shelley Exeter, Shurtleff's executive assistant, leads an exciting life trying to jam all the charities, political events, speeches, legal work, meetings, and audiences Shurtleff wants to accomplish into a twenty-four-hour day to further his career. Shurtleff was also deep into research for his historical novel about Dred Scott, a project he'd dreamed about completing for years. He was traveling extensively to interview Scott's descendants and personally visit the locales in his story. And after an unprecedented three terms as attorney general, each won by exponentially higher margins, Shurtleff was contemplating a run for either the U.S. Senate or the Utah governor's mansion.

The UEP case had gone on a lot longer than anyone could have imagined. It was eating up resources, it was not any fun at all, and honestly, Shurtleff was increasingly uncomfortable with his role. "There has to be an end to any war," he said levelly. "When you're in one, you have to know how to end it." Asked how much time he personally spent on the UEP case, he answered with airy indifference, "Not very much time at all." His careless shrug was

---

*   Lindberg and Goddard had also taken the FLDS-chaperoned Short Creek tour. In addition, Goddard and Shurtleff had appeared in town once together in an effort to convince FLDS residents that they did not walk on cloven hoofs.

accompanied by a frown that said that he intended to keep it that way. One way or another, he wanted FLDS off his plate.

By May 2009, six months after UEP mediations had begun, Shurtleff's waning interest in forcing FLDS to obey court orders was exactly what anti-FLDS activists and attorneys were worried about. When he'd visited Short Creek in December, Shurtleff received the full *National Geographic* version of FLDS. The happy children sledding in the pristine snow, the wholesome farm, and the home-baked bread were all a far cry from his first FLDS encounter in which he felt the need to display his gun to get service in a restaurant. A sage Willie Jessop explained, "If people are working off of bad intelligence, then everybody makes presumptions and gets into things that are very difficult to get out of. We're excited because we feel like it's the first time we feel like we have the opportunity to provide something besides a perspective of only hate groups against us."

During the happy tour and his sushi dinner with the attorney general, Jessop presumably skipped any discussion of the escalating FLDS campaign of harassment, assault, and intimidation being waged against non-FLDS residents. The tour probably did not include the broken windows and doors and other vandalism to non-FLDS homes nor Isaac Wyler's treasured dead horses that had been released into traffic. But if Shurtleff had tuned into Channel 4 during December, he might have seen Brent Hunsaker's reports on the systematic, disturbing escalation of FLDS hostilities against Short Creek residents who had left the sect but had returned to the area, living under Lindberg and Wisan's protection in homes for which they had signed UEP occupancy agreements.

In just one example, Matt and Genevive Hainline went on camera describing the pervasive FLDS threats and unwelcome, uninvited intrusions onto their property. After the report aired, their side door was kicked in with force enough to rip it off its frame. When they called the Colorado City marshal to report the vandalism, the responding officer challenged their right to be on the property at all, resulting in a screaming match on the street. When the Hainlines produced their occupancy agreement with the UEP, Colorado City manager Dave Darger donned his "building inspector" hat and condemned the Hainlines' home, which they were in the process of renovating, for "electrical and plumbing problems."

Like others, the Hainlines tried to reach the Utah Attorney General's Office by voicing their concerns at Safety Net Committee meetings. The Safety Net Committee was a program Shurtleff implemented to accomplish a number

of goals. The committee, which was supposed to comprise people representing the spectrum of positions on polygamy in Utah, was intended to promote
understanding and tolerance among the groups and teach polygamists about
signs of child abuse and the dangers of underage marriage. The Safety Net
was headed by social worker Pat Merkley and overseen by Shurtleff's talented press officer Paul Murphy. The intelligent, warm-natured Murphy was
utterly convinced that the Safety Net approach was the only sane solution for
Utah's more out-there polygamist groups. Although Murphy was working
several full-time jobs in the Attorney General's Office, he threw himself into
Safety Net, making the ten-hour round-trip drive to the FLDS meeting site at
least once a month.

Anti-FLDS activists appreciated Murphy's dedication, but they were
uneasy with Safety Net from the beginning. Activists believed the committee's literature bent over backward and forward to mollify polygamists,
never taking a forceful stand on the illegality of polygamy or underage
marriage.* Initial literature released by the Safety Net Committee demonstrated an eagerness to appease FLDS sensibilities the activists found
disturbing. Prominently affiliated with Safety Net decisions were Mary
Batchelor and Anne Wilde, founders of the pro-polygamy Plural Voices,
a group hoping to decriminalize the practice glorified in a collection of
essays the group published from "freelance" polygamous women called
Voices in Harmony.**

Elaine Tyler of Hope Organization says she attended Safety Net
Committee meetings for a while but was quickly disenchanted. "What did it
for me was when Safety Net said they'd be returning any underage girls who
escaped to them back to their parents," she said sourly, raising both hands in
an exasperated shrug. "I mean, what the hell? The girls think they're finally
coming to authorities who will help them, and they just get sent back like

---

* Over the course of a few years, Safety Net Committee literature was revised several times.
Activists saw each revision as a dumbing down of language until the pamphlets almost seemed
to condone polygamy as an alternative lifestyle.

** Although Batchelor and Wilde began their married lives in plural relationships, neither had
been in a polygamous marriage for more than twenty years. Wilde had several sister wives, but
she rarely saw them because she traveled exclusively with her husband. She lived alone after she
was widowed. While asserting that nobody was closer to her than her one sister wife, Batchelor
becomes emotional discussing the "walking on eggshells" plural life fraught with bitter jealousy. Batchelor's sister wife divorced the couple after only a few years of marriage and is now
an antipolygamy activist in Salt Lake City.

always? Who could be a party to *that*? We just figured it was more of the same. Giving FLDS a nod and a wink, as usual."

An equally frustrated Murphy responded, "I don't think people realize how much work and effort Mark's office has put into this very delicate situation. You're never going to get anywhere by just arresting these people. You can arrest them all day long and you're not going to change *attitudes*, which is what we're trying to do. Mark was everybody's hero when he got into this with the Rod Holm case—the first FLDS prosecution in the state. Now that he's trying to do something a little quieter, everybody is complaining about him. It's completely unfair."

But "unfair" is how Genevive and Matt Hainline assess their reception at the Safety Net Committee when they appeared to complain about FLDS vandalism and harassment. The Hainlines felt they were dismissed as rabble-rousers by dominant committee members like Batchelor and Wilde, who offered vague observations and no action. "We're concerned that everybody is treated fairly," said Wilde of the Hainlines problems, cold comfort for non-FLDS residents who reported being stalked as they went about their daily lives, constantly harassed by FLDS representatives knocking (or not) on their doors with taunts and orders to get out.

Keeping the FLDS-controlled utilities on in their homes was a constant struggle. Groups of FLDS men would surround non-FLDS individuals, refusing to allow them to pass. Things got dangerous as black SUVs with tinted windows forced non-FLDS drivers—sometimes ferrying children—off the roads and then sped away. It was sometimes brother against brother or father against son, and the police force refused to take reports or intervene. In fact, non-FLDS members attempting to make a complaint report were in danger of being arrested themselves on any available charge, ranging from trespassing to disturbing the peace.

Of special ire to FLDS leaders was the irrepressible Isaac Wyler, who'd posted the hated tax and eviction notices for Satan's accountant, Bruce Wisan. From prison, Warren Jeffs continued moving FLDS people around the country at whim, creating many unpredictable vacancies in UEP properties abandoned when their residents were relocated. Part of Wyler's job was to establish which properties were vacant and available for occupancy applications. Typically, Wyler accomplished this by eyeballing houses with obvious signs of neglect and abandonment—houses with impassably overgrown lawns, for instance, or broken windows in winter. He'd then knock on all the doors, sometimes over a course of several days. If there was no response, Wyler was legally empowered to enter the residences, inspecting them for signs of life. If he found none, he installed a UEP lock and placed the property on the "available" list.

Wyler often sought a second opinion from excommunicated FLDS accountant Jethro Barlow, who also worked for Wisan. Barlow was doing his level best to keep track of which houses were occupied, but with Warren Jeffs moving everybody around six Western states in midnight cattle drives and the sect's refusal to cooperate, it was dicey work. For FLDS, which ignored all court authority and wanted to keep all residencies secret, Wyler's activities had been highly irritating for a long time, and finally, the Colorado City police arrested him for trespassing as he was changing the locks on an abandoned trailer.

For anyone relying on the *Tribune* for information, the incident would have sounded as if the rampaging Wyler smashed his way into the home of a defenseless and terrified widow. But for anyone else, the facts were a little different. "That house was absolutely vacant!" declared a defiant Wyler, "It was falling apart! There was nothing but trash on the floor! Nobody lived there, and nobody was there when I went in!"

Not according to FLDS. As sect leaders had in the past, and would in the future, a resident was produced as soon as a property was either declared vacant or assigned to someone who'd qualified for an occupancy agreement. In this case, FLDS produced two residents for two dwellings Wyler allegedly invaded, one of whom claimed Wyler had tried to extort $500 from her to change her locks back. The FLDS-generated police report filed by officer Sam Johnson asserted that Wyler was spotted by the other trailer's elusive resident, Aaron Nielsen, as Nielsen was making inexplicable drive-bys of his own home. On one pass, he saw Wyler, a man he knew, on the lawn. On the second drive-by, Wyler was in the house. Nobody explains why Nielsen didn't stop at his own house to ask Wyler what he was doing but instead drove to the police station to report the break in.*

The unsavvy Wyler unwisely agreed to a bench trial in nearby Moccasin, where polygamist sympathizer judge Mitchell Kalauli unsurprisingly found him guilty of trespassing in March 2009, sentencing him to probation and a

---

* Attached to this report was another incident eight months earlier in which Wyler was confronted changing the locks on empty buildings. In a warning every officer in a small town must know, officer Jonathan Roundy invoked inside-baseball lawyer-speak to discuss what are commonly known as civil rights violations. "I informed him he is setting himself up for a 1983 class action law suite [*sic*] along with the fiduciary," Roundy wrote.

$400 fine. Attempting to defend himself, Wyler testified at his trial that he'd made every effort to locate any resident for the property and that he'd even phoned Bruce Wisan in Salt Lake City to describe the situation, receiving the fiduciary's legally empowered permission to enter the trailer and change the locks.

Fair enough. In April, Colorado City attorney Ken Brendel charged Bruce Wisan and ex-FLDS accountant Jethro Barlow too: six misdemeanor counts against Wisan involving solicitation to trespass and four for Barlow, whom Wyler had also called for advice that day. Getting back to his "town manager" hat, Dave Darger cut a report to the FLDS city council advising them that "the charges are not merely related to isolated instances, but is [sic] a culmination of a situation spinning out of control." The intriguing concept of charging people criminally for generally out-of-control situations is new for American jurisprudence, a system that stubbornly insists that criminal charges be attached to a specific event with specific victims.

This was one of many problems a puzzled Mohave County presiding judge Richard Weiss was having after Wisan's and Barlow's lawyers managed to wrench their trespassing cases away from the FLDS courts. In an unusually long and detailed memo that only set a hearing date, Weiss wrote:

> This Court discerns that perhaps the state has no witness other than an agent of the defendant. . . . If there are no complaining witnesses (which infers neither victim was present at the day and time of the alleged offenses) it is difficult for the state to show the requisite indicia or proof beyond a reasonable doubt for the state to further proceed with this case. Similarly, there is a question whether the assigned prosecutor is or has made himself a witness, which may require disqualification of the prosecutor's office. Further, it is not clear whether the state has complied with its disclosure requirements, including, but not limited to, whether it has any exculpatory evidence not yet disclosed.

Typical of any legal action involving FLDS, the Wisan/Barlow misdemeanor trespassing case is still mired in the courts more than a year after the offending incident occurred. In February 2011, Wisan and Barlow endured a strange bench trial before Arizona judge pro tem Paul Julien. Judge Julien, who proceeded despite the defendants' objections that their attorney was not present, allowed transcripts of previous proceedings to be introduced as evidence even though the witnesses from those proceedings were available, meaning the defendants were deprived of their rights to cross-examine a witness. Julien promised a decision within a month, but Wisan and Barlow's attorney Bill Walker has promised that any guilty verdict will be appealed. "I filed immediately for a hearing on a bench trial that violated black letter law," Walker said. "We'll pursue this even if Julien doesn't grant a hearing."

From the time Brendel brought charges, however, the *Tribune* has echoed FLDS filing documents constantly describing Wyler as "convicted" and Wisan as additionally "indicted," while ignoring or downplaying the FLDS assaults on nonmembers that went on and on.

In March 2009, Shane Stubbs, Ruth Stubbs's brother, and his associate Seth Cooke, went to tend a field they'd just planted with a $10,000 cash crop. A normal workday turned to anguish when they arrived to find two FLDS men on tractors merrily plowing under their freshly sown seed, destroying the crop. Stubbs and Cooke had gone through UEP channels, receiving an occupancy agreement to farm the land. When they discovered Clarence Jessop and Thomas Jessop astride their tractors in the field, they called the local police and Jethro Barlow, who was still on the phone with a live tape recorder when FLDS officer Helaman Barlow arrived. Officer Barlow blithely refused to stop the destruction, nor would he accept the UEP occupancy agreement as evidence that Stubbs and Cooke were legally entitled to plant the field. "What does it take to get these guys to quit doing this?" a despairing Cooke demanded of Officer Barlow. "Do I have to go and get my .270 and start shooting people?"

An indignant Brooke Adams would reprint the taped conversation in her *Tribune* blog as evidence that the invader non-FLDS people had graduated to "death threats," but if Cooke's hopelessness carried violent overtones, Officer Barlow was remarkably unperturbed. He hung out contentedly for nearly a half hour watching the Jessop men destroy the crop, pleased to inform Cooke the land dispute was a civil matter requiring a "court order" for him to even think about intervening. Of course, the occupancy agreement *was* the court order, but it would soon be revealed that the FLDS city attorney was instructing all the Short Creek cops to ignore non-FLDS complaints with the nonsensical explanation that their problems were "a civil matter."

Eventually, Officer Barlow ambled off along with the Jessop men, who left after destroying only most of the field, but they reappeared the following morning to finish the job. Stubbs and Cooke had called the non-FLDS Mohave County police the day before, but the distance between Short Creek and the rest of the world was still daunting, and the county police had not arrived in time. The next day, however, Mohave County deputies arrived to catch the plow-happy men red-handed. Apparently panicking when the deputies strode into the field, the Jessop men tried to evade capture by nearly running one of the cops down, putting him in a very bad mood. "He [Jessop] was very uncooperative," Mohave County sheriff's spokeswoman Trish Carter said. "He would not turn the engine off. He would not say who he was. He was taken into custody." Of the arrests, an indignant Willie Jessop opined, "It's the church's land. They've been farming it for thirty years. When did they get terminated for being on it?"

It seemed to have again slipped Jessop's mind that he was party to a lawsuit trying to undo the fact that FLDS had been terminated from doing whatever its leaders wanted with the land by court order, three years earlier. "They [FLDS] do not recognize anybody's authority," said a weary Jeffrey Shields. "They don't recognize the court's authority. They don't recognize the fiduciary's authority. They don't recognize the attorney general's author- ity. They just ignore everything."

Amid all of this, activists and non-FLDS residents of Short Creek were getting very edgy about Mark Shurtleff. While the Utah Attorney General's Office continued to an optimistic drumbeat about the good progress being made in negotiations, Wisan and Goddard seemed nervous under unusually persistent questioning from reporters, unable or unwilling to confirm the excellent news coming out of Shurtleff's office. Finally, after yet another optimistic prediction, the Arizona Attorney General's Office took the unusual step of publicly refuting the good predictions, warning that the par- ties were "miles apart." Rumors that Shurtleff was caving to FLDS demands to have their trust back alarmed all non-FLDS residents in Short Creek. "What we're afraid of is that the FLDS people are going to take it all the way and start another trust," said eighty-one-year-old Ben Bistline. "Then we'll all get evicted."

In May, a large group of non-FLDS protestors arrived at the Utah Capitol Building to protest what they saw as Shurtleff's impending capitulation. Shurtleff was in his office that day and, informed of the protest, bounded down the capitol's elegant marble stairs to wade into the placard-carrying crowd in trademark style, cornering anyone he could to assert he was taking everyone's position into consideration. Press secretary Paul Murphy said,

"I understand the concerns and the fears, but in the middle of negotiations, there are a thousand different scenarios and options. I think, as hard as it is, people need to wait and see what is hammered out."

But what Shurtleff had hammered out with FLDS was shocking to anti-FLDS activists, far worse than they could have imagined. "Agreement Would Give Colorado City Property Control to FLDS," cried the May 25, 2009, edition of the *Mohave Daily News*, the only newspaper to cut to the chase on what Shurtleff had agreed to with FLDS but not the only ones floored by the negotiations' outcome. Jaws dropped in three states when Shurtleff allied himself with FLDS, presenting a settlement that would return the majority of UEP property back to the people who'd looted and abandoned it to begin with. As proposed, the settlement basically pushed the reset button, ignoring all the reforms and court orders of the past three years.

The only concession made to non-FLDS people who'd relied upon the authority of the courts to plan their lives was a small parcel of land set aside for them, which activists immediately pointed out was like assigning them to a religious ghetto that FLDS would wall off, harass, and probably refuse running water or electricity. FLDS members were already illegally fencing off property and blocking access to public roads and parks. Recently, they'd denied the grieving parents of a dead infant the right to bury the child in the town cemetery with all his other relatives, turning a mere anguish into a situation of macabre cruelty. Wisan had to step in personally to get the unburied baby laid to rest.

"The court should reject the settlement proposals submitted thus far," was the first sentence of Arizona attorney general Terry Goddard's response to the proposal. "The settlement proposed by the Fundamentalist Church of Jesus Christ of Latter Day Saints (the "FLDS") and the Utah Attorney General pose insurmountable jurisdictional, constitutional, and equitable hurdles." Part of the proposal Goddard urged the court to reject was Shurtleff's request for a court order forcing Wisan to accept the agreement. What had been a private spat was about to go public.

In his forty-two-page response, a painfully diplomatic Bruce Wisan also urged Judge Lindberg to reject the settlement, noting that, among other things, it threw out the window Lindberg's legal reforms demanding the trust be administered with religious neutrality. Whereas he was amenable to distributing lands to FLDS members who had only recently decided to participate, he pointed out that Shurtleff's plan would return everything to

Warren Jeffs and others who created the mess to begin with. There was little doubt what FLDS intended to do with the non-FLDS people they could now safely corral for torment. Even without the power Shurtleff now wanted to give the sect, FLDS had recently started building unauthorized walls around properties, cordoning off public roads and parks, and restricting the water supply by removing critical well equipment in the dead of night. Wisan did not think FLDS should be "rewarded" for spitting in the face of court orders and the laws of the land.

After waiting three years, FLDS should not be allowed to turn back time because they'd proved they could be menacing. "Having been the object of unwarranted criticism, harassment, false testimony, and frivolous civil and criminal attacks," Wisan's attorney, Jeffrey Shields, wrote, "he [Wisan] is genuinely concerned about additional legal attacks based on false testimony by those seeking to punish him for his role in accepting the Court's appointment. . . . Such attacks may further be motivated by the desire to send a message to others—'Don't mess with us.'"

It is worth noting that Mark Shurtleff never shrank from heated criticism that his proposal was an "FLDS/Utah Attorney General" plan, the implication being that the attorney general of Utah was in bed with FLDS. Such characterizations didn't bother Shurtleff because by this time he had decided that Wisan's brusque tone and rash statements had left him no choice but to deal with FLDS the way he had. "The guy called himself the State Ordained Bishop!" Shurtleff scoffed with incredulity. "He said he was the SOB working for Mark Shurtleff," he added, pointing at his own chest. "Me! Can you believe that?" He stared open-mouthed and wide-eyed, beside himself with umbrage. "It was just . . . unacceptable," he sputtered. "You cannot deal with people that way."

Shurtleff was also furious that Wisan had sold some dairy cows owned by the UEP trust while the settlement talks were in progress. Actually, it was more like Wisan had pawned the cows, because there was a deadline before which the trust could repurchase the animals, but FLDS launched a legal bombardment (in defiance of the stand-down order) claiming the cows were "sacred" and irreplaceable and now all the FLDS members would be deprived of "wholesome milk."

The usual flood of back-and-forth motions took place, with Wisan pointing out that the cows fitting the "sacred" parameters of age and use FLDS described had, in fact, *not* been pawned but were still mooing away at the UEP dairy. Wisan's pawned cows were the ones past their dairy prime. Even if FLDS hadn't messed up and assigned sacredity to the wrong bunch of cows (a fact that did not prevent them from pursuing the argument), the fiduciary didn't believe any of the cows were sacred. If they were, they must have obtained that status after pawning, because in three years nobody had said anything about any sacred cows and no cows had been treated differently than any others.

Discussing the sacred cow debacle, Shurtleff's restless frustration was plain. He paced, waved his arms, and slapped his forehead at the dumbness of it all. It wasn't really the cow pawning that bothered him, but the timing. The sacred cows threatened to screw up his FLDS "settlement." Like Tim Bodily, Shurtleff was fed up with all the petty sniping and endless litigation, although he wasn't above his own gamesmanship. To punish Wisan for the cows, Shurtleff withheld $192,000 in occupancy payments from the trust.* But getting back to the big picture, Shurtleff was deadly serious. "There has to be an end to any war," he repeated. "When you start one, you better have an end game."

Still hotly denying he was retreating from anything, Shurtleff insisted that Wisan's ham-fisted dealings with FLDS had rendered him useless in effecting the court's orders. He admitted that he met with FLDS leaders, supporting their desire to get Wisan fired. "I told them to bring me the evidence of real malfeasance—not just personality complaints but *real* evidence that Bruce was breaking rules or laws." Shurtleff declared defiantly: "And yeah. I said if they had real evidence, I'd go into court with it and ask to have him removed myself." No evidence of malfeasance against Wisan was ever presented. "They [FLDS] came back to me with a list of petty complaints dealing mostly with his demeanor," said a disgusted Shurtleff.

Shurtleff was not concerned that critics found his provision for a board to oversee land claims laughable. He did not dispute the probability that the board would be quickly taken over by FLDS leaders who would undoubtedly refuse to allow former FLDS members to reclaim their homes while driving those already there away with brutal harassment. "Ninety percent

---

*   The $192,000 was another wormhole more complicated than any one event. FLDS had been refusing to make the court-ordered monthly UEP occupancy payments, but when the sect sensed Shurtleff would capitulate to their demands, they instantly produced the back payments to mollify their new ally. Wisan refused to accept the payments because FLDS lawyers said they were being made "under protest," a phrase Wisan interpreted as a promise for more litigation. An exasperated Shurtleff took the check as a middleman, but when he found out about the cows, he withheld the money. Eventually, Lindberg was forced to issue a formal court order directing Shurtleff to give Wisan the payments.

of the people living out there *are* FLDS," he shrugged with startling indifference. "It'll probably always be that way."

Advanced by all FLDS supporters, the argument that a clear majority
of any population should be entitled to decide their own destinies comes
with the assumption that FLDS is like a harmless gated community merely
writing its own bylaws for lawn maintenance. It ignores the fact that even
gated communities must comply with federal, state, and county laws in
the country they inhabit and that a great number of the bylaws FLDS has
incorporated constitute serious felonies that were "shamefully," as Shurtleff
himself said, ignored by authorities for a good half century. Shurtleff's position also assumed that FLDS had a right to be at the negotiating table at all,
a premise that contradicted court orders in effect for the past three years
when Lindberg reformed the trust and removed the derelict FLDS administrators. But these arguments, too, no longer seemed to interest the Utah
attorney general.

"I do not have the constitutional authority to tell people what to think,"
Shurtleff stated evenly, a fair point, but in returning all property to Warren
Jeffs, Shurtleff was apparently content to leave telling people what to think
up to the prophet who taped public sex acts with twelve-year-old girls.
"Unlike the fiduciary and the Arizona attorney general," Shurtleff went
on with creeping sarcasm, "I'm not in the business of conducting social
experiments."

"Mark drank the Kool-Aid," observed Dan Fischer, a common belief that
infuriated Shurtleff. Eyes flashing, Shurtleff asserted that his office has been
"right down the middle" from the start. "I never said I was on *anybody's*
side," he spat. "Just because FLDS didn't show up at first doesn't mean I was
on the *other* side of it. Just because only one side was talking didn't mean I
was on it."

Given Shurtleff's past statements describing FLDS as a "criminal
enterprise" involved with child rape and wholesale fraud and his vow to
investigate the sect under organized crime statutes, it seems reasonable that
FLDS activists would assume that the Utah attorney general was not planning to restore UEP lands to the sect that made no secret of the fact it would
return to business as usual. "I guess he forgot what he told us down here in
Texas, too," drawled Kathy Mankin, Randy's wife and business partner.

And there's another troubling problem with Shurtleff's "right down
the middle" stance. By the time FLDS got involved, there was no middle.
The case had been decided in 2005. A final order had been signed in 2006.

A fiduciary had been appointed to distribute the assets to the rightful beneficiaries—the lowly membership that had built the multimillion-dollar estate, not the leaders dining at the five-star Painted Pony restaurant in St. George and riding around in private planes. Asked why FLDS should be excused from laws concerning appeal deadlines and allowed to relitigate a case settled three years earlier, Shurtleff offered a winning smile, holding up both hands to signal surrender to the point. "Well," he said genially, "I don't think our laws should be so inflexible as to allow no exceptions every once in awhile, because those people out there are victims of Warren Jeffs, too. They're in this mess because they listened to his bull."

But Judge Lindberg did not share Shurtleff's resignation to an inevitable, indefinite FLDS country ignoring all laws of the land as they siphoned U.S. tax dollars on the Utah/Arizona border. On July 22, 2009, Lindberg rejected the Shurtleff/FLDS proposal in a six-page order that seesawed between "appreciation" for "good faith efforts" and rebuke. Lindberg's decision agreed with Wisan's points and made an additional, fairly important observation: giving the FLDS "church" land would be against the law. Not only would it violate religious neutrality, but FLDS demanded that its followers break the law by practicing polygamy. Under Utah law, a trust wasn't allowed to promote law breaking.

"[T]he Utah A.G./FLDS proposal decidedly favors the FLDS Church and its adherents to the detriment of other potential trust beneficiaries," Lindberg wrote. "The FLDS Church as an entity is not a recognized Trust participant, yet under the Utah A.G./FLDS proposal the vast majority of Trust land—including the Berry Knoll Farm, the Harker Farm, all vacant residential lots, all commercial lots, Cottonwood Park, the zoo, the majority of the cemetery, and the Gap/Apple Valley property would be directly transferred to the FLDS Church. . . . This is hardly a neutral allocation of benefits among potential beneficiaries." For the normally careful and mild-mannered Lindberg, the wording was harsh. Asked about the public defeat, Shurtleff offered the careless shrug of a man accustomed to rolling with the punches. "Win some, lose some," he said without inflection, but he is outraged by the subsequent commentary.

Lindberg's rejection of Shurtleff's settlement plan meant the Berry Knoll sale was back on the table, and that meant FLDS was going back to the future with a whole new set of lawsuits and emergency petitions, eight law firms cranking out enough paper to choke a herd of elephants. Up until the settlement talks, Arizona had been content to play a supporting role to Shurtleff's office, but the Utah attorney general's perceived withdrawal from the stage left Wisan and Lindberg twisting slowly in the wind. It was a depressing time for anti-FLDS activists and non-FLDS Short Creek residents who'd seen the man who'd dared to break fifty years of silent acquiescence to FLDS with the Rod Holm prosecution as their champion and only hope. Who could replace him? Wisan was broke. Lindberg was straitjacketed in the appeals courts, and besides, she was only a judge, not an advocate. Who would stop this FLDS juggernaut now?

In Phoenix, Arizona, attorney general Terry Goddard watched the deteriorating situation with sorrowful resignation and not a little anger. Fighting FLDS wasn't what he'd had in mind when he'd run for his office, but he simply couldn't let it end this way. He told Bill Richards to suit up.

Arizona was taking the field.

24

ARIZONA RISING

Should not I take my tea and coffee, my beef and pork, and every other good thing, and put it into the hands of the men who sweat over the rock for the Temple, instead of feeding men, women, and children who do not strive to do all they are capable of doing? I am tried on that point, and I must say that if there is anything in the world that bothers me, it is the whining of women and children to prevent me from doing that which I know I ought to do.
— Brigham Young, *Journal of Discourses*, Vol. 5

Please keep me advised on the Wendell Musser case. . . . I saw in a vision a few nights ago a fierce and violent wolf running toward me to devour me, and as I climbed a ladder up to a platform to enter a house of safety, this wolf grew in size and ferocity, and leaped up where I was; but as he rose up, I was empowered to strike him down and he fell. Other wolves were following him to attack me, but I was delivered. I was shown this first attacker was Wendell Musser, a traitor. I know the Lord can deliver me and us. He has knowledge of the houses in hiding.
— Warren Jeffs, Purgatory jail, May 5, 2007

Jethro Barlow sat behind his desk in a home office within the Short Creek house he built, was ejected from, and managed to reclaim with Bruce Wisan's help. Now working for Wisan, the slender, bespectacled former FLDS accountant was nearly eclipsed by the towers of paperwork required for his work, reams of paper teetering on every available surface, stacked on the floor, creating paper canyons with only narrow paths for walking.

Behind him were shelves bulging with books in a community that has banned reading. Barlow is an educated man in a community that has banned education. He discussed the theories of philosophers in a community that prohibits thought. He drew easily upon events in world history in a community in which young people haven't a clue what the American Revolution might be or that there is a country called China or a place called Washington, D.C., much less who lives there. Living every day of his life required all the

mental and physical courage Barlow could muster to proceed in a community that hated him and wished him dead. As things got worse and worse
in town, Barlow never knew if or when someone would take it upon themselves to make the wishing real.

Seven years ago, Barlow was on his way to church with his two wives
and nineteen children. When he reached the portal, his children were
allowed inside, but childhood friends, family, and men he'd known and
worked with his entire life barred his entry in devastating silence, turning their backs to him to demonstrate that he no longer existed. Warren
Jeffs had fingered Barlow as a dangerous traitor, a threat to the salvation
of every soul in Short Creek. Everything the fifty-three-year-old man had
worked for was to be stripped from him, his wives and children reassigned.
Even though he still lives there, no one in Short Creek has spoken to him
since. "It's hard sometimes," he said in understatement. "You go to the
store for milk, and everybody turns away. You go to the post office, and
everybody looks right past you, like you're invisible. People I've known all
my life. It's hard."

Barlow was fortunate. One of his wives and half of his children decided
to stick by him, refusing reassignment, becoming outcasts themselves, not
that the ones who remained fared much better. "They were treated like lep-
ers," Barlow said stoically. Ironically, the probable reasons Warren Jeffs found
Jethro Barlow to be a threat were the tools that brought him through the dark
time. With advanced business degrees, Barlow was too educated, too widely
traveled, too seasoned to believe that Jeffs was anything but an increasingly
paranoid, power-mad son of a rich, indulgent father. "The *dreams*," Barlow
said with a pained smile. "Here was a man who acted on *dreams*. Maybe thousands of lives—children, women, girls, men—were destroyed for this man's
dreams. It was just . . . bizarre."

Barlow's job now is to help others whose lives were taken by Jeffs while
daring to hope the community he loves can be restored to some semblance
of normality. "I know some things have to change," he conceded. "But there
was so much good here. It was a loving, peaceful place with so many good
people. They're still good. They've just been led completely awry by Warren
Jeffs and his gang."

Barlow believed the problems in Short Creek extend well beyond the obvious. "Everyone's focused on the young girls, and that's valid," he said. "But
there has been a whole class of young men created—maybe thousands—
with no educations, no social skills, and no hope. Some of them are already

in their thirties. They're too terrified to even meet a girl's eyes. They're afraid of half the human population! They've been made into eunuchs, with no families, no futures. What's going to happen to them? What happens to them when they're too old to work construction and FLDS throws them away too?"

As he spoke, the quiet accountant became angry. "I told that to Mark Shurtleff!" he exclaimed. "I asked him, 'How can you walk away? What are you going to do about these men?' I told Mark, 'You know what? They're going to call them *Shurtleff's shirtless.*' He got very angry with me. Very angry. But that's what this whole class of men will be when they can't work and they're cut loose. Shurtleff's shirtless." Barlow shifted behind a stack of papers to hide his creeping emotion. "Excuse me for a moment," he said, abruptly exiting the room.

By fall 2009, Barlow's despair over the Utah attorney general's perceived capitulation to FLDS was shared by nearly everyone who thought the sect destructive. The man who had prosecuted Rod Holm, promised RICO investigations of the sect, and gone to Texas declaring that he was "ashamed" of Utah's nonexistent track record curbing a host of FLDS excesses now openly undermined fiduciary Bruce Wisan and by extension the court orders he enforced.

"Where's Utah?" became the question on websites following the UEP case as Wisan and Lindberg seemed to be answering the new attacks without the Utah Attorney General's Office.

FLDS was able to get off only one emergency petition before Lindberg held another hearing on the Berry Knoll sale on July 29, just a few days after rejecting the Utah/FLDS settlement proposal. In court pleadings to the Utah supreme and U.S. district courts, FLDS lawyers furiously asserted that Lindberg and Wisan were in open cahoots with "a rival religious group," a queer description for the FLDS breakaway sect living in nearby Centennial Park, to whom the judge and fiduciary were conspiring to sell Berry Knoll.* On August 24, Lindberg once again accommodated FLDS by ordering Wisan to sell the property in a competitive bidding process, but the gesture didn't stop the accusations or the lawsuits.

---

*   The attorneys referred to Ken Knudsen, an FLDS member in Centennial Park who was a potential buyer but who had not yet contracted to purchase Berry Knoll Farm. Nevertheless, FLDS lawyers would continue to characterize the proposed sale of Berry Knoll as a sinister, done-deal conspiracy between Wisan and a rival religious group.

New FLDS "movants" joined old ones to declare "ecclesiastical" authority over Berry Knoll, awarded them in sacred religious "stewardships" by
FLDS elders who hadn't seen the necessity for conveyance deeds. Hildale
attorney Peter Stirba returned with a hard-to-understand motion to
intervene in the Berry Knoll sale on behalf of the twin cities and its soon-
to-be-suspect water department. The twin cities had proclaimed themselves
"neutral" about Berry Knoll when it looked like FLDS would retain control
over the property, but now any sale would spell unmitigated disaster for
Short Creek, whose residents Stirba could envision withering on the streets
from dehydration as a rival religious group stole their water. Of course, the
motion carried the monotonous demands to remove Lindberg and Wisan
from the case.

There were a number of legal problems with Stirba's sudden water wor-
ries, which would eventually be one cornerstone of a federal civil rights
lawsuit. Chief among them were the facts that municipalities have no
authority to interfere in private land sales, and water rights in Arizona (and
most of the West) are not tied to land ownership. Either one of these would
seem to make the twin cities' challenge moot, but Stirba plowed forward,
complaining that Lindberg had "abused her discretion" when she did not
accept FLDS's assertions that the area's water was hopelessly low, preventing any new hookups for non-FLDS families. Lindberg instead considered
the reams of contradictory evidence presented by engineers hired by Wisan
and the Arizona attorney general.

Appealing Lindberg's decision in another emergency petition to the
Utah Supreme Court, Stirba seemed to feel the justices would agree with
him that only Hildale's point of view should be considered. He complained
to the high court that Lindberg's consideration of "opposing views of the
water supply system" constituted bias against the sect. "The threat that the
twin cities experience a catastrophe due to the loss of their water supply is
real and should not be minimized or dismissed," Stirba direly warned.

Developing a wry, if-I-don't-laugh-I'll-cry humor that would characterize many of Arizona's increasingly pointed opposition motions, the
assistant attorneys general wrote that Stirba's presentation "suffers from
multiple errors," stopping just short of calling him a liar. With "suspect
facts," they wrote, Stirba's arguments were "disingenuous, misleading,
and incomplete."

Meanwhile, the FLDS law firm of Snow, Christensen, and Martineau
had another lawsuit in Utah's Third District Court with remarkable new

clients.* "Rulon Jeffs Back from the Dead," declared the *Eldorado Success* in a sour headline that might have been playful if Randy Mankin didn't feel so disgusted. Mankin, who'd been watching the UEP case as closely as anyone, remarked, "The whole thing was kind of crazy to watch. The Utah courts must be gluttons for punishment."

Rod Parker's new, old clients were the estate of Rulon Jeffs, represented by executor Leroy Jeffs; the FLDS Church; the corporation of the president of FLDS; the corporation of the presiding bishop of FLDS; Warren Jeffs; Truman Barlow; Leroy Jeffs; James K. Zitting; and William E. Timpson.** The idea of being sued by the imprisoned Warren Jeffs, who'd created this swamp to begin with, was almost too much for Wisan.

"This Court is faced with a watershed event," Wisan wrote in a December 2009 motion begging Lindberg to begin ending the madness by granting six Wisan demands that FLDS be either forced to comply with court orders or be held in contempt of court. "These requests come as the latest wave in a continued blitzkrieg against the fiduciary by the former trustees and those acting in concert with them. . . . If ever there is a case of unclean hands, this is it."

Demonstrating his point, Wisan included without comment bombshell pages of photocopied canceled checks from Peter Stirba's Twin Cities Water Company to his legal pleadings. Somehow, Wisan's subpoenas for the checks had slipped past FLDS's otherwise ferocious refusals to comply with court orders, leaving the fiduciary in possession of what looked like evidence that the water company was another FLDS slush fund. Like the Colorado City Unified School District, water company revenues had disappeared into personal FLDS bank accounts, "tithing," the "bishop's storehouse," and other FLDS destinations to the tune of $3.2 million.

The Twin Cities Water Company had made no expenditures on maintenance, infrastructure, or any other capital outlay expected of water companies in the desert. It appeared that the FLDS members in charge of

---

* Although Lindberg had disqualified Parker a year earlier, he continued his participation under the stay of that order made by the Utah Supreme Court, which had not ruled on the matter. Parker would also nonsensically argue that he was not in violation of Lindberg's verbal litigation stand-down order in November 2008 or her written stand-down order in March 2009 because he was not a participant in the UEP case, even though every motion he filed addressed the UEP case.

** All the named clients were the derelict former trustees of the UEP trust ousted in the 2005 Utah attorney general petition. There is some uncertainty about the William E. Timpson moniker, which is thought to be an alias of Willie Jessop.

the water collected money from billing and deposited it directly into FLDS concerns, such as the "Bishop's Storehouse" controlled by Warren Jeffs. Authorities would later discover a handwritten letter to Jeffs, composed by a water company employee, asking if these practices should be abandoned or left in place after his unsettling arrest.

Wisan's motion also listed thirteen separate FLDS court actions launched from three lawsuits, including more ever-popular motions to vacate the trust and remove Lindberg and Wisan from their posts.* In October, FLDS attorney Ken Okazaki filed a petition for extraordinary writ in the Utah Supreme Court in a new complaint, this time representing "the FLDS, an association of individuals," who Okazaki later explained were "faithful members" of FLDS. Rod Parker's emergency petition to lift a stay imposed in 2008 was also on the table, but on November 3, the Utah Supreme Court seemed to have had enough.

In an unusually long opinion, the court dismissed Parker's emergency, writing that it was taking the opportunity "to clarify the scope and purpose" of emergency writs. The rule "did not purport to supplant" the regular court system, the court advised. "Moreover, because the abbreviated response deadline has the effect of placing a substantial burden on respondents, a Rule 8A petition should not incorporate requests for relief that require something less than emergency treatment. . . . For the same reason, Rule 8A should not be employed as a means for harassing or unjustifiably burdening respondents when ordinary procedural mechanisms would be adequate. This includes the circumstances where the 'emergency' has arisen from petitioner's own unjustified delay in seeking relief."

The justices may not only have been reacting to the three-year delay in FLDS challenges to the reformed trust but also the fact that they seemed to wait weeks after rulings, filing their emergencies at the last possible moment. "The petitioners have created their own emergency," Arizona's Bill Richards responded wearily to one emergency petition. But if the Supreme Court thought their icy tone would produce a little restraint from FLDS, they had misunderstood the overall plan to move the UEP case out of Lindberg's court and into theirs. FLDS attorney Stephen Clark filed

---

*   Wisan was also sued in federal court in Utah and Arizona by two lawyerless FLDS men who filed what can only be described as pages of nonsensical rambling. Wisan's attorneys were forced to answer the complaints, and the men kept filing nonexistent "recusitation" [sic] motions after the cases were dismissed. One of the men sought $250 million and tax-exempt status for FLDS as damages.

another Rule 8A emergency petition a mere three weeks after the rebuke. It was accompanied by a request to shorten the time available for responses, increasing the very "substantial burden" upon Wisan and others the high court had warned against.

In late 2009, even the superior organizational skills of Utah attorney general paralegal Rexine Pitcher was taxed as she ran out of office space for the tsunami of legal filings. Tim Bodily had gone to Mark Shurtleff to tell him he was at the end of his emotional rope, a condition with which Shurtleff sympathized. With Utah in a transitional state, Pitcher answered harried phone calls from her counterparts in Arizona. "They're trying to get up to speed," she confided. "I mean, look at this!" She extended her arms, circling slowly in a 360-degree circle so that an observer can get the full effect of the floor-to-ceiling boxes in one of the rooms stuffed with paper. With no hubris, Pitcher said she is the Arizona caller's best bet for locating a file. "They need copies of a particular court ruling for one of their pleadings," she said empathetically. "It's like, 'You're our last hope.'" She expelled air through closed lips, making a horse noise. "Boy, do I ever know that feeling."

Although Utah continued responding to the barrage of FLDS litigation, the pleadings were shorter and more aloof, while Arizona's picked up bite and verve. Mark Shurtleff's prosecution of Rod Holm, petition to save the UEP trust from default judgments, and subsequent fiery public speeches lambasting FLDS had garnered the Utah attorney general lavish international press, but an argument could be made that the attention resulted because Mormon Utah, with its polygamous roots, had never moved on polygamy before and indeed still tolerated its wide practice across the state. Even Shurtleff expressed ambivalence about the necessity for antibigamy statutes for consenting adults.

The 1953 raid was a publicity disaster for Arizona, but the state never actually tolerated the open practice of plural marriage. Outside of Short Creek, there are no pockets of open polygamy in Arizona the way there are in Utah, where people like Shurtleff grew up attending school with the children of polygamous families and accept the practice as a real, if odd, part of Utah life. In Arizona, children thought to be of polygamous families in the public schools would trigger visits from state social workers.

While it is true that Phoenix *New Times* had to goad her a little, Governor Napolitano received little credit for quietly signing the law that empowered Goddard to raid Colorado City again in 2005, this time looking for evidence not of polygamy but of FLDS using the school district as a private slush fund, vanishing tens of millions of tax dollars into FLDS bank accounts. Mohave County attorney Matt Smith had indicted eight FLDS men, including Warren Jeffs, before Utah had done so. And as it turns out, Roger Hoole harbored doubts that Shurtleff even had the stomach for a Warren Jeffs indictment, despite all the tough talk. "We took Elissa [Wall]'s case to Brock Belnap," said Roger Hoole of the 2007 criminal case in St. George that resulted in Jeffs's Utah conviction, "because we didn't trust Mark Shurtleff to do the right thing."

The Mormon Church did not abolish polygamy voluntarily, and there is always speculation that a state that began as a theocracy still dominated by the LDS Church may not have much of an appetite for discouraging a tenet of their founding prophet. LDS has not struck polygamy from the all-important *Doctrines and Covenants*, and polygamy is still viewed as part of the afterlife. Church leaders may be embarrassed and uncomfortable with groups like FLDS, but their public statements regarding polygamy are tepid at best. And although Mark Shurtleff becomes downright hostile when asked if LDS desires play into state government decisions, others are less certain there is no influence. "Nothing happens in Utah without LDS," journalist and author Jon Talton stated flatly, as if suggestions to the contrary are ludicrous. "They wouldn't have to spell it out for him [Shurtleff]. It would be a look from his Bishop, a suggestion about future political ambitions, a nod from the pulpit. Anything that said: 'This [FLDS] thing has gone on long enough. Time to get rid of it.'"

In Utah, where polygamy is not a queer idea but one no further away than many families' great-grandparents, the situation is unique. But there can be no question that most politicians in America would rather walk barefoot over hot coals than deal with a religiously charged scenario like the one presented by FLDS. Perhaps Shurtleff was not forced to consider LDS in his decisions, but every politician considers a political climate.

Both Napolitano and Goddard always had a significant, lopsidedly powerful, and ultraconservative Mormon population influencing the Maricopa County Republican Party, already one of the most stringently right-wing parties in the country. But Goddard now is navigating more white water than Napolitano ever imagined.

Like Napolitano, Goddard had the governor's mansion on his mind when he took the Attorney General's Office, but when Arizona took a harder-than-ever right turn in 2008, a series of events would leave Goddard standing alone in the middle of the political intersection. The drastic political climate in Arizona meant Goddard was about to be faced, on a nearly monthly basis, with the kind of stark, principles-over-politics choices few American politicians must ever make.

When president Barack Obama tapped Napolitano to head the Homeland Security Department, conservative Republican Jan Brewer was in line for the vacated governor's seat. Brewer was something of an unknown with a relatively quiet career in state government in which she focused on fiscal health. However, once in office, she began to court the far right of Arizona's Republicans. In less than six months, Goddard plummeted in polls from a comfortable lead over Brewer to a twenty-point deficit, and he ultimately lost his bid for governor in the 2010 midterm elections. He had nothing to gain politically by facing off against FLDS and further irritating the Maricopa County right wing, but at the end of 2009, that's exactly what Goddard did. "I don't think there's any question that Attorney General Goddard acted on his principles, not his political ambition," says Talton. After allowing Utah to take the lead in the UEP case for years, Goddard couldn't stomach the direction in which the case had veered over the summer. In December 2009 and January 2010, Arizona assistant attorney general Bill Richards filed an eruption of sharply worded legal retorts to the boatload of various pending FLDS lawsuits and emergency writs.

By the end of 2009, individual court filings in the UEP case could run hundreds of pages with attachments. As a graphic illustration of the sect's numbing appetite for litigation, Bruce Wisan filed a motion that included most of the lawsuits and corresponding motions for one thing or another associated with them, a single filing that ate up more than two thousand pages. Wisan's astounding filing also demonstrated Arizona's dominance in the battle, but Shurtleff might have been smarting under the withering criticism directed at his proposed UEP settlement, and he was taking heat on another front. The *Tribune* might have ignored Wisan's apparent evidence that Hildale's water company had misappropriated $3.2 million, but other media outlets questioned why Shurtleff was not following up on that lead.

Out of the blue sky, in January 2010, Shurtleff sent a tart letter to FLDS's three lead attorneys, warning them to settle the UEP case in thirty days or else. "I was tired of being their patsy," Shurtleff told a shocked Adams in an interview she posted on her blog, which, along with her Twitter account, was used increasingly as a news reporting vehicle. But Adams wasn't the only one startled by Shurtleff's letter, which led evening news broadcasts

across the state. "It came out of nowhere," complained Rod Parker, who
was waylaid by a news camera crew in the parking lot.

The exasperated tone of Shurtleff's letter illustrated the treacherous
nature of any negotiations with FLDS. "If your client has trouble with the
fact that the proposal comes from the Special Fiduciary," Shurtleff wrote
three FLDS attorneys, "then let's call it my proposal. . . . This matter has
gone on long enough. Please do not call me on the 29th day and say that
your clients will accept settlement if the following long list of items are
changed. I want a final settlement . . . not a new round of negotiations to
commence in 30 days. . . . The suggestion of tweaking or massaging the
proposal is not an invitation to make wholesale revisions."

Shurtleff then issued a threat to end his benign neglect of the UEP trust
case. "If your clients are not willing to accept this offer, I will assume that
they have no intention, or at least do not have the ability to resolve this
matter. . . . In the event that you are unable to reach a commitment to settle under these [Wisan's] guidelines, I believe it is necessary for my Office
to support the rule of law which includes supporting those actions of the
Arizona Attorney General's Office and the Special Fiduciary which are consistent with court orders." While FLDS activists wondered if this statement
weren't some kind of admission that Shurtleff had *not* been following the
rule of law for the past months, Shurtleff concluded his thoughts with a
final punch in the mouth. "Regardless of the Trust matters, I believe that
serious issues must also be addressed with the local governments, and we
are prepared to seek a disincorporation of the city of Hildale with the legislature if necessary."

The new compromise Shurtleff referenced was very nearly what FLDS
had wanted all along. It allowed any FLDS member who received a deed
from the trust to turn around and give it right back to FLDS. Given the fact
that the sect still had not been awarded legal standing to participate in the
UEP case at all—and might never be—the compromise was something of a
gift, and Shurtleff knew it. Most FLDS members *would* return their land to
the leadership, leaving only a minority of "interlopers and intermeddlers,"
as Parker called non-FLDS people, but Wisan's compromise still wasn't
enough for FLDS and was rejected out of hand.

"He [Shurtleff] knows Wisan's proposal is unacceptable to FLDS," said
Parker, adding that all Wisan proposals were "impossible." Why couldn't
FLDS take back most of the land and allow a few people their own property
deeds? Because Wisan refused to allow a half dozen or more stern-faced

FLDS elders to stand around the room glaring when timid individuals came in to sign up for the program. Parker explained that the elders' presence was imperative to offer "guidance" to naive FLDS members Wisan was trying to snooker into accepting clear property deeds to their own homes.

In a statement demonstrating that the Utah Attorney General's Office grasped the situation perfectly, assistant attorney general Jerrold Jensen told the *Deseret News*, "It's not politics. What's prompted this [letter] is their [FLDS's] refusal to make any movement toward settlement. All they want to do is file motion after motion in court." Jensen added that his boss was also concerned about the tsunamis of cash FLDS was showering on their top-drawer attorneys, fees that had to be paid by the lowly FLDS membership, though how that was accomplished remains a mystery.* Ironically, and sadly, the membership also had to pay Bruce Wisan's fees, which were increasingly used to defend the UEP trust against attacks by FLDS lawyers paid by the bottom-rung membership caught in a vicious cycle of suing themselves over and over for the same things.

"We think it's an abhorrent situation, and we'd like to see it settled," Jensen concluded. Wisan wasn't even happy about the compromise plan—it would take a boatload of courage for any individual FLDS member to step forward against Warren Jeffs's orders—but the fiduciary was still tired of being sued.

After Shurtleff's perceived FLDS ennui following his shocking summer alliance with FLDS, the threat letter was received with tempered jubilation from Short Creek's non-FLDS residents under increasing physical and legal harassment from the FLDS residents, police, city government, and utilities. "We thought maybe he'd seen the light," says Colorado City resident Jinjer Cooke. In a year, the deplorable living conditions FLDS entities had imposed upon the Cooke family would explode in court, but for now the Cookes watched Shurtleff's thirty-day deadline come and go without a peep, while no moves were made in the legislature to disincorporate Hildale or anything else FLDS controlled.

---

* FLDS businesses were probably "consecrating" funds that also could have been used to pay taxes and other bills, which may have been done in Texas but not Short Creek. In addition, there was a widely accepted rumor that every FLDS household was required to fork over $1,000 a month to a sort of prophet's defense fund. If true, the practice could have raked in hundreds of thousands a month, but since up to 80 percent of the FLDS membership subsisted on welfare, the required payments would have presumably subjected families to severe hardship while again paying Warren Jeffs's way with tax dollars.

The inauspicious passing of the second settlement deadline left the Utah Attorney General's Office with only one remaining threat. In his January letter, Shurtleff warned that if no settlement were reached, he would find it "necessary" to join the Arizona attorney general's vigorous defense of Lindberg's court orders. The threat was no idle dalliance. Three weeks earlier, Arizona pivoted from a primarily defensive position, asking Lindberg to take the "litigation stand down order" cuffs off so that the Arizona attorney general could start draining the swamp. "The Petitioners, FLDS, Lyle Jeffs, and Willie Jessop attempt improperly through emergency petitions to wrest administration of the United Effort Plan Trust entirely away from the Third Judicial District and vest responsibility for fact-finding and administration of the Trust in the appellate courts," wrote Bill Richards.

Specifically, Richards asked Lindberg to allow Arizona to issue subpoenas, warrants, and deposition orders and to utilize other law enforcement tools to get to the bottom of what, exactly, FLDS was doing in Short Creek. The water company, city government, police department, zoning matters, property confiscations—anything up for discussion, Arizona wanted to dive in and find hard evidence. The December 30 motion to discover represented an all-in, all-the-way commitment from Arizona never before assumed. It provoked mighty howling from the FLDS camp, who charged that Goddard was on a religious persecution witch hunt.

In his opposition motions, Parker called Arizona's motion for discovery a "motion to expand litigation." An unperturbed Richards dryly conceded that FLDS attorneys, who had ignored all court orders, knew a little something about expanding litigation, but he insisted mildly that Arizona only wanted to clarify the UEP situations by replacing hyperbolic language with hard facts, adding that the shrill responses from FLDS attorneys to a little discovery motion "raises suspicion that there is something to hide."

Weighing in at some three hundred pages, Arizona's monster discovery motion took its place with the towers of other UEP documents on Lindberg's desk, but Terry Goddard was not in a waiting mood.

25

THREE STRIKES IN TEXAS

Elders, never love your wives one hair's breadth further than they adore the Gospel, never love them so but that you can leave them at a moment's notice without shedding a tear. Should you love a child any more than this? No. Here are Apostles and Prophets who are destined to be exalted with the Gods, to become rulers in the kingdoms of our Father, to become equal with the Father and the Son, and will you let your affections be unduly placed on anything this side of that kingdom and glory? If you do, you disgrace your calling and Priesthood.

—Brigham Young, *Journal of Discourses*, Vol. 3

The Lord showed me they were going to take away our lands and houses. He showed me that it was the intention of our enemies to pull me and many people into court and turn traitor by bearing witness in court of my father's doings and my doings concerning the Celestial Law of Marriage. . . . And I say to you brethren, no person no court, no government on the face of the whole earth has the right or authority to bring God into question what he has His prophets do.

—Warren Jeffs, February 21, 2005

A pparently confused by the muted public reaction to the 2008 Texas raid on the YFZ ranch, FLDS doubled down on efforts to enlighten Americans to the fact that members of a persecuted minority religion were one short stutter step away from being loaded onto the trains bound for concentration camps, an image Willie Jessop invoked with regularity at press conferences. FLDS websites such as FLDSTruth.org published heartbreaking videos of children being separated from their mothers, and the case of one underage girl—Warren Jeffs's sixteen-year-old daughter, Teresa— became an FLDS battle cry.

FLDS records seized in the 2008 raid indicated that Teresa's father had "sealed" her to thirty-eight-year-old Raymond Merril Jessop a day after she turned fifteen, a fact supported by Teresa's own diary and a slew of deleted photographs recovered from a computer showing the girl snuggling and kissing with her "husband."

Teresa denied everything. She was assigned attorney Natalie Malonis as her guardian *ad litem*. "Natalie was one of the only lawyers out there who got it," Roger Hoole said. "Most of them didn't have a clue what they were dealing with, didn't care, and didn't make an effort to get educated, but Natalie figured it out early." For her comprehension, Malonis would pay dearly.

Malonis understood that, to have any chance of getting through to her young client, she had to first remove Teresa from the pressures of the sect. Malonis got a restraining order against Teresa's mother, Annette Jeffs, and sect spokesman Willie Jessop, who was coaching Teresa as to how to behave in court. For a while, Malonis felt she was making some progress helping Teresa understand her situation and her options, which included education. But Willie successfully sued to lift the order against Annette, and once Teresa's mother started reminding her daughter about FLDS salvation, things went downhill fast.

The job of a guardian *ad litem* is to do what is best for the underage client, which is not necessarily what the underage client wants done. Now under the influence of her dedicated FLDS mother, Teresa stopped thinking about her options and started demanding that Malonis do what she demanded: return her to the YFZ ranch, where, she claimed, her "husband" didn't exist. This, Malonis refused to do. Whether it was Teresa's idea or not, the girl's subsequent battle to fire Malonis went public, along with Malonis's personal e-mails between herself and her client. Much the same way it had with Dr. Dan Fischer, FLDS launched a smear campaign against Malonis, digging up some nasty divorce records and portraying her as a slothful drug addict with depraved morals trying to convert an innocent young girl to her sickening lifestyle.

Teresa was successful in severing Malonis from her case, and she was not the only young girl FLDS exploited to generate '53 raid–style publicity for the heavy-handed actions of Texas Child Protective Services that had been condemned by the Texas courts. Text messages from FLDS sent to fourteen-year-old Merrianne Jessop and read by CPS workers advised the girl to "stay angry. We need you to keep crying, pout, sleep in. Crying will get you what you want."

FLDS released a wrenching tape of another young girl, said to be fourteen years old, being separated from her mother, who has driven her as instructed to be delivered to a shelter. In a tape that seems endless, the blond girl writhes and weeps, inexplicably alone in the backseat of a car as expressionless CPS workers wait outside helplessly for her to emerge. The girl looks out of her mind with anguish, in danger of some sort of catatonic breakdown as she sobs and clutches at car upholstery. Eventually, she is gently extracted by women in prairie dresses, whose faces are never really clear. Although they were undoubtedly present, FLDS men are, as usual, not shown at all. The poor girl clings pitiably to the women, weeping uncontrollably for what seems like hours before the tape cuts off.

The girl's agony is undeniable, and perhaps it is justifiable to release video showing the real-life results of the raid, but there is also the sense that the filmmaker relishes the girl's suffering, allowing it to go on for way too long, that the girl's misery could have been significantly abbreviated with a word of comfort or at least her removal from the backseat of the car for an embrace before she brought herself to near collapse.

Armed with weapons like the tape and Natalie Malonis's ugly divorce records, Willie Jessop stomped the countryside with the Holocaust comparisons, but the hoped-for public outcry still refused to materialize. What the sect got instead was something they hadn't expected: a governor with more blustery verve than Jessop. Ultraconservative Texas governor Rick Perry wasn't remotely interested in FLDS's claimed civil rights violations or the fact that two Texas courts had deemed the raid to be excessive. Instead, Perry went on a full-blown offensive that a surprised Jessop called "shocking."

Attending a trade conference in La Baule, France, Perry said that he wasn't much interested in "fine legal lines" and that Texas would continue to "send a message" to people who liked underage sex. "The state of Texas has an obligation to young women who are forced into marriage and underage sex—to protect them," Perry stated. "That's my bottom line on this." Lest anyone sense equivocation, Perry added: "If you are going to conduct yourself that way, we are going to prosecute you. If you don't want to be prosecuted for those activities, then maybe Texas is not the place you need to consider calling home."

Over the next year, Perry would continue inviting FLDS members to pack their bags while offering unswerving support for the actions of Child Protective Services and the Texas Rangers. After Judge Walther exonerated the search warrants in October 2009, Texas wasted no time getting down to business with the twelve FLDS men it had in its dock. Before the month was out, Raymond Merril Jessop, charged with assault on a child in his "marriage" to an underage girl, was facing trial.

Walther hadn't felt the urge for a lot of handwringing over pretrial challenges brought by FLDS attorneys with the same gusto they brought to the Utah cases. FLDS charges that the Texas grand jury that had handed down the indictments was unconstitutional because the selection process discriminated against Hispanics were denied in short order. Others were submitted, argued, and ruled upon. The trial started three days after an exhaustive jury selection, as it was difficult to locate anyone in Schleicher County, or all of Texas for that mattter, who hadn't heard of the YFZ raid. In fact, Randy Mankin was the first juror excused from the pool, yet FLDS had not made strong efforts to get the trial moved out of Eldorado.

Curiously, the FLDS men and their attorneys did not think the YFZ ranch's rocky relationship with Eldorado and Schleicher County had damaged their standing with the actual citizens. To the contrary, they believed Eldorado residents would understand Jessop's actions once they understood that he was an honorable man, but that conclusion couldn't have been reached by reading the *Success*. "I Didn't Do Nuthin', and It Won't Happen Again," mocked a headline on one of Randy's "Over the Back Fence" columns, in which he compared Willie Jessop's recent promises that FLDS would cease underage marriages to a prankster grade school friend who, when caught red-handed at his misdeeds, would deny all wrongdoing, falsely promising future good behavior.

Nevertheless, Jessop's attorneys, Gerald Goldstein and Mark Stevens, launched a spirited defense, presenting evidence of Jessop's good character and deep faith when they weren't bringing a stream of challenges to other evidence out of the jury's sight. For two weeks, the trial lurched forward in jerky fits and starts as defense lawyers objected to such things as using the word "polygamy" before the jurors. Agreements reached between prosecutor Eric Nichols and the defense team before bedtime were discarded in the morning, and Judge Walther was obliged to rule on continuous legal challenges throughout.

Understandably, the defense didn't want the jury to know that Jessop had nine wives, at least four of whom were nursing or pregnant at the time of the charged offense. Even worse, Jessop's victim was the sixteen-year-old girl who endured three agonizing days of labor because Warren Jeffs refused to allow her to be transported to a hospital. Walther allowed prosecutors to introduce evidence from Jeffs's seized dictations, which were leaking out in courts everywhere at an alarming, infuriating rate, too fast for FLDS attorneys desperate to keep the damning records secret. In the dictations, Jeffs explains that he knew the girl had been "struggling" for three days, but he was no dummy.

"I knew that the girl being sixteen years old, if she went to the hospital, they could put Raymond in jeapordy [*sic*] of prosecution as the government is looking for any reason to come against us there," Jeffs wrote.

In most regards, the cases that followed would require essentially the same defense, but since Jessop was the first one out of the gate, his attorneys had to test-drive everything they had. This included scaled-down O. J. Simpson–type attacks on the DNA evidence and questioning the intent and meaning of FLDS family records seized in the raid. To combat the latter, prosecutors put Rebecca Musser on the stand.

Warren Jeffs had selected the lovely Rebecca for one of his ailing father's wives. While Rulon was alive, Rebecca was secluded in the Jeffses' massive Short Creek compound, part of a largely untouched harem created by Warren, who she apparently detested. When Rulon died, Warren tapped Rebecca for his bed, but she was unable to bear the thought. She fled with an FLDS man she later married. As the wife of a former prophet, Rebecca had credibility compounded by her collected, steady, and unflappable demeanor in the witness box. Her graphic testimony of life within FLDS and translation of the records would continue to devastate FLDS defense teams in trial after trial. She is so hated by FLDS that the state of Texas finds it prudent to provide for her personal security, but a fearless Rebecca continues to testify when called.

An understanding prosecutor, Nichols urged jurors to disregard testimony given by current FLDS members who, Nichols said, meant well but "don't know what you know." He may have also hoped that Rebecca Musser would provide a kind of substitution for the young girls who were refusing to testify against their "husbands." In what is always a major hurdle for polygamy prosecutions, Nichols had no tearful victims asking jurors for justice. In all of FLDS history, only Ruth Stubbs and Elissa Wall had ever made it to the witness stand, and Ruth got cold feet more than once.

If Texas assistant attorney general Eric Nichols was nervous about the absence of victims, he didn't show it. The cool-headed, methodical Nichols, who would handle all twelve FLDS cases, announced early and often that no man's religion was on trial in Texas—the rape of a young girl was. Systematically, Nichols laid before jurors all the evidence from the YFZ raid that defense attorneys had desperately tried to keep out: the priesthood records, the bishop's records, DNA results, and photographs. As for the lack of a victim, Nichols displayed photographs of the babies produced by the unions, urging jurors to think of them as "the snow on the ground that tells you what happened outside last night."

On the day the jury came back, Jessop was apparently in a jocular mood. He reportedly bantered with his jailors, advising them not to squander food by making up an evening meal for him, because he wouldn't be back. "He really thought he was going to walk out of that courthouse with probation at the worst," said a marveling Randy Mankin. "I don't know what that says, but he really believed there would be no penalty."

In another bewildering testament to the faith FLDS placed in the local population to which the sect had lied and obstructed while building YFZ, FLDS defendants requested the Texas option allowing the jury to fix the sentence after sitting through another lengthy evidentiary hearing in which prosecutors argue for more time and defense attorneys for less. Jessop's charge was probation eligible, meaning he could have walked away from the courthouse that day and been home for dinner, but that didn't happen. The jury fixed a penalty of ten years in prison and an $8,000 fine, a shock to the systems of FLDS leaders. Although Willie Jessop downplayed the sentence as "bittersweet" because it meant an appeal removed from the dastardly Judge Walther would commence, Mankin disagreed that FLDS was sanguine. "They [FLDS leaders and lawyers] were absolutely stunned," said Mankin, still not quite believing it. "They were *stunned*. I really don't know what they thought would happen, but I don't think they expected so much time."

A month after Jessop's conviction, the second trial began right on schedule. In December 2009, another Schleicher County jury found Allan Eugene Keate, fifty-seven, guilty of sexual abuse of a child. Keate was sentenced to thirty-three years in prison.

Even though Michael Emack, fifty-eight, got his trial moved to neighboring Tom Green County, the defendant had seen enough writing on the wall. Saying he wanted to preserve his dignity, Emack pleaded guilty to sexual assault of a child in January 2010, receiving a relatively light sentence of seven years in the plea bargain.

Merril Leroy Jessop, thirty-five, was still willing to roll the dice. Jessop was facing enhancements on a potential sentence because he'd taken an underage bride after Texas changed its laws, but he still proceeded with his March trial in San Angelo, about forty miles from Eldorado. By now the wind had gone out of the pretrial motion sails, and trials were taking only a few days. Jessop was convicted, and the San Angelo jury deliberated only an hour before imposing a staggering seventy-five-year sentence. They hadn't thought twice before taking those enhancements to heart.

The shocking sentence may have persuaded Lehi Barlow Jeffs, twenty-nine, to plead no contest to child rape charges, receiving eight years in a plea bargain. But Abram Harker Jeffs, thirty-seven, proceeded to trial, this time back in Schleicher County, where defense attorneys may have correctly assessed a more charitable atmosphere. Abram Jeffs was convicted, but he only received seventeen years in prison. Overruling vociferous defense arguments in October 2010, Judge Walther agreed with prosecutors that Schleicher County was suffering from "juror fatigue," moving the trial of Keith William Dutson to neighboring Tom Green County. In early November, Dutson was convicted of sexual assault upon a child, the seventh of the twelve men indicted after the 2008 raid to be convicted.

"I feel bad about Michael Emack myself," admitted Hoole. "I'm told he is a nice man who never deserved Warren Jeffs. It's awful that things like these huge sentences have to happen, but you know, they *do* have to happen. Nobody seems able to get their attention any other way."

But the intensity of FLDS attention is debatable. Ordered to pay child support to his ex-wife Carolyn and their seven children still with her, FLDS elder Merril Jessop failed to appear for court hearings and is in substantial default, including nonpayments for the care of a disabled son. All of the convictions are on appeal, but suddenly the defendants, who could pay top dollar for lawyers before, are asking the court to declare them indigent and appoint lawyers to be paid for by taxpayers.

These directives were undoubtedly coming from Warren Jeffs. If it wasn't already common knowledge that Jeffs was pulling the strings from prison, Wisan had filed motions specifically stating it. Jeffs's damaging dictations continued to be attached as evidence to court filings—public documents anyone can see but no Salt Lake City newspaper excerpted for their readers' edification. Frustrated and angry by the dearth of coverage detrimental to FLDS, Hoole put together an editor-friendly presentation on Jeffs's more astounding orders, to no avail.

But in Texas, they weren't having it. Texas attorney general Greg Abbott fought the indigency petitions hard. Attached to his court pleadings were pages of an ongoing FBI forensic examination of FLDS finances. Even incomplete, the pages showed some of the defendants in control of literally millions of dollars.

To date, Judge Walther has denied all the petitions, save one allowing Emack to receive a free transcription of his trial. She has denied all motions for new trials, putting the FLDS convictions before the Texas Court of Appeals. Nichols is on schedule to do a trial a month until it's over. There are twelve cases total, including Warren Jeffs's. Of the seven cases Nichols has already won, the only defendants who didn't get walloped with decades of jail time are the ones for whom the terrible government—Nichols and Judge Walther themselves—offered the more lenient punishments.

Texas governor Rick Perry, however, is still not satisfied. After the raid, the population at YFZ dropped dramatically. It was quietly hoped that FLDS would return to Utah, but Warren Jeffs committed tens of millions to the Texas project, which was still considered the new Zion where one could achieve an afterlife. Over the past few years, the population at YFZ has inched up, prompting Perry to mumble about helping people pack their bags.

That may be exactly what a new Schleicher grand jury convened in July 2010 had in mind. Texas assistant attorney general Eric Nichols is this time reportedly hoping for indictments against FLDS for financial fraud. As 2010 ended, Mankin noted that Nichols was empowered to convene as many grand juries as he wished. Meanwhile, various oversight and government agencies within Schleicher County do their part to discourage FLDS migration to the YFZ ranch. In February 2011, the Plateau Underground Water Conservation and Control District Board denied FLDS's request for an exemption to water well spacing requirements. The sect wanted to sink a new well within one hundred feet of an existing one, an ambition met with a chorus of complaints from FLDS's ranching neighbors. In denying the exemption, board member Phil McCormick remarked that the sect's explanation for why they needed the new well "didn't work" for him.

26

THE LIVES OF OTHERS

Why cannot we behold all things in space? Because there is a curtain dropped, which makes them out of sight to us. Why cannot we behold the inhabitants in Kolob, or the inhabitants in any of those distant planets? For the same reason; because there is a curtain dropped that interrupts our vision. So it is something that intervenes between us and them, which we cannot penetrate. We are short sighted and deprived of the knowledge which we might have. I might say this is right, without offering any explanation.
—Brigham Young, *Journal of Discourses*, Vol. 1

I thank our Heavenly Father. Through these days I have had quorums of ladies trained and prepared in the fulness [sic] of the Celestial Law, reading through the revelations of the Lord has given on how to be heavenly wives having experience by my direction of the Lord. I have sent David Allred to find houses.
—Warren Jeffs, "Record of President Warren Jeffs," January 15, 2005

In some religiously neutral history books, there is a story describing Brigham Young's reaction to a makeshift memorial monument erected two years after the Mountain Meadows Massacre to honor those murdered in the 1857 event. In the killing field still interrupted with jutting human bones and blowing with the locks of a woman's long hair or a child's pinafore, U.S. Army major James H. Carleton and his troops had gathered up the remains of thirty-four people and buried them in a ditch the doomed emigrants had themselves dug for protection. Carleton's troops lugged what large rocks could be scavenged to build a crude twelve foot tower topped by a twelve-foot cedar cross. A slab of granite laid against the side of the cairn read, "Here 120 men, women, and children were massacred in cold blood early September, 1857. They were from Arkansas." The biblical inscription on the cross read, "Vengeance is mine; I will repay, saith the Lord."

About three years after early Utah Mormons executed more than 120 people, Young rode by the poignant monument on horseback, accompanied by his usual enormous entourage. Stopping his horse, he looked at the uneven tower of rock with a cold eye, then spurred his mount on, calling over his shoulder, "Vengeance is mine, saith the Lord. And I have had a little."

There was no need for elaboration. The folks in Young's troupe banking on his particular brand of salvation knew their prophet's commentary was an order to rip the sad monument to pieces and scatter the pieces hither and yon, so that it could not be easily reconstructed. They did so without hesitation as a smug Young rode off with his back to the destruction, carrying plausible deniability in his top-notch saddlebags.* It was that way with Young and, it is said, with Joseph Smith. Their more unsavory orders were obtuse and untraceable but innately understood by their devotees, who executed them to a T out of their leaders' sights and presumably without their knowledge, at least so far as anyone could prove in a court of law.

More than a century later, obtuse orders, no matter how despicable, were still followed without a thought in Short Creek. In early winter 2009, Jinjer Cooke was driving along one of Short Creek's sandy roads on her way home in a truck with four children under age ten she'd just collected from school. Brigham Young had been right about the climate out St. George way, and while vicious snowstorms raged in Salt Lake City, the weather in Short Creek that day was sunny and mild—sweater weather, though patches of snow dotted the reddish ground.

Jinjer, who had never belonged to FLDS, had just made a turn toward the UEP property that the sect was trying to run her family off when an imposing black SUV with dark tinted windows swerved in behind her at frightening speed. Jinjer did not have to guess at the intentions of those inside. As calmly as she could, she instructed the whimpering children, who also knew the intent of the gigantic black vehicle, to get into seat belts or

---

*   Some years later the U.S. Calvary rebuilt the destroyed monument and kept stubbornly rebuilding it over the next seventy years of continued vandalism. In 1932, a monument was left standing. After more than a century of denying Mormon culpability for the slaughter, LDS president Gordon Hinckley finally visited the site in 1998, inviting the Paiute Indians to join the Mormons in asking forgiveness. The tribe refused, its chief saying, "That's *their* history, not ours." LDS then joined with descendants of the murdered pioneers to design and install a proper monument, but frictions arose when the descendants demanded that an unsanitized historical account of the event appear at the site. A permanent monument involving a replica of the original stone cairn surrounded by a wall with the names of the victims and a small plaza was jointly dedicated in 1999 by LDS and the descendants of the victims. At their request, LDS expanded the monument in May 2009. It contains an accurate account of the slaughter and is listed on the National Register of Historical Places.

onto the floorboards. She tried to decide if speeding up would make what was about to happen worse.

Since she could not outrun the sinister SUV and taking the slippery sandy roads at high speeds was unsafe, Jinjer put her truck in the middle of the narrow road, hoping the SUV's occupants would think twice about risking their own rollover by crowding forward on a street bordered by ditches, but she knew the strategy was wishful thinking. Whoever was there had been lying in wait, acting on orders implied or otherwise, orders they could not afford to fail. She could not fight the terror as the black behemoth made its move, gunning up on her right bumper with no regard for the drop on their right side.

With the children wailing, Jinjer blinked first, instinctively moving away from the SUV while, to her horror, speeding up. Now they were side by side on the slim road, the other driver's identity obscured by the black windows, showroom extras selected to preserve the attackers' cowardly anonymity. Jinjer didn't know if she was under assault by one person or a dozen as she watched her front left tire inching closer to the ditch drop-off, unable to stop what was happening. She said a quick prayer as the tire slid off and the steering wheel jerked from her control as the truck skidded into the ditch, thumped to a stop, and died. The children screamed as the black SUV sped away, disappearing in a cloud of flying dust with no concern whatsoever about what manner of broken bodies their assault might have produced.

There were no injuries that day. Jinjer called the Colorado City police, who refused to take her report or look for the assailants, whom the FLDS cops said Jinjer could not prove existed. For all they knew, Jinjer could have driven the truck full of children into a ditch on purpose. Recounting her scare months later, a stony-faced Jinjer shrugged. "I didn't expect anything else," she said dully. "It's what they always do, but I try to report everything to keep a record." She shrugged again. "It doesn't do much good 'cause they won't file the reports."

Jinjer reported the latest assault to her husband, Ron, another agonizing reminder of the devastating accident that left him severely disabled, living in a wheelchair with multiple physical and mental impairments rendering him unable to pick up the children and brave the attacks himself. Now thirty-five, Ron had been an FLDS member until he realized he was slated to become a sect worker-bee eunuch, never allowed to marry and raise a family. He left Short Creek at age eighteen, married Jinjer, and found construction work to support his growing family. Returning to Short Creek had not been in his plans, but disaster struck on a 2005 work site when a runaway heavy construction truck plowed into Ron head-on.

Barely alive when they pulled him out from under the vehicle, Ron survived but with permanently disabling injuries, including spinal cord and traumatic brain injuries, facial paralysis, and multiple injuries requiring catheters and other supporting medical equipment. After the accident, he heard about the UEP trust reformation. Since he'd worked wage-free for FLDS for many years, he thought he might qualify as a trust beneficiary. If he did, he might be able to secure a safe home in a beautiful locale for his family, something close to his own family and friends that would be otherwise extremely difficult in his current circumstances.

Using the system established by Bruce Wisan, Ron applied for housing as a trust beneficiary. He was approved. In 2007, Ron and Jinjer began looking at homes available in the UEP inventory—that is, homes for which no occupancy agreements had been signed and that were certified vacant or abandoned by Isaac Wyler and Jethro Barlow. The fiduciary had control of these homes, including keys to all door locks, so there was no issue whatsoever of current residency.

In 2008, Ron and Jinjer signed an occupancy agreement for the only home in Short Creek that required few modifications to accommodate Ron's handicaps. The hallways were wide enough for a wheelchair, and it had enough bedrooms. The house had been abandoned while portions were still under construction, perfect for the Cookes because it could be finished with a handicap-friendly bathroom. The Cookes planned to let their children finish the school year in May, then move onto the property abutting a stunning vermillion cliff, living in a travel trailer for no more than a month while construction on the modest, blue clapboard home was completed by Ron's brother Seth Cooke. Cooke was a member of the UEP advisory board who was present during the Shane Stubbs field plowing debacle and issued the *Tribune*-characterized "death threats" in despair over his loss.*

Today, the Cookes are still living in a life-threatening hell. The family of five is squeezed into a deteriorating trailer no bigger than a midsize U-Haul hitch crammed with medical equipment and a wheelchair that leave little room to move—conditions imposed by a mystifying tangle of FLDS city government, utility companies, and affiliated businesses that charge the Cookes thousands of dollars for the tortures they bring upon the family.

---

*   After the *Tribune* story ran, Seth Cooke was fired from his position on the UEP board.

The city government has refused to allow the Cookes to finish their home, producing an array of bewildering paperwork snafus somehow connected to the home's previous—and they say current—resident. As always, FLDS produced the resident as soon as the Cookes signed papers for the house, though the sect is apparently not claiming he was living in the home at the time the Cookes tried to take possession, only that he intended to live there. Water has been denied to a man who must clean catheters daily because there allegedly isn't enough of it. The family is denied electricity as well, not that they have much room for electronics. Meanwhile, an unauthorized FLDS building project involving a triplex "for the elderly" constructed within weeks during January 2010 was hooked up right away.* Electricity was provided quickly to the FLDS project as well.

Like other non-FLDS residents, the Cookes are followed and harassed. Groups of men appear on the property to menace them and their children. And in the most recent outrageous incident, the FLDS water company accused them of stealing water the company doesn't even own. The attorneys general of Utah and Arizona assert that water rights in Short Creek belong to the UEP trust, no matter how many goofy quitclaim deeds Willie Jessop files or phony irrigation companies FLDS creates. The subject of the FLDS water company's diversion of at least $3.2 million from the UEP trust was the whole point of Bruce Wisan's court filing demonstrating the theft with canceled checks.

Nevertheless, in May 2010, a backhoe appeared on the Cookes' property to "investigate" the family's "theft" of water FLDS itself had illegally denied them for two years. The investigation consisted of digging a meteor-sized crater in their yard. Backhoe operator Scott Jessop was accompanied by Colorado City marshal Helaman Barlow of Shane Stubbs field plowing fame. FLDS member Helaman Barlow was confronted by UEP administrator Jethro Barlow, who lived a short distance from the Cookes and had been called by a panicked Jinjer. Also appearing for the Cookes was Ron's brother Seth, who parked his car in the middle of the Cookes' yard to prevent digging.

Jethro Barlow told FLDS officer Helaman Barlow that any digging on UEP property to investigate the theft of UEP assets was illegal, as

---

*   FLDS insists that the triplex received water from an alternate source, but the fact remains that water has been provided to many new FLDS-approved homes and denied to those holding leases with the court, discrepancies the sect will soon be forced to explain in U.S. District Court in Prescott, Arizona, where Bill Walker has filed a lawsuit on behalf of the Cookes.

in against the law Officer Barlow was sworn to uphold. The FLDS cop insisted he was "authorized," probably the same way Brigham Young's men were authorized to destroy a monument. Officer Barlow refused to wait for the arrival of Mohave County deputies en route, and when Seth Cooke refused to move his car, Officer Barlow handcuffed him, threatening him with something like the same kangaroo court fate inflicted upon the hapless Isaac Wyler who "trespassed" in vacant UEP homes. Seth relented. The handcuffs came off so he could move the car, whereupon digging commenced. A giant hole was left in the Cookes' front yard, though Officer Barlow never "investigated" the crater. Several days later, the Cookes received a bill for the mess, hundreds of dollars they owed "South Side Irrigation Co. Inc.," a phantom corporation registered in neither Utah nor Arizona.

Five months before Officer Helaman's backhoe investigation, Tucson attorney Bill Walker, who is not a tall man, was forced to duck as he entered the Cookes' cramped trailer. Alerted to the Cooke's predicament by Pennie Petersen, Walker had come to meet with the family and view the deplorable conditions firsthand. Ron Cooke, his wheelchair wedged into a corner against a bed consuming a third of the space, struggled to lean forward far enough to greet the attorney, who was visibly shaken by the Cookes' enforced squalor.

Crammed with Ron's teetering, life-sustaining medical devices, the tiny space is suffocating, unfit for a family of dogs, much less a human family of four. Jinjer must haul water every day, cooking either outside or on a dangerous set of hot plates jimmied into an overhang at the front of the trailer, powered by a coughing gas generator spewing fumes around the rotting picnic table Jinjer uses as a parlor outdoors. The Cookes' only connections to the outside world are their outdated cell phones and an ancient, unreliable laptop precariously perched on a TV dinner tray. Even in the chair, it is evident Cooke is a football player–sized man. He gripped Walker's hand with a steady gaze and a set, determined jaw. "Welcome," he said, refusing to surrender his dignity.

In the nippy January air outside the trailer, a stoic Jinjer smoked half a Marlboro, saving the rest for later. She said she did not want to let FLDS chase them off the property, but they weren't getting much help preventing it. "I don't know what's going to happen," she said without inflection. "Ron . . . he's angry. He wants to keep fighting, and so do I. . . . It's not right. But how long can we go without water or power? Ron is sick. He doesn't want that to matter, but it does." Carefully pocketing the half cigarette, she made another observation. "*Christians*," she scoffed. "That's what these people call themselves. *Christians*."

When Bill emerged from the trailer, Jinjer presented him with a neatly organized manila file folder, a record of everything that had happened to the Cooke family since their arrival two years ago. The correspondence with FLDS government agencies and utilities. The denied building permits. Thousands in payments to the water company, which took their money and still refused to hook them up. She did not include the assault incidents, because there are no police records, only her word and similar tales told by others in the Cookes' predicament. Because of Bruce Wisan's programs, there are more of them in Short Creek than ever before—people who have come to reclaim their lives—but they are still vastly outnumbered and, they believe, deserted by government agents like Mark Shurtleff. "I don't know what happened to Mark," Jinjer said. "But he sure left *us* to the wolves."

By "us" Jinjer means the roughly fifty people like herself: Isaac Wyler, the Chatwins, Jethro Barlow, Shane Stubbs, and others who managed to stay in Short Creek and the hundreds, possibly thousands, who would like to return but are afraid. The experiences of the Cookes and other non-FLDS residents amply illustrate that, even if one could get water and electricity, there is no law enforcement protection for non-FLDS residents, period. Theft and vandalism of property, the killing of livestock or pets, and even dangerous personal assaults rule the day in the FLDS-controlled twin cities.

At a meeting of non-FLDS residents in the Chatwin home, stories of discrimination and harassment tumble out of the adults like turbulent, converging rivers, tales impossible to separate over the roar. Several have been run off the road. Several have been surrounded by groups of FLDS men, pinned outside their front doors. All live in fear of FLDS. They wonder if the FLDS habit of leaving mutilated dead animals in vehicles or on doorsteps will escalate to something much worse.

But without knowing who put them there, when, or why, dead animals aren't proof in any court of law. Unidentified SUVs with unidentified drivers crowding families into ditches aren't proof. When it comes to evidence that can be presented in a court of law, the perpetrators of assaults against non-FLDS residents and property seem knowledgeable about how to dance just outside the circle. "It's beyond outrageous," Walker stated, red-faced with anger. "These people are getting mauled out here, and there's *no law enforcement*."

Under those lawless circumstances, Walker was uncertain if he could mount a lawsuit on behalf of the Cookes, but he was about to get an unexpected assist. As it turned out, the Cookes had filed a boilerplate discrimination complaint with the Arizona Attorney General's Office. Any Attorney General's Office receives dozens of these handwritten form complaints in a month. The Cookes had not called particular attention to theirs, but the Arizona prosecutors had followed up on this one. Scrupulously. The struggle to force FLDS to follow the laws of the land was about to gain a new dimension.

27

THE LIGHT

Just ask yourselves, historians, when was monogamy introduced on to the face of the earth? When those buccaneers, who settled on the peninsula where Rome now stands, could not steal women enough to have two or three apiece, they passed a law that a man should have but one woman. . . . This was the rise, start and foundation of the doctrine of monogamy; and never till then was there a law passed that we have any knowledge of, that a man should have but one wife.

—Brigham Young, *Journal of Discourses*, Vol. 12

At 1 o'clock you said, "Oh my, Oh my. Will there be any faith left among the young people. How I yearn to talk to them. The Lord is showing me the young girls of this community, those who are pure and righteous will be taken care of at a younger age. As the government finds out about this, it will bring such a great pressure upon us, upon the families of these girls, upon me, and also upon the girls who are placed in marriage." You said, "The Lord will take care of them as they seek unto Him and yearn to stay clean and pure. And I will teach the young people that there is no such thing as an underage Priesthood marriage but that it is a protection for them if they will look at it right and seek unto the Lord for a testimony. The Lord will have me do this, get more young girls married. . . . The halfhearted will rage and this band of Gadianton robbers will become more hardened.* They will become more forceful as they see they are not getting any blessings, because

---

* In the *Book of Mormon*, the Gadianton Robbers are a secret society of evil conspirators formed around 52 B.C. by Nephite supporters of Paanchi, who made an unsuccessful bid to become a chief judge. Paanchi was executed when he refused to accept the election of his brother, Pahoran II. A Paanchi supporter named Kishkumen then assassinated Pahoran II, swearing a pact of silence around the deed, the foundation of the underground criminal sect whose most prolific leader was a man named Gadianton. The robbers made significant converts with both Nephites and Lamanites, and the secret band is resurrected and reinvented throughout Mormon history. Today, they are thought to be living in Utah, Arizona, and Nevada and were allegedly seen near St. George in 1962. After 9/11, LDS president Gordon Hinckley suggested that the attack might be linked to the Gadianton Robbers, against whom the whole world would now finally be forced to unite.

from now on, only those who have Zion in their hearts will obtain the blessing of
Celestial Marriage."
                    —Naomie Jeffs reading her transcript of a "heavenly session,"
                        "Record of Preseident Warren Jeffs," November 24, 2003

In the early morning hours of April 6, 2010, approximately twenty-five
Arizona and Utah law enforcement officers rumbled into Short Creek with
search warrants tucked into their just-in-case flak jackets. Spreading out, they
hit five fire stations, which had done so well securing hundreds of thousands
of dollars in Homeland Security grants, and two residences, carrying off cartons of records and computers. Four of the five fire stations were located in
Colorado City and the other in Hildale. The private residences belonged to
the Colorado City fire chief, Jake Barlow, and Colorado City's man of many
hats, Dave Darger, who, for these purposes, was the "elected town treasurer."
A subsequent Mohave County sheriff's office press release advised that the
cops were seeking evidence of misuse of public funds and ongoing "fraudu-
lent schemes."

An affidavit supporting the warrant surprisingly revealed that Mohave
County had been investigating the FLDS fire departments for financial wrongdoing since 2008. The twenty-two-page, single-spaced document compiled by
Mohave County attorney's office investigator W. T. Flanagan with assistance
from Gary Engels discussed in eye-popping detail the various frauds uncov-
ered so far in a review of bank and credit card statements as well as invoices
and records "dealing with the expenses and purchases by Barlow and Darger
with CCFD public monies beginning around September 2004 to June 2009."

Most astonishing in the recovered documents was the brazen cool with
which Barlow and Darger spent public monies to furnish their homes, pay for
vacations and expensive dining, and buy socks and candy. They transferred
tens of thousands to their personal bank accounts—an excellent indicator
the men were completely unfamiliar with the concept of public account-
ability. Amazingly, the *Tribune* could find fault only with the Danish hams
and smoked salmon purchased close to Christmas. Brooke Adams speculated the items were meant for an innocent holiday party but conceded that
even such benign purchases with tax dollars would be artless and wrong.
However, Adams reassured her blog readers, Jeffs's Arizona attorney, Mike
Picaretta, had promised her an explanation for the hams, if not the tens of
thousands of Darger and Barlow's personal expenses.

The explanation never came, but Goddard's office announced they'd not forgotten about the canceled checks from the FLDS water department either. After the checks surfaced, Mark Shurtleff had promised an investigation, but like the thirty-day UEP settlement deadline letter, no one had heard anything about it since. Proceeding on the legal assumption that the water was deemed part of the UEP trust, the Arizona attorney general could exercise investigative authority over fraud in that department as well, but Goddard's office had something more immediate in mind.

On June 25, 2010, a month after the Cooke backhoe "investigation," Arizona assistant attorney general Sandra Kane filed a civil rights discrimination lawsuit against three FLDS utility companies, the City of Hildale, and the town of Colorado City, plus (presumably FLDS) unnamed John Does and John Doe corporations "to remedy Defendant's discriminatory and unlawful housing practices, provide appropriate relief to aggrieved persons, and vindicate the public interest."

The case was specifically brought on behalf of Ron and Jinjer Cooke, who'd summoned the intestinal fortitude to go public after filing a formal complaint. Months earlier, the Arizona AG's office had responded to their original complaint by filing a "reasonable cause" document in court, a potential prelude to a real lawsuit that had concluded that the Short Creek city governments and utility companies were engaging in widespread, religiously based discrimination, implying there were other victims out there who could found a class action suit.

The "reasonable cause" document should have alerted FLDS leaders that they were skating on paper-thin ice and needed to rectify the Cooke situation without delay, but men who deposit thousands of tax dollars directly into their bank accounts are apparently untroubled by flags of civil rights lawsuits from the state's attorney general. Kane's actionable twenty-six-page lawsuit on behalf of the Cookes set forth in intimate detail and with scrupulous documentation the twisted history of the FLDS campaign against the Cookes, and the "John Does" listed as unknown perpetrators meant Kane could add more defendants as they were discovered in the ensuing investigation.*

---

* A copy of the detailed complaint CV2010-020375 filed in Maricopa County can be found along with other significant court filings at a variety of websites, including Hope Organization and FLDS Texas. Hope Organization lists the filings at the bottom of categories listed under the Media Archive or Current Events heading. Arizona also maintains an online courts web page, as does Utah, though access at the latter is more limited.

It was not the first civil rights complaint Goddard had lodged against the sect. Years earlier, Arizona had sued two FLDS restaurants for refusing to serve non-FLDS patrons—the situation Shurtleff resolved by displaying a badge and gun. Smartly, the restaurants caved, signing an agreement to stop the practice. A mollified Goddard went on his way, and the eatery proprietors went on theirs with some, but not total, compliance.

It seems unlikely that partial compliance will be satisfactory in the Cooke matter. The Arizona filing was the backup Bill Walker needed to file an individual federal discrimination suit on behalf of the Cookes, also with an eye toward a class action. In June 2010, Walker filed in U.S. District Court in Prescott, Arizona, with a case so strong FLDS attorneys uncharacteristically offered to pay thousands for a mediator to get rid of it. "Naturally I was open to settling," said abnormally mild-mannered Walker, "but they were going to have to pay substantial damages and guarantee the hookups as well as an end to the harassment. I didn't think they'd be able to do all of that to my satisfaction, but I was gratified they wanted to come to the table at all."

No one was surprised when FLDS refused even the most humanitarian of the Cookes' demands, and the family remains without water or electricity to this day. The Cookes also report that the threat of two lawsuits has not dented FLDS sect members' enthusiasm for trespass, vandalism, and intimidation. Though there isn't much to vandalize, things get mysteriously broken around the Cooke property, and Jinjer Cooke has confronted armed men peeping in her windows or milling about her front yard more than a few times. "Someone," Walker states evenly, "is going to get hurt." That is also the conclusion of the Arizona Attorney General's Office, which in October 2010 asked for and received permission to join in Bill Walker's federal suit, an extraordinary show of support and assistance for the Cookes, but the help might not end there. In October 2010, Mark Shurtleff filed court papers announcing that he was assigning more prosecutors to FLDS-related cases. Reportedly, the Utah Attorney General's Office is also considering joining Bill Walker's federal case, which is currently active in the U.S. District Court in Prescott, Arizona.

Meanwhile, two-year-old misdemeanor criminal charges against Warren Jeffs in Arizona were dropped in June 2010, and Jeffs began fighting extradition to Texas. A triumphant Mike Picaretta asserts the charges had to be dropped when he discovered that one of the state's witnesses, former FLDS midwife Jane Blackmore, had reconstructed medical records for Elissa Wall. In submitting the records, Blackmore had falsely testified they were originals, which

Picaretta believes calls all subsequent testimony into question, even though the accuracy of the reconstructed records are not in dispute.

But Mohave County attorney Matt Smith says Picaretta's aggressive pursuit of state witnesses' personal and financial affairs left them all uneager to take the stand for a trial in which Jeffs would suffer no penalty. Picaretta's flood of pretrial motions, including a monster motion challenging the Texas YFZ search warrant completely unrelated to Jeffs's Arizona charges, meant that Warren Jeffs had already served more time in Arizona waiting for trial than any judge could impose as a sentence for a guilty verdict.* In any event, says Smith, Warren Jeffs was a pain-in-the-butt prisoner Arizona was delighted to return to Utah. "All the fasting and everything," a creeped out Smith told Mike Watkiss. "He had to be force-fed sometimes. . . . It was just a strain on the system."

When he was arrested in Nevada in 2006, Warren Jeffs didn't fuss about returning to his home state, but he felt a great deal differently about returning to his new land of Zion. In Texas, he faced two counts of rape of twelve-year-old girls, with penalty enhancements because he'd "married" them after Texas upped its consent laws. If convicted, Jeffs faced ninety-nine years in a Texas penitentiary. He would never be released in this lifetime. "We're looking forward to having him," remarked Randy Mankin.

In a slap-to-the-face July 2010 decision that refocused a hot spotlight on Utah's mushy view of polygamy in general and its worst results in particular, the Utah Supreme Court reversed Warren Jeffs's conviction for facilitating the rapes of Elissa Wall, citing faulty jury instructions. The high court's supporting contortionist logic mystified legal commentators and enraged activists. Bill Walker fairly shouts his objections to the decision. "First of all, Jeffs was convicted because he occupied a position of trust in Elissa's life. He was her spiritual advisor. His word carried great weight, and when he ordered her to submit, she was afraid not to do it. Jeffs knew that.

"Basically, this decision says that the jury had to find that the rapist— Allen Steed—was *also* in a position of trust. That there had to be jury instructions to that. It's *absurd*! It *makes no sense*! Why does the *rapist* have to be in a position of trust? What does *that* have to do with Warren's position of trust? How does it change in any way what Warren Jeffs did to the victim?" Bill snorts derisively. "It *doesn't*. The answer is: *it doesn't*, and this is

---

* Although FLDS activists charged that Picaretta was unscrupulously intimidating the state's witnesses, all the actions Picaretta took are allowed under Arizona law. Utah law does not allow the probing of state's witnesses to the same degree as Arizona.

just one big excuse to give Jeffs another shot at freedom with another jury that will hopefully get it. I can't see anybody reading this convoluted opinion without concluding that this court was just grasping at straws to let this guy off and send a message that they weren't really interested in polygamy. And that's the good spin."

CNN legal analyst and author Jeffrey Toobin appeared on *Anderson Cooper 360* with former FLDS plural wife Carolyn Jessop and author Jon Krakauer to challenge the decision and its true intentions. Condemnations from activists like Krakauer and Jessop were to be expected, but the Jeffs reversal pulled the normally reserved and circumspect Toobin out of his shell. "You know, I'm not someone who does a lot of trashing of judges," said Toobin. "I think judges generally do a good job, do their best. This opinion, I find a disgrace. I had to read this opinion twice even to understand what they were saying was wrong with these jury instructions. It is the very definition of a technicality. It has nothing to do with his [Jeffs's] guilt or innocence. . . . It is an appalling, appalling decision."

In Salt Lake City, Roger Hoole echoed these sentiments, sighing into his phone. "It's just a terrible decision on its face, but it's also a terrible decision for Utah," he says mournfully. "It just makes us look like we really aren't serious about child rape or abandonment, let alone polygamy. Warren Jeffs is a criminal. What he did has nothing to do with religion, and yet, I think that somewhere in the justices' subconscious, they thought it did.* We have that problem in Utah. Being Mormon, it's hard to separate the polygamy from the religion deep down. I'm afraid of what might happen in Short Creek and places like it if we continue to do that."

The *Tribune* printed extensive and jubilant reactions from Jeffs's defense team and Willie Jessop. Soured by Toobin's comments, angry Jeffs defense attorney Walter Bugdon challenged: "What's technical about a jury instruction? It's one of the most important things in a trial." And Jessop vocalized what activists feared. With so many FLDS appeals in the UEP case pending before the Utah Supreme Court, Jessop triumphantly observed that the higher courts had always been true-blue FLDS friends. "We've always had luck in the higher courts," he told Brooke Adams.

Unsurprised Texans received news of the Jeffs reversal in Utah with amused disdain. "Well," said an unconcerned Kathy Mankin, "I don't think anybody here was exactly shocked." After the reversal, Jeffs's lawyers

---

*   Four of Utah's five Supreme Court justices are Mormon.

exclaimed that they could not wait another second to scamper over to the Purgatory jail to deliver the joyous news, but behind the beaming faces had to lurk cognition that Jeffs's legal future remained essentially unchanged. The Utah Supreme Court hadn't erased the Utah charges. The trial reversal meant Jeffs could be retried for the Elissa Wall rapes, a prospect of heinous expense, but even if Utah did not retry Jeffs, Texas awaited with their almost-one-hundred-year-sentence crimes. Kathy speculates, "What if Utah doesn't try him again? We'll just get him that much quicker."

Indeed, Texas governor Rick Perry wasn't even waiting for Utah to make up its mind. On July 29, 2010, only two days after the reversal, Perry sent the extradition paperwork off to Utah's governor, Gary Herbert, requesting that Warren Jeffs be transferred to answer for his crimes in Texas. Warren Jeffs's lawyers had promised to fight extradition, and the Utah appellate courts were not inspiring confidence in the Lone Star State, so to erase any possibility of unfortunate, loophole misunderstandings, Perry sent along twenty-eight pages of excruciating details identifying Jeffs and the charges against him. "Texas to Jeffs: Come on Down!" read a headline in the *Success*.

Mark Shurtleff had a decision to make. After issuing the standard "we're disappointed" statement regarding the reversal, he had to weigh the exorbitant hundreds of thousands of dollars required to try Jeffs again against the possible outcome. Normally, the wear and tear upon the victim forced to relive the experience would also be considered, but Elissa Wall held a press conference the day of the opinion stating her unequivocal intentions to testify as often as the Utah appellate courts deemed necessary. She wasn't going anywhere.

And then there was the touchy political situation. The Utah Supreme Court opinion put Mark Shurtleff in a bad box. He'd railed against Warren Jeffs, always careful to separate the crimes against children from any religion. What would it look like if he just chucked it in now? What would it mean for the nation's perception of Utah? If Shurtleff didn't retry Jeffs, would the numbers of Americans equating Mormons and polygamy shoot through the roof? It was a question rarely discussed in the open on the American national scene, but now Toobin spoke to it on *Anderson Cooper 360*. Asked if he thought Utah's appellate decision was politically motivated, Toobin said he couldn't be certain, *but* "given the magnitude of these charges and given the fact that these jury instructions don't even relate to the core issue, I am bewildered by this decision. And it certainly bears looking into—whether there is some political connection between these judges."

Krakauer was less restrained. "I, for one, do not doubt that there may have been a political basis for this [Supreme Court] decision," Krakauer stated, "given the five members of the—the five justices on the Supreme Court's close ties to the LDS Church and the LDS Church's own concerns with sexual abuse and what this says about, you know, how you can tie some-one who compelled the abuse but didn't actually commit the rape, how he can be held accountable. That's—that's a scary thing for some members high up in the LDS Church." With the unmistakable implications of *that* statement still sizzling on the national airwaves, Krakauer tossed another bombshell of heretofore unknown evidence Texas planned to use in their management of Warren Jeffs.

"And in the evidence," Krakauer said, "in the raid of 2008, they uncov-ered a treasure trove of evidence, including a tape recording and a transcript of Warren raping a twelve-year-old girl. Actually, she'd been eleven until twenty-four days earlier. She had been forced to marry Jeffs. She was raped in the temple on a special bed. Two of Jeffs's older wives participated in the rape. It was tape recorded. Every grunt and perverted prayer and command to this girl."

Mark Shurtleff had no public reaction to Krakauer's allegations, but less than two weeks after the Utah Supreme Court reversal, he announced he would petition the high court for a rehearing on the Jeffs reversal. However, Shurtleff's petition did *not* ask the justices to change their minds and rein-state the conviction, only to offer more detailed guidelines about jury instructions the high court found unacceptable. At this writing, Utah has not decided if it will retry Warren Jeffs for the rapes of Elissa Wall.

Texas, however, was unequivocal. Governor Rick Perry, who won reelec-tion in the November 2010 midterms, reportedly had a plane on constant standby, ready to whisk Texas Ranger Nick Hanna away to Utah to collect Warren Jeffs the instant Texas's extradition request was granted. In two flail-ing, fifty-page efforts to quash the extradition warrant, Jeffs's attorneys argued that he could not be sent to Texas until the situation in Utah, where Jeffs was now effectively presumed innocent, was resolved with either a new trial or dismissal of the Utah charges. The latter, they argued, was the only foresee-able outcome, given the Utah Supreme Court's reversal, and Jeffs's detention violated all manner of his rights. But, the attorneys argued, Jeffs's predicament was so much more sinister than mere constitutional violations.

"In an apparent effort to destroy the prophet of an unpopular religion," began the memorandum of October 8, 2010, "the states of Utah and Texas, by their governors, have entered into an Executive Agreement that effectively strips Warren Steed Jeffs (Mr. Jeffs) of his constitutional rights to a speedy, public trial; to present a defense; to access and explore the evidence against him; to due process of law; to counsel; and to reasonable bail. By doing so, they have abused their discretion, failed to uphold their highest and fundamental duty to sustain the constitutions of both state and country, and intentionally refused Mr. Jeffs the enjoyment of rights to which he is entitled. *They have shrouded their ungodly alliance in the semantics of extradition law.* . . . [emphasis added]

"Although there are those even among our own who would seek to destroy it, America's strength remains in its devotion to the protection of the individual and his rights, even if—and indeed, especially if—that protection requires the governmental body to give way."

FLDS Texas, a premier anti-FLDS website whose contributors rarely shrink from merciless sarcasm, posted the "ungodly alliance" memorandum without comment, leaving readers to wonder when the separation of church and state had been abolished on Warren Jeffs's behalf or why the legal proceedings for a man incarcerated because he'd never particularly cared for the character or laws of the United States were now jeopardizing the country's very soul with "extradition semantics."

Apparently unalarmed by these imminent threats to Americanism, Utah assistant attorney general Craig L. Barlow, newly assigned to the FLDS cases, answered each of Jeffs's pleadings point by point in straight-talking language. In the end, though, Barlow's reply could be summed up in one of his opening sentences: "Jeffs's motion to quash the Governor's Warrant should be denied based on . . . its lack of legal and factual merit."

After three months of legal wrangling, Warren Jeffs was extradited to Texas in early December 2010. Prosecutor Nichols announced he would comply with provisions guaranteeing defendants speedy trials and try Jeffs before the remaining four FLDS men charged after the 2008 raid. Though he'd had months to do it, Jeffs had failed to hire a Texas attorney, refusing to sign routine legal documents without one present. An undeterred Judge Walther set a trial date of January 24, 2011.

In the following weeks, Jeffs hired and then fired several Texas lawyers, finally settling on prominent Fort Worth attorney Jeff Kearney in early February. Kearney, who secured an acquittal for a Branch Davidian cult member accused of murdering a federal agent during the infamous 1993 raid in Waco, did not join Jeffs at the defense table until FLDS member John Wayman wrote a check in the courtroom. Waiving Jeffs's right to a speedy trial, Kearney persuaded Walther that the voluminous evidence in the case merited a lengthy extension. Jeffs is slated to stand trial on two counts of sexual assault on a minor on July 25, 2011. Walther set October 3, 2011, for Jeffs's bigamy trial, but Kearney all but promised he'd be seeking extensions on both dates.

Meanwhile, Warren Jeffs's paranoia continued unchecked. In a mass excommunication from his jail cell that dwarfed the shocking ejections in 2004, Jeffs threw thirty men out of FLDS, many of them high-ranking officers who had stood by him for years. They included Wendell Nielsen, Merril Jessop, and even the staunchly reliable attack dog Willie Jessop. A good percentage of the disenfranchised men had up to thirty wives and dozens of children, now up for reassignment to strangers. Observers noted that many of the excommunicated men could have been in a position to take Warren's place if the membership ever tired of following a convicted felon from prison.

28

END GAME

The FLDS have tried to stop me and my dad from using our leases with Mr. Wisan since they had problems in Texas. In the summer of 2008 they even have plowed our wheat up. They have grazed their cattle and sheep on it. They have shut the water off so we could not irrigate. They chased our cows and horses out onto the highway, removed gates, tore down fences and have done lots of different things to harass us and stop us. . . . WE are the ones being harmed. No harm will take place if my Red Winter Wheat [sic] is stored in a silo next to someone else's White Winter Wheat [sic]. . . . Where is the law and order? We are only farmers, not lawyers, this is our plea to the court for legal enforcement of our lease.

—Shane Stubbs, letter to Utah Fifth District Judge James Shumate,
after FLDS sought a restraining order preventing
Stubbs from using his leased grain silos, July 16, 2010

The Bishop informed me yesterday, and updated me today, about an event which took place Sunday, where Marvin Wyler, an apostate, tried to take over a house, next to him, on the UEP land [sic] the bishop, William Jessop, had Lyle gather twenty or more men, it ened [sic] up about forty men, and they had prayer circle and then they stood firm that they would not surrender UEP homes. . . . The apostates backed off, withdrew their things that they had stored in this house, and the bishop put someone else in the house.

—Warren Jeffs, "Record of President Warren Jeffs," July 28, 2005

In his early thirties, John is married with two young children and has a good job as a construction crew supervisor in the Phoenix area. His wife knows little of his past. When they were courting, John says his future wife was naturally curious about the family he hadn't seen in over a decade, prodding him gently for information. The little he told her was upsetting enough to convince her that she didn't need to learn anything else. John's children know nothing of FLDS, and John wants to keep it that way.

Although John feels like he's successfully put FLDS in his life's rearview mirror, he's been unable to squelch some curiosity about the ongoing UEP fight and Warren Jeffs's arrest. John knew Pennie Petersen when he was growing up in FLDS. In the beginning of 2010, Pennie, who keeps track of most FLDS defectors as best she can, contacted John to ask if he might have anything—any evidence at all—that might help the non-FLDS residents of Short Creek struggling to regain their homes. John's first instinct was to run for the hills—he was certain he didn't possess anything of value anyway. But after a few nights of restless sleep, he changed his mind, deciding he owed it to people less fortunate than he'd been to help in whatever way he could. In January, he drove to an upscale hotel near Phoenix's Sky Harbor Airport for a meeting with Bill Walker, lugging a small, battered suitcase stuffed with tattered papers.

Even though he fled many years ago, John is afraid that if the sect knew where he was, they would fill his new life and that of his young family with misery. He doesn't know what form it would take, whether it would be simple harassment, like hang-up calls in the dead of night, or something worse, but he's seen other defectors hassled to within an inch of their sanity. Amid assurances that his identity would be kept secret, John let slip just how deep the fear runs. "The blood atonement thing," he shrugs in an unsuccessful stab at nonchalance. "I don't know how serious that is, but I know the other stuff they're capable of."

Though he acknowledges he would have been thrown out of FLDS eventually for his freethinking ways, John left the sect under his own steam after independently deciding that no loving God would sanction the cruelty, hatred, fear, and despair the FLDS leadership inflicted upon its membership. Twelve years ago, when John was eighteen, he rose before dawn, making a stealthy exit from his family home where everything he held dear and everyone he loved in the world still slumbered. His battered heart was breaking to pieces; uncontrollable, silent tears stained his smooth face as he padded across the kitchen in his stocking feet, carrying his shoes. Those and the clothes on his back were the only possessions John took to his black pickup truck. Cracking the door with the care of a thief, he slid inside and shifted to neutral, allowing the vehicle to roll quietly down the driveway before turning the ignition key.

"I was afraid that if my mother found me, she'd manage to convince me to stay," John explains. "Even though I didn't believe the religion anymore, I would have stayed for her. I love her. I love my whole family still." As he drove away, he didn't dare even check the rearview mirror as he abandoned his body to convulsing sobs. "I knew I would never see them again," he says of his mother, father, brothers, and sisters, his eyes focused sharply on something in space.

"To them, I am dead," he states. "In fact, in their minds it would be better if I *was* dead. They wouldn't have given me something to eat if I were starving or tossed me a line if I were drowning. They wouldn't acknowledge me at all. I knew all that when I left. It nearly killed me, but if I'd stayed, I really would have died inside." Like all other FLDS defectors who have told their stories, John recounts the emotional carnage in a jarring, dull monotone. The flat delivery is accompanied by a dead poker face, the inscrutable expression all FLDS members must wear to protect their thoughts from the caprice of a mad prophet.

Almost reluctantly, John admits that barely a day passes in which he doesn't worry about the siblings he left behind. It is a secret torture of his soul he shares with no one, but if what he's got in the case can do anything to free them, Bill Walker is welcome to it. As John unpacks the case, Walker points to a stack of old Alta Academy yearbooks— the FLDS school in Salt Lake City at which Warren Jeffs was principal. "Take them," John orders, sliding the stack across the table with a mixture of disgust and anger. "I don't know why I kept them. Maybe today is why. I just thought . . ." He trails off, returning the unspoken thought to the shadows of memory. "I hope they can help you," he continues briskly, as if he's completed an unpleasant task. John doesn't seem aware that he is vigorously wiping his hands on his jeans, as if rubbing them clean. He adds, "Don't worry about getting those back to me."

The yearbooks contain no startling revelations save one: the haunting faces of hundreds and hundreds of children, boys and girls staring out from page after page after page. FLDS doctrine holds that each one of them is the property of the prophet to do with as he pleases, whatever he pleases. The fates of the children in the yearbooks are unknown. There are so many, it is overwhelming.

John cannot answer the question most people unfamiliar with FLDS always ask. "I don't know why I saw through it and others don't," he says. "I don't know why I got up the courage to leave and others can't. It's impossible to explain to outside people what kind of control the group has over you. I gave up trying a long time ago. People say, 'Why don't you just leave? Why don't you call the police?' and they can't understand when you tell them why. You just don't *know* anything else. Everything else is terrifying and evil, and you're taught to be afraid of everything that isn't in the group. There's no way to explain it to people. They can't understand it. But I do. I know. I know most people cannot get out without help. A lot of help.

"I don't know what happened with me. I don't know. I just knew that a loving God wouldn't want people to feel that bad and hate so much. Nobody should be afraid all the time, scared that anything they do could lose their families and get them sent to hell. It shouldn't have felt like dying to be close to God. I didn't believe it anymore. And of course," he smiles thinly, "I wanted a family. When I left, things weren't as bad as they are now with all the little girls being married off and everything, but I could see where it was going even then." John's smile turns sardonic. "I knew my family didn't have the right Israelite bloodlines. I knew the Jeffses weren't going to be giving me a wife.

"I don't hold it against my family," he continues, staring out through wounded eyes. "I can't. I know what that power is that FLDS has. My family can't help it. They can't think any other way." He looks at the stack of yearbooks at the table's edge dejectedly. "What do you think will happen with Warren?" John asks. "'Cause keeping him in jail would be a good step. I mean, it won't solve everything. There's other guys out there to carry on but it's a good step. He never came after me, but I was pretty big, pretty strong. He may have known I'd fight, but I heard a lot of stories about kids who couldn't. Warren's a really destructive man. A bad man, I think. That's just my opinion," he injects with quick modesty, "but I know a lot of people are being hurt."

That's the conclusion that Terry Goddard reached in July 2010, when he filed an emergency report with Judge Lindberg, saying the FLDS war on nonmembers was out of control. Overwrought emergency writs and emergency hearings are an FLDS attorney's bread and butter, but most other lawyers don't like to take the sparkle off their emergencies by declaring them with the regularity of daybreak. That goes double for career litigators like attorneys general, whose careers compel them to appear in court often before judges who might become irked by a plethora of nonurgent emergencies.* There had been a dozen emergencies in the UEP case, but in this actual emergency, people could start getting hurt.

Assistant attorney general Bill Richards provided video of FLDS men plowing under fields as the police stood by as well as evidence that planted

---

* Even Goddard's "emergency report" did not request an emergency hearing but rather a "recommendation for expedited status conference."

fields were deliberately overrun by FLDS livestock and that non-FLDS live-stock were being driven from their fields into open country, as Isaac Wyler's horses had been. There was evidence of vandalism, theft of UEP property, illegal fencing and blocking of public roads, widespread housing and utility discrimination, and illegal capping of wells. There were videos of the FLDS cops helping FLDS members break into non-FLDS properties.

In short, FLDS and their representatives were proceeding as if the trust reformation had never occurred, violating dozens of court orders with flab-bergasting aplomb. Just as disturbing as anything else was Richards's allegation that Colorado City attorney Ken Brendel, prosecutor of the famed Wyler/Wisan/Barlow trespassing case, was flirting with malfeasance by instructing the FLDS police force how to ignore laws unless they benefitted FLDS. Since Brendel presumably graduated from a law school, he should have known that Lindberg's court orders were enforceable law, but instead the FLDS prosecutor instructed the cops to disregard all non-FLDS complaints with catchy phrases like "It's a civil matter" or "I need to see a court order," when the leases were themselves court orders. Naturally, the complaints of FLDS members were to be taken very seriously and "interlopers" arrested.

Informed sources outside the Arizona Attorney General's Office say the report was a public effort to light a fire under Judge Lindberg, who was presumed to be delaying rulings on critical discovery motions the Arizona attorney general had filed six months earlier while she awaited various deci-sions from the Utah Supreme Court. It looked like the FLDS strategy of paralyzing Lindberg by jerking the case out of her hands and into the court that had reversed Warren Jeffs's conviction was working, but Arizona wasn't content with the arrangement. There was no law in Short Creek, and bad things were happening.

Specifically, Richards needed a decision on his December request to lift Lindberg's stand-down order and allow the Arizona AG to commence discov-ering (and proving) what was really going on in Short Creek. While Richards understood that Lindberg might want to know if the Utah Supreme Court intended to upend the entire UEP case before she made anymore rulings, Richards argued that non-FLDS Short Creek residents didn't have the luxury of time. No matter how many FLDS emergencies were on appeal, the trust still had to be administered and non-FLDS members protected from what looked like imminent harm.

Perpetually unconcerned by laws, it wasn't long before FLDS made Richards's case for him. When threats, vandalism, and harassment failed to dislodge Matt and Genevive Hainline from their UEP leased property, tax-supported FLDS bureaucrats rezoned the property, rearranging the property lines so that the Hainlines could not step into their backyard without trespassing.

Perhaps the creative rezoners knew that the Hainlines would be forced to enter their backyard if they wanted to get to their pickup trucks, and when Genevive Hainline did just that, the industrious FLDS cops were waiting, handcuffs at the ready. As Genevive entered her truck she was swarmed by FLDS cops eager to arrest her on the sect's ever-popular trespassing charge. Genevive refused to submit, back talking as she attempted to scramble out of reach atop the vehicle's roof, but she wasn't quick enough. In the ensuing struggle, two FLDS cops dragged her from the truck, wrestling the screaming mother of two to the ground while a third, police chief Jonathan Roundy, tried unsuccessfully to force the video camera–wielding Andrew Chatwin out of viewfinder range, unhooking his own handcuffs for incentive. Both Mike Watkiss and Brent Hunsaker ran the footage, while the *Tribune* used the incident to imply Bruce Wisan was engaging in unsavory activities again.

The Hainlines weren't the only ones with problems. Shane Stubbs, who'd leased two UEP granaries to store his wheat harvest, was slapped with an FLDS restraining order for trespassing on an FLDS bishop's property. Tons of his wheat were removed from the granary, transported from town, and unceremoniously dumped in the desert and along roadsides.

The granary episode was another depressing illustration of FLDS court tactics. Requesting the restraining order against Shane Stubbs from Ruth's old judge, Fifth District judge James Shumate, FLDS attorney Rod Parker argued several points. First, Stubbs was an abusive, dangerous person who'd been scaring the wits out of Warren Jeffs's brother, Lyle, who was also one of the "movants" in several of the FLDS suits against UEP. Second, Stubbs did not have a "valid lease" for the silos, an astounding continuation of FLDS and their attorneys' refusal to acknowledge Lindberg's orders. Third, whereas the silos might be *situated* on UEP land, they were in fact the personal property of Lyle Jeffs, new information to everyone. Finally, Stubbs's use of the silos interfered with Lyle Jeffs's constitutional rights to discharge his duties as an FLDS bishop in charge of making sure his people had enough food.

To his motion, Parker attached an affidavit from FLDS member Chad Johnson, who said he was in charge of maintaining the granaries, keeping them clean and in good working order. Johnson charged that Shane Stubbs used a bolt cutter to sever locks placed on the properties. Worse than that, Johnson went on, was the fact that Stubbs "put filthy red grain of a very low quality" near the "approximately 60,000 lbs. of high quality white" FLDS grain already there.

Johnson then speculated that *if* Stubbs had engaged the milling machinery and *if* the filthy red apostate grain had mixed with the pure white FLDS grain—if those things had happened—then FLDS's food supply would be destroyed and the silos would have required a complete overhaul and sanitization. The conjuring of imaginary catastrophes are the bedrock of FLDS emergency petitions, and like other speculative disasters in FLDS pleadings, the scenario Johnson presented never happened. Still, FLDS continues to monopolize hundreds of court hours with "what if" or nonexistent episodes presented to uninitiated judges who often have no way of knowing that the facts in the court pleadings are speculative at best and something far worse by some interpretations.

"We feel that you have been hustled and lied to by the FLDS, Rod Parker, Kenneth Okazaki, and Lyle Jeffs," Shane Stubbs wrote to Judge Shumate. Arizona's Bill Richards included the note in supplement to the emergency report to Lindberg, citing the Stubbs situation as yet another example of the FLDS brick wall Richards could not dismantle with hands tied behind his back.

Judges rely upon lawyers to tell them the truth, even if shaded in favor of their clients. Even Parker had to recognize that his claim that Stubbs had no valid lease for the silos was wildly disingenuous, even misleading. Even a hardcore FLDS supporter with deep-seated hatred for the reformed UEP trust would have to admit the UEP leases were at least contestable. Johnson's multiple, overwrought descriptions of "filthy red wheat" might lead a judge to conclude there was something very wrong about red wheat. In fact, varieties of red wheat (winter, spring, hard, soft) are grown more than any other sort in the United States, used to bake the bread and pastries on any grocery store shelf.

Omissions of fact, another pesky FLDS pleading problem, popped up in the restraining order. There are twenty-three grain silos on UEP property. Shane Stubbs had a lease for four of them, two of which were still empty. Lyle Jeffs selected the two silos Stubbs had used to become his personal property and fill with grain. Despite Jeffs's claims that he was responsible for feeding his people by filling the silos, they had all been empty for five years, right up until the time Stubbs decided to lease them.

Such childishness is part of what drove Utah's Tim Bodily up the wall, but Parker's newly enunciated theory of personal property situated on UEP property threatened to explode litigation in the already monstrously obese case into outer space. FLDS attorneys had always nibbled around the edges of the personal property notion, but since Wisan wasn't interested in furniture, linens, or what is usually associated with personal holdings, defining the private property in a way that could thwart the trust administration had proved elusive.* But the silo incident seemed to be like a lightbulb going off. It might just be possible to muddy the property assignments by treating every silo, bush, tree, or car sitting on the property as a separate concern.

In February 2011, unverified posts on the FLDS Texas website revealed the misery in Short Creek was deepening as FLDS leaders required all members to inventory every single item in their homes, down to the number and colors of crayons. If true, the inventories might be used in the same way FLDS approached the granary situation. The granary, FLDS claimed, was private property and therefore the land upon which it sat could not be leased. If FLDS intends to litigate each piece of personal property on every parcel of land, the explosion of cases in the courts will take decades to resolve.

However, in the summer of 2010 Lindberg was tackling other problems. Arizona's emergency report had apparently succeeded in lighting a fire within the judge as well as under her. In response to the petition, Lindberg held a telephone-conference hearing between all the parties on July 22. The contentious hearing produced several blows to FLDS. Lindberg granted Arizona's six-month-old request to investigate problems in Short Creek, and she practically ordered Richards to bring her affidavits that would enable her to hold the contempt of court hearings Wisan had asked for a year earlier. Topping a long list for contempt of court candidates was Colorado City attorney Ken Brendel, who'd been essentially instructing the FLDS police department in evasive maneuvers.

The telephone conference held by Judge Lindberg is emblematic of the entire UEP/FLDS quagmire. After first denying they'd been properly noticed for the hearing, FLDS attorneys continuously reminded Lindberg that the case was essentially with her betters in the higher courts. Then Rod Parker got to the heart of the issue, which was that FLDS didn't recognize

---

*   In five years of court supervision of the UEP trust, there had never been a bare hint that administrators would assert a control claim over individual property such as cars. However, Rod Parker continued to raise "what if" propositions in court, painting scenarios in which Wisan would rip clothing from closets and confiscate flatware under authority of the trust.

the court orders at all. "You know," Parker told Lindberg, "the fiduciary . . . [and] Arizona [are] taking the position that they are basically dictators down there and that people with property rights can simply be ignored."

"Excuse me," Lindberg attempted to interrupt, as Parker continued talking over her. "Excuse me. Excuse me," Lindberg persisted. After some back and forth, Lindberg got to her heart of the matter. "Just a moment," she told Parker. "There is no preexisting property rights of any alleged beneficiary to any land or to anything in the UEP. OK? There is no pre-existing right, period. There is none." She later added, "Any agreement, any written agreement entered into by the special fiduciary, regardless of how denominated at this point, is the order of the Court, and it is to be enforced and it is to be protected."

But by whom? The police forces in the twin cities were actively undermin-ing the court's orders, coached by the town prosecutor, who was arresting non-FLDS people for trespassing. As Bill Richards repeated again and again in the telephone conference, the so-called law enforcement in Short Creek was exactly the problem.

After Lindberg green-lighted the Arizona attorney general to conduct an investigation, Richards began sending out notices to take depositions, most of them from FLDS cops in the twin cities, along with city prosecu-tor Ken Brendel. Incredibly, Hildale attorney Blake Hamilton, who with Peter Stirba was representing Brendel and the police, informed Richards that the cops and prosecutor would not submit to depositions unless they were given broad immunity for anything they might say. As sworn police officers dodged the attorney general's process servers, hiding out in sheds or fleeing town when Richards's men approached with notices for depositions, an incredulous Richards wondered what sorts of crimes these guys knew they'd committed to be demanding immunity in the same manner as com-mon criminals.

"I am uncertain why you or your clients would be motivated to try and prevent anyone from advising a criminal court of any conflict involving a government prosecutor [Colorado City prosecutor Ken Brendel] if such evi-dence arose," Richards wrote Hamilton on August 17, 2010. He continued, "It is equally curious that your police clients seek a protective order. They are sworn police officers, and are well aware of their obligations as such. It is difficult to understand why police officers might demand that the testi-mony they give related to their actions as public officials be kept sequestered absent their consent to release."

Richards flatly refused to offer any deals or immunity to the cops, and the cops kept hiding. To date, Richards has been forced to go to court several times for orders demanding that the twin cities supply the work schedules of the men in question, so that they may be served their deposition papers. Richards has won every effort, but the battle to get the FLDS cops deposed continues.

After the Texas raid, Nevada senator Harry Reid convened judicial committee hearings on FLDS, ostensibly to look into the possibility of a task force of federal cops empowered to bypass the red tape (and reluctance) of state and local laws and get something done in Short Creek. Mark Shurtleff's terrible motorcycle accident prevented him from testifying, but he didn't think much of Reid's hearings anyway. "Harry's a Mormon, and he was just embarrassed," Shurtleff said dismissively. "He held those hearings to make it look like he was doing something about an embarrassing situation to him personally as a Mormon."

Along with a dozen others, Terry Goddard did testify, at length and with somber passion. Goddard said there was only one way to stop FLDS leaders from usurping U.S. tax dollars to arrogantly ignore every law on the books while running their own private country headed by a jailed despot of questionable mental stability. The FLDS law enforcement branches must be decertified once and for all and replaced by federal cops, judges, and prosecutors. It was the only way to ensure that the rule of law would also finally be applied to a lawless sect ignored for fifty years and to protect young girls and boys and the non-FLDS families now living in Short Creek. It was, Goddard repeated gravely, the only way.

With his dramatic views of states' rights, Shurtleff probably wouldn't care for Goddard's solution, although one detractor wryly observed that there was nothing wrong with Shurtleff's extreme view of states' rights save for the fact that "his side lost the Civil War." But Shurtleff seemed to have been right about Reid's attention span for FLDS. Not a single thing came of the vaunted hearings. Although Reid prevailed against his Tea Party challenger in the November 2010 midterms, his difficulty in doing so speaks to the senate majority leader's ongoing problems, which are so pervasive that he may not even remember that he once cared enough to call hearings about FLDS.

Claims of persecution, tactics of obstruction, delay, emergencies galore, and endless appeals seemed to be working out well for FLDS, whose attorneys had put their faith in the less FLDS-educated Utah Supreme Court to circumvent the Utah and Arizona attorneys general, the fiduciary, and the Third District Court judge acquainted intimately with the situation in Short Creek. After the numbing August 23 Utah Supreme Court reversal of Warren Jeffs's criminal convictions, it seemed reasonable for FLDS lawyers to start popping champagne corks over the possible outcome of the myriad UEP appeals they'd laid before the same court, but that very week the court issued FLDS heartache instead of jubilation.

On August 27, 2010, a mere four days after the Jeffs reversal, the Utah Supreme Court denied all FLDS petitions save one, which they ruled was not "ripe" for consideration. In its decision, the court gave a single reason for the denials, one of the issues those on the other side had been raising for three years: FLDS was too late in challenging the law upon which others had in good faith relied to move forward with their lives. Changing things now would be grossly unfair to those people, not to mention causing savage emotional and financial damage. "In sum," the court wrote, "many individuals have relied upon the district court's final order from over three years ago, and the FLDS Association has given no adequate explanation for its delay in appealing or otherwise petitioning for relief. The FLDS Association has shown a lack of diligence in challenging the modification of the Trust, and this lack of diligence has operated to the detriment of others. . . . Accordingly, we dismiss the FLDS Association's Trust modification claims pursuant to the doctrine of laches."

The "doctrine of laches" invoked by the court is hard to get around. "Laches" is one of those black letter, settled components of law that asserts that a party may not simply ignore or remain inexplicably silent as legal decisions are made and then come into court years later and damage others by claiming those legal decisions were wrong. There are conditions under which laches may be forgiven, but they include high bar circumstances such as being insane or an infant at the time of the original proceedings. And the court's conclusions about the one petition it did not deny provided little good news for FLDS.

"The FLDS Association does not allege that either the district court or the special fiduciary has actually used religion as a factor in determining how to parse out property," the justices wrote. "It does not cite any instance where an active FLDS member received a lesser delegation of property because of his or her religious beliefs." The justices concluded therefore that FLDS claims that they were being targeted for extermination were "hypothetical." If evidence of discrimination became available in the future, the justices would consider it then.

Despite Parker's assertion that the opinion was "not all bad," it's hard to see where the good in it lies from the FLDS perspective. The killer laches designation will apply to any future challenges FLDS might entertain for the UEP case. After the telephone conference in July, FLDS attorneys filed another flurry of motions to get Lindberg kicked off the case, all efforts that became effectively moot after the laches decision, which also untied the hands of both Lindberg and Wisan, who may now proceed without a saw swinging over their heads.

After the July 22 hearing, Lindberg agreed to have Wisan set up an entirely new system by which property claims could be evaluated. Wrangling over what that system will look like began in November 2010, but one thing seems evident from the pleadings. If they can, FLDS will contest every property decision, including what's on the property, in court. Already, items like automobiles and household goods—elements nobody in their wildest dreams considered to be part of the UEP picture—have been mentioned as potential battlegrounds.

In Texas, time marches on. Governor Rick Perry won reelection in the November 2010 midterms, and Perry's feelings about FLDS have been unequivocal. He wants the sect out of his state. Assistant attorney general Eric Nichols continues prosecuting the twelve men indicted after the 2008 raid, which will cap off with the prosecution of Warren Jeffs in the spring or summer of 2011. Nichols announced that he was leaving the Texas Attorney General's Office in February 2011, but he has been appointed special prosecutor for the Jeffs case, at least.

Though most anti-FLDS activists consider Mark Shurtleff's performance uneven at best, it was the Utah attorney general who started the ball rolling to begin with, and no one can dismiss that. Shurtleff, the conservative Mormon, was the first authority to successfully require FLDS to conform to law since the 1953 raid, first with the prosecution of FLDS polygamous policeman Rod Holm and later by assuming temporary control of a trust being looted and mismanaged by its "trustees." Without Shurtleff, there wouldn't be any kind of reformation under way in Short Creek, where Warren Jeffs may very well have remained firmly ensconsed, as he ejected little boys and married little girls in a frenzy, while continuing to soak taxpayers to finance a host of other illegal activities.

Instead, Shurtleff's diligence forced the FLDS prophet's flight to Texas, where authorities were eventually able to secure evidence of his personal crimes that could keep him in prison for the next hundred years. Current

FLDS residents of Short Creek may see Shurtleff as the source of their destruction, but he is actually the source of their salvation. Without him, FLDS members would have most probably lost everything as Jeffs decimated the trust lands upon which their homes are built and "pruned" families according to their bloodlines and blind loyalty, no laughing allowed.

Likewise, non-FLDS members currently unhappy with Mark Shurtleff wouldn't have a leg to stand on—no matter how wobbly—if he had not decided to take action against the derelict UEP trustees in 2005. Today, especially in light of the laches decision, families destroyed and disenfranchised by Warren Jeffs have at least a shot at regaining some of what was stolen from them. The strength of Shurtleff's commitment to the notion that FLDS join the rest of the country in the twenty-first century may have vacillated at times, particularly in the summer of 2009 when he seemed ready to chuck it in by returning most of the UEP lands to Warren Jeffs. But he lost that fight gracefully and backed off the position entirely in the following months. As 2010 neared its end, Shurtleff's office demonstrated renewed interest for the UEP case, assigning more prosecutors and joining more vigorously—and frequently—in positions taken by Arizona and Wisan.

Mark Shurtleff has two years left in his term, but in Arizona, the November 2010 midterm election results spell uncertainty for the future of continuing legal actions against FLDS, something the sect may have been counting on all along. In the past, FLDS has banked on the fact that they could outlast their opposition, private parties that would either run out of money or governmental agencies that would change in elections.

In many ways, Arizona attorney general Terry Goddard was more dangerous to FLDS than Mark Shurtleff. Under Goddard, the scope of FLDS activities open for legal attention was expanded to include discrimination, fraud, and malfeasance with public funds. Goddard removed the public schools from FLDS, eliminating an important cash cow. He filed a number of civil rights violations cases, culminating with the ongoing cases on behalf of the Cooke family. And he ordered a two-year financial investigation of the sect's misappropriation of tax dollars, culminating in a dull May 2010 Short Creek raid in which police carted off computers instead of children. Are future indictments and prosecution jeopardized by the fact that Goddard, who had to step down as attorney general to run for governor, lost his election to Republican Jan Brewer? No one knows.

The hysteria-whipped immigration debate in Arizona may have also contributed to the defeat of Democrat Felicia Rotellini's bid to take Goddard's place. Though Rotellini stated she would defend Arizona's draconian immigration law in court (Goddard said he would not), the Democrat did not support the law. Her opponent, the victorious Republican Tom Horne, was an enthusiastic supporter of the law, but his long-term commitment to pursuing the UEP case remains to be seen. Arizona assistant attorney general Bill Richards—Goddard's point man on FLDS—left the office at the end of 2010 to further his career in private practice. At this writing, Arizona has passed the UEP trust baton to assistant attorneys general Michael H. Hinson and Mark P. Bookholder, while Arizona assistant attorney general Sandra Kane continues pursuing the Cookes' civil rights action in federal court with Bill Walker.

The new Arizona attorneys general could be going backward into the future, as FLDS has successfully restarted the entire UEP case in federal court. The FLDS federal suit, a larger version of the sect's state challenges to the UEP's reformation, had been on hold in the U.S. District Court for five years, an FLDS safety net should they lose in the state courts. When that loss became reality, FLDS attorneys sprinted back to the federal courthouse to begin again. Their first priority was halting the sale of Berry Knoll Farm, but the federal suit aims to relitigate all the issues everyone thought had been settled by the Utah Supreme Court's laches decision.

In what many considered a shocking development, U.S. district judge Dee Benson granted FLDS an injunction prohibiting the sale of Berry Knoll in mid-December 2010. Benson also blocked the critical, ongoing efforts to subdivide UEP properties until he could rule on the suits' larger issues, but it was his unsolicited statements from the bench that produced the most cold sweat on the parties who have worked to force FLDS to follow the law.

"Whether the state is entitled to be in this [FLDS] arena at all . . . I think that's a very important constitutional question," Benson said.

Others questioned whether the federal courts even possessed the authority to review a matter settled by the state. Most parties involved with the suit suspected that Benson wanted to rule in favor of FLDS but would never be able to concoct the legal authority necessary for him to do so.

But Benson shocked everyone, ruling in February 2011 that the state of Utah had possessed no authority to interfere with an "established church" when it assumed temporary control of the UEP trust in 2005, and that such an action was unconstitutional. In other words, FLDS is a religion protected by the U.S. Constitution.

Benson seemed unconcerned with the criminal conduct within the "established church," writing, "The defendants speak at long length about how bad—even criminal—Warren Jeffs' behavior was, but they say little that is relevant to defend their own wholesale interference with an established church." His forty-eight-page decision scolded Lindberg for her part in violating FLDS's First Amendment rights and asserted that the Utah Supreme Court was wrong when it determined that FLDS had waited too long to start challenging the reformed trust, and therefore the all-important laches decision was moot. Benson ordered a stay of the Berry Knoll land sale, already under way.

Amazed by Benson's invasion of state authority, Shurtleff's prosecutors appeared before the federal judge in March, asking him to stay the injunction until the Utah Supreme Court could weigh in, but they were met with hostility and sarcasm. "You're violating the Constitution every day," Benson declared from the bench. "So why should I care about what the Utah Supreme Court is doing?"

Most observers, however, believe that a panel of federal appeals court judges will care when it hears appeals of Benson's order. "Benson's statements from the bench were stunning, way over the line," said Bill Walker. "He didn't even require FLDS to post a bond with the injunction as required by federal law. I don't see any way that this order can stand."

The lives of thousands of underage girls and boys as well as men and women, FLDS and non-FLDS, hang in the balance. They don't live only in Short Creek but also in Canada, Idaho, Colorado, Texas, California, New Mexico, South Dakota, and possibly Mexico. Despite his blunt personal presentation, it is a fact that weighs on Bruce Wisan every day. "I want to help those people who want it," he said, almost desperately, in his Salt Lake City office. "I want to help give those people who want it a secure place to live and a chance to have their lives without someone like Warren Jeffs watching every move they make."

Additionally, there is a generational situation. Under the Jeffses' iron-fisted rule, several generations of FLDS children were raised with minimal or nonexistent educations. Barely able to read and write, they are socially dysfunctional. To this day, on Warren Jeffs's orders from prison, the sect continues to discharge hundreds of unwanted boys and young men into a society they fear and cannot negotiate.

As part of one court filing, Wisan included the remarks of the judge to those men arrested in the 1953 raid. In his lengthy sentencing remarks on November 30, 1953, in Kingman, Arizona, judge Robert S. Tullar lamented the fact that "fanaticism flourishes in ignorance," yet the FLDS "gentlemen" before him were not ignorant at all but men of "keen intelligence, pleasant personality, industry and optimism" who insisted upon assigning thirteen-year-old girls to fifty-year-old men when they'd been repeatedly told to stop.

"Well, most of the clamor and outcry have died away," Tullar began his remarks at a sentencing fifty-eight years ago. "In this remote corner of this remote state, in this quiet courtroom, the time has come for you gentlemen to face up to the majesty of democratic government, to the dignity of the law, and to the power of the people. . . .

"Your conspiracy to violate our law was entered into with deliberate purpose and with a full awareness of the extent and nature of the offense. You selected, as one of your number has boldly stated, a location not easily accessible to law enforcement officials—a place where your crimes might longer escape official notice; a place on a state border impossible to approach without giving warning; a place where, upon the approach of the officers of the law, it was easy for you to slip out your back doors, sneak through the woods and be across the state line out of reach. . . . Your selection of Short Creek as the place for your stand brands the United Effort Plan with pusillanimity."

Conceding that he was "no theologian," Tullar nevertheless informed the men before him that he had studied the biblical authority for polygamy their lawyers cited as an affirmative defense, "cross-indexed and leading to many books, chapters, and verses," but Tullar could not agree that the Bible required men to practice polygamy.

"The Devil, of course, can cite scriptures," Tullar observed dryly. He continued, "Nor gentlemen, in this day and age, can polygamy be defended upon an ethical or sociological basis. Law may be defined as the rules of conduct which enable man to live peaceably with his fellow man. The law evolves in direct ratio to the society it serves. Our society today is composed of men and women with equal rights and freedoms. In this country today the woman is not told whom to marry or when. She is not forced into an unwanted union by her father, her pastor or the deacons of her church."

The judge told the FLDS men that he did not believe the states of Arizona and Utah could not put an end to polygamy. "I believe that we can, and we will. Our immediate success depends upon action by our sister state of Utah. . . . I call upon the Utah authorities to act promptly and aggressively in this matter, so that they may have the respect and regard of law abiders that Arizona now has."

And finally, this: "Gentlemen, our way of life does not permit the practice of polygamy in America today. You gentlemen had to be stopped. You

were fairly treated. There has been no persecution, even though your crime
has been enormous, particularly because you have caused little children to
suffer. . . . I have heard not one word of repentance, despite the tragedies you
have brought down on these innocent children. There has been no promise
to reform."

Fifty-eight years later, there still isn't.

Epilogue
RUTH ACROSS THE RUBICON

In the winter of 2010, the girl who started everything does not keep abreast of FLDS court developments. Ruth Stubbs lives only a dozen miles from her honeymoon suite at the Mark Twain hotel from a decade earlier, but she doesn't think about that day anymore and hasn't for a long time. Ruth is truly married now, to another FLDS defector who crafted the iron wood-burning stove in the couple's immaculate Apple Valley manufactured home himself. She prepares a soft fried egg for a robust baby boy watching her every move with lip smacking attention from his high chair, one of her five children.

"I'm afraid I haven't lost all the baby weight from him yet," she apologizes self-consciously, but she looks beautiful, radiant even. Bill Walker was right. Ruth's pictures do not do her justice. In person, she exudes good will, optimism, and honesty. She answers every question I ask, including the uncomfortable extortion and perjury questions, with a straight-on, eyeball-to-eyeball gaze and without hesitation. "Stupid, stupid, stupid," she says of the extortion, her face coloring with embarrassment. "I really didn't think they [her brothers] would go through with it, but yeah, they told me about it. I'll admit I needed money. I was regretting that I didn't sue 'em when I could," she shakes her head again but does not look away. "Stupid," she repeats. "I apologize to everybody. I'm very ashamed."

Ruth willingly hands over diaries—sixty single-spaced typewritten pages—the story of her life. It's an extraordinary effort for a girl pulled out of the fifth grade, and she's far from finished. "I'm writing it for the kids," she explains. "For when they're much older, 'course. When they can understand it, 'cause I didn't leave anything out. I figure they will have a lot of questions about what's happened. I want them to know the whole truth, even stuff about me."

Winston and Maranda, two of the three children she had with Rod Holm, suddenly burst down the hallway in a tumble of giggles and shrieks, flying through the kitchen with their friends ferried to Ruth's home for a playdate. Pursing her lips in disapproval, the girl a Utah court-appointed psychologist once deemed too narcissistic and dumb to be a fit mother calls Maranda to her side, kneeling before the girl to explain eye to eye that the interruption was rude and too boisterous for indoor play. The eight-year-old, blue-eyed blond with her mother's thick French braids nods soberly, flashes a brilliant smile just like her mother's, and retreats as calmly as she can manage into the unseen back rooms where her friends and happy bedlam await. In a different scenario, the giggling child would be only a few years away from her assignment to an old man's bed.

"I've been meaning to tell ya," Ruth says to her former attorney, Bill Walker, as she drags a box of old photographs over to the sofa. "Rod called and said he's OK with my husband adopting Winston and Maranda." She says it so casually, it's almost hard to remember that FLDS and Rod Holm assaulted Ruth's character in a blowout custody battle that led to Holm's indictment, tipping Warren Jeffs toward abandoning Short Creek and the UEP trust, which led to the court takeover and the massive social upheaval in the twin cities today. She hands me a stack of pictures. "That's me as a little girl," she says, eyes dancing with good memories. "I used to have a lot more," she remembers sadly, "but they took 'em all away when they gave me to Rod." She says that as if everybody gets "given" to somebody to have sex and children.

"So, what's the deal with Holm?" Bill redirects her, perusing his own stack of photographs. "He wants to get out of court-ordered child support by having another man take charge of his children?"

"Yeah, well. He doesn't pay it anyway," she responded. "He hasn't seen the kids in three years." A frown interrupts her cheerful features. "Sometimes it's hard to explain to the kids, but I'm like, 'Whatever, dude.' But then the other day Rod said he might have to go back to court, take the kids back, if we didn't do the adoption thing. Said he had a good case and I was a bad mother. The usual." She sighs, tapping another picture of children in a campsite. Carefully, Bill places the photographs he is holding on the sofa, his face flooded with disbelief.

"Rod Holm is threatening you?" he gapes.

"Well, it just started," Ruth offers, as if the newness of a threat to snatch her children back into FLDS mitigates matters. Bill throws his hands up, imploring the heavens. "It never ends with these people," he cries as Ruth nibbles her bottom lip. "Well!" Bill resumes, shaking his head, starting a trademark cackle that floods his opponents' hearts with cold dread. "I guess you better tell him to call your lawyer the next time. Don't talk to him, Ruth. Understand? Just tell him to call your lawyer."

"Really?" Ruth gasps, and only in the explosion of her relief does the depth of her worry become apparent. "He can't do it, can he, Bill?" she asks, searching Walker's face for evidence of worry, but there is none.

Bill retrieves the photographs. "Not, my dear, while I'm around," he states.

Not every FLDS woman has a lawyer handy when the threats start, and Ruth knows it. "I consider myself one of the luckiest people in the world," she exclaims. "I can't change what happened to me, but I got out of it, and I'm a better person. Thank God I had help and I got out. Now I've got the best damn husband in the world, and we love each other. I've got my family and friends. My children are *free*! They're gonna go to school and have real lives. I'm a *real* person. I'm *happy*."

A DOZEN MILES from Ruth's home in Apple Valley, Jethro Barlow lives in his UEP-leased Short Creek home just down the street from where Ruth once lived with Rod Holm. Barlow works from dusk to dawn trying to ensure that other FLDS members might someday be allowed to experience Ruth's happy freedom. Asked how he envisions FLDS without a prophet controlling every aspect of members' lives, Barlow leaps from his chair, shoving stacks of paper aside on a nearby desk to lay out an organizational chart he's come up with for a reborn FLDS.

It's a complicated chart, but it looks a lot like democracy.

Acknowledgments

The legal story of FLDS was unfolding during the research for this book, and it continues to do so. Keeping up with multiple developments sometimes occurring daily from across the country required the generous assistance of busy people who took the time to keep me current with court documents and other news.

Special thanks to the talented Jaqueline Meacham, Roger Hoole's paralegal, who for ten months doggedly kept me abreast of court filings that sometimes came at the rate of four a day. I'm grateful to Rexine Pitcher, paralegal extraordinaire to Utah assistant attorney general Tim Bodily, who cheerfully accepted the daunting task of getting me up to speed on the oceanic UEP lawsuit, already under way for five years when I arrived. Without her help, understanding that massive case would have been far more difficult and taken twice as long.

Also in the Utah Attorney General's Office, heartfelt thanks to the remarkable Shelley Exeter, executive assistant to Mark Shurtleff. Shelley already has the difficult task of trying to manage the schedule of her energetic boss, but she always made certain I had whatever access I needed. Thanks, too, to Shurtleff's tireless information officer, Paul Murphy, who encouraged me to explore avenues I might have overlooked without his input, and to Mark Shurtleff himself, who suffered through days of interviews without complaint.

A special thanks to amazing historian and writer Will Bagley, who selflessly always made time amid his own writing, research, speaking engagements, and travel to answer questions and clarify the complex history of early Mormons.

Many other individuals in Utah assisted me in gaining access to people and documents but fear retaliation from FLDS's aggressive attorneys if they are named. They know who they are, and I thank them for their time and help.

In Texas, I am eternally grateful to fellow journalist Kathy Mankin, whose broad knowledge and ferocious devotion to facts about FLDS in Texas and elsewhere were invaluable in accurately reconstructing the events in Eldorado. Though she has plenty to do running the *Eldorado Success*, Kathy always had time to help me with research and proof for errors.

In acknowledgments, all writers say they have the best agent and editors in the business, but mine really are. Thanks beyond measure to Jane Dystel, a force of nature who saw the story in this chain of events before I did and guided me to a complete concept, then found a home for it in a crashed economy—and what a home. Chicago Review Press senior editor Jerry Pohlen is insightful, intelligent, flexible, honest, patient, funny, encouraging, supportive, and always available to take my calls, and he possesses the kind of sharp eye for detail and form that can save a writer's hide, as he did mine more times than I'd care to admit. That goes double for editors Lisa Reardon and Claire Podulka, who together gave my work one of the most thorough, thoughtful line edits I've experienced in my thirty years of journalism. I can only imagine how much work these two invested to make me look good, and I'm thankful for it.

Bibliography

Books

Bachelor, Mary, Marianne Watson, and Anne Wilde. *Voices in Harmony; Contemporary Women Celebrate Plural Marriage*. Salt Lake City: Principle Voices, 2001.

Bagley, Will. *Blood of the Prophets: Brigham Young and the Massacre at Mountain Meadows*. Norman: University of Oklahoma Press, 2002.

Bennion, Janet. *Desert Patriarchy: Mormon and Mennonite Communities in the Chihuahua Valley*. Tucson: University of Arizona Press, 2004.

Bigler, David L. *Doing the Works of Abraham: Mormon Polygamy, Its Origin, Practice and Demise*. Norman, OK: The Arthur H. Clark Comany, 2009.

———. *Fort Limhi: The Mormon Adventure in Oregon Territory 1855–1858*. Spokane, WA: The Arthur H. Clark Company, 2003.

——— *The Mormon Theocracy in the American West 1847–1896*. Norman, OK: The Arthur H. Clark Company, 2007.

Bistline, Benjamin G. *The Polygamists: A History of Colorado City, Arizona*. Scottsdale, AZ: Agreka, 2004.

Bloom, Harold. *The American Religion*. New York: Chu Hartley Publishers, 1992.

Brodie, Fawn M. *No Man Knows My History: The Life of Joseph Smith*. New York: First Vintage Books, 1995.

Brooks, Juanita. *John Doyle Lee: Zealot, Pioneer, Builder, Scapegoat*. Logan: Utah State University Press, 1992.

———. *The Mountain Meadows Massacre*. Norman: University of Oklahoma Press, 2003.

Bushman, Richard Lyman. *Joseph Smith, Rough Stone Rolling: A Cultural Biography of Mormonism's Founder*. New York: Vintage Books, 2005.

Compton, Todd. *In Sacred Loneliness, The Plural Wives of Joseph Smith*. Salt Lake City: Signature Books, 1997.

Gilmore, Mikal. *Shot in the Heart*. New York: Doubleday, 1994.

Givens, Terryl L. *By the Hand of Mormon: The American Scripture that Launched a New World Religion*. New York: Oxford University Press, 2002.

Hassan, Steven. *Combatting Cult Mind Control*. Rochester, VT: Park Street Press, 1990.

Jeffs, Brent W. *Lost Boy*. With Maia Szalavitz. New York: Broadway Books, 2009.

Jenkins, Philip. *Mystics and Messiahs: Cults and New Religions in American History*. Oxford University Press, 2000.

Jessop, Carolyn. *Escape*. With Laura Pulizter. New York: Broadway Books, 2007.

Jessop, Flora. *Church of Lies*. With Paul R. Brown. San Francisco: Jossey-Bass, 2009.

Krakauer, Jon. *Under the Banner of Heaven: A Story of Violent Faith*. New York: Anchor Books, 2004.

Lee, John D. *Mormonism Unveiled: The Life and Confession of John D. Lee and the Complete Life of Brigham Young*. Albuquerque: University of New Mexico Press, 2008.

Llewellyn, John R. *Polygamy's Rape of Rachel Strong: Protected Environment for Predators*. Scottsdale, AZ: Agreka, 2006.

Moore-Emmett, Andrea. *God's Brothel*. San Francisco: Pince-nez Press, 2004.

O'Dea, Thomas. *The Mormons*. Chicago: The University of Chicago Press, 1957.

Ostling, Richard N., and Joan K. Ostling. *Mormon America: The Power and the Promise*. New York: Harper One, 2007.

Quinn, D. Michael. *Early Mormonism and the Magic World View*. Salt Lake City: Signature Books, 1998.

———. *The Mormon Hierarchy: Extensions of Power*. Salt Lake City: Signature Books, 1997.

———. *The Mormon Hierarchy: Origins of Power*. Salt Lake City: Signature Books, 1994.

Sargant, William. *Battle for the Mind: A Physiology of Conversion and Brain-Washing*. Cambridge, MA: Malor Books, 1997.

Shurtleff, Mark. *Am I Not a Man? The Dred Scott Story*. Orem, UT: Valor Publishing Group, 2009.

Singular, Stephen. *When Men Become Gods: Mormon Polygamist Warren Jeffs, His Cult of Fear, and the Women Who Fought Back*. New York: St. Martin's Press, 2008.

Smith, Joseph Jr. *The Book of Mormon*. Independence, MO: Herald Publishing House, 2002.

———. *Doctrine and Covenants*. Independence, MO: Herald Publishing House, 2007.

———. *Pearl of Great Price*. Whitefish, MT: Kessinger Publishing, 2003.

Solomon, Dorothy Allred. *Daughter of the Saints: Growing Up in Polygamy*. New York: W. W. Norton & Company, 2003.

Sonntag Bradley, Martha. *Kidnapped from That Land: The Government Raids on the Short Creek Polygamists*. Salt Lake City: University of Utah Press, 1993.

Stegner, Wallace. *The Gathering of Zion: The Story of the Mormon Trail*. Lincoln: University of Nebraska Press, 1964.

———. *Mormon Country*. Lincoln: University of Nebraska Press, 1970.

Van Wagoner, Richard S. *Mormon Polygamy: A History*. Salt Lake City: Signature Books, 1989.

Wall, Elissa. *Stolen Innocence*. With Lisa Pulitzer. New York: William Morrow, 2008.

Newspapers

Arizona Daily Star

Arizona Republic

Dallas Morning News

Denver Post

Deseret News

Eldorado Success

Houston Chronicle

Kingman Miner

Los Angeles Times

New York Times

Phoenix New Times

Salt Lake Tribune

San Angelo [Texas] *Times-Standard*

[St. George, Utah] *Spectrum*

Magazine Articles

Author unknown, "The Lonely Men of Short Creek." *Life*, 1953.

Anderson, Scott, with photos by Stephanie Sinclair. "Polygamy in America." *National Geographic*, February 2010.

Tresinowski, Alex, Darla Atlas, Anne Lang, and Cary Cardwell, with photos by David Burnett. "The Children of the Cult." *People*, March 2009.

Documentaries

Merten, Jennilyn, and Tyler Measom. *Sons of Perdition*. Leftturn Films, 2010.

Reidelbach, Dot, and Laurie Allen. *Banking on Heaven*. Over the Moon Productions, 2007.

Rubin, Daphna, and Olivia Ahnemann. *Inside Polygamy: Life in Bountiful*. Hoggard Films for National Geographic Channels, 2010.

Watkiss, Mike. *The Colorado City Underground Railroad*, 2010.

Whitney, Helen. *The Mormons*. "The American Experience," PBS Home Video, 2007.

Websites

The Church of Latter-Day Saints of Jesus Christ
www.lds.org

FLDS 101
http://flds101.blogspot.com

FLDS Texas
http://texasflds.wordpress.com

FLDS Truth.org
www.fldstruth.org

The Hope Organization
www.childbrides.org

MormonFundamentalism.com
www.mormonfundamentalism.com

Mormon Think
www.mormonthink.com

Mormon Quotes
www.mormonquotes.com

MyEldorado
www.myeldorado.net

Recovery from Mormonism
www.exmormon.org

Rethinking Mormonism
www.i4m.com/think

Court Cases

Utah: Third District

In the Matter of the United Effort Plan Trust (Dated November 9, 1942, Amended April 10, 1946, and Amended and Restated November 3, 1998); and Its Trustees, Including Known Trustees Truman Barlow, Warren Jeffs, Leroy Jeffs, Winston Blackmore, James Zitting and William E. Jessop a/k/a William E. Timpson and Doe Trustees I Through IX, 053900848 (May 2005).

M.J. v. Warren Jeffs et al., 070916524 (December 2005).

Bruce R. Wisan, as the Court Appointed Fiduciary of the United Effort Plan v. Warren Jeffs et al., 060908716 (May 2006).

The Fundamentalist Church of Jesus Christ of Latter Day Saints et al. v. Bruce Wisan as the Court Appointed Fidcuiary of the United Effort Plan and John Does, 080918199 (August 2008).

Snow, Christensen & Martineau, William Jessop, Dan Johnson and Merlin Jessop v. Bruce Wisan as Court Appointed Fiduciary of the United Effort Plan and Denise Posse Lindberg, Third District Court Judge, 053900848 (November 2008).

State of Utah v. Warren Steed Jeffs [extradition case], 101401820 (October 2010).

Utah: Fifth District

Rodney H. Holm v. Ruth M. Stubbs, 014500891 (May 2002).

State of Utah v. Rodney Hans Holm, 021501054 (October 2002).

Bruce R. Wisan, as the Court Appointed Fiduciary of the United Effort Plan v. Aspen Management Investments LLC et al., 050909669 (May 2005).

State of Utah v. Warren Steed Jeffs, 061500526 (April 2006).

Bruce R. Wisan, as the Court Appointed Fiduciary of the United Effort Plan v. City of Hildale, Twin City Water Authority, a Utah Corporation, and Russell Shirts, County Recorder for Washington County, Utah. Other Party, Lowther & Associates, 070500105 (January 2007).

Bruce R. Wisan, as the Court Appointed Fiduciary of the United Effort Plan v. Colorado City Improvement Association, a Utah Corporation, 07503037 (December 2007).

Commercial Services of Perry Inc. v. Bruce R. Wisan, as the Court Appointed Fiduciary of the United Effort Plan, and William Barlow, 080500593 (February 2008).

Harker Farms Inc. v. Sterling Harker and William Harker, 080500259 (March 2008).

Sterling J. Harker, an Individual, and William S. Harker, an Individual v. the United Effort Plan et al., 080500225 (March 2008).

Ammon Parley Harker, Benjamin Harker, et al. v. Harker & Sons, LC, Harker Farms, Inc., John and Jane Does I Through X, and John Doe Entities I Through X, 080500538 (July 2008).

United Effort Plan Trust by Bruce R. Wisan, as the Court Appointed Fiduciary of the United Effort Plan v. Guy Steed, Ilene Steed, and John Does I Through X, 080502167 (August 2008).

Guy Steed and Ilene Steed v. Bruce Wisan, as the Court Appointed Fiduciary of the United Effort Plan, John and Jane Does I through X, and John and Jane Doe Entities I through X, 080502450 (September 2008).

Utah: U.S. District Court (Salt Lake City)

Fundamentalist Church of Jesus Christ of Latter Day Saints, an Association of Individuals v. Bruce R. Wisan, Special Fiduciary of the United Effort Plan Trust; Mark Shurtleff, Attorney General for the State of Utah; Thomas C. Horne, Attorney General for the State of Arizona; Denise Posse Lindberg, Judge of the Third Judicial District Court of Salt Lake County, State of Utah, 2:08-CV-00772-DB (October 2008).

Guy A. Ream v. Judge Denise Lindberg, Mark Shurtleff, Bruce Wisan, State of Utah, 2:09 CV-00856-CW (September 2009).

Utah: Supreme Court

Rulon Jeffs, Fundamentalist Church of Jesus Christ of Latter Day Saints v. David Stubbs et al., 960454 (September 1998).

State of Utah v. Rodney Hans Holm, 20030847 (May 2005).

SCM [Snow, Christensen & Martineau], Raymond Scott Berry, Willie Jessop, Dan Johnson, and Merlin Jessop v. Denise Posse Lindberg, Third District Court Judge, 20091006-SC, 060908716, 053900848-DC (November 2008).

SCM, Willie Jessop, Merril Stubbs, and Dan Johnson v. Lindberg, 20080928-SC, DC 053900848, 060908716 (November 2008).

Willie Jessop, Dan Johnson, Merlin Jessop, Lyle Jeffs, and James Oler v. Denise Posse Lindberg, Third District Court Judge, 20090691-SC (053900848-DC) (August 2009).

Twin Cities City Hildale Utah and City of Colorado City, Arizona v. Denise Posse Lindberg, Third District Court Judge, 20090781-SC (053900848-DC) (September 2009).

The Fundamentalist Church of Jesus Christ of Latter Day Saints, an Association of Individuals, Lyle Jeffs, an Individual; and Willie Jessop, an Individual v. Denise Posse Lindberg, Third District Court Judge, 20090859-SC (053900848-DC) (October 2009).

Jessop et al., v. Denise Posse Lindberg, Third District Court Judge, formerly 20080928-SC (053900848-DC, 060908716-DC) (December 2009).

Arizona: Superior Court (Mohave County)

State of Arizona v. Dale Barlow, CR-2005-0647 (May 2005).

State of Arizona v. Kelly Fischer, CR-2005-0648 (May 2005).

State of Arizona v. Warren Jeffs, CR-2007-0743 (June 2005).

William Jessop, a Married Man, Daniel Johnson, a Married Man, Merlin Jessop, a Married Man, Elmer L. Johnson, a Married Man, and John and Jane Does I through X v. Bruce R. Wisan, Special Fiduciary of the United Effort Plan Trust, CV-2008-2047 (November 2008).

State of Arizona v. Bruce Wisan and Jethro Jessop Barlow, CR-2009-0012/0015 (consolidated with CR-2009-0012) (February 2010).

Bruce R. Wisan, Jethro Barlow v. Justice of the Peace Benjamin Haney and the Town of Colorado City Municipal Court and Town of Colorado City Attorney's Office, No. CV-2010-00330 (March 2010).

In the Matter of the United Effort Plan and Its Trustees, Including Known Trustees Truman Barlow, Warren Jeffs, Leroy Jeffs, Winston Blackmore, James Zitting, and William E. Jessop a/k/a William E. Timpson and Doe Trustees I through IX, CV 2010 1928 (September 2010).

Arizona: U.S. District Court (Prescott)

Roland Cook v. Mr. Bruce Wisan and the Mormon Church, CV-09-8152-PCT-LDA (September 2009).

Ronald Cooke and Jinjer Cooke, Husband and Wife, Plaintiffs, and the State of Arizona ex rel Terry Goddard et al. v. Town of Colorado City, Arizona; City of Hildale, Utah; Colorado City Utilities; Twin City Water Authority, a Utah Non-Profit, No. 10-CV-08105-PCT-JAT (October 2010).

Texas: Fifty-First District Court (Schleicher County)

State of Texas v. Warren Steed Jeffs, Nos. 990, 997 and 1007 (September 2008).

State of Texas v. Raymond Merril Jessop, No. 991 (September 2008).

State of Texas v. Allan Eugene Keate, No. 992 (September 2008).

State of Texas v. Michael George Emack, No. 993 (September 2008).

State of Texas v. Merril Leroy Jessop, No. 995 (September 2008).

State of Texas v. Dr. Lloyd Barlow, No. 996 (September 2008).

State of Texas v. Lehi Barlow Jeffs a/k/a Lehi Barlow Allred, No. 1000 (September 2008).

State of Texas v. Abram Harker Jeffs, No. 1002 (September 2008).

State of Texas v. Keith William Dutson, Jr., No. 1004 (September 2008).

State of Texas v. Leroy Johnson Steed, No. 1019 (September 2008).

Index